Contents

What Is a Document?

To the historian, a document is, quite simply, any sort of historical evidence. It is a primary source, the raw material of history. A document may be more than the expected government paperwork, such as a treaty or passport. It is also a letter, diary, will, grocery list, newspaper article, recipe, memoir, oral history, school yearbook, map, chart, architectural plan, poster, musical score, play script, novel, political cartoon, painting, photograph—even an object.

Using primary sources allows us not just to read *about* history, but to read history itself. It allows us to immerse ourselves in the look and feel of an era gone by, to understand its people and their language, whether verbal or visual. And it allows us to take an active, hands-on role in (re)constructing history.

Using primary sources requires us to use our powers of detection to ferret out the relevant facts and to draw conclusions from them; just as Agatha Christie uses the scores in a bridge game to determine the identity of a murderer, the historian uses facts from a variety of sources—some, perhaps, seemingly inconsequential—to build a historical case.

The poet W. H. Auden wrote that history was the study of questions. Primary sources force us to ask questions—and then, by answering them, to construct a narrative or an argument that makes sense to us. Moreover, as we draw on the many sources from "the dustbin of history," we can endow that narrative with character, personality, and texture—all the elements that make history so endlessly intriguing.

Cartoon

This political cartoon addresses the issue of church and state. It illustrates the Supreme Court's role in balancing the demands of the First Amendment of the Constitution and the desires of the religious population.

Illustration

Illustrations from children's books, such as this alphabet from the *New England Primer*, tell us how children were educated and also what the religious and moral values of the time were.

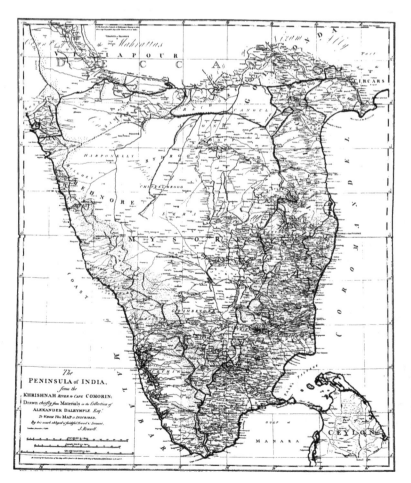

Treaty

A government document such as this 1805 treaty can reveal not only the details of government policy, but also information about the people who signed it. Here, the Indians' names were written in English transliteration by U.S. officials; the Indians added pictographs to the right of their names.

Map

A 1788 British map of India shows the region prior to British colonization, an indication of the kingdoms and provinces whose ethnic divisions would resurface later in India's history.

Object

In this 15th-century ewer, both the physical materials of brass and silver and the iconic depiction of heaven as a forest display the refinement of the owner, an Egyptian sultan's wife. Objects, along with manuscripts and printed materials, provide evidence about the past.

How to Read a Document

In this book, you will encounter a wide variety of documents—everything from political cartoons to written laws and court decisions, poems and satires, advertisements and petitions, photographs and posters, letters and diary entries, meeting reports and manifestoes, and a few three-dimensional objects. Each offers a snapshot of a particular moment in history; each exists because someone preserved it; together, they enable historians and history students to reconstruct a version of the past, an interpretation of historical events and developments. History is, after all, the interpretation of the past based on the evidence that has survived. Just as you could not reconstruct your own life story without consulting surviving evidence—your memory, a scrapbook or photo album, school report cards, interviews with family members, your email or text archive—historians can retrieve "the past" only through the documentary record.

Only some documentary traces of past events have survived, as our ancestors made decisions about what was important and discarded the rest. Because women and girls in the past were less likely than boys and men to have the opportunity to learn to read and write, and even then, because women's documents were often judged to be less important than men's, there remain fewer traces of women's past experiences than of men's. Gaps and silences in surviving materials are particularly noticeable when we seek information about women from groups (such as slaves) denied the right to become literate. Understanding the history of women's rights means analyzing documents about women as well as those written by women, and bringing to bear on the documents the same analytical and critical perspectives that historians employ as key tools of their work.

In other words, reading the documents in this book requires active engagement with them, and a willingness to notice things and ask questions about them. Historians start with basic questions: Who made or produced the document and for what purpose? When? What was the intended audience at that time? What type of document is it? What information does the document convey? Does it reveal a perspective, limitation, or bias that I need to be aware of? Is this the only or best source for the topic covered? Having asked these and other questions, historians strive to place historical documents within larger historical contexts or frameworks.

The two documents on the opposite page offer specific examples of the process. Both are from the same historical decade, 1900–1910,

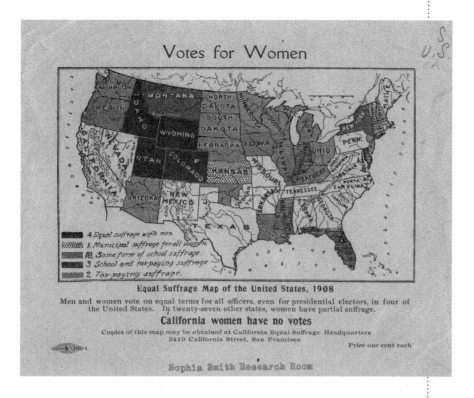

National American Woman Suffrage Association (NAWSA) statement, 1903.

"The National American Woman Suffrage Association is seeking to do away with the requirement of a sex qualification for suffrage. What other qualifications shall be asked for it leaves to each State. The southern women most active in it have always in their own State emphasized that granting suffrage to women who can read and write and who pay taxes would insure white supremacy without resorting to any methods of doubtful constitutionality. The Louisiana association asks for the ballot for educated and taxpaying women only and its officers believe that in this lies 'the only permanent and honorable solution of the race question.'"

and both provide evidence about one example of a women's rights issue: the effort to win women's suffrage. Analyzing them individually and placing them in conversation with each other can be revealing and instructive about the possibilities and limitations of studying any one document, and the need to read attentively.

Topic

Both the 1908 map and the 1903 statement convey information about the quest for full voting rights for women. In devising the map, rather than simply depict states with full voting rights as opposed to states where women did not have full suffrage, the artist chose to complicate the story by identifying five separate types of suffrage possibilities, and to leave blank states or territories where no women could vote (New Mexico and Arizona were territories in 1908). When the California Equal Suffrage Association printed the map and offered copies for sale, California suffragists were engaged in a campaign to convince the state's male legislators and voters to enfranchise women. That effort succeeded when a 1911 voter referendum on woman suffrage passed. The other document, a statement from the National American Woman Suffrage Association (NAWSA), which issued the statement at an annual meeting in 1903, constituted a response to a New Orleans newspaper's comments on how full suffrage for women might affect "the race question."

Context

Historical context is crucial to understanding the choices the creators made when drafting these documents. Between the 1870s and 1910, suffragists focused their efforts at the state and territorial levels. By presenting visual information on the spread of suffrage rights, and the willingness of states near California to institute full suffrage, the map-maker likely hoped to demonstrate that full suffrage would not be the threatening move that antisuffragists claimed it would be, and perhaps also convince viewers that the state was in danger of getting behind the times. The patterns evident in the map, including the widespread availability of "school suffrage" (women could vote for and run for school board and school superintendent positions) and "municipal suffrage" (in cities, women could vote for mayors and city council members) provide reminders that women were winning suffrage rights during the "Progressive" era when reform of schools and city politics was widely discussed. Suffragists' claim that women voters would "clean up" politics emerged within that context. State-level suffrage mobilization provides an important context for understanding the 1903 statement, too, but so does the spread of white supremacy throughout the South in the decades after Reconstruction, and its entrenchment in voting and segregation laws in the decades after 1890. When Southern white suffragists sought voting rights, they worked to win suffrage for themselves while keeping African Americans (both men and women) disfranchised.

Details

Both documents include interesting details, some of which may require additional explanation. In the map, there are geographical patterns to the winning of suffrage that a reader should analyze and try to explain. Both documents leave out information that readers may need in order to understand what the documents are saying. An attentive reader notices all types of details, both those that are in the document and those that are absent. The map does not include either Alaska or Hawaii, for example, and its reference to "tax-paying suffrage" may be puzzling to readers who know that few states had income or sales taxes in 1908. Poll taxes, however, fees imposed upon voters before they could vote, were widespread throughout the South. The 1903 statement's reference to "other qualifications" for voting and its assurance that NAWSA "leaves to each State" a decision on those qualifications raises questions about what happened to the organization's earlier commitment to universal suffrage. One might wonder what Susan B. Anthony, who had retired from the organization's presidency, would have thought about it.

Language

Historical documents often include unfamiliar terms, words that have changed meaning over time, or words that carry unspoken assumptions. Writers often use the word "women" without modifying or clarifying adjectives. The NAWSA statement's use of the term "southern women," for instance, hides its racial exclusivity; what the statement actually means is "southern white women." Although the rest of the statement, with its reference to "insur[ing] white supremacy," makes the reference clear, other documents are often not so transparent. In addition, people in the past often used the singular "woman" or "Woman" where modern writers would use the plural term "women." An attentive reader will always ask herself or himself *which* women are included in the word and which are not. Because women vary widely in their historical experiences, historians do not assume that women share one universal experience or that there is a singular essence to being female.

Women's Rights in
the United States

A HISTORY IN DOCUMENTS

Introduction

The history of women's rights in the United States is in part a story of achievement over seemingly insurmountable obstacles. At various times, claims to rights that later came to seem perfectly reasonable, even natural, were ridiculed and fiercely contested. Women's right to vote, for instance, while briefly seen as acceptable for some New Jersey women in 1776, had become ludicrous by the lights of most public commentators of the 1840s and 1850s. For women to vote was as unnatural as for hens to crow or men to give birth. Girls' claims to any but the most rudimentary or traditional of educations often met with opposition and the argument that, as future wives and mothers, they did not need or want a challenging curriculum, or the contention that demanding study would ruin their health. And the idea that married women might legally control their own property, wages, and even their bodies, so widely assumed today, in earlier eras was deemed unthinkable. By contrast, most Americans in the 21st century accept without much question that women and men should enjoy comparable legal, economic, educational, sexual, and individual rights, that they should be, in other words, equal citizens.

On one level, then, this book tells the story of how the unimaginable became imaginable, the imaginable became possible, and the possible became real. It explores how the very notion of equal citizenship for women and men came into being. In doing so, it sketches a history of rights denied as well as rights exercised, rights lost as well as rights won. The voting rights enjoyed by a few women in early-republic New Jersey were kept from most of the female population because of legal status and social class (only free single or widowed adult women property-holders could vote). And when those few women voters lost their rights in 1807, they joined the rest of the female population in their exclusion, on account of sex, from the political arena. Another century would pass before "woman" and "voter" could occupy the same space on the page. Even after the ratification of the Nineteenth Amendment in 1920, intersecting systems of inequality based on race and ethnicity kept some women (along with some men) off the voting rolls. In the South, the Amendment did little for African American women, who shared legal disfranchisement with African American men. Women could still lose other rights simply by marrying, as they had since English Common Law crossed the Atlantic with the colonists. Such losses were occasionally stunning: in 1915, the U.S. Supreme Court affirmed that American women (but not men) could be stripped of their citizenship when they married citizens of other countries.

The history of women's rights has almost uniformly been one of different rights for different women. For much of American history, single women (including widows) enjoyed different rights from married women, whether to ownership of property or access to education and jobs. Until well into the 20th century, it was perfectly legal for employers to refuse to hire married women and to fire those who wed. Etiquette books routinely advised brides to send in their resignation letters two weeks before the wedding date. During the Great Depression of the 1930s, federal government policy forbade the hiring of both members of a married couple, forcing women either to resign upon marriage or hide any evidence of their marriages. At the same time, single women could be and were excluded from the rights of the married. Until 1962, single mothers were denied Aid to Dependent Children (welfare) under the Social Security Act, and until the 1970s, physicians could legally refuse to prescribe contraceptives to single women.

Throughout American history, women's access to rights has been either facilitated or (more often) restricted by such factors as race, class, ethnicity, nationality, and sexuality. Whereas free women living under English Common Law in the colonies had few opportunities to control land or property outright, those who lived under Spanish or French law were generally able to inherit and pass on their own land. By custom, Native American women often controlled communal lands, both because they were the primary food producers for their communities and because their societies were matrilineal (people traced their lineage through their mothers). Customary practices, however, generally fell by the wayside when male leaders of Native groups made treaties with state and federal governments; formalized laws and written constitutions proved largely dismissive of women's traditional rights. And when the United States conquered or purchased, and then annexed, territories that had been part of Spain, France, or Mexico, the legal status of women's property rights often came into question. Despite conventional language encompassing all women under a unitary "Woman," poor women have seldom enjoyed the same access to rights that their better-off sisters have taken for granted. At a time when 20th-century middle-class women were beginning to assume that they could make their own decisions on matters of fertility and family planning, poor and minority women were still being sterilized without their consent. Lesbian identification has historically been sufficient to deprive individuals of basic rights, and only recently have changes in some states' laws and in the interpretation of the U.S. Constitution allowed same-sex partners to claim the same marriage rights as heterosexuals.

Just as women never formed a uniform group when it came to exercising legal, political, economic, and personal rights, they were never unified in their pursuit of equal rights, or even in their definition of the term "equal rights." In all of the great crusades to guarantee full citizenship and equal status to women—the suffrage movement, the effort to add an Equal Rights Amendment (ERA) to the Constitution, the demand that women enjoy the same right to self-ownership as men—there have been women on both sides. Often, the privileges they enjoyed as members of a particular racial or social group, and the fear of losing those privileges, were enough to convince some women to oppose making other women their equals. Many female anti-suffrage leaders were white native-born middle- and upper-class women who believed that the influence they enjoyed would disappear overnight once all women could vote. Similarly, Phyllis Schlafly, in opposing an ERA, excluded many women from her definition of "we" when she proclaimed in 1974: "American women have never had it so good. Why should we lower ourselves to 'equal rights' when we already have the status of special privilege?"

Men, too, have been both pro- and anti-suffrage, pro- and anti-ERA, and for and against women's rights to reproductive and other freedoms. It took a particularly strong or perhaps self-aware man to refuse the favors that law, custom, and established gender hierarchies awarded him, favors that assumed his superior rights and privileges over the women in his life, and often over women in general as well. But such men can be found in the documents in this volume, whether voting to enfranchise women, rejecting the idea that their brides must take their names and pledge to obey them, or standing side by side with their mothers, sisters, and daughters in challenging unfair or discriminatory laws and practices.

The history of women's quest for rights and full citizenship includes innumerable stories of heroic individuals: Anne Hutchinson defending her right to teach Puritan women on religious topics in the 1630s; Abigail Adams questioning her husband John on wives' legal rights in the 1770s; schoolgirl Priscilla Mason standing up for girls' educational rights in the 1790s; teacher Maria Stewart speaking to mixed male and female audiences in the 1830s; feminist Frederick Douglass explaining to lecture audiences "why I am a woman's rights man" in the 1880s; suffragist Alice Paul enduring force-feeding in prison as punishment for picketing the White House in 1917; lawyer Pauli Murray refusing to allow either racial or gender discrimination in the 1940s to curb her ambitions; retiree Lily Ledbetter asserting in 2008 women's right to receive fair pensions. Through singular actions, both famous and ordinary women and men have actively pursued women's full citizenship.

But a crucial element in that pursuit has been collective action on behalf of all women through organized social movements. When a women's rights movement arose in the 1840s, its adherents sought to rework the legal and constitutional fabric of the United States in order to guarantee women full citizenship. Envisioning and designing a new pattern, remaking and expanding whole sections of law and policy, was an arduous and ever-changing challenge. It remains so today. For it was—and is—women's willingness to identify with other women with whom one had nothing in common but the social experience of being female, that propelled much of the historical change chronicled in the documents in this volume. Generations of women's rights activists have taken up the challenge laid down in the 1840s, though they have not always agreed on goals, tactics, or priorities. The questions of which women's rights should take precedence in the struggle and which women were most rights-deprived never found easy agreement. In the 19th century, African American and white women found common cause in the struggle to end slavery, but then divided over priorities once that battle was won. In the early 20th century, women and men who termed themselves "feminists" pressed for women's "emancipation," thereby differentiating themselves from contemporaries whose primary goals were constitutional amendments guaranteeing women's suffrage and equal legal rights.

In later decades, advocates of "women's liberation" developed different ideals and programs from those who spoke of "women's rights" to join the mainstream of American society. In recent years, the call of "global feminism," echoing the interest of earlier activists in "international" concerns, has engaged women's rights supporters in efforts to achieve gender equality around the world, while also exposing differences over how to reach that goal.

What gender equality might look like has long been a contested issue; it is likely to remain contentious for the foreseeable future, both locally and globally. When Judith Sargent Murray wrote "On the Equality of the Sexes" in the Revolutionary era, she focused primarily on the equal capacities of women's and men's brains, hence girls' equal right to be educated. Sarah Grimké's *Letters on the Equality of the Sexes* (1836) staked out an important claim to the sexes' equal moral abilities and responsibilities, a claim that led logically to women's right to speak on the important political issues of the day. Debates over adding an Equal Rights Amendment (ERA) to the U.S. Constitution, in both the 1920s and the 1970s, often got tangled up in the question of whether making women equal to men meant making them the same as men; was equality a trap that precluded consideration of differences in the sexes' life experiences? Many of the documents in this book invite consideration of those issues.

Above all, the documents remind us that the history of women's rights is a history of struggle. Seldom have women simply been granted rights; most often women's rights advocates have advanced their cause through long and arduous campaigns accompanied by setbacks and disagreements. On occasion, as with the failed 1970s effort to ratify an ERA (the text of which appears on this book's cover), effort and struggle have been insufficient to stave off defeat. Throughout, advocates have sought to define, negotiate, and expand the boundaries of women's citizenship under ever-changing historical circumstances. The sources collected here place women's individual and collective strivings within those contexts and provide reminders of both how difficult and how remarkable the struggle has been.

Note on Sources and Interpretation

For many years, historians envisioned the history of women's rights largely as the history of the women's rights *movement* with its emphasis on political rights, especially the right to vote. In framing the story, they relied upon sources generated by the individuals who had populated that movement, most notably the six-volume *History of Woman Suffrage,* edited by Elizabeth Cady Stanton, Susan B. Anthony, Matilda Joslyn Gage, and others who were active in the National Woman Suffrage Association (NWSA). While that massive project was hugely significant, it was also incomplete, because the editors downplayed or ignored the work of activists in the rival American Woman Suffrage Association (AWSA) and its affiliates. By writing of "woman" and "the woman movement" in the singular, the editors posited a false unity among women as a group. Likewise, by focusing on the right to vote, they presented a narrower history than the one they themselves had lived. By giving prominence to 1848 and 1920 as key turning points in women's collective struggles for rights, they helped form the idea that women's rights activism occurred in "waves," with a "first wave" culminating in the Nineteenth Amendment to the Constitution, and a "second wave" emerging during the 1960s. Finally, the focus on suffrage conferred an aura of inevitability to the goal, even as the participants understood that few achievements in history are inevitable—or irreversible.

Elements of that original history have been challenged, particularly by historians studying African American and working-class women, with the result that in recent years historians have fundamentally reworked their understandings both of "women's rights" and of women's rights movements. Particularly important was the arrival of women's history as a subject of study in U.S. colleges and universities during the 1970s. As historians sought to study women in all their variety, they ferreted out an extraordinary range of new source materials in order to produce histories that would reflect the complexity of women's experiences in the past. In the process, they broadened their understanding of rights, rethought earlier characterizations of women's rights movements, and challenged the waves metaphor as limiting and restricting. Recent historians have paid close attention to the ways in which the women's experiences *as women* were inseparable from their experiences as members of racial, ethnic, and sexual majorities or minorities. One cannot analyze African American women's access to rights, for instance, without a clear awareness of how their access was shaped by the simultaneous, intersecting social facts of race and gender. Understanding white women's demands for rights requires seeing that, even as they faced gender inequality, they often enjoyed racial privilege. The complexities of women's intersectional identities can hardly be captured by a metaphor of waves, just as that trope has often concealed important conflicts among women over rights and priorities.

Although it is unlikely that historians and history textbooks will discard the metaphor of waves any time soon, in this volume I have avoided using it, preferring instead the more flexible concept of citizenship as a way of discussing women's variable access to rights, and their collective efforts to dismantle systems of gender hierarchy and promote gender equality. Those efforts were never confined to a few chronological eras, as the waves metaphor might imply. To be sure, citizenship itself is an ambiguous concept, subject to varied and shifting meanings, and capable of hiding exclusions based on racial or sexual identity. Moreover, the historical "path to women's full citizenship," as historian Nancy Cott has observed, is both "uneven and unfinished." Still, the concept of citizenship facilitates a nuanced understanding of how women's access to rights served to include them in the body politic, while lack of access excluded and diminished them. Using the concept offers a way to cover far-flung efforts to secure women's rights, whether by union members seeking a voice in organizational decisions, abolitionists pressing for equal rights for former slaves, or suffragists demanding the right to vote as the keystone of citizenship. Political and legal rights nevertheless remain central concerns of many documents presented here, because for so many women voting and civic equality symbolized access to full citizenship and the ability to press legislators for redress of other grievances. Because the effort to attain those rights did not begin in 1848 nor end in 1920, the documents trace a long history, including women's use of partial suffrage and their struggles to secure voting rights when gender exclusion stemmed from racial or ethnic categorization.

Recent historical work confirms that the struggle for suffrage and other women's rights in the United States did not occur in isolation. In the early nineteenth century, European and American activists met at antislavery conventions where women's rights concerns were on the agenda; after returning home, they corresponded with each other and exchanged information and ideas. In later years, international conferences brought together suffragists and women's rights activists from many parts of the globe. Most recently, United Nations–sponsored conferences have focused attention on global women's rights struggles. While the sources found in this volume focus on the United States, covering both individual strivings for rights and broader movements designed to end institutional, legal, and customary practices that denied equal citizenship to women, Americans' involvement in broader global struggles also receives due attention.

Monclova, y Maio 4,, de 1770 años.

Testim.º de Escriptura, que de Ma
ria, Clemencia, Quintana, y flore s.
hiro âel Señor, B.r D.n Miguel, Sanchez,
Navarro. Cura por S.M. Com.do de S.to
ôficio, Vicario, y Juez ê.co, de Esta Villa
de Sant.o de la monclova, y Sus âgreg.s
de Una Casa, y pedaso de tierra, que
le Vendió enprecio, y Cantidad, de ôchen
ta p.s fñâ. Ante el Cap.n de Milicias
D.n fran.co flores, de Abrego. Then.te Gral.
de Gov.or enlo politico, de Esta dha Vi
lla, y Su Jurisdiccion, p.or S.M. (que
Dios gûê.) Como â dentro Severan los
Requisitos, que Se jncluien en ella

CHAPTER 1

Law and Custom in the Colonies

What rights, if any, did women have in the American colonies? The answer depends upon which women we consider, the sources from which they derived their rights, and where they lived in North America.

In thinking about women's rights in colonial America, it is important to remember that modern ideas about rights and citizenship were absent. European colonists were subjects, not citizens: both women and men owed allegiance to a monarch, and most women were also subject to the authority of a husband or father. The notion that governments were obliged to honor and defend individuals' rights evolved slowly; indeed, the very idea that individuals should have equal rights under the law lay far in the future. Not until the time of the American Revolution did Americans articulate such principles, let alone attempt to put them into practice. In the colonies, different groups of women had access to varying sorts of rights, rights that themselves derived from variable sources, including laws, customs, practices, and codes of conduct.

Native American groups followed customary practices that reflected shared ideas about members' rights and obligations to each other and to the group. European settlers, on the other hand, whether they came from England, Holland, Spain, or France, brought varied traditions of written law with them. British Common Law was the basis for the legal systems of the British North American colonies; the Dutch, Spanish, and French based theirs on Roman law. But whether shaped by customary practice or written law, women's access to rights depended on **gender** *(the social and cultural meanings that societies give to biological sex), and on* **patriarchy** *(a gender system that prizes men and masculinity more highly than women and femininity), but especially on social rank or* **status** *(being free or unfree, and possessing or lacking property and power). Neither law nor custom remained static, however; both changed as Europeans settled permanently in North America, interacted with Native Americans, and introduced African slavery into their colonies.*

Economic and Political Rights

Upon their arrival in North America, European observers were especially struck by stark differences between the roles of Indian and European women in economic production, land use, and resource distribution. Native people did not divide Mother Earth into fenced-off parcels; instead they owned land communally and tied land ownership to use. Farming was largely women's work in the Americas, and women used the land to produce much of the food consumed in kinship groups and villages. Women also preserved and prepared the meat and fish that men gathered on expeditions. They built and decorated houses, made furniture, led sugar maple-making expeditions, and worked alongside men in fur-trading operations. Most Native societies were **matrilineal** (tracing one's kinship and descent through one's mother), and many Indian origin stories and spiritual narratives included female deities. The combination of matrilineal descent with significant power both to produce and to distribute basic food items meant that women as a group had important customary rights. In addition, some individual women enjoyed higher status and greater rights than others, usually as older heads of matrilineal households ("matrons"), as religious figures, or as healers. But even in societies that were **patrilineal** (tracing one's kinship and descent through one's father), such as the Algonkian-speaking Kickapoo, women and men observed customs that paired privileges with mutual obligations.

When European commentators, such as William Wood, who sought to encourage English emigration to the colonies, described Algonkian women's customary roles and rights, they did so through a haze of European gender ideas that clouded their vision. In particular, because observers like Wood did not comprehend or value the complementary economic roles that women and men fulfilled, they often portrayed Indian men as "lazy" because they were hunters. In England, hunting was a sport, and enjoyed largely for leisure. Nevertheless, despite the biases evident in the language of Wood's 1634 book, *New England's Prospect,* his description provided a glimpse of Indian women's varied work roles and customary rights.

"Of Their Women, Their Dispositions, Employments, Usage by Their Husbands, Their Apparel, and Modesty

To satisfie the curious eye of women-readers, who otherwise might thinke their sex forgotten, or not worthy a record, let them peruse these few lines, wherein they may see their owne happinesse, if weighed in the womans ballance of these ruder *Indians*, who scorne the tuterings of their wives, or to admit them as their equals, though their qualities and industrious deservings may justly claime the preheminence, and command better usage and more conjugall esteeme, their persons and features being every way correspondent, their qualifications more excellent, being more loving, pittiful, and modest, milde, provident, and laborious than their lazie husbands. Their employments be many: First their building of houses, whose frames are formed like our garden-arbours, something more round, very strong and handsome, covered with close-wrought mats of their owne weaving, which deny entrance to any drop of raine, though it come both fierce and long, neither can the piercing North winde find a crannie, through which he can conveigh his cooling breath, they be warmer than our *English* houses; at the top is a square hole for the smoakes evacuation.... [A]n other work is their planting of corne, wherein they exceede our *English* husband-men, keeping it so cleare with their Clamme shell-hoes, as if it were a garden rather than a corne-field, not suffering a choaking weede to advance his audacious head above their infant corne, or an undermining worme to spoile his **spurnes** [tree roots]. Their corne being ripe, they gather it, and drying it hard in the Sunne, conveigh it to their barnes, which be great holes digged in the ground in forme of a brasse pot, seeled with rinds of trees . . . An other of their employments is their Summer processions to get Lobsters for their husbands, wherewith they baite their hookes when they goe a fishing for Basse or Codfish. This is an everyday's walke, be the weather cold or hot, the waters rough or calme, they must dive sometimes over head and eares for a Lobster, which often shakes them by their hands with a churlish nippe and bids them adiew. The tide being spent, they trudge home two or three miles, with a hundred weight of Lobsters at their backs, and if none, a hundred scoules meete them at home, and a hungry belly for two dayes after. Their husbands having caught any fish, they bring it in their boates as farre as they can by water, and there leave it; as it was their care to catch it, so it must be their wives paines to fetch it home, or fast: which done, they must dresse it and cooke it, dish it,

Peter Lindeström drew an Algonkian (Lenape) family in 1691, differentiating the man from the woman primarily by the implements they carried: gourds for the woman and arrows for the man.

"I had then been with the Indians four summers and four winters, and had become so far accustomed to their mode of living, habits and dispositions, that my anxiety to get away, to be set at liberty, and leave them, had almost subsided. With them was my home; my family was there, and there I had many friends.... Our labor was not severe; and that of one year was exactly similar, in almost every respect, to that of the others.... In the summer season, we planted, tended and harvested our corn, and generally had our children with us; but had no master to oversee or drive us, so that we could work as leisurely as we pleased."

—Mary Jemison, a white Pennsylvania woman captured in 1758 and later married to a Delaware Indian, remembering Algonkian women's work patterns

and present it, see it eaten over their shoulders; and their **loggerships** [sluggards, that is, husbands] having filled their paunches, their sweete lullabies scramble for their scrappes. In the Summer these *Indian* women when Lobsters be in their plenty and prime, they drie them to keepe for Winter, erecting scaffolds in the hot sun-shine, making fires likewise underneath them, by whose smoake the flies are expelled, till the substance remain hard and drie. In this manner they dry Basse and other fishes without salt, cutting them very thinne to dry suddainley before the flies spoile them, or the raine moist them, having a speciall care to hang them in their smokie houses, in the night and dankish weather.

In summer they gather **flagges** [reeds, rushes], of which they make Matts for houses, and Hempe and Rushes, with dyeing stuffe of which they make curious baskets with intermixed colours and protractures of antique Imagerie: These baskets be of all sizes from a quart to a quarter, in which they carry their luggage. In winter time they are their husbands Caterers, trudging to the Clamm bankes for their belly timber, and their Porters to lugge home their Venison which their lazieness exposes to the Woolves till they impose it upon their wives shoulders. They likewise sew their husbands shooes, and weave coates of Turkie feathers, besides all their ordinary household drudgerie which daily lies upon them."

Among some Indian groups, women's customary right to control land, including the production and distribution of its bounty, translated into political power. Huron clan mothers, who headed up households populated by their daughters, sons-in-law, and grandchildren, had traditional rights to select village chiefs and to send their men into battle against chosen enemies. Although women themselves rarely served as chiefs or warriors, the role of chief was inherited through the female line. Nevertheless, European observers, who came from societies where women's political power always derived from their kinship with or sexual relationship to men, struggled to describe what they saw when they observed politics among Native people. A French priest, Pierre de Charlevoix, conveyed his impressions of Huron women's political roles in a letter to an unidentified woman that he included in his 1721 book *Journal of a Voyage to North America*.

"It must be agreed, Madam, that the nearer we view our Indians, the more good qualities we discover in them: most of the principles which serve to regulate their conduct, the general maxims by which they govern themselves, and the essential part of their character, discover nothing of the barbarian...."

Amongst the Hurons, where [the] dignity [of the chief] is hereditary, the succession is continued through the women, so that at the death of a chief, it is not his own, but his sister's son who succeeds him; or, in default of which, his nearest relation in the female line. When the whole branch happens to be extinct, the noblest matron of the tribe or in the nation chuses the person she approves of most, and declares him chief. . . .

Nay more, each family has a right to chuse a counsellor of its own, and an assistant to the chief, who is to watch for their interest; and without whose consent the chief can undertake nothing. These counsellors are, above all things, to have an eye to the public treasury; and it is properly they who determine the uses it is to be put to. They are invested with this character in a general council, but they do not acquaint their allies with it, as they do at the elections and installations of their chief. Amongst the Huron nations, the women name the counsellors, and often chuse persons of their own sex. . . .

The women have the chief authority amongst all the nations of the Huron language; if we except the Iroquois canton of Onneyouth, in which it is in both sexes alternately. But if this be their lawful constitution, their practice is seldom agreeable to it. In fact, the men never tell the women any thing they would have to be kept secret; and rarely any affair of consequence is communicated to them, though all is done in their name, and the chiefs are no more than their lieutenants. . . . I have been however assured, that they always deliberate first on whatever is proposed in council; and that they afterwards give the result of their deliberation to the chiefs, who make the report of it to the general council, composed of the elders; but in all probability this done only for form's sake, and with the restrictions I have already mentioned. The warriors likewise conclude nothing of importance which concerns the nation or town; all being subject to the examination and controul of the council of the elders, who judge in the last resource. . . .

Each tribe has an orator in every town, which orators are the only persons who have a liberty to speak in the public councils and general assemblies: they always speak well and to the purpose. . . . On some occasions, the women have an orator, who speaks in their name, or rather acts as their interpreter."

In 1724, a Jesuit missionary, Joseph-François Lafitau, published his analysis contradicting Charlevoix somewhat on the extent of women's influence among the Iroquois, of whom the Huron were one component.

"Nothing is more real, however, than the women's superiority. It is they who really maintain the tribe, the nobility of blood, the genealogical tree, the order of generations and conservation of the families. In them resides all the real authority: the lands, fields and all their harvest belong to them; they are the soul of the councils, the arbiters of peace and war; they hold the taxes and the public treasure; it is to them that the slaves are entrusted; they arrange the marriages; the children are under their authority; and the order of succession is founded on their blood. The men, on the contrary, are entirely isolated and limited to themselves. Their children are strangers to them. Everything perishes with them. A woman alone gives continuity to the household, but, if there are only men in the lodge, however many they may be, whatever number of children they may have, their family dies out with them. And, although the chiefs are chosen among them, they are purely honorary. The Council of Elders which transacts all the business does not work for itself. It seems that they serve only to represent and aid the women in the matters in which decorum does not permit the latter to appear or act. . . .

[To recapitulate:] the real authority is in the women's hands, but they choose chiefs in their families to represent them and be, as it were, the repositories of this authority with the senate [council]. The women choose their chiefs among their maternal brothers or their own children and it is the latter's brothers or their nephews who succeed them in the mother's household."

Among the British settlers, only men, and only some of them, had any formal right to participate in public affairs, political discussion, or decision-making. Voting was a privilege of property-ownership, and in some colonies, church membership. Still, an occasional woman property-owner, such as Margaret Brent, sought voting privileges on the basis of her status as a possessor of substantial lands and servants. The minutes of the Maryland Assembly recorded her 1648 quest.

"Came Mistress Margarett Brent and requested to have vote in the howse for her selfe and voyce allso for that att the last Court 3rd Jan: it was ordered that the said Mrs Brent was to be lookd uppon and received as his Lordships Attorney. The Governor denied that the said Mrs Brent should have any vote in the howse. And the said Mrs Brent protested against all proceedings in this present Assembly, unlesse shee may be present and have vote as aforesaid."

"Our ancestors considered it a great offence to reject the counsels of their women, particularly [those] of the female governesses. They were esteemed the mistresses of the soil. *Who*, said our forefathers, bring us into being. *Who*, cultivate our land, kindle our fires, and boil our pots, but the women? . . . They are the life of the nation."

—Oneida leader Good Peter's 1788 address to New York Governor Clinton

Margaret Brent: Born in England in 1601, Margaret Brent arrived in Maryland in 1638 with two brothers, her sister Mary, and a group of servants; the sisters promptly claimed 2,000 acres of land and established a profitable farm. Soon, Margaret was lending money to other settlers and pursuing them into court for non-payment. In an eight-year period she appeared in court 134 times. In 1647, upon the death of the colony's governor, she became executor of his estate, with power of attorney. Her request for two votes in the colonial assembly was based upon those two positions. Eventually, Brent and her sister left Maryland for Virginia, where she established a plantation she named "Peace"; she died there in 1671.

Among European settlers, a woman's marital status had a profound effect on her economic and legal rights, whether she sought to control, inherit, and bequeath property or undertake independent legal actions, such as writing a will or running a business. Under English Common Law, which was the basis of law in the British colonies, a single woman (never-married or widowed), designated a *feme sole*, could stand "alone" or "solo" before the law, while a married woman was a *feme covert*, that is, she was literally "covered" by her husband and had no rights separately from him. Margaret Brent remained single her entire life; as a *feme sole*, she escaped the limitations of *coverture*. That legal principle was summed up by the English legal expert William Blackstone in his 1765 *Commentaries on the Laws of England,* which remained foundational in British and American law until well into the 20th century.

"By marriage, the husband and wife are one person in law: that is, the very being or legal existence of the woman is suspended during the marriage, or at least is incorporated and consolidated into that of the husband: under whose wing, protection, and cover, she performs every thing; and is therefore called in our law-french a feme-covert; is said to be covert-baron, or under the protection and influence of her husband, her baron or lord; and her condition during her marriage is called her coverture. Upon this principle, of an union of person in husband and wife, depend almost all the legal rights, duties and disabilities, that either of them acquire by the marriage....

[By] *marriage*, ... those **chattels** [real and personal property], which belonged formerly to the wife, are by act of law vested in the husband, with the same degree of property and with the same powers, as the wife, when sole, had over them....

As to *chattels personal* ... in *possession* which the wife hath in her own right, as ready money, jewels, household goods, and the like, the husband hath therein an immediate and absolute property, devolved to him by the marriage, not only potentially but in fact, which never again can revert in the wife or her representative....

If the wife be injured in her person or her property, she can bring no action for redress without her husband's concurrence, and in his name as well as her own: neither can she be sued, without making the husband a defendant....

[A] married woman is not only utterly incapable of devising *lands*, being excepted out of the statute of wills, but also she is incapable of making a testament of *chattels*, without the license of her husband.... Yet by her husband's license she may make a **testament** [a will]....

The husband also (by the old law) might give his wife moderate correction. For, as he is to answer for her misbehaviour, the law thought it reasonable to intrust him with this power of restraining her, by domestic chastisement, . . . But, with us, . . . this power of correction began to be doubted: and a wife may now have security of the peace against her husband; . . .

[E]ven the disabilities, which the wife lies under, are for the most part intended for her protection and benefit. So great a favourite is the female sex of the laws of England."

In principle, coverture meant that any movable property a woman brought to her marriage, even her clothing and cooking tools, became her husband's, though he could not arbitrarily dispose of those personal possessions. Once she was married, if she owned land or other real estate, her husband had the right to collect any rents or profits on it; if she earned wages, they were his. But practice differed from principle, and in practice, married women could get around the extraordinarily restrictive demands of coverture and exercise some economic rights independently of their husbands. Equity Law existed alongside Common Law in both England and her colonies, providing loopholes for situations where Common Law was too restrictive. Different colonies administered Equity Law differently, but in all colonies, wives could use it to relax somewhat the bonds of matrimony. Prenuptial contracts were one example. Although nowadays the term "prenup" conjures up images of wealthy celebrities entering marriage while simultaneously preparing for the possibility of divorce, in the British colonies, prenuptial contracts were most often used by widows entering second marriages. In 1670, New England farm wife Beatrice Plummer, who had inherited land, real estate, livestock, and household goods from her first husband, William Cantlebury, confirmed the prenuptial contract that she and her second husband, Francis Plummer, made before their marriage.

"Agreement, dated Nov. 25, 1670, between Francis Plummer of Newbury and Beatrice, his wife, confirming the contract made before marriage that if Plummer should die before the said Beatrice, the latter was to have all the estate that was properly hers before marriage, and also to have the new room, half the orchard, half the apples, and her **thirds** [dower right] of the land of said Francis during her life, also firewood out of said Francis Plummer's twenty acres near the little river and the garden as it is now enclosed. If said Beatrice deceased before him, that she should have power to dispose of what estate was hers before marriage to any of her relatives, and if anybody claimed any debts due from William Cantlebury, deceased, said Beatrice's estate was to pay such debts and not the estate of said Plummer, her now husband.

Witness: Richard Dole and Anthony Somerby. . . .

An inventory of the goods to belong to Beatrice, the wife of Francis Plumer or to her heirs: a horse & mare & cattell soe many as was prised to him at 35li. to be paid within one year after the decease of either the said Francis or Beatrice; two Ruggs, four blancketts, two paire of sheets of cotten & linnen, pr. of fine sheets of six yards a peice in them, one feather bed, one brass kettle, an Iron kettle, a paire of sheets more, one chest with a coffer with wearing linnen in them, petticoats, wascoats, two pillows, foure platters, a basen, pewter pint pott, a paire of old curtaines & vallens.

The house and land at Salem that was William Cantleburyes is the proper estate of the said Beatrice, and Francis Plumer has no interest in it as shown by the marriage contract between the said Francis Plumer and Beatrice; besides four cattell and four sheep, and also what is due by bills from Joseph Plumer, Daniell Thurston and Robt. Long, also Francis Plumer agreed not to require anything for keeping his wife's grandchild for the time past to this day.

Dated Nov. 25, 1670 Francis (his mark) Plumer.

Witness: Richard Dole, Anthony Somerby."

Another legal loophole, "feme sole trader" laws, permitted wives to carry on businesses in their husbands' absence. In effect, they allowed a married woman (a *feme covert*) to behave, legally, as though she were single (a *feme sole*). Such laws seemed especially imperative in the colonies, where a traveling husband could be lost without a trace at sea, or a devious lout could light out for another colony, leaving his wife and children without resources. Pennsylvania's law, enacted in 1718, evoked the specter of desertion and other possibilities, clarified the rights of *feme sole* traders, and made abundantly clear the legislators' reasons for providing wives with those rights.

"Whereas it often happens that mariners and others, whose circumstances as well as vocations oblige them to go to sea, leave their wives in a way of shop-keeping: and such of them as are industrious, and take due care to pay the merchants they gain so much credit with, as to be well supplied with shop-goods from time to time, whereby they get a competent maintenance for themselves and children, and have been enabled to discharge considerable debts, left unpaid by their husbands at their going away; but some of those husbands, having so far lost sight of their duty to their wives and tender children, that their affections are turned to those, who, in all probability, will put them upon measures, not only to waste what they may get abroad, but misapply such effects as they leave in this province: For preventing whereof, and to the end that the estates belonging to such absent husbands may be secured for the maintenance of their wives and children, and that the goods and effects which such wives acquire, or are entrusted to sell in their husband's absence, may be preserved for satisfying of those who so entrust them, Be it enacted, That where any mariners or others are gone, or hereafter shall go, to sea, leaving their wives at shop-keeping, or to work for their livelihood at any other trade in this province, all such wives shall be deemed, adjudged and taken, and are hereby declared to be, as feme-sole traders, and shall have ability and are by this act enabled, to sue and be sued, plead and be impleaded at law, in any court or courts of this province, during their husbands' natural lives, without naming their husbands in such suits, pleas or actions: And when judgments are given against such wives for any debts contracted, or sums of money due from them, since their husbands left them, executions shall be awarded against the goods and chattels in the possession of such wives, or in the hands or possession of others in trust for them, and not against the goods and chattels of their husbands; unless it may appear to the court where those executions are returnable, that such wives have, out of their separate stock or profit of their trade, paid debts which were contracted by their husbands, or laid out money for the necessary support and maintenance of themselves and children; then, and in such case, executions shall be levied upon the estate, real and personal, of such husbands, to the value so paid or laid out, and no more. . . .

[I]f such absent husband shall happen to suffer shipwreck, or be by sickness or other casualty disabled to maintain himself, then, and in such case, and not otherwise, it shall be lawful for such distressed husband to sell or mortgage so much of his said estate, as shall be necessary to relieve him, and bring him home again to his family, any thing herein contained to the contrary notwithstanding. . . .

But if such absent husband, having his health and liberty, stays away so long from his wife and children, without making such provision for their maintenance before or after his going away, till they are like to become chargeable to the town or place where they inhabit; or in case such husband doth live or shall live in adultery, or cohabit unlawfully with another woman, and refuses or neglects, within seven years next after his going to sea, or departing this province, to return to his wife, and cohabit with her again; then, and in every such case, the lands, tenements and estate, belonging to such husbands, shall be and are hereby made liable and subject to be seized and taken in execution, to satisfy any sum or sums of money, which the wives of such husbands, or guardians of their children, shall necessarily expend or lay out for their support and maintenance. . . ."

Like "feme sole trader" laws, statutes providing a dower, or endowment, to a widow, and guaranteeing her a dower right, the right to use one-third of her late husband's real property during widowhood, were intended to ensure that wives were not left without any source of economic support. Long a part of English legal tradition, the "widow's third" acquired particular importance in the colonies, where high death and disease rates made daily life uncertain and unstable and many men died before they could make wills bequeathing more than the customary third. In a will, a husband could leave all or most of his worldly goods to his widow, as William Cantlebury did for Beatrice Plummer; in the absence of a will, a widow inherited only the right to use her "third." In order to support herself and any minor children (who would normally be their father's direct heirs), a widow could use her "third" to carry on her husband's work, whether he had been a farmer, a blacksmith, a sail-maker, or a leather-tanner. Or, more likely, she could rent out the property, or use slaves or servants or local hired hands to work it. Connecticut's law, written in 1672, spelled out the widow's entitlement and obligations when it came to her "dower."

"That there may be suitable provision made for the maintenance and comfortable support of widows, after the decease of their husbands, Be it enacted . . . that every married woman, living with her husband in this state, or absent elsewhere from him with his consent, or through his mere default, or by inevitable providence; or in case of divorce where she is the innocent party, that shall not before marriage be estated by way of jointure in some houses, lands, tenements or hereditaments for term of life . . . shall immediately upon, and after the death of her husband, have right, title and interest by way of dower, in and unto one third part of the real estate of her said deceased husband, in houses and lands which he stood possessed of in his own right, at the time of his decease, to be to her during her natural life: the remainder of the estate shall be disposed of according to the will of the deceased. . . .

And for the more easy, and speedy ascertaining of such rights of dower, It is further enacted, That upon the death of any man possessed of any real estate . . . which his widow . . . hath a right of dower in, if the person, or persons that by law have a right to inherit said estate, do not within sixty days next after the death of said husband, by three sufficient freeholders of the same county; to be appointed by the judge of probate ... and sworn for that purpose, set out, and ascertain such right of dower, that then such widow may make her complaint to the judge of probate ... which judge shall decree, and order that such woman's dowry shall be set out, and ascertained by three sufficient freeholders of the county ... and upon approbation thereof by said judge, such dower shall remain fixed and certain. ...

And every widow so endowed ... shall maintain all such houses, buildings, fences, and inclosures as shall be assigned, and set out to her for her dowry; and shall leave the same in good and sufficient repair."

Spanish, French, and Dutch law differed from English Common Law on these matters. In colonies such as New Amsterdam, Florida, and New Mexico, where the traditions of Roman law prevailed, and in Louisiana, which followed the customary laws of Paris, married women kept property they brought into a marriage, and co-owned any property acquired during it, in some cases including their late husbands' personal property as well. The legal principle of "community property" derives from that tradition, as an 1851 summary of the 1680 marriage law makes clear.

"The law recognizes a partnership between the husband and wife as to the property acquired during marriage, and which exists until expressly renounced. ... To this community belong:

1. All the property of whatever nature which the spouses acquire by their own labor and industry.
2. The fruits and income of the individual property of the husband and wife.
3. Whatever the husband does gain by the exercise of a profession or office, e.g., as a judge, lawyer, physician, &c. ...

The property owned by either husband or wife before marriage does not belong to the community. ... Property acquired by either after marriage by a gratuitous title, such as inheritance, donation, or bequest, does not belong to the community. ...

Husband and wife are entitled to an equal share in the community. ... At the same time both are liable, in equal proportion, for the losses and debts incurred during its existence. ..."

Because marriage did not subject wives to coverture, married women property-owners in Spanish and French colonies had the right to administer and protect any property they brought into a marriage. When Doña Maria Clemencia Quintana y Flores of Monclova, Mexico, sold the adobe house and adjacent land that she had inherited from her mother, a

ten-page "testimonio de escriptura," or statement of deed, recorded the 1770 transaction in detail. The first page read:

"Monclova, May 4, 1770

Testimony of deed, made by Doña Maria Clemencia Quintana y Flores to Señor Beneficiado Don Miguel Sanchez Navarro, Priest by his Majesty, Commissary of the Santo Oficio, Vicar, and Ecclesiastic Judge of the city of Santiago de la Monclova and its aggregates, for a house, and a piece of land, sold for the price and amount of eight hundred eighty pesos. Given before the Military Captain Don Francisco Flores de Abrego, Lieutenant General Governor for political matters of this city and its jurisdiction, by his Majesty whom God protects. The following pages specify the conditions."

The combination of Roman and Parisian law with Catholic religious tradition, however, meant that colonial French and Spanish women were expected to defer and be obedient to husbands and fathers, whose patriarchal authority was paramount. Even though they had greater rights to own and control property than women subject to English Common Law, wives were still subject to husbands' authority and were required to secure their husbands' permission to conduct any business related to their property. Husbands, in turn, held the obligation to protect their wives and dependents and to provide for them, as stipulated in the 18th century code of Spanish laws.

"Husband and wife owe each other mutual fidelity, aid, and carnal cohabitation.... The husband is the head of the family, and must provide for its wants.... The wife must obey her husband, and reside where he

Married women's names. Both England and Spain were patrilineal societies, but only English women completely lost their surnames when they married. Spanish women retained their own names, then added on their husbands' names. Doña María Clemencia Quintana's adding of "y Flores" or "and Flores" to her name was typical of the practice.

Facsimile of "testimonio."

thinks proper. The authority of the husband, however, is not one of violence, but of protection. . . .

The husband alone administers the property of the conjugal partnership, during the existence of the marriage, and he can sell and dispose of the same as he thinks proper, provided always he does so without the intention of injuring his wife. . . . This power, however, must be exercised in the lifetime of the husband and gives him no power of control over the community property, not his own, by last will and testament."

Regulating Marriage, Sexuality, and Divorce

European colonists viewed marriage as a lifetime commitment. Because the family constituted the basic economic and social unit of society, permanent marriage bonds were essential for controlling and transmitting property and guaranteeing that children were legitimate. Moreover, for Catholics, marriage was a sacred as well as a worldly event (in the Catholic tradition, marriage is a sacrament). Regulating marriage thus emerged as a central concern for colonial rulers. The question of who was permitted to marry whom, and under what circumstances, became especially complicated in the colonies, when women and men of different ethnic and geographical origins sought to marry. In 1614, Virginians celebrated the union of Pocahontas, an Algonkian leader's daughter, and John Rolfe, an English landowner; the birth of their son, Thomas, seemed to promise a bright future for such Native-English alliances. But by the 1660s, the arrival of thousands of enslaved Africans in Virginia and the reality of sexual liaisons among English, Native, and African colonists, led the House of Burgesses to pass a series of laws restricting the right to marry across racial lines—and eventually prohibiting marriages between women like Pocahontas and men like John Rolfe, along with marriages across categories such as "black" and "white."

"[1691] . . . for the prevention of that abominable mixture and spurious issue which hereafter may encrease in this dominion, as well by negroes, mulattoes, and Indians intermarrying with English, or other white women, as by their unlawful accompanying with one another, Be it enacted . . . that . . . whatsoever English or other white man or woman being free shall intermarry with a negroe, mulatto or Indian man or woman bond or free shall within three months after such marriage be banished and removed from this dominion forever. . . .

And be it further enacted . . . That if any English woman being free shall have a bastard child by any negro or mulatto, she pay the sume of fifteen pounds sterling, within one moneth after such bastard child shall be born, to the Church wardens of the parish … and in default of such payments she shall be taken into the possession of said Church wardens and disposed of for five yeares, and the said fine of fifteen pounds, or whatever the woman shall be disposed of for, shall be paid, one third part to their majesties … and one other third part to the use of the parish … and the other third part to the informer, and that such bastard child be bound out as a servant by the said Church wardens untill he or she shall attaine the age of thirty yeares, and in case such English woman that shall have such bastard child be a servant, she shall be sold by the said church wardens, (after her time is expired that she ought by law to serve her master) for five yeares, and the money she shall be sold for divided as is before appointed, and the child to serve as aforesaid.

[1705] *And be it further enacted*, That no minister of the church of England, or other minister, or person whatsoever, within this colony and dominion, shall hereafter wittingly presume to marry a white man with a negro or mulatto woman; or to marry a white woman with a negro or mulatto man, upon pain of forfeiting or paying, for every such marriage the sum of ten thousand pounds of tobacco. . . ."

In French-governed Louisiana (1699–1766) and Spanish-governed New Mexico (1598–1820), similar concerns about regulating marriage emerged. The French "Code Noir," proclaimed in 1724, specifically prohibited "white" French subjects from marrying "Blacks." Unlike British colonial law, it provided clear sanctions against slave masters who sexually abused their own slaves.

"We forbid our white subjects of either sex from contracting marriage with the Blacks, under penalty of punishment and arbitrary fine; and all cures, priests, or secular or regular missionaries, and even the chaplains of ships, from marrying them. We also forbid our said white subjects, and even the manumitted or free born Blacks, from living in concubinage with slaves. We desire that those who have had one or several children from a similar conjunction, together with the masters who will have permitted them, are each sentenced to a fine of three hundred livres. And, if they are masters of the slave with whom they have had the said children, we desire that, in addition to the fine, they are deprived of the slave as well as of the children, and that they [the slaves] are awarded to the hospital of the place, without ever being able to be manumitted. We do not intend however that the present article applies, when the

In 1967, the Supreme Court, in the case of *Loving v. Virginia,* lifted the last of such restrictions on heterosexual marriage.

Although Spanish authorities did not initially restrict marriages across ethnic or racial lines, they did regulate marriages to ensure that the bride and groom were of similar *calidad*, a Spanish term roughly translatable as "quality," referring to an individual's social status or rank and possession (or lack) of property and rights, as well as age, racial designation, occupation, and legitimacy or illegitimacy. In the 1760s, they began to redefine *calidad* to focus increasingly on racial characteristics in the belief that it was important to maintain a family's "*limpieza de sangre*" or pure bloodline. Such ideas relied on socially invented categories of "blood" and "race" similar to those found in Virginia's laws and in the Code Noir. As a result, high-status women and men in New Mexico, arguing that there was no available potential spouse of the same *calidad* or "purity" of aristocratic lineage, sought to bypass other marriage restrictions, such as the Catholic prohibition on first-cousin marriage. "I cannot find another person with whom to contract marriage who is my blood equal," said Don Pedro Sánchez in 1761, seeking to marry his cousin Doña Efigenia Durán y Chávez. "The purity of our families has always been conserved with honor and without mixture with castes; and the love which I have for him" were the reasons Doña Serafina Chávez gave in 1836 for wanting to marry her cousin Don José Torres.

Spanish painting illustrating *calidad*.

black man, manumitted or free, who was not married during his concubinage with his slave, shall marry, in forms prescribed by the Church, the cited slave, who will be manumitted in this way, and the children rendered free and legitimate."

Because of their views on marriage, the English, French, and Spanish rendered the right to divorce essentially non-existent, though couples could seek church or civil annulments for marriages that were, for various reasons, "null and void." Europeans were surprised, and usually horrified, to discover that Native American groups did not share their understanding of the marital bond, and that, indeed, women often had the right both to initiate marital separation and to remarry. The comments of Englishman John Lawson, from his 1709 survey of back-country Native Americans, were fairly non-judgmental for their time.

"As for the Indian Marriages, I have read and heard of a great deal of Form and Ceremony used, which I never saw, nor yet could learn in the Time I have been amongst them, any otherwise than I shall here give you an Account of: which is as follows.

When any young *Indian* has a Mind for such a Girl to his Wife, he, or some one for him, goes to the Young Woman's Parents, if living; if not, to her nearest Relations; where they make Offers of the Match betwixt the Couple. The Relations reply, they will consider of it, which serves for a sufficient Answer, till there be a second Meeting about the Marriage, which is generally brought into Debate before all the Relations (that are old People) on both Sides: and sometimes the King, with all his great Men, give their Opinions therein. If it be agreed on, and the young Woman approve thereof, (for these Savages never give their Children in Marriage, without their own Consent) the Man pays so much for his Wife: and the handsomer she is, the greater Price she bears....

The Marriages of these *Indians* are no farther binding, than the Man and Woman agree together. Either of them has Liberty to leave the other, upon any frivolous Excuse they can make; yet whosoever takes the Woman that was another Man's before, and bought by him, as they all are, must certainly pay to her former Husband, whatsoever he gave for her....

The Woman is not punish'd for Adultery, but 'tis the Man that makes the injur'd Person Satisfaction, which is the Law of Nations practis'd amongst them all; and he that strives to evade such Satisfaction as the Husband demands, lives daily in Danger of his Life; yet when discharg'd, all Animosity is laid aside, and the Cuckold is very well pleased with his Bargain, whilst the Rival is laugh'd at by the whole Nation, for carrying on his Intrigue with no better Conduct, than to be discover'd and pay so dear for his Pleasure.

The *Indians* say, that the Woman is a weak Creature, and easily drawn away by the Man's Persuasion: for that Reason, they lay no Blame upon her, but the Man (that ought to be Master of his Passion) for persuading her to it."

European colonists' prohibition on divorce was not complete, however. Among the Puritans who settled New England and the Dutch Calvinists in New York, marriage was a civil contract, not a sacrament, and could be broken in certain instances. Connecticut, which had the most liberal divorce policy in the colonies, permitted individuals to petition for a divorce from the superior court, under the specific conditions spelled out in a 1667 statute, "An Act Relating to Bills of Divorce."

"Marriages among the Indians are not, as with us, contracted for life; it is understood on both sides that the parties are not to live together any longer than they shall be pleased with each other. The husband may put away [divorce] his wife whenever he pleases, and the woman may in like manner abandon her husband."

—Moravian missionary John Heckewelder's observations on marriage and divorce among Ohio's Delaware Indians in the 1770s

"Be it enacted . . . that no bill of divorce shall be granted to any man or woman, lawfully married, but in the case of adultery, or fraudulent contract, or wilful desertion for three years with total neglect of duty; or in case of seven years absence of one party not heard of: after due enquiry is made, and the matter certified to the superior court, in which case the other party may be deemed and accounted single and unmarried. And in that case, and in all other cases afore-mentioned, a bill of divorce may be granted by the superior court to the aggrieved party; who may then lawfully marry or be married again."

Between 1750 and 1797, 839 divorce cases made their way through Connecticut's courts. The legal ground most commonly cited? Desertion. In more than half of all cases it was the only cause mentioned, and women filed over 80 percent of petitions citing desertion. In other words, when women had the right to divorce, they used it to deal with absconding husbands or those who disappeared at sea, never to be heard from again. Other Connecticut women sought divorces from bigamous spouses, and more than 10 percent of women's divorce petitions involved physical abuse or extreme cruelty. Ruth Crary had not heard from her absent husband, Roger, in over three years when she filed her 1791 divorce petition.

Mary Dewey's husband Elias not only deserted her but remarried in Rhode Island; her divorce petition revealed that she felt forced to go "begging from house to house for support for her and her infant child."

—Mary Dewey of Connecticut, 1764

Sarah Johnson's husband John eventually deserted her, but not before "beating, striking, kicking and stamping upon her, pulling her hair and buffeting and spitting in her Face in a most angry, malicious manner."

—Sarah Johnson of Connecticut, 1770

"To the Hon Superior Court of the State of Connecticut now sitting at Windham—the Petition of Ruth Crary—of Ashford in the County afores'd Humbly Sheweth that she was on the 21st day of April 1785 Lawfully joined in Marriage with Roger Crary of Said Ashford with whom she lived in a Due Discharge of the Marriage Covenant on her Part untill on or about the first day of May AD 1788 when the said Roger Crary for reasons wholly unknown to the Petitioner did Absent himself from the Family and Friendships of your Petitioner and hath gone to some parts of the world unknown to the Pet. leaving her wholly Destitute of Support, and he hath continued so to absent himself to the Present time and thereupon the Petitioner Prays your Honrs to Grant her a Bill of Divorce from him the said Roger Crary and that the Petition[er] be declared single and unmarried and She as in Duty bound shall Pray.

Dated at Ashford the 23rd day of September AD 1791"

With a full divorce, such as that allowed by Connecticut law, the parties could remarry. Short of that, legal separation was at times permissible. Separations "from bed and board," without the option of remarriage, were available even in colonies, such as New Mexico and Louisiana, where Catholicism was the dominant religion, but the requirements were highly restrictive. Under Louisiana's *Coutume de Paris* (customary Parisian law), a wife could ask for a separation only if her husband's

cruelty threatened "her life, her sanity, or her tranquility to such a degree that cohabitation became intolerable." In the British colonies, a legal separation required direct petition either to Chancery Court (equity courts, which did not exist in all colonies) or to the colonial legislature. In 1678, the Maryland Governor and Governor's Council acted as a court of chancery in granting a legal separation to Robert and Elizabeth Leshley, a well-off couple who had been feuding for two long years. The decision did not mention Elizabeth's sensational accusation that Robert had engaged in "buggery" (anal sex) but required Robert to provide yearly "maintenance" (alimony) to support Elizabeth for the rest of her life.

"To the Honble Thomas Notley Esqr Ltt Genll & Chiefe Governor of Maryland

The Humble Peticōn of Robert Leshley Humbly Sheweth. That Yor Peticōners wife being a woman of an Implacable turbulent Spiritt has at severall times unjustly & wrongfully made Divers complaints and Accusations against yor Pett before severall of his Lo[rdships] Justices of the peace of Calvert County but finding they tooke not the effect she hoped for, and that her Designe of procureing a considerable part of yor Petrs Estate to be allowed her for a maintenance with which she might live at her pleasure where she listed and quite Desert the family and concerns of yor Petr was wholly frustrated, she hath since very falsly injuriously & maliciously accused yor Petr of Buggery to the greate scandal & irreparable prejudice of yor Petrs credit and reputation wch he Does & alwaies shall Esteeme of greater price & value then his Life.

Wherfore yor Peticōner humbly prayeth, that yor Honor will be gratiously pleased to grant him a Warrant, that she may be brought before yor Honor and her complaints & accusations against yor Petr heard and Examined before yor Honor whereby yor Petr may purge and cleanse himself of that grevious scandall cast upon him and that for the future he may live more peaceably & comfortably either with his said Wife or by allowing her such a maintenance as yor Honor shall ordr and Command....

Upon heareing and Examination of the whole matter the Substance gathered from thence was that the Peticōner & his wife having had severall Differences betweene them wch could not be composed Did severall Declare that they were fully resolved never any more to live together, She Desireing an allowance proportionable to what she had at her Intermarriage with him. He Declared himself willing to allow her such a reasonable maintenance as the Governor and Councell should think fitt to award her with Due

Under English common law, all divorce suits were "fault" divorces; that is, one party had to sue the other, and one party had to be found at fault for causing the marriage to break down.

consideration had to his Capacity. The wch at last they both referred to the Discretion of the Govrnor and Councell to ordr therein what to them should seeme meete wch they would submit to.

The Governor and Councell haveing Duely and maturely considered the prmisses Did ordr viz. . . .

Whereas appeared before the Governor and Councell this Day Robert Leshley of Calvert County & Elizabeth his wife, and Did both jointly and severally openly Declare that for severall Differences between them both publick and private they were fully resolved never to cohabitt together again, . . . It is Ordered.

That the said Robert Leshley pay or cause to be paid yearly and every yeare unto the said Elizabeth his wife for and Dureing her naturall life the just summe of two thousand pounds of tobacco for a maintenance and no more."

Whether seeking divorce or separation, individuals needed economic and educational resources to be able to write petitions, appear before courts, and defend their rights. Women sometimes took things into their own hands and abandoned abusive, absent, or adulterous husbands without bothering to see a lawyer or appear before a judge or legislative committee. Some left their marriages to seek happiness in another man's arms. Such informal divorces, not sanctioned by or recorded in law, allowed women to extricate themselves from problematic marriages but could plunge them and their children into serious economic crisis if they had no means of support, whether from paid labor, a new husband, or parents. Newspaper notices from angry husbands refusing to provide economic support for wives who "eloped" from their "bed and board" open a window into this practice. On occasion, wives or fathers-in-law posted competing notices, seeking to argue their side of the story. The men's and women's language reveals how husbands such as Jonathan Staples (married to the delightfully named Freelove) and wives such as Katherine Kirkpatrick understood the rights and obligations of both parties within patriarchal marriage.

"Whereas Katherine, the Wife of John Kirkpatrick, of Charles-Town, Maryland, hath eloped from his Bed and Board, without any just Cause known to him; having robbed and plundered his House, and left nothing worth mentioning, at the Time he was at the Point of Death. These are to forewarn all Persons not to trust her on his Account, for he will pay no Debts of her contracting after the 28th of May, 1768.

John Kirkpatrick"

"Whereas John Kirkpatrick, of Charles-Town, Maryland, did, in an Advertisement, published in the Pennsylvania Gazette, No. 2061, advertise that I Katherine his Wife, had eloped from his Bed and Board, after plundering his House of every Thing worth mentioning, and that without any just Cause given by him; all which Facts are false, and without any Foundation; in Truth, and in Justice to my Character, I take this Method to acquaint the Public, that I never eloped, nor ever had any Intention so to do, until forced by Ill Treatment to leave his House, for the Security of my Life which his Son James was Witness to; and that I intend to prosecute him, according to Law, for the Falsities contained in his Advertisement.

Katherine Kirkpatrick"

"Whereas Catherine, the wife of John Kirkpatrick, of Charlestown, Maryland, did publish in the Pennsylvania Gazette, No. 2068, that I had falsely accused her of eloping from me, and plundering my house, and has industriously spread abroad that she took nothing with her but what she tied up in a handkerchief; but I can prove and will be qualified to it, if required, that she has taken, in money and effects, in the value of 301 pounds 9 shillings and twopence; nevertheless if she will bring back what goods she has left, I will receive her again, and

Jonathan Staples thought that it was the "advice and persuasion of some evil-minded persons" that made his wife, Freelove, "elope" from his "bed and board" in 1764.

When Nathaniel Sands' wife, Jane, left her marriage in 1735, it was for another man.

Whereas *Jane* the Wife of *Nathaniel Sands* of *Long Island*, in the Province of *New-York*, is eloped from her Husbands Bed and Board, in Company with one *William Davies*, in the Sloop Carolina, *John Blair* Master, to *N. Carolina*, and has taken with her a Negro Woman, and all the Houshold Furniture of the said *Nathaniel Sands*. These are therefore to forewarn all Persons not to trust the said *Jane* on Account of her Husband, for he will not pay any Debts she shall contract during her Elopement.

if she does not I hereby forbid all persons to trust her on my account, for I will pay no debts of her contracting, until I give her her former Credit under my hand.

John Kirkpatrick"

The codification of slavery and indentured servitude in colonial law offers a stark example of the process whereby early flexibility gave way to legal rigidity in the expanding European empires in the New World. Various forms of unfreedom were commonplace throughout Europe and her colonies (as indeed they were among many Native people, who often used war captives as servants), but with the arrival of growing numbers of African slaves and servants in the French, Spanish, Dutch, and English colonies in the mid-17th century, lawmakers faced questions about Africans' status in law, as well as the status of their children. In the English colonies, they responded with new laws specifying, as Virginia's law did, first, that slavery would be a permanent—and inheritable—condition and, second, that the inheritance would be matrilineal.

"[1662] Whereas some doubts have arrisen whether children got by any Englishman upon a negro woman should be slave or ffree, Be it therefore enacted and declared by this present grand assembly, that all children borne in this country shalbe held bond or free only according to the condition of the mother, And that if any christian shall committ ffornication with a negro man or woman, hee or shee soe offending shall pay double the ffines imposed by the former act."

Other laws separated European from African women by making all of the latter subject to taxation ("tythable"), even if they became free, but taxing only female indentured servants who did field work. Lawmakers thereby created a chasm between the rights of free white women and those of free black women.

"[1662] Whereas diverse persons purchase women servants to work in the ground that thereby they may avoyd the payment of levies, *Be it henceforth enacted by the authority aforesaid* that all women servants whose common imployment is working in the crop shalbe reputed tythable, and levies paid for them accordingly; and that every master of a family if he give not an accompt of such in his list of tythables shalbe fined as for other concealments. . . .

[1668] Whereas some doubts, have arisen whether negro women set free were still to be accompted tithable according to a former act, *It is declared by this grand assembly* that negro women, though permitted to enjoy their ffreedome yet ought not in all respects to be admitted to a full fruition of the exemptions and impunities of the English, and are still liable to payment of taxes."

Religion and Education

In only one arena—religion—might colonial Americans have used the term "equal" or "equality" in discussing women in relationship to men. European settlers came from religious traditions that assumed the spiritual equality of the sexes, the belief that both women and men possessed souls that were equal before God. But rare indeed was a claim that equality in the spiritual realm should extend to the world of daily living. Instead, women were routinely enjoined to submit to male authority in all the lawful things of this world, including religious instruction and speech. A woman who insisted upon her right to interpret religious texts or sermons for the benefit of other women, in separate religious meetings, might find herself, as Anne Hutchinson of Puritan Massachusetts did in 1636, put on trial, convicted of heresy, excommunicated from the church, and banished from the colony. The trial transcript revealed a deep-seated hostility to female claims to religious authority among male leaders such as Governor John Winthrop, as well as Hutchinson's assumption, because of her family's status in the colony, that unlike most women, she had the right to speak on religious matters.

"Mr. Winthrop, governor: Mrs. Hutchinson, you are called here as one of those that have troubled the peace of the commonwealth and the churches here; you are known to be a woman that hath had a great share in the promoting and divulging of those opinions that are causes of this trouble. . . . [Y]ou have spoken divers things as we have been informed very prejudicial to the honour of the churches and ministers thereof, and you have maintained a meeting and an assembly in your house that hath been condemned by the general assembly as a thing not tolerable nor comely in the sight of God nor fitting for your sex, . . . therefore

A group of Maryland's free women of color challenged that colony's taxation policy in 1688 and won: "The peticon of Sarah Driggers and the rest all Negroes desiring that they might be putt out of the list of Tythables from paying any Taxes as being free borne Negroes whereupon it was the same day Ordered that the four women be exempted and that the mn [men pay] taxes for this yeare and that they bring a Certificate under the Ministers hands where they formerly did live or were borne that they are free Negroes and baptized."

—Somerset County Court
proceedings, 1690–1691

we have thought good to send for you to understand how things are, that if you be in an erroneous way we may reduce you that so you may become a profitable member here among us, otherwise if you be obstinate in your course that then the court may take such course that you may trouble us no further. . . .

Mrs. Hutchinson: I am called here to answer before you but I hear no things laid to my charge.

Gov: I have told you some already and more I can tell you.

Mrs. H: Name one, Sir.

Gov: Have I not named some already?

Mrs. H: What have I said or done?

Gov: Why for your doings, this you did harbour and countenance those that are parties in this faction that you have heard of.

Mrs. H: That is [a] matter of conscience, Sir.

Gov: Your conscience you must keep or it must be kept for you. . . .

Gov: Why do you keep such a meeting at your house as you do every week upon a set day?

Mrs. H: It is lawful for me to do so, as it is all your practices and can you find a warrant for yourself and condemn me for the same thing? . . .

Gov: For this, that you appeal to our practice you need no confutation. If your meeting had answered to the former it had not been offensive, but I will say that there was no meeting of women alone, but your meeting is of another sort for there are sometimes men among you.

Mrs. H: There was never any man with us.

Gov: Well, admit there was no man at your meeting and that you was sorry for it, there is no warrant for your doings, and by what warrant do you continue such a course?

Mrs. H: I conceive there lyes a clear rule in Titus [a reference to Titus, 2: 3–5, 'Bid the older women . . . to train the young women'], that the elder women should instruct the younger and then I must have a time wherein I must do it. . . . Will it please you to answer me this and to give a rule, for then I will willingly submit to any truth. If any come to my house to be instructed in the ways of God what rule have I to put them away? . . .

Gov: [B]ut suppose that a man should come and say Mrs. Hutchinson I hear that you are a woman that God hath given his grace unto and you have knowledge in the word of God I pray instruct me a little, ought you not to instruct this man?

Mrs. H: I think I may. Do you think it not lawful for me to teach women and why do you call me to teach the court?

Gov: We do not call you to teach the court but to lay open yourself.

Mrs. H: I desire you that you would then set me down a rule by which I may put them away that come unto me and so have peace in so doing.

Gov: You must shew your rule to receive them.

Mrs. H: I have done it. . . . [I]f you look upon the rule in Titus it is a rule to me. If you convince me that it is no rule I shall yield.

Gov: You know that there is no rule that crosses another, but this rule crosses that in the Corinthians [a reference to I Corinthians 14: 34, 35, 'women should keep silence in the churches']. But you must take it in this sense that elder women must instruct the younger about their business, and to love their husbands and not to make them to clash.

Mrs. H. I do not *conceive* but that it is meant for some publick times. . . .

Gov: Your course is not to be *suffered* for, besides that we find such a course as this to be greatly prejudicial to the state, besides the occasion that it is to seduce many honest persons that are called to those meetings and your opinions being known to be different from the word of God may seduce many simple souls that resort unto you, besides that the occasion which hath come of late hath come from none but such as have frequented your meetings, so that now they are flown off from magistrates and ministers and this since they have come to you, and besides that it will not well stand with the commonwealth that families should be neglected for so many neighbours and dames and so much time spent, we see no rule of God for this, we see not that any should have authority to set up any other exercises besides what authority hath already set up and so what hurt comes of this you will be guilty of and we for suffering you.

Mrs. H: Sir, I do not believe that to be so."

Intelligent and accomplished women, such as Winthrop's acquaintance Anne Bradstreet, bristled at the views he expressed. In her poems, such as "The Prologue" from 1650, she used wit and humor to skewer views like Winthrop's.

"I am obnoxious to each carping tongue,
Who sayes, my hand a needle better fits,
A Poets Pen, all scorne, I should thus wrong;
For such despight they cast on female wits:

John Winthrop's casual comment in a 1645 journal entry reflected his views on the dangers of intellect in women:

"[April 13, 1645]: Mr. Hopkins, the governor of Hartford upon Connecticut, came to Boston, and brought his wife with him, (a godly young woman and of special parts), who was fallen into a sad infirmity, the loss of her understanding and reason, which had been growing upon her divers years, by occasion of her giving herself wholly to reading and writing, and had written many books. Her husband being very loving and tender of her was loath to grieve her; but he saw his error, when it was too late, for if she had attended her household affairs, and such things as belong to women, and not gone out of her way and calling to meddle in such things as are proper for men, whose minds are stronger, etc., she had kept her wits, and might have improved them usefully and honorably in the place God had set her."

Anne Dudley Bradstreet, born in England in 1612, was the first American to publish a book of poetry. Although she did not have formal schooling, Bradstreet was well educated in the classical literature of her day, as her poetic allusions and references reveal. In 1630, the eighteen-year-old Anne Bradstreet left England with her parents and her husband, Simon, to venture to Massachusetts Bay Colony, in order to participate in the Puritan experiment in building what the group's leader, John Winthrop, termed a "city upon a hill." Bradstreet led a busy life in the new colony as the mother of eight children and as an unpublished poet; interestingly, because both her father and her husband served as public officials in Massachusetts Bay, they were among the men who questioned and convicted Anne Hutchinson. In 1650, her first volume of poetry was published anonymously in England under the title *The Tenth Muse Lately Sprung Up in America*. Today, her poetry is valued for its beauty, wit, and skill; in it she occasionally commented on the situation of women within a patriarchal culture. She died in North Andover, Massachusetts, in 1672.

If what I doe prove well, it wo'nt advance,
They'l say it's stolne, or else, it was by chance.

But sure the anti[que] *Greeks* were far more milde,
Else of our Sex, why feigned they those nine
And poesy made, *Calliope's* owne childe,
So 'mongst the rest, they plac'd the Arts divine:
But this weake knot, they will full soon untye,
The *Greeks* did nought, but play the fools & lye.

Let *Greeks* be *Greeks*, and women what they are,
Men have precedency, and still excell,
It is but vaine unjustly to wage war,
Men can doe best, and Women know it well;
Preheminence in each, and all is yours;
Yet grant some small acknowledgement of ours."

Anne Hutchinson, John Winthrop, and Anne Bradstreet represented one tradition within Protestant Christianity—Puritanism—but a newer Protestant group—Quakers—permitted women the right to speak and preach on religious subjects. Because they believed that each individual had access to an "inner light" through which God's spirit could speak directly, Quakers took a very different approach to religious authority from that taken by religious groups that required a priest, minister, or rabbi to interpret God's word to believers. Quakers ordained no ministers, selected no particular individual to serve as a spiritual intermediary between worshippers and their God; instead, any member of the congregation (the "meeting") who felt moved by the spirit could speak. In one Philadelphia Quaker meeting, between 1745 and 1746, women took advantage of that opportunity to deliver 40 percent of all prayers and sermons. As this letter (c. 1675) from a group of English Quaker women to their colonial sisters makes clear, belief that the souls of the sexes were equal in God's eyes could be the basis for women's collective authority through separate women's meetings. The Quaker women's interpretation of the Scriptures, especially the letter of Titus, offers a clear contrast with the Puritan views voiced at Anne Hutchinson's trial.

"Dear Sisters,

In the blessed unity in the Spirit of grace our Souls Salute you who are sanctified in Christ Jesus, and called to be Saints.... To you that are of the true seed of the promise of God in the beginning, that was to bruise the Serpent's head, and which is fulfilled in Christ Jesus of which we are made partakers, which is the seed the promise is to; which the Apostle spoke of and said, God sent forth his Son made of a woman, made under the Law to redeem.... To you all every where, where this may come, is this written....

And that every particular of us, may be ready, and willing to answer what the lord requires of us; in our several places and conditions ... for we are all the children of God by faith in Christ Jesus, where there is neither male nor female &c. but we are all one in Christ Jesus.... So here is the blessed Image of the living God, restored againe, in which he made them male and female in the beginning: and in this his own Image God blessed them both, and said unto them increase and multiply, and replenish the earth, and subdue it, and have dominion over ... the earth.... And in this dominion and power, the lord God is establishing his own seed, in the male and female, over the head of the serpent, and over his seed, and power. And he makes no difference in the seed, between the male and the female....

And let us therefore ... meet together, and keep our womens meetings, in the name and power, and fear of the lord Jesus, whose servants and handmaids we are, in the good order of the Gospel meet....

And so here in the power and spirit of the Lord God, women comes to be coheires [co-heirs], and fellow laborers, in the Gospell, as it was in the Apostles dayes who entreated his true yoakfellowes, to help those women that laboured with him in the Gospell, phill: 4.3. and also in his epistle to Timothy 5.3. he exhorted the elder women, that they should be as mothers, and the younger as sisters in all purity.

And in Titus: 2.3: the Aged women likewise that they be as becometh holiness, and teachers of good things; and that they teach the younger women to be sober, to love their husbands, to love their children, to be discreet, Chast, keepers at home, Good, Obedient to their own husbands; that the word of God be not Blasphemed....

And though wee be looked upon as the weaker vessels, yet strong and powerfull is God, whose strength is made perfect in weakness, he can make us good and bold, and valliant Souldiers of Jesus Christ."

While Protestants, such as Puritans and Quakers, predominated in the British colonies, Catholicism was the religion of New France and New Spain. The Catholic tradition of a male, and celibate, priesthood could have a contradictory effect on women's right to speak and teach on religious subjects. On the one hand, all lay individuals needed priests as

intermediaries between themselves and their God; only priests could celebrate the Mass, the central worship event in Catholicism, and only they could perform other sacred rituals, such as administering the sacraments. On the other hand, deeply religious women could commit themselves to lives of celibacy and service by joining a religious order and going to live in a convent. Convents were self-governing women's institutions, often with extensive property holdings, such as schools or hospitals and even slaves, managed by women (under the nominal guidance of a priest or bishop). In her letters to her father, the French-born Ursuline sister Marie Madeleine Hachard, who helped found the first Catholic convent in New Orleans in 1727, described the group's plans for a school and their belief that they could save pupils' souls.

[New Orleans, October 27, 1727] "We do not expect to take possession of our monastery and the hospital for a year, or perhaps longer, for the workers are not as numerous here as in France, especially since they want to construct it to last; all will be in brick. While waiting, they built us a small lodging area in our residence for extern students and for lodging the boarders.... There are already more than thirty boarders from here and Belize and the surrounding area who insisted on being received. The parents are carried away with joy to see us, saying that they no longer worry that they will return to France since they have here what they need to educate their daughters.... We hope that our establishment will be for the glory of God and that, in time, it will produce great good for the salvation of souls. This has been our principal aim."

Within their educational institutions, religious women exercised their right to teach on religious topics, and to interpret Catholic doctrine to students and lay women. A second letter from Sister Marie Madeleine Hachard to her father reflects the special spiritual knowledge and authority that nuns claimed. She believed that, by instructing local girls (black, white, and Native, free and enslaved), the Ursulines elevated womanhood—and especially motherhood—to a position of spiritual importance, while helping to alter the girls' worldly aspirations. Religious beliefs thus provided a rationale for women's right to education, and religious teaching institutions supplied a venue. Women needed to be educated in order to train their children properly in religious matters. Still, throughout the colonies women were less likely than men to be able to read and write.

[New Orleans, January 1, 1728] "Our little community grows from day to day. We have twenty boarders, of whom eight today made their first communion, three ladies also board, and three orphans that we took through charity. We also have seven slave boarders to

In New Mexico, Catholic women's devotion to the Virgin Mary reflected her importance as a female role model. Painting on hide, "Nuestra Señora de Guadalupe," New Mexico, 18th century.

instruct for baptism and first communion, besides a great number of day students, female blacks and female savages who come for two hours a day for instruction. The custom here is to marry the girls from age twelve to fourteen. Before our arrival, many married before they even knew how many Gods there are. Judge the rest. But since we have been here, none of them have been married without having come to receive our instructions. . . . The boarders, ranging from twelve to fifteen years of age, have never been to Confession or even to Mass. They were raised on their habitations, five to six leagues from this city, and in consequence without any spiritual succor. They had never heard anyone speak of God. When we tell them the most common things, for them they are oracles that come out of our mouths. We have the consolation to find in them great docility and a strong desire to be instructed. All would like to be nuns, which is not to the liking of Reverend de Beaubois, our very worthy **superior** [the sisters' religious supervisor, the Jesuit priest Ignace-Nicolas de Beaubois]. He finds it more proper for them to become Christian mothers who, by their good example, will finally establish religion in the country."

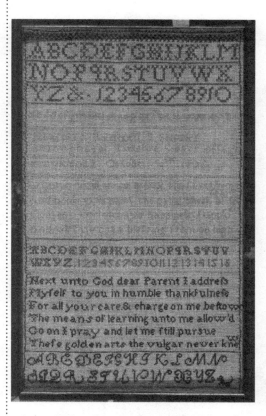

In her 1756 sewing sampler, Ataresta Learned gave thanks for the educational opportunity she enjoyed.

CHAPTER 2

Revolutionary Ideals and Realities

In the Declaration of Independence (1776), when Thomas Jefferson wrote that "all men are created equal" and that it was "self-evident" that they possessed "certain unalienable rights," he made claims that were radically new for the time. In a republic, people would be equal citizens, not a monarch's subjects. France's "Declaration of the Rights of Man and Citizen" (1789) stated flatly that "men are born and remain free and equal in rights" while Haiti's 1805 Constitution "irrefutably established . . . equality before the law" for all citizens. Historians argue about whether women—or even "all men"—were included in Jefferson's statements, but the basic principles that he and his counterparts articulated represented a significant new departure in thinking about human rights and human equality. If monarchy as a system of government was to be rejected because it created inequality and hierarchy by setting one individual, by virtue of birth alone, above all others, then what justification was there for other systems of hierarchy, including the hierarchy of slave and master and the hierarchy of gender?

Girls and women were among those who took to heart the American Revolution's principles of independence, freedom, liberty, equality, and rights by raising questions about how universal the principles were. As they did so, they invoked new concepts, especially "woman's rights" and "the equality of the sexes." A white Philadelphia schoolgirl, Priscilla Mason, employed Revolutionary principles to argue not only for girls' right to education but also for their right to use their educations in professions such as the Law. At age twenty, Phillis Wheatley, African-born and about to be released from slavery, engaged Revolutionary ideas to proclaim her love of freedom, while a still-enslaved woman in her forties, Elizabeth Freeman, used them to argue for her right—and that of all slaves in Massachusetts—to be free people. Abigail Adams had the rights of married women in particular on her mind when she asked her husband John to "remember the ladies" in the "new code of laws" that would be written after American "independancy" was declared; "remember all Men would be tyrants if they could," she wrote. And in 1779, the writer Judith Sargent Murray argued explicitly for "the equality of the sexes" in an essay that she eventually published in 1790. But the meaning of concepts such as equality in the new republic was open to debate. It remained unclear what rights women would have and what "equality of the sexes" entailed. Free women might be citizens of the new republic, but it was not at all obvious what sort of citizenship they would enjoy, and which women would gain access to new rights or new versions of equality.

Women in Wartime

Women's claims to rights derived, in part, from their participation in the War for Independence (1775–1783) and pre-war political activism. Traditionally, it was men's responsibility to take up arms in defense of the nation—their "public virtue," or patriotism—that served as the basis for their rights as citizens. Women now sought to change the definition of patriotism to include their own labor as economic producers and consumers, fund-raisers, thinkers, and mothers. Although some women, like some men, remained loyal to England, and some sought to remain neutral, those who endorsed the Patriot cause, sometimes calling themselves "Daughters of Liberty," took up the work of boycotting British goods, raising money for the Continental Army, or expressing their sentiments in letters and poems. In doing so, they took a political stance and asserted themselves in support of male political leaders, who viewed the boycotts as crucial to resisting illegitimate British taxation schemes. In 1770 in Boston, "300 Mistresses of Families" including "Ladies of the highest Rank and Influence" pledged to boycott tea.

"Boston, January 31, 1770.

At a Time when our invaluable Rights and Privileges are attacked in an unconstitutional and most alarming Manner, and as we find we are reproached for not being so ready as could be desired, to lend our Assistance, we think it our Duty perfectly to concur with the true Friends of Liberty, to all the Measures they have taken to save this ill used Country from Ruin and Slavery: And particularly, we join with the very respectable Body of Merchants and other Inhabitants of this Town, who met in Faneuil-Hall the 23d of this Instant, in their Resolutions, *totally* to abstain from the Use of TEA: And as the greatest Part of the Revenue arising by Virtue of the late Acts, is produced from the Duty paid upon Tea, which Revenue is wholly expended to support the American Board of Commissioners: We the Subscribers do strictly engage, that we will *totally* abstain from the Use of that Article (Sickness excepted) not only in our respective Families; but that we will absolutely refuse it, if it should be offered to us upon any Occasion whatsoever. This Agreement we chearfully come into, as we believe the very distressed Situation of our Country requires it, and we do hereby oblige ourselves religiously to observe it, till the late Revenue Acts are repealed."

A statement signed by a group of fifty-one women in Edenton, North Carolina, confirms that consumer boycotts, led by women and focusing especially on tea, were widespread throughout the thirteen colonies by the time the First Continental Congress met in Philadelphia in 1774.

"The provincial deputies of North Carolina, having resolved not to drink any more tea, nor wear any more British cloth, etc., many ladies of this province have determined to give a memorable proof of their patriotism, and have accordingly entered into the following honorable and spirited association:

'As we cannot be indifferent on any occasion that appears nearly to affect the peace and happiness of our country, and as it has been thought necessary, for the public good, to enter into several particular resolves by a meeting of members deputed from the whole province, it is a duty which we owe, not only to our near and dear connections, who have concurred in them, but to ourselves, who are essentially interested in their welfare, to do everything, as far as lies in our power, to testify to our sincere adherence to the same; and we do therefore accordingly subscribe this paper as a witness of our fixed intention and solemn determination to do so.'"

The seemingly routine way in which women joined men in political protest represented a new Revolutionary-era acceptance of political activity by women, as well as a new willingness to include women in the body politic. Women's involvement in the Patriot cause gave them a

Broadside announcing a boycott by Boston's Sons and Daughters of Liberty, 1770.

The Edenton women's statement prompted a satirical British cartoon. In caricaturing their position, the artist ridiculed both the statement and the broader involvement of women in politics, employing various stereotypes, from the female politician who neglects her motherly role to the conviction that political activism makes women masculine. The box-like items on the floor and in the hands of the woman in the upper left are tea canisters. The text reads: "We the Ladys of Edenton do hereby solemnly Engage not to conform to that Pernicious Custom of Drinking Tea, or that we the aforesaid Ladys will not promote ye wear of any Manufacture from England untill such time that all Acts which tend to Enslave this our Native Country shall be Repealed."

A SOCIETY of PATRIOTIC LADIES.

venue for expressing their political views; their participation was both crucial and controversial. Hannah Griffitts, a poet and member of a Quaker women's intellectual and literary circle, in lines addressed to "the Daughters of Liberty," underscored the significance of women's primary roles in the boycotts—as consumers who rejected British products and as makers of homespun cloth. She also revealed her political knowledge and sharp wit. (Despite her support for women's rights and her duty to join the opposition to British taxation measures, when war broke out in 1775, Griffitts adhered to Quaker pacifist principles and to her family's loyalty to the king.)

> "Since the Men, from a Party or fear of a Frown,
> Are kept by a *Sugar-Plumb* quietly down,
> Supinely asleep–and depriv'd of their Sight,
> Are stripp'd of their Freedom, and robb'd of their Right;

If the Sons, so degenerate the Blessings despise,
Let the *Daughters of Liberty*, nobly arise;
And tho' we've no Voice but a Negative here,
The Use of the *Taxables*, let us forebear;–
(Then Merchants import till your Stores are all full.
May the Buyers be few, and your Traffick be dull!)
Stand firmly resolv'd, and bid *Grenville* to see,
That rather than Freedom we part with our *Tea*,
And well as we love the dear Draught when a-dry,
As American Patriots,–our Taste we deny– . . . ."

For enslaved women, the right to freedom was more likely to come from participation in the war on the side of the British than the Patriots. As a wartime measure, the Royal governor of Virginia, Lord Dunmore, offered freedom to the slaves held by American rebels. The chaos and disruption that wartime brought afforded both women and men the opportunity to achieve their freedom. That opportunity attracted enslaved women such as Sally, described in a runaway ad posted by a Virginia slaveholder. Reading between the lines, a researcher can learn something about why Sally fled, including her hopes and dreams, and the circumstances that made freedom seem possible.

"FIFTEEN POUNDS REWARD. RUN away from Williamsburg in July, 1781, at the time when the British army left it, a **likely** [strong, capable] negro woman named SALLY, about twenty four years of age, five feet four or five inches high, square made, and very black; has a scar on the back of one of her hands, one of her upper fore teeth broke, a round scar on her breast, occasioned by a burn, and stammers very much when surprised. I was informed she left York at the time the French legion marched up the county, and has not been heard of since. The above reward will be given to any person that will deliver her to me if taken in this state, and if brought from any other, thirty pounds. JOHN SAUNDERS."

Ads, such as one for Amia Wood, who ran away in 1782, can also reveal the importance of family ties to slaves' decisions, and the skills that might enable them to support themselves in freedom.

"TWENTY **PISTOLES** [**pistole: a Spanish gold coin**] REWARD. FOR bringing home the two Negroes hereafter described, belonging to the subscriber in Chesterfield County, near the Falls of the James River, viz. A black fellow by the name of PETER, frequently called PETER WOOD, about 37 or 38 years of age, 5 feet 8 or 9 inches high, has a smiling countenance, a little pitted with the small-pox which he formerly had in the West Indies; some of his

Portrait miniature of Anna Green Winslow. Writing in her diary in 1772, twelve-year-old Bostonian Anna Green Winslow embraced wearing homespun as a patriotic act: "As I am (as we say) a daughter of liberty I chuse to wear as much of our own manufactory as pocible."

"I do further declare all indentured Servants, Negroes, or others, (appertaining to Rebels,) free that are able and willing to bear Arms, they joining His Majesty's Troops as soon as may be. . . ."
—Lord Dunmore's Proclamation, November 7, 1775

"Sentiments of an American Woman." As the war wore on, the passionate attachment of Patriot women to the cause of independence found expression in their support of the Continental Army. In 1780, a group of elite women in Philadelphia, led by Esther DeBerdt Reed, the wife of Pennsylvania's president, and Sarah Franklin Bache, Benjamin Franklin's daughter, created a Ladies Association that raised $300,000 (in war-inflated currency) for the benefit of the soldiers. In doing so, the women had to defend their right to speak and act in a political cause. Esther Reed did so in a broadside published as "Sentiments of an American Woman." Reed's deep knowledge of history was evident in the way she brought to bear historical precedents, especially Old Testament figures, classical-era matrons, and recent monarchs, to make a claim for women's political involvement.

THE SENTIMENTS of an AMERICAN WOMAN.

ON the commencement of actual war, the Women of America manifested a firm resolution to contribute as much as could depend on them, to the deliverance of their country. Animated by the purest patriotism, they are sensible of sorrow at this day, in not offering more than barren wishes for the success of so glorious a Revolution. They aspire to render themselves more really useful; and this sentiment is universal from the north to the south of the Thirteen United States. Our ambition is kindled by the fame of those heroines of antiquity, who have rendered their sex illustrious, and have proved to the universe, that, if the weakness of our Constitution, if opinion and manners did not forbid us to march to glory by the same paths as the Men, we should at least equal, and sometimes surpass them in our love for the public good. I glory in all that which my sex has done great and commendable. I call to mind with enthusiasm and with admiration, all those acts of courage, of constancy and patriotism, which history has transmitted to us: The people favoured by Heaven, preserved from destruction by the virtues, the zeal and the resolution of Deborah, of Judith, of Esther! The fortitude of the mother of the Macchabees, in giving up her sons to die before her eyes: Rome saved from the fury of a victorious enemy by the efforts of Volumnia, and other Roman Ladies: So many famous sieges where the Women have been seen forgetting the weakness of their sex, building new walls, digging trenches with their feeble hands, furnishing arms to their defenders, they themselves darting the missile weapons on the enemy, resigning the ornaments of their apparel, and their fortune, to fill the public treasury, and to hasten the deliverance of their country; burying themselves under its ruins; throwing themselves into the flames rather than submit to the disgrace of humiliation before a proud enemy.

Born for liberty, disdaining to bear the irons of a tyrannic Government, we associate ourselves to the grandeur of those Sovereigns, cherished and revered, who have held with so much splendour the scepter of the greatest States, The Batildas, the Elizabeths, the Maries, the Catharines, who have extended the empire of liberty, and contented to reign by sweetness and justice, have broken the chains of slavery, forged by tyrants in the times of ignorance and barbarity. The Spanish Women, do they not make, at this moment, the most patriotic sacrifices, to encrease the means of victory in the hands of their Sovereign. He is a friend to the French Nation. They are our allies. We call to mind, doubly interested, that it was a French Maid who kindled up amongst her fellow-citizens, the flame of patriotism buried under long misfortunes: It was the Maid of Orleans who drove from the kingdom of France the ancestors of those same British, whose odious yoke we have just shaken off; and whom it is necessary that we drive from this Continent.

But I must limit myself to the recollection of this small number of atchievements. Who knows if persons disposed to censure, and sometimes too severely with regard to us, may not disapprove our appearing acquainted even with the actions of which our sex boasts? We are at least certain, that he cannot be a good citizen who will not applaud our efforts for the relief of the armies which defend our lives, our possessions, our liberty? The situation of our soldiery has been represented to me; the evils inseparable from war, and the firm and generous spirit which has enabled them to support these. But it has been said, that they may apprehend, that, in the course of a long war, the view of their distresses may be lost, and their services be forgotten. Forgotten! never; I can answer in the name of all my sex. Brave Americans, your disinterestedness, your courage, and your constancy will always be dear to America, as long as she shall preserve her virtue.

We know that at a distance from the theatre of war, if we enjoy any tranquility, it is the fruit of your watchings, your labours, your dangers. If I live happy in the midst of my family; if my husband cultivates his field, and reaps his harvest in peace; if, surrounded with my children, I myself nourish the youngest, and press it to my bosom, without being affraid of seeing myself separated from it, by a ferocious enemy; if the house in which we dwell; if our barns, our orchards are safe at the present time from the hands of those incendiaries, it is to you that we owe it. And shall we hesitate to evidence to you our gratitude? Shall we hesitate to wear a cloathing more simple; hair dressed less elegant, while at the price of this small privation, we shall deserve your benedictions. Who, amongst us, will not renounce with the highest pleasure, those vain ornaments, when she shall consider that the valiant defenders of America will be able to draw some advantage from the money which she may have laid out in these; that they will be better defended from the rigours of the seasons, that after their painful toils, they will receive some extraordinary and unexpected relief; that these presents will perhaps be valued by them at a greater price, when they will have it in their power to say: *This is the offering of the Ladies.* The time is arrived to display the same sentiments which animated us at the beginning of the Revolution, when we renounced the use of teas, however agreeable to our taste, rather than receive them from our persecutors; when we made it appear to them that we placed former necessaries in the rank of superfluities, when our liberty was interested; when our republican and laborious hands spun the flax, prepared the linen intended for the use of our soldiers; when exiles and fugitives we supported with courage all the evils which are the concomitants of war. Let us not lose a moment; let us be engaged to offer the homage of our gratitude at the altar of military valour, and you, our brave deliverers, while mercenary slaves combat to cause you to share with them, the irons with which they are loaded, receive with a free hand our offering, the purest which can be presented to your virtue,

By An AMERICAN WOMAN.

fingers are contracted by a burn on the right hand when young; he is a very good sawyer, and has worked a little as a rough carpenter; famous for running away. Also a very likely black girl, wife to the above fellow and taken off by him, about 18 or 19 years old, middle size, by the name of AMIA. I expect as they were with the British both at Portsmouth and York that she has had the small-pox. She is a fine spinner and Weaver, has never had a child, and I am informed has holes in her ears for rings. Those Negroes were seen in the town of Gloucester the night after the surrender of the enemy, and I have some reason to believe they are in that County now. . . . FRANCIS SMITH. Jan. 24, 1782."

Women of the Republic: Debates over Women's Rights and Equality

If wartime patriotism gave women a claim to certain rights, especially the right to speak and act on political issues, the republican philosophy that shaped the American Revolution became a crucial source for women's claims to rights. A republic, after all, was a form of government based on the political equality of its citizens, and upon their consent to be governed. Moreover, the founding documents of the American republic, including the state constitutions, the U.S. Constitution, and the Bill of Rights, set republican ideals down in writing and outlined the basic rights of citizens. Small wonder, then, that the American Revolution sparked a wide-ranging debate over the rights of women in a republic and the meaning of "equality" when it came to both gender and freedom. The debate took place in living rooms and coffee houses, in city kitchens and farmyards, in newspaper columns and legislative halls. Perhaps the most famous private conversation was that between Abigail Adams and her husband, John. While John Adams was attending the Second Continental Congress in Philadelphia in 1776, Abigail Adams wrote to him about her hope that a "new Code of Laws" written for the new republic would "Remember the Ladies," especially wives, who under coverture suffered from the "unlimited power" of husbands. "All Men would be tyrants if they could," she warned. Her letters display her deep familiarity with republican ideals and her desire for women's inclusion in the process of lawmaking, as well as her concern for vulnerable women trapped in abusive marriages. John Adams's response to her was playful, but in letters to his friend James Sullivan, he made it clear that he took his wife's arguments seriously, and thought through the implications of forming a government based on "the consent of the people" but excluding women from voting and other rights of direct

"The contributions of the association you represent have exceeded what could have been expected, and the spirit that animated the members of it, entitles them to an equal place with any one who have preceded them in the walk of female patriotism."

—Letter of General George Washington to the Ladies Association, February 13, 1781 participation. In the end, he relied upon two related principles, property-holding and "independence," as the key determinants of which citizens should have the right to vote.

Abigail Adams to John Adams, Braintree, March 31, 1776

"—I long to hear that you have declared an independancy—and by the way in the new Code of Laws which I suppose it will be necessary for you to make I desire you would Remember the Ladies, & be more generous & favourable to them than your ancestors. Do not put such unlimited power into the hands of the Husbands. Remember all Men would be tyrants if they could. If perticuliar care and attention is not paid to the Laidies we are determined to foment a Rebelion, and will not hold ourselves bound by any Laws in which we have no voice, or Representation.

That your Sex are Naturally Tyrannical is a Truth so thoroughly established as to admit of no dispute, but such of you as wish to be happy willingly give up the harsh title of Master for the more tender & endearing one of Friend. Why then, not put it out of the power of the vicious & the Lawless to use us with cruelty & indignity with impunity. Men of Sense in all Ages abhor those customs which treat us only as the vassals of your Sex. Regard us then as Beings placed by providence under your protection & in immitation of the Supreem Being make use of that power only for our happiness."

John Adams to Abigail Adams, April 14, 1776

"As to your extraordinary Code of Laws, I cannot but laugh. We have been told that our Struggle has loosened the bands of Government every where. That Children and Apprentices were disobedient—that schools and Colledges were grown turbulent—that Indians slighted their Guardians and Negroes grew insolent to their Masters. But your Letter was the first Intimation that another Tribe more numerous and powerfull than all the rest were grown discontented.—This is rather too coarse a Compliment but you are so saucy, I wont blot it out.

Depend upon it, We know better than to repeal our Masculine systems. Altho they are in full Force, you know they are little more than Theory. We dare not exert our Power in its full Latitude. We are obliged to go fair, and softly, and in Practice you know We are the subjects. We have only the Name of Masters, and rather than give up this, which would compleatly subject Us to the Despotism of the Peticoat, I hope General Washington, and all our brave Heroes would fight."

John Adams to James Sullivan, Philadelphia, May 26, 1776

"It is certain, in theory, that the only moral foundation of government is, the consent of the people. But to what an extent shall we carry this principle? Shall we say that every individual of the community, old and young, male and female, as well as rich and poor, must consent, expressly, to every act of legislation? No, you will say, this is impossible. How, then, does the right arise in the majority to govern the minority, against their will? Whence arises the right of the men to govern the women, without their consent? . . .

The same reasoning which will induce you to admit all men who have no property, to vote, with those who have . . . for, generally speaking, women and children have as good judgments, and as independent minds, as those men who are wholly destitute of property; these last being to all intents and purposes as much dependent upon others, who will please to feed, clothe, and employ them, as women are upon their husbands, or children on their parents. . . .

Depend upon it, Sir, it is dangerous to open so fruitful a source of controversy and altercation as would be opened by attempting to alter the qualifications of voters; there will be no end of it. New claims will arise; women will demand a vote; lads from twelve to twenty-one will think their rights not enough attended to; and every man who has not a farthing, will demand an equal voice with any other, in all acts of state. It tends to confound and destroy all distinctions, and prostrate all ranks to one common level."

In Pennsylvania, the poet Susanna Wright had had similar issues on her mind for some time. Born in 1697, she carried on an extensive correspondence with a large Quaker circle, including Hannah Griffitts, all the while managing her father's household at Wright's Ferry and experimenting with silkworm production. Sometime before 1779, Wright composed a poem for her friend Elizabeth Norris, criticizing the standard argument for men's "right to govern womankind" (Eve's role in Adam's fall), asserting the equality of women's and men's mental capacities ("there is no sex in soul"), and challenging women to resist the "soothing flattery" of any man who, given the opportunity, "reigns tyrant" over them.

"Since Adam, by our first fair Mother won
To share her fate,—to Taste, & be undone,
And that great Law, whence no appeal must lye,
Pronounc'd a Doom, That He should Rule—& Die,
The Partial Race, rejoyceing to fulfill
This Pleasing Dictate of Almighty will
(With no Superior virtue in their Mind),

Assert Their Right to Govern womankind.
But womankind, call Reason to their aid,
And Question, when or where, that Law was made,
That Law Divine,—(a Plausible pretence)
Oft urg'd with none, & oft with Little Sense,
from wisdom's Source, no origen could draw,
That form'd the Men, to keep the sesc [sex] in awe;
Say, Reason govern all the might[y] frame,
And Reason rules in every one, the same,
No Right, has man, his equal, to Controul,
Since, all agree, There is no sex in soul;
Weak woman, thus, in agreement grown strong,
Shakes off the yoke her Parents wore too long;
But, He, who arguments, in vain, had try'd,
Hopes still for conquest, from the yielding side,
Soft soothing flattery & Persuasion tries,
and by a feign'd submission, Seeks to rise,
Steals, unperceiv'd—to the Unguarded heart,
And There Reigns Tyrant,—...

All you can do,—is but to Let him see
That woman still, shall sure his equal be. . . ."

Other forms of "tyranny" preoccupied Phillis Wheatley, whose remarkable life, encompassing enslavement, education, and eventual liberation, and whose career as a published poet presented a formidable challenge to Patriots who would not—or could not—extend their notions of equality to Americans of African descent. To anyone who believed Africans incapable of freedom, Wheatley's 1773 volume, *Poems on Various Subjects, Religious and Moral*, represented a rebuke. Appearing first in London, the book was soon available in print on both sides of the ocean. In a poem addressed to the earl of Dartmouth, who supported the publication of her book in London, and who she hoped would be sympathetic to the Patriot cause, Wheatley commented directly on the contrast between freedom and tyranny. But she also explained how her own personal story enabled her to feel, and to explain to others, the experience of being enslaved.

"To the Right Honourable WILLIAM, Earl of DARTMOUTH,

Hail, happy day, when, smiling like the morn,
Fair *Freedom* rose *New-England* to adorn:
The northern clime beneath her genial ray,
Dartmouth, congratulates thy blissful sway; ...

No more, *America*, in mournful strain
Of wrongs, and grievance unredress'd complain,
No longer shall thou dread the iron chain,
Which wanton *Tyranny* with lawless hand
Has made, and with it meant t' enslave the land.
Should you, my lord, while you peruse my song,
Wonder from whence my love of Freedom sprung,
Whence flow these wishes for the common good,
By feeling hearts alone best understood,
I, young in life, by seeming cruel fate
Was snatch'd from *Afric's* fancy'd happy seat:
What pangs excruciating must molest,
What sorrows labour in my parent's breast?
Steel'd was that soul and by no misery mov'd
That from a father seiz'd his babe belov'd:
Such, such my case. And can I then but pray
Others may never feel tyrannic sway?"

Published according to Act of Parliament. Sept.ʳ 1.1773 by Archᵈ Bell.
Bookseller Nº 8 near the Saracens Head Aldgate.

Frontispiece portrait of Phillis Wheatley, accompanying 1773 volume, *Poems on Various Subjects*. **Phillis Wheatley** was born about 1753 in West Africa, probably along the Gambia River. Her African name is unknown. When she was seven or eight, she was enslaved and transported on the slave ship *Phillis* to Boston, where Susanna and John Wheatley purchased her in 1761. In their household, she learned to read and write, acquired a working knowledge of Latin, and began to write poetry. Her first poem was published in 1765. In 1773, she traveled to London with the Wheatleys; there, Phillis Wheatley found patrons who helped her publish her collection *Poems on Various Subjects* and introduced her to high circles in politics and the aristocracy. More important, during that visit various "friends in England" prevailed upon the Wheatleys to free Phillis from slavery. Upon her return to Boston, she advocated unambiguously for freedom—both the freedom of the United States from Great Britain, and the freedom of Africans from bondage. Her portrait presents Wheatley as a writer and thinker, dressed in simple garb; her skin color reminds the viewer of her African origin.

Discussions about human rights were trans-Atlantic in nature. When the conversation turned to women, increasingly two phrases came into common usage: "the rights of woman" and "the equality of the sexes." In England in 1792, Mary Wollstonecraft published her stunning and widely circulated book, *A Vindication of the Rights of Woman*; it quickly crossed the Atlantic and entered the libraries and parlors of American women and men. In France, the Marquis de Condorcet protested on behalf of women's political rights in his 1790 essay, "On the Admission of Women to the Rights of Citizenship" while his countrywoman, Olympe de Gouges, no fan of the new French republic, wrote "The Declaration of the Rights of Woman and the Female Citizen" in 1791. And in 1798 the American novelist and schoolmaster Charles Brockden Brown published a novel, *Alcuin: A Dialogue*, echoing Mary Wollstonecraft's argument about the sources of women's *in*equality. Most of the key themes in these publications can be found in Judith Sargent Murray's essays. In her essays, including "On the Equality of the Sexes," published in 1790, Murray posed questions that echo down the ages: Are women's and men's minds mostly similar or mostly different? Are the seeming inequalities between the sexes based in biology or society? What would happen if girls were educated as much and as well as boys? And can women be *both* different from *and* equal to men?

"... May not the intellectual powers be ranged under their four heads—imagination, reason, memory, and judgement. The province of imagination has long since been surrendered up to us, and we have been crowned undoubted sovereigns of the regions of fancy. Invention is perhaps the most arduous effort of the mind;

FRONTISPIECE.

Publish'd at Philad.ª Dec.ʳ 1.ˢᵗ 1792.

Frontispiece, *Lady's Magazine*, Philadelphia, December 1792. In the same issue, the editors reprinted portions of Mary Wollstonecraft's *A Vindication of the Rights of Woman*. The figure in the foreground, "The Genius of the Ladies Magazine," accompanied by the "Genius of Emulation," presents Liberty with a scroll labeled "Rights of Woman." By invoking imagery from ancient Rome and Greece, women displayed their erudition and learning while also using the same intellectual frame of reference as that of the men who were developing laws and constitutions for the new American republic. That framework and their attainments, in turn, enabled them to advance important arguments for women's political rights and to validate the demand for improved education for girls.

this branch of imagination hath been particularly ceded to us, and we have been time out of mind invested with that creative faculty. Observe the variety of fashions (here I bar the contemptuous smile) which distinguish and adorn the female world. . . .

Are we deficient in reason? We can only reason from what we know, and if opportunity of acquiring knowledge hath been denied us, the inferiority of our sex cannot fairly be deduced from thence. . . . May we not trace [the] source [of men's superiority in judgment] in the difference of education, and continued advantages? Will it be said that the judgment of a male of two years old, is more sage than that of a female's of the same age? I believe the reverse is generally observed to be true. But from that period what partiality! how is the one exalted, and the other depressed, by the contrary modes of education which are adopted! the one is taught to aspire, and the other is early confined and limited. As their years increase, the sister must be wholly domesticated, while the brother is led by the hand through all the flowery paths of science. Grant that their minds are by nature equal, yet who shall wonder at the *apparent* superiority, if indeed custom becomes *second nature*. . . . Now, was she permitted the same instructors as her brother, (with an eye however to their particular departments) for the employment of a rational mind an ample field would be opened. . . .

Yes, ye lordly, ye haughty sex, our souls are by nature *equal* to yours; the same breath of God animates, enlivens, and invigorates us; and that we are not fallen lower than yourselves, let those witness who have greatly towered above the various discouragements by which they have been so heavily oppressed. . . ."

In another essay, Murray expressed her faith that young women, the "daughters of Columbia," would produce "a new era in female history" by pursuing intellectual challenges and cultivating their capacity for reason.

"I expect to see our young women forming a new era in female history. They will oppose themselves to every trivial and unworthy monopolizer of time; and it will be apparent, that the adorning their persons is not with them a *primary* object. . . . Such, I predict, will be the daughters of Columbia; and my gladdened spirit rejoices in the prospect. A sensible and informed woman—companionable and serious—possessing also a facility of temper, and united to a congenial mind—blest with competency—and rearing to maturity a promising family of children—Surely the wide globe cannot produce a scene more truly interesting. . . . *The idea of the incapability* of women is, we conceive, in this *enlightened age*, totally *inadmissible*; and we have concluded, that establishing the *expediency* of admitting them to share the blessings of equality, will remove every obstacle to their advancement. . . . [T]he sexes are congenial; they are copyists of each other; and their opinions and their habits are elevated or degraded, animated or depressed, by precisely the same circumstances. . . . [Thus,] a candid investigation, effectually establish[es] the female right to that *equality with their brethren, which, it is conceived, is assigned them in the Order of Nature.*"

"Female academies are everywhere establishing," Murray noted with pleasure, pinning her hopes for a better future on the equality of girls' education with boys'. Young women who delivered commencement addresses at such academies took up the point, and elaborated upon it, as Priscilla Mason did when she delivered a "Salutatory Oration" at the Young Ladies Academy of Philadelphia in 1793. In her audience, in addition to her classmates, were the school's (male) trustees, students' parents, and other Philadelphians who attended out of curiosity or interest. Mason laid claim to eloquence as a feminine skill, using her own powers of oratory to do so. Oratory or elocution was a subject commonly taught at girls' and boys' academies and seminaries. But Mason went farther: she raised the question of the uses to which women should put their eloquence and knowledge, and what customs and beliefs were holding them back, including Biblical arguments against women's religious leadership. Finally, she offered concrete proposals for ways in which women should use their skills for the public good.

"A female, young and inexperienced, addressing a **promiscuous [mixed-sex]** assembly, is a novelty which requires an apology, as some may suppose. I therefore, with submission, beg leave to offer a few thoughts in vindication of female eloquence. . . . Although the free exercise of this natural talent, is a part of the rights of woman,

Newspaper ad for Mary Wollstonecraft's *A Vindication of the Rights of Woman*, Boston, 1792.

"I have read a large Octava volume, intitled The Rights of Woman, By Mary Wolstonecroft. in very many of her sentiments, she, as some of our friends say, *speaks my mind*, in some others, I do not, altogether coincide with her—I am not for quite so much independance."

—Elizabeth Drinker diary entry, Philadelphia, April 22, 1796

"I have just finished reading the rights of Woman to your father, i.e. as much of it as I could read, for I was often obliged to stop, & pass over, & frequently to cough & stammer it. He is as much disgusted with the book as I am, & calls the author a vulgar, impudent Hussy."

—Alice Izard, writing to her daughter Margaret Manigault of South Carolina, 1801

Judith Sargent Stevens Murray was born into a wealthy merchant family in Gloucester, Massachusetts, in 1751, and received her splendid education at the side of a brother who was preparing to enter Harvard University. Married at age eighteen to a sea captain, John Stevens, and widowed when Stevens died in the West Indies in 1786, she married the Universalist minister John Murray in 1788 and lived in Boston during most of her writing days. It was the Murray family's economic distress that prompted her to publish collections of her work, most notably the three-volume *The Gleaner*, in hopes of raising money by subscription, and indeed both John Adams and Martha Washington were subscribers. Judith Sargent Murray's writing career encompassed poetry, fiction, plays, and political essays. A firm patriot during and after the Revolutionary War, Murray wrote extensively on the position of women in the new republic and the need for a proper education to prepare their daughters for republican equality. Her own daughter Julia (a son died in infancy) married a wealthy Mississippi planter, Adam Louis Bingamon, in 1812; Murray lived with the Bingamons from 1815 until her death in 1820. It is perhaps ironic that, despite her passionate writings on the topics of women's economic freedom and equality, Judith Sargent Murray spent her final years on a slave plantation in Natchez.

and must be allowed by the courtesy of Europe and America too; yet it . . . should rest like the sword in the scabbard, to be used only when occasion requires.—Leaving my sex in full possession of this prerogative, I claim for them the further right of being heard on more proper occasions—of addressing the reason as well as the fears of the other sex. . . .

Our high and mighty Lords (thanks to their arbitrary constitutions) have denied us the means of knowledge, and then reproached us for the want of it. Being the stronger party, they early seized the sceptre and the sword; with these they gave laws to society; they denied women the advantage of a liberal education; forbid them to exercise their talents on those great occasions, which would serve to improve them. They doom'd the sex to servile or frivolous employments, on purpose to degrade their minds, that they themselves might hold unrivall'd, the power and pre-eminence they had usurped. Happily, a more liberal way of thinking begins to prevail. The sources of knowledge are gradually opening to our sex. Some have already availed themselves of the privilege so far, as to wipe off our reproach in some measure. . . .

But supposing now that we posses'd all the talents of the orator, in the highest perfection; where shall we find a theatre for the display of them? The Church, the Bar, and the Senate are shut against us. Who shut them? *Man*; despotic man, first made us incapable of the duty, and then forbid us the exercise. Let us by suitable education, qualify ourselves for those high departments—they will open before us. . . .

But Paul forbids it! Contemptible little body! The girls laughed at the deformed creature. To be revenged, he declares war against the whole sex: advises men not to marry them; and has the insolence to order them to keep silence in the Church—: afraid, I suppose, that they would say something against celibacy, or ridicule the old bachelor.

With respect to the bar, . . . I am assured that there is nothing in our laws or constitution, to prohibit the licensure of female Attornies; and sure our judges have too much gallantry, to urge *prescription* in bar of their claim. . . .

It would be worthy the wisdom of Congress, to consider whether a [senate of women] established at the seat of our Federal Government, would not be a public benefit. . . . Such a Senate, composed of women most noted for wisdom, learning and taste, delegated from every part of the Union, would give dignity, and

"Scenes from a Seminary for Young Ladies": A drawing illustrated the seriousness and intensity with which girls approached the new educational opportunities afforded them.

independence to our manners; uniformity, and even authority to our fashions.... It would call forth all that is human—all that is *divine* in the soul of woman; and having proved them equally capable with the other sex, would lead to their equal participation of honor and office."

The idea of women serving in public office proved a ripe topic for satire in the newspapers of Priscilla Mason's day. A fictional dialogue appearing in a Philadelphia newspaper in 1791 made fun of politically minded "young ladies."

"I happened lately to be in the company of several young ladies, where the following curious conversation took place:—

Sophia: Mercy on our poor Congress! I really fear that some of them will return home crack-brained or hysteric. Our body politic is so very sore that it cannot bear to be handled, though ever so gently;—every part cries *touch me not....*

Charlotte: Indeed I sincerely pity our national guardians.—Their pupils are more whimsical than young girls, and some of them as froward [sic] as naughty boys.... I suppose that we young women must learn militia duty, and turn out with both musket and bayonet.

Thalestris: Upon my word, I long for this happy change of affairs. We shall then expunge the odious *obey* from the wedding ceremony.... Then, my girls, we shall first be absolute mistresses of our houses, and then in a very short time govern the State also. We shall in this western hemisphere set up a FEMALE

EMPIRE, that shall laugh at all the male governments in the world. . . . I anticipate the glorious day when American ladies shall be Commanders, Presidents of Congress, Ambassadors, Governors, Secretaries of State, Professors, Judges, Preachers; when the golden age of the Poets, and the millenium of the Christians shall be realized in America.

Amelia: Yet, Ladies, you must, in the execution of this splendid plan, employ the men, at least in subordinate parts.

Thalestris: Yes, yes, . . . they shall cook for us, make our shoes, knit stockings, wash our linen, &c. &c.

Amelia: But will they submit to this inferiority?

Roxana: *Inferior minds* will be fitted for inferior stations."

What Difference Did the Revolution Make?

Historians agree that public discussions about equality and rights called attention to the mismatch between Revolutionary ideology and republican practice. They do not agree, however, on what overall effects the Revolution had on women's rights. Clearly, women (that is, free women) were citizens of the new republic; they were included in the U.S. Constitution's opening words "We, the People," as well as among the "people" whose rights were spelled out in the first ten amendments, the Bill of Rights. As "persons," women were counted in the decennial census of population, upon which a state's representation in the House of Representatives depended. And much later, when women began to run for the House and the Senate, no constitutional amendment was required to alter the Constitution's use of male pronouns for representatives and senators. Yet when women's—especially wives'—rights as citizens came into conflict with the principle of coverture, it was in the state constitutions and laws and in local court decisions that the issues were hashed out. In the 1805 case of *Martin v. Massachusetts*, a state court directly addressed the question of married women's citizenship, asking whether the late Anna Martin should have had her property confiscated when she and her Loyalist husband left the United States during the Revolutionary War. Arguing for Anna Martin's son James, lawyer George Blake suggested that coverture required that a married woman be treated only secondarily as a citizen; she was first and foremost a wife (that is, subject to her husband) whose obligations to her husband took priority over her obligations to her country. James Sullivan, who had discussed married women's rights with John Adams thirty years earlier, argued for the state of Massachusetts that wives were indeed citizens with independent legal existences. Judge Theodore Sedgwick's decision took Blake's side. In his view, as a married woman, Anna Martin owed her first "duty of obedience" to her husband; indeed, it would be a "violation of her marriage vows" were she to "rebel against the will" of her husband.

"[George Blake:] Upon the strict principles of law, a *feme covert* is not a member; has no *political relation* to the *state* any more than an *alien*.... The legislature *intended* to exclude *femes-covert* and infants from the operation of the act [the 1779 Massachusetts Confiscation Act addressed to 'every inhabitant and member of the state']; otherwise the word *inhabitant* would have been used alone, and not coupled with the word *member*.... And can it be supposed, in the case before the Court, that the legislature contemplated the case of a wife withdrawing with her husband? It ought not to be, and surely was not intended that she should be exposed to the loss of all her property for withdrawing from the government with her husband. If he commanded it, she was bound to obey him, by a law paramount to all other laws—the law of God."

"[James Sullivan:] The same reasoning would go to prove that the *Constitution* of the Commonwealth does not extend to women—secures them no rights, no privileges; for it has no words in the feminine gender; it would prove that a great variety of crimes ... could not be committed by women, because the statutes had used only the words *him* and *his*.... Who are members of the body politic? are not all the *citizens*, members...? Cannot a *feme-covert*...commit treason; and if so, there is no one act mentioned in the statute which she is not capable of performing."

"[Theodore Sedgwick:] [W]e are called upon ... to say whether a *feme-covert*, for *any* of these acts, *performed with her husband*, is within the intention of the statute; and I think that she is not.... Can we believe that a wife ... should lose her own property, and forfeit the inheritance of her children ... [and] be considered as criminal because she permitted her husband to elect his own and her place of residence? Because she did not, in violation of her marriage vows, rebel against the will of her husband? ... A *wife* who left the country in the company of her husband did not *withdraw* herself; but was, if I may so express it, withdrawn by him. She did not deprive the government of the benefit of her personal services; she had none to render; none were exacted of her...."

Abigail Adams's hope that the republic, with its emphasis on independence and equality, would have a "New Code of Laws" providing married women with new rights, went largely unfulfilled. In the Revolution's aftermath, state legislatures made few alterations in wives' rights, with

"In the theory of our Constitution women are calculated as political beings. They are numbered in the census of inhabitants ... and the Representatives are apportioned among the people according to their numbers, reckoning the females as well as the males. Though, therefore, women do not vote, they are nevertheless represented in the national government to their full amount."

—New York Senator Samuel Mitchill to Catharine Akerly Mitchill, 1804 two exceptions: erasing the provision of English marriage law that a wife who killed her husband committed *petit treason*, or the killing of her rightful ruler, whereas a husband who killed his wife committed simple murder; and marginally expanding access to divorce. A few state legislatures began for the first time to hear divorce suits; a few others began to allow courts to hear them, or to permit the use of extreme cruelty as a ground for divorce. Abigail Bayley's divorce petition to a New Hampshire court in 1793 concealed in the bland language of the law the years of horrific abuse she endured from her husband. The "adultery" of her petition referred to his incestuous rape of their daughter Phoebe.

*D*ivorce Laws: Pennsylvania's 1785 divorce law, considered very liberal for the time, permitted the state supreme court to grant divorces in cases "where one party is under natural or legal incapacities of faithfully discharging the matrimonial vow, or is guilty of acts and deeds inconsistent with the nature thereof, . . . [in order to] give relief to the innocent and injured person." Permissible grounds for a full divorce included impotence, bigamy, adultery, or desertion for four years, but cruel treatment warranted only a separation "from bed and board." After 1804, Pennsylvania's county courts of common pleas could also hear divorce cases. Indiana's 1818 and 1824 divorce laws went further, permitting circuit courts to grant full divorce for impotence, bigamy, adultery, desertion for two years, conviction of a felony, extreme cruelty, and "in any other case, where the court in their discretion, shall consider it just and reasonable that a divorce should be granted." South Carolina, on the other hand, completely forbade divorce until 1868.

Bayley divorce document.

"Abigail Bayley of Landaff in the County of Grafton, wife of Asa Bayley of Landaff aforesaid Esquire humbly shews that she was lawfully married to the said Asa on the fifteenth day of April Anno Domini 1767 that they lived together as husband and wife till he repeatedly violated the marriage covenant by committing adultery and otherwise by cruelly injuring abusing and illtreating your petitioner. That more than two years ago, the said Asa fearing the pains and penalties of the law for his many heinous and flagrant transgressions thereof absconded to places remote and unknown to your petitioner and hath utterly forsaken her and neglected and refused in any wise to perform the duties of an husband unto her Wherefore she prays your honors to grant her a bill of divorcement. The said Asa Bayley being legally notified doth not appear and the said Abigail appears and verifies the facts set forth in said petition. It is therefore considered by the court that the prayer of said petition be granted and that the said Abigail and Asa be and hereby are divorced from the bonds of Matrimony."

British Common Law remained the basis for American law. Blackstone's *Commentaries* taught existing precedents to new generations of lawyers whose training involved "reading law" by memorizing and then carrying Blackstone about with them, and American judges wrote new interpretations of marital coverture based on Blackstone. Perhaps the most widely read American jurist of the new republic was Tapping Reeve of Connecticut, whose *Law of Baron and Femme* (first published in 1816) joined Blackstone in lawyers' saddlebags and brief cases and spelled out the American version of the law of coverture.

"The husband, by marriage, acquires an absolute title to all the personal property of the wife, which she had in possession at the time of the marriage; such as money, goods or chattels personal of any kind. These, by the marriage, become his property, as completely as the property which he purchases with his money; and such property can never again belong to the wife, . . . unless it be given to her by his will; and in case of the death of the husband, this property does not return to the wife, but vests in his executors. . . . By the death of the husband the wife becomes entitled, during her life, to one-third part of the real estate of inheritance of which the husband was seised during coverture. This estate is termed *dower*. . . . If any man should carry away the wife of another man, it is a trespass,

WHEREAS William Gillcust has forbid any Person trusting me on his Account: I think it my Duty to declare, that I should not expect to obtain any Credit on his Account, were I inclined to make the Attempt, till he has paid the Debts *of his own contracting*; and that I am unconscious of having conducted myself in a "disorderly Manner," unless refusing to live with him, till he will provide for his Wife and Children with *his Earnings*, instead of squandering them by Intemperance, and associating with lewd Women, can be deemed disorderly Conduct in me.
CATHARINE GILLCUST.
Providence, October 8, 1803.

The dramatic increase in newspaper notices of wives who had "eloped" from their husbands' "bed and board" may have reflected new ideals about Americans' personal "pursuit of happiness." For women like Catharine Gillcust, republican ideology about freedom and independence may have made the "bonds" of matrimony look like bondage, and changed their views about their basic rights within the marriage relationship, including their rights to economic support and to protection from abuse.

"As the husband is the guardian of the wife, and bound to protect and maintain her, the law has given him a reasonable superiority and control over her person, and he may even put gentle restraints upon her liberty, if her conduct be such as to require it."
—James Kent, *Commentaries on American Law*, 1827

Writing to her husband in 1782, Abigail Adams expressed her frustration with the mismatch between women's patriotic service and the lack of real changes in their legal status: "Even in the freest countrys our property is subject to the controul and disposal of our partners, to whom the Laws have given a soverign Authority. Deprived of a voice in Legislation, obliged to submit to those Laws which are imposed upon us, is it not sufficient to make us indifferent to the publick Welfare? Yet all History and every age exhibit Instances of patriotick virtue in the female Sex; which considering our situation equals the most Heroick of yours."

"All men are born free and equal, and have certain natural, essential, and unalienable rights...."

—Massachusetts State Constitution, 1780

for which a recovery of damages may be had by the husband.... The case of the wife, as respects her liability to punishment for crimes, is different from any other which exists in society. Children or servants are punishable for crimes which they commit in obedience to the command of their parents or masters, or by their coercion; but a wife is, in many cases, privileged from punishment, for offences against the law of society; provided she commits the offence by the coercion of the husband. His command to commit the offence, is in law deemed coercion."

The persistence of slavery seemed to some Americans the most egregious example of how republican practice deviated from republican principles. Others considered that the Constitution guaranteed them the freedom to own slaves. The latter group eventually prevailed: in 1810, the United States had more enslaved people than in 1775. Still, the states north of Delaware, where slavery was less economically central than elsewhere, altered their laws to end slavery. As freedom began to seem possible, enslaved people made known their views. In Massachusetts, Elizabeth Freeman, often called "Mum Bett" or "Mumbet," helped bring slavery to an immediate end. In 1781, Freeman, along with an enslaved man named Brom, enlisted an attorney to sue for their freedom on the grounds that the state constitution prohibited slavery. She won. A subsequent 1783 suit led Massachusetts to end all slavery in the state. Mumbet became a paid servant in the household of her attorney, Judge Theodore Sedgwick, who later decided the case of *Martin v. Massachusetts*. Sedgwick's daughter, the noted novelist Catherine Maria Sedgwick, wrote this account of Elizabeth Freeman's decision.

"Her name was Elizabeth Freeman—transmuted to 'Betty'—and afterwards contracted ... to 'Mum-Bett' by which name she was best known.... MumBett's character was composed of few & strong elements. Action was the law of her nature, & conscious of superiority to all around her, she felt servitude intolerable. It was not the work—work was play to her, ... but it was the galling of the harness, the irrepressible longing for liberty. I have heard her say, with an emphatic shake of the head.... 'Any time, any time while I was a slave, if one minute's freedom had been offered to me, and I had been told I must die at the end of that minute, I would have taken it—just to stand one minute on God's *airth* a free woman—I would.

It was soon after the close of the revolutionary war that she chanced at the village 'meeting house,' in Sheffield [Massachusetts], to hear the Declaration of Independence read. She went the next day to the office of Mr. Theodore Sedgwick.... 'Sir,' said she, 'I heard that paper read yesterday that says "all men are born equal, and that every man has a right to freedom." I am not a dumb *critter*; won't the law give me my freedom?' . . . [He] immediately instituted a suit in behalf of the extraordinary plaintiff; a decree was obtained in her favour . . . and on this decision was based the freedom of the few slaves remaining in Massachusetts."

In one state—New Jersey—Revolutionary ideals were temporarily put into gender- and race-neutral practice. There, a provision of the 1776 state constitution permitted "all inhabitants of this Colony, of full age who are worth fifty pounds proclamation money, clear estate in the same" to vote as independent property holders. A small number of single and widowed women (and free black men) qualified, and between 1776 and 1807, they exercised their right to vote. In 1807, however, a controversy over *how* women were voting led the state legislature to reverse itself and restrict voting to men. In doing so, they were susceptible to arguments such as those put forward in an 1802 letter to a newspaper by a "Friend to the Ladies," whose distinctly unfriendly views echoed Revolutionary-era caricatures of "female politicians."

Ivory miniature of Elizabeth Freeman.

"Among the numerous striking scenes which our election presents to the disinterested observer, none is more amusing than the sight of whole wagon loads of those 'privileged fair', who for the lucky circumstance of being possessed of 50 pounds, and of being disengaged at the age of 21, are entitled to vote. What a blissful week has the preceding one been for them! How respectfully attentive each young federalist and republican has been to the fair elector! How ready to offer them his horses, his carriage, to drag them in triumph to the election ground! Oh sweet week! why do you not last the whole year round!

However pleasing these reflections may be to the Ladies it must be owned that the inconveniences attending the practice far outweigh the benefits derived from it. We may well be allowed to assert, without being accused of detraction, that those votes are rarely if ever unbiassed. Timid and pliant, unskilled in politics, unacquainted with the real merits of the several candidates, and almost always placed under the dependence or care of a father, an uncle, a brother &c, they will of course be directed or persuaded by them; and the man who brings his two daughters, his mother, and his aunt to the election, really gives five votes instead of one. How will an obedient daughter dare to vote against the sentiments of her father? and how can a fair one refuse her lover, who on his knees beseeches her by her beauty, by his passion, to give her vote to Lambert or Anderson?

When our legislators passed the act by which the females are entitled to share in our elections, they were not aware of its inconveniences, and acted from a principle of justice, deeming it right that every free person who pays a tax should have a vote. But from the moment when party spirit began to rear its hideous head, the female vote became its passive tools, and the ill consequences of their admission have increased yearly. . . .

Let not our fair conclude that I wish to see them deprived of their rights. Let them rather consider that female reserve and delicacy are incompatible with the duties of a free elector, that a female politician is often subject to ridicule, and they will recognize in the writer of this a sincere

Friend to the Ladies."

Barred by law and custom from direct political participation, women nevertheless claimed their right to be included in the body politic through expressing their political opinions, petitioning legislatures for favors, or seeking to influence the men in their lives. Few were as effective as Margaret Bayard Smith, a New Yorker whose marriage to a newspaper editor brought her to Washington, D.C., during the Jefferson administration. A graduate of one of the female academies that Judith Sargent Murray championed, Bayard Smith possessed—by dint of her excellent education, high social status, and marital connections—ready access to the leading politicians of her day. Her letters to family members reveal how elite white women blended socializing and politics in their parlors, and in the halls of Congress and the Supreme Court, and how the shift to a more "democratic" politics engaged women as well as men. Bayard Smith did not entirely approve of the effect that women's presence had on male leaders, yet she recognized that their access to deliberative arenas was significant in the new republic.

[March 13, 1814] "Washington possesses a peculiar interest and to an active, reflective, and ambitious mind, has more attractions than any other place in America. This interest is daily increasing, and with the importance and expansion of our nation, this is the theatre on which its most interesting interests are discuss'd, by its ablest sons. . . . The house of representatives is the lounging place of both sexes, where acquaintance is as easily made as at public amusements. And the drawing-room,—that centre of attraction,—affords opportunity of seeing all these whom fashion, fame, beauty, wealth or talents, have render'd celebrated. . . . The last evening we were there, the room was empty, there were not above 50 or 60 persons,—after tea we adjourned to the music room, which is comparatively small, 3 or 4 sophas surrounded the fire and we form'd quite a social circle.... For myself, seated in one corner of a sopha, conversation with 4 or 5 agreeable and intelligent men pass'd the time most pleasantly away."

"Curiosity led me against my judgement, to join the female crowd who throng the [Supreme] court room. A place in which I think women have no business. The effect of female admiration and attention has been very obvious, but it is a doubt to me whether it has been beneficial, indeed I believe otherwise.... [A] gentleman told me, that one day Mr. [William Pinkney] had finished his argument and was just about seating himself when Mrs. [Dolley] Madison and a train of ladies enter'd,—he recommenced, went over the same ground, using fewer arguments, but scattering more flowers. And the day I was there I am certain he thought more of the female part of his audience than of the court.... The women here are taking a station in society which is not known elsewhere. On every public occasion, a launch, an oration, an inauguration, in the court, in the representative hall, as well as the drawing room, they are treated with mark'd distinction. Last night Mr. Ogilvie while he censured the frivolous, elevated the rest of our sex, not only to an equality but I think to a superiority to the other sex. I think the manners here different from those in other places. At the drawing room, at our parties, few ladies ever sit. Our rooms are always so crowded, that few more could find a place in the rooms, the consequence is, the ladies and gentlemen stand and walk about the rooms, in mingled groups, which certainly produces more ease, freedom and equality than in these rooms where ladies sit and wait for gentlemen to approach and converse."

[January 26, 1830] "[N]ever were the amphitheatres of Rome more crowded by the highest ranks of both sexes than the senate chamber is. Every seat, every inch of ground, even the steps, were *compactly* filled, and yet not space enough for the ladies—the Senators were obliged to relinquish their chairs of State to the fair auditors who literally sat in the Senate. One lady sat in Col. Hayne's seat, while he stood by her side speaking.... Our government is becoming every day more and more democratic, the rulers of the people are truly their servants and among those rulers women are gaining more than their share of power."

Whereas New Jersey's voting women enjoyed political power and citizenship status on an equal legal footing with voting men, the political influence that women like Margaret Bayard Smith exercised depended upon their connections to powerful men. Still, on an imaginary balance

Between 1789 and 1820, women submitted at least 246 individual petitions to Congress, the vast bulk of them seeking compensation or pensions related to the Revolution. Like other individuals and groups of women, they understood that they possessed the right to petition their rulers, and they used it.

sheet of Revolutionary gains and losses, both groups could be said to have gained. Native women, on the other hand, lost many of their customary rights during the decades after 1790. Extensive land loss was a legacy of the Revolution for all Native groups within the boundaries of the United States, but women experienced that loss with particular poignancy because of their traditional role as farmers and custodians of Mother Earth. Between 1795 and 1842, for instance, the Oneidas (an Iroquois-speaking group) entered into twenty-four land treaties with New York State, each of which diminished the amount of land the group controlled. By 1855, only 161 Oneidas remained in the group's traditional territory. In such treaties, women's rights to the land were almost uniformly ignored, despite the matrons' pleas for inclusion. Among the Cherokee, who sought to protect their lands by writing a Constitution, the very process of codifying traditional practices in writing had the destructive consequences of obliterating matrons' access to political leadership and economic authority and introducing elements of coverture into Cherokee law. In 1817, the Cherokee women's council, led by Nancy Ward, petitioned the all-male leadership both to protect their traditional lands and to resist any schemes designed to remove the Cherokee "over the Mississippi."

"Amovey [Tenn.] in Council 2nd May 1817

A True Copy} The Cherokee ladys now being present at the meeting of the Chiefs and warriors in council have thought it their duties as mothers to address their beloved Chiefs and warriors now assembled.

Our beloved children and head men of the Cherokee nation we address you warriors in council we have raised all of you on the land which we now have, which God gave us to inhabit and raise provisions we know that our country has once been extensive but by repeated sales has become circumscribed to a small tract and [we] never thought it our duty to interfere with the disposition of it till now, if a father or mother was to sell all their lands which they had to depend on which their children had to raise their living on which would be indeed bad and to be removed to another country we do not wish to go to an unknown country [to] which have understood some of our children wish to go over the Mississippi but this act of our children would be like destroying your mothers. Your mothers your sisters ask and beg of you not to part with any more of our lands, we say ours you are descendants and take pity on our request, but keep it for our growing children for it was the good will of our creator to place us here and you know our father the great president will not allow his white children to take our country away only keep your hands off of paper talks for it is our own country for if it was not they would not ask you to put your hands to paper for it would be impossible to remove us all for as soon as one child is raised we have others in our arms for such is our situation and will consider our circumstance.

Therefore children don't part with any more of our lands but continue on it and enlarge your farms and cultivate and raise corn and cotton and we your mothers and sisters will make clothing for you which our father the president has recommended to us we don't charge anybody for selling our lands, but we have heard such intentions of our children but your talks become true at last and it was our desire to forewarn you all not to part with our lands.

Nancy Ward to her children Warriors to take pity and listen to the talks of your sisters, although I am very old yet cannot but pity the situation in which you will hear of their minds. I have great many grand children which [I] wish them to do well on our land.

Nancy Ward

Attested
A McCoy Clk.}
Thos. Wilson Secty}

Jenny McIntosh	Widow Tarpin
Caty Harlan	Ally Critington
Elizabeth walker	Cun, o, ah
Susanna Fox	Miss Asty walker
Widow Gunrod	Mrs. M. Morgan
Widow Woman Holder	Mrs. Nancy Fields"

When the United States purchased Louisiana from France, the question of how American law would affect women's rights to own property and wages was particularly pressing for the Ursuline nuns of New Orleans, who had been accustomed to the economic rights that Spanish and French law afforded them. They wrote to Thomas Jefferson in 1804, whose response reassured them.

"Washington May the 15 1804

To the Soeur Therese de St Xavior Farjon superior, and the Nuns of the order of St. Ursula at New Orleans

I have received, holy sisters, the letter you have written me wherein you express anxiety for the property vested in your institution by the former governments of Louisiana. The principles of the constitution and government of the United states are a sure guarantee to you that it will be preserved to you sacred and

Nancy Ward (c. 1738–1822): Born Nanye'hi in present-day Tennessee, Nancy Ward was close to eighty years of age when she delivered the Cherokee women's petition to the all-male council. Her authority and power derived both from her status as an elder and from her achievements as a traditional Cherokee War Woman, a designation she won through bravery in battle. During the Revolutionary War, although most Cherokee sided with the British, Nancy Ward, who had adopted an English name in the late 1750s, supported the Patriot cause. In the post-war years, she emerged as a spokesperson for Cherokee women in their dealings with treaty negotiators, even as the policies of the U.S. government eliminated any formal role for matrons like herself in the treaty-making process. Although her death in 1822 spared her the experience of removal along the "Trail of Tears," Nancy Ward lived long enough to see the traditional position of Cherokee War Woman eliminated, the traditional authority of Cherokee matrons eroded, and the land she sought to defend ceded to others.

Jefferson's letter.

inviolate, and that your institution will be permitted to govern itself according to it's [sic] own voluntary rules without interference from the civil authority. Whatever diversity of shade may appear in the religious opinions of our fellow citizens, the charitable objects of your constitution cannot be indifferent to any, and it's [sic] furtherance of the wholesome purposes of society, by training up it's [sic] younger members in the way they should go, cannot fail to ensure it the patronage of the government it is under. Be assured it will meet all the protection which my office can give it.

I salute you, holy sisters, with friendship & respect.

[Signed] Thomas Jefferson"

The Revolution's ambiguous legacy was evident in the title of Hannah Mather Crocker's 1818 book, *Observations on the Real Rights of Women, with Their Appropriate Duties, Agreeable to Scripture, Reason and Common Sense.* By combining a discussion of women's "real rights" with an insistence that they fulfill their "appropriate duties," Crocker, a granddaughter of the Puritan divine Cotton Mather, endorsed women's right to pursue intellectual cultivation but only so long as they remained within an appropriate female "sphere."

"There can be no doubt, that in most cases, [women's] judgment may be equal with the other sex; perhaps even on the subject of law, politics or religion, they may form good judgment, but it would be morally improper, and physically very incorrect, for the female character to claim the statesman's birth, or ascend the rostrum to gain the loud applause of men, although their powers of mind may be equal to the task. . . .

Much abstruse study or metaphysical reasoning seldom agrees with the natural vivacity or the slender frame of many females, therefore the moral and physical distinction of the sex must be allowed; if the powers of the mind are fully equal, they must still estimate the rights of men, and own it their prerogative exclusively to contend for public honours and preferment, either in church or state, and females may console themselves and feel happy, that by the moral distinction of the sexes they are called to move in a sphere of life remote from those masculine contentions, although they hold equal right with them of studying every branch of science, even jurisprudence.

But it would be morally wrong, and physically imprudent, for any woman to attempt pleading at the bar of justice, as no law can give her the right of deviating from the strictest rules of rectitude and decorum. . . .

It must be woman's prerogative to shine in the domestic circle, and her appropriate duty to teach and regulate the opening mind of her little flock, . . . The surest foundation to secure the female's right, must be in family government, as without that, women can have no established right. This must be the touchstone of the matrimonial faith; and on this depends very much the safety and happiness of a free republic."

A c. 1800 drawing entitled "Keep within Compass," and adapted from an earlier European sketch, suggested that post-Revolutionary women should stay within their proper "compass" or "sphere"; those who did not were liable to the vices depicted around the edges: drinking, child neglect, prostitution, and crime.

CONSTITUTION AND BY-LAWS

OF THE

ABYSSINIAN BENEVOLENT DAUGHTERS

OF

ESTHER ASSOCIATION,

OF THE

CITY OF NEW YORK.

Adopted April 19, 1839.

Printed at the Office of the Colored American.

CHAPTER 3

Women's Rights Movements

Although Revolutionary-era Americans spoke about "the rights of woman," they created no social movement aimed at securing those rights. Such a movement still lay in the future. Nevertheless, in the early years of the new republic, Americans understood free women as rights-bearing individuals, and individual women exercised their limited citizenship rights, including the right to freedom of religion and speech and the right to petition their rulers. Women also fulfilled their citizenship responsibilities by paying taxes and supporting local, state, and national governments in ways large and small. Some women even collectively gained expanded rights and responsibilities as leaders of the volunteer organizations that proliferated after 1800. In such groups, they not only exercised their right to assemble peaceably and discuss issues of broad public concern, but they wrote constitutions and elected officers, raised money and invested it, and occasionally sought political favors for their organizations. Free women, both white and African American, both individually and collectively, exercised their limited citizenship rights. Only some, however, explicitly endorsed "woman's rights" as a cause.

That cause remained controversial throughout the decades before 1860, particularly because of the close connections between it and the movement to abolish slavery. The rights of enslaved women to freedom, to self-ownership, to safety from sexual assault and violence, and to family security were constant themes in abolitionist commentaries. Outside of abolitionist and women's rights circles, whether on the public stage, around the kitchen table, or in the print media, ordinary women and men conversed about the nature of free women's citizenship rights. Individual women might have sought their rights to property or inheritance, but not all connected their solitary struggles to the broader concerns of women as a group. It was certainly possible to hear women's voices prominently within the chorus of vocal opponents of women's rights, those who preferred to speak of women's "influence" and "duties" rather than rights. Even within the circles of those who embraced the cause, divisions over goals, priorities, strategies, and tactics occurred as activists debated which rights *should take precedence, and* which women *were most rights-deprived. By the end of the Civil War in 1865, the question of which women and men were entitled to equal civil and political rights, including the full privileges of citizenship, had become a central topic of public debate. In the 1860s, too, the ratification of the Fourteenth and Fifteenth Amendments created a new constitutional context, one in which the right to vote emerged for many as the key right for which women's rights advocates would struggle. Even so, two rival organizations vied for pre-eminence in the suffrage cause. Nineteenth-century Americans may have written and spoken in the singular about "Woman's Rights," but there was always a plurality of movements, approaches, issues, discussion arenas, and definitions.*

Discussing/Debating Women's Rights

Between the 1820s and the 1840s, a variety of individuals spoke out in the cause of women's rights. One was Scots-born Frances Wright, who after her first visit to the United States in 1819–1820 traveled back and forth across the Atlantic, writing and lecturing on the abolition of slavery, women's educational and personal rights, the rights of working people, and religious freethought. Her public lectures given in 1828 and 1829 made her famous, and eventually infamous, as did her scandalous personal life, because she was pregnant when she married in 1831. Like Mary Wollstonecraft, she was a radical, rationalist, Enlightenment-inspired freethinker whose ideas were often dismissed because moralists condemned her life choices. She especially called upon American men to champion women's equality in education and in marriage.

"I shall venture the assertion that, until women assume the place in society which good sense and good feeling alike assign to them, human improvement must advance but feebly. It is in vain that we would circumscribe the power of one half of our race and that half by far the most important and influential. If they exert it not for good, they will for evil; if they advance not knowledge, they will perpetuate ignorance.... How many, how omnipotent are the interests which engage men to break the mental chains of women! How many, how dear are the interests which engage them to exalt rather than lower their condition, to multiply their solid acquirements, to respect their liberties, to make them their equals, to wish them even their superiors!... Let them not imagine that they know aught of the delights which **intercourse** [**social interaction or communication**] with the other sex can give ... until power is annihilated on one side, fear and obedience on the other, and both restored to their birthright—equality. Let none think that affection can reign without it; or friendship, or esteem. Jealousies, envyings, suspicions, reserves, deceptions—these are the fruits of inequality. Go, then! and remove the evil first from the minds of women, then from their condition, and then from your laws."

During her sojourn in New York City, Frances Wright may have met Louise Mitchell, another advocate of working women's rights. In 1831, Mitchell addressed a group of her sister needleworkers—"tailoresses"— who had gone on strike in order to improve their wages. Mitchell was a voice for women's economic rights in an era when women uniformly received less pay than men for the same or similar work, and were excluded from almost all well-paying jobs.

"If union is strength, why should we be weak? Let this be our motto, 'United we stand, divided we fall'—and suffer me to urge the necessity of a free and candid avowal of opinion on the part of the members respecting every subject in discussion; let each individual consider this her duty, as well as her right. I am aware that many are averse to this measure[,] feeling themselves incapacitated for public business, and acknowledging their inability to act without the aid of men—but they would do well to remember who are our *oppressors*—and it would be worse than useless to seek redress through *their* instrumentality. Let us, then, have more confidence in our own abilities, and less to the sincerity of men.

'Tis true that custom and education have assisted to intimidate us, but our energies once aroused, we shall find ourselves less deficient than we want to believe and have we not sufficient excitement to arouse those energies? ... Understandably a great number (from their hitherto secluded lives) feel a reluctance to come forward, fearful of having their names made public. Excuse me, if I say

Robert Dale Owen, a colleague and admirer of Wright, echoed her views on women's rights in his own essays: "Are not all women 'endowed with certain unalienable rights, among which are life, liberty, and the pursuit of happiness'? ... Do not marriages as well as governments 'derive their just powers from the consent' of the contracting parties? ... Is not divorce, is not revolution, a virtuous act, when kings and husbands play the despot?"

—*Free Enquirer*, 1829

"[Frances Wright is] a bold blasphemer, a voluptuous priestess of licentiousness.... Casting off all restraint, she would break down all the barriers to virtue, and reduce the world to one grand theatre of vice and sensuality in its most loathsome form."

—New York *Commercial Advertiser*, November 7, 1829

The Salem, Massachusetts, *Gazette* of February 25, 1831, chose to make fun of the women's concerns by suggesting that they should seek marriage, not improved wages, as a way to improve their economic circumstances: "The tailoresses of New York city have had a meeting, with a view of forming a society for bettering their condition. That would have been done, perhaps, more readily, if they had invited the tailors and a 'justice of the peace,' or 'minister.'"

I consider this timidity unworthy of us, for in my estimation, the publicity of a respectable name can be nothing to the lady, or the cause she advocates; and is not this cause worthy to be advocated by all who bear the name of women? Are we not a species of the human race, and is not this a free country? Then why may we not enjoy this freedom? Because we have been taught to believe ourselves far less noble and far less wise than the other sex? They have taken advantage of this weakness and tyrant-like have stepped from one ascendancy to another 'til finally, and without resistance, they have us in their power; and severely have they used that power; nay they have even trampled us under their feet (comparatively speaking) and women have made no resistance.

Our supposed helplessness has heretofore caused us to remain silent and submissive, but I hope and believe our eyes are now open to a scene of misery too glaring to be overlooked and too painful to be submitted to. When we complain to our employers and others of the inequality of our wages with that of men, the excuse is, they have families to support from which females are exempt. Now this is either a sad mistake or a willful oversight. How many females are there who have families to support and how many single men who have none and who, having no other use for the fruits of their employers' generosity, they, childlike, waste it while the industrious mother having the care of a helpless offspring finds (with all the economies she is necessitated to practice) the scanty reward of her labors scarcely sufficient to support nature...."

Maria W. Miller Stewart's voice was heard in Boston by members of the city's free African American community. In lectures delivered in 1831 and 1832, she asserted the rights of all African Americans to full citizenship and women's right to take leadership roles in their communities. Stewart underlined how the intersection between race and sex in their lives made available fundamentally different economic and educational opportunities to Northern free African American as compared to white women. To challenge her critics, she invoked biblical precedents for women's public leadership.

"All the nations of the earth are crying out for liberty and equality. Away, away with tyranny and oppression!... This is the land of freedom. The press is at liberty. Every man has a right to express his opinion. Many think, because your skins are tinged with a sable hue, that you are an inferior race of beings; but God does not consider you as such. He hath formed and fashioned you in his own glorious image, and hath bestowed upon you reason and strong powers of intellect . . . and according to the Constitution of these United States, he hath made all men free and equal. . . .

O, ye daughters of Africa, awake! Awake! Arise! No longer sleep nor slumber, but distinguish yourselves. Show forth to the world that ye are endowed with noble and exalted faculties. . . . How long shall the fair daughters of Africa be compelled to bury their minds and talents beneath a load of iron pots and kettles? . . . Methinks I heard a spiritual interrogation— 'Who shall go forward, and take off the reproach that is cast upon the people of color? Shall it be a woman?' And my heart made this reply—'If it is thy will, be it even so, Lord Jesus!' . . . I can but die for expressing my sentiments; and I am as willing to die by the sword as the pestilence; for I am a true born American; your blood flows in my veins, and your spirit fires my breast . . ."

"[D]oubtless many are the prayers that have ascended to Heaven from Afric's daughters for strength to perform their work. Oh, many are the tears that have been shed for the want of that strength! Most of our color have dragged out a miserable existence of servitude from the cradle to the grave. And what literary acquirements can be made, or useful knowledge derived, from either maps, books, or charts, by those who continually drudge from Monday morning until Sunday noon? O, ye fairer sisters, whose hands are never soiled, whose nerves and muscles are never strained, go learn by experience! Had we had the opportunity that you have had, to improve our moral and mental faculties, what would have hindered our intellects from being as bright, and our manners from being as dignified as yours? Had it been our lot to have been nursed in the lap of affluence and ease, and to have basked beneath the smiles and sunshine of fortune, should we not have naturally supposed that we were never made to toil? . . ."

"What if I am a woman; is not the God of ancient times the God of these modern days? Did he not raise up Deborah, to be a mother, and a judge in Israel? Did not queen Esther save the lives of the Jews? . . . St. Paul declared that it was a shame for a woman to speak in public. . . . Did St. Paul but know of our wrongs and deprivations, I presume he would make no objections to our pleading in public for our rights."

CONSTITUTION AND BY-LAWS

OF THE

ABYSSINIAN BENEVOLENT DAUGHTERS

OF

ESTHER ASSOCIATION,

OF THE

CITY OF NEW YORK.

Adopted April 19, 1839.

Printed at the Office of the Colored American.

Constitution and By-Laws of the Abyssinian Benevolent Daughters of Esther Association (New York, 1839). Free African American women's "noble and exalted faculties" were reflected in the voluntary societies they organized to assist their communities and to fight against slavery.

"We would have every arbitrary barrier thrown down. We would have every path laid open to woman as freely as to man. As the friend of the [N]egro assumes that one man cannot, by right, hold another in bondage, so should the friend of woman assume that man cannot, by right, lay even well-meant restrictions on woman."

—Margaret Fuller, *The Dial*, 1843

Other voices focused specifically on the question of married women's legal rights. The practice of coverture, severely restricting wives' ability to hold their own income or property, seemed increasingly out of touch with economic realities in the rapidly growing commercial economy. In addition, older legal loopholes (such as equity courts) that had in earlier times permitted women to escape coverture's fetters were becoming less available and more expensive. Most voices calling for legal change were those of fathers concerned about protecting family assets from wastrel sons-in-law or their creditors, as was the case in Mississippi, which enacted the first Married Women's Property Act in 1839 (property that included slaves). But an occasional state legislator, such as New York's Thomas Herttell, a freethinker, argued for legal reform on grounds of general principle.

"By virtue of existing laws, *unmarried* females can acquire, manage, and dispose of their estate both real and personal, and can exercise all the rights and powers relative thereto, as are possessed and exercised by *men*. This is as it ought to be. The doctrine, or just and moral principle of 'equal rights' cannot consistently, and does not righteously justify laws, giving to one *sex* power and privileges relative to property which are denied to the other. . . . Not so with *married* women. Existing laws divest them of rights which are retained and exercised not only by the male, but by the *un*married portion of the female sex. By marriage, the wife's personal property . . . becomes vested in her husband, and she is as fully deprived of her title to it, and her right to use or dispose of it, . . . as if she instead of being *married*, had been sold a *slave* to a *master*. . . . But what have married women done that they should be . . . deprived of the rights of property, which is held sacred and inviolate in the cases of *unmarried* women, and males, married and unmarried? Why, to be sure, they got married! *That*, they had a right to do. . . . [S]hall married women be deprived of their rights, and dispossessed of their property, barely for having exercised a natural and inalienable right?"

Even as Thomas Herttell rose in the New York state legislature to argue for his legislation (which eventually lost), women within the radical anti-slavery movement (abolitionists) had begun to precipitate a full-scale debate over women's rights. Foremost among them were two white sisters from South Carolina, Sarah and Angelina Grimké. A religious conversion experience led Sarah to reject her family's slave-produced wealth and privilege, move to Philadelphia, and join the Society of Friends (Quakers). Angelina followed, and together the sisters became Quaker ministers and then joined the abolitionist crusade. Their intimate knowledge of slavery made them extraordinarily effective writers and public speakers; in both written and spoken words, they appealed

"I went from house to house with a petition for signatures simply asking our Legislature to allow married women to hold real estate in their own name. What did I meet with? Why, the very name exposed one to ridicule, if not to worse treatment. . . . [There were] five signatures attached to the first petition, in 1837!"

—Ernestine Potowski Rose, who left her native Poland in 1827 and arrived in New York in 1836, recalling her work in support of Herttell's legislation

specifically to women to work against slavery. In a series of letters published in 1836, Angelina connected antislavery activism with women's rights.

"The investigation of the rights of the slave has led me to a better understanding of my own. I have found the Anti-Slavery cause to be the high school of morals in our land—the school in which *human rights* are more fully investigated, and better understood and taught, than in any other.... Human beings have *rights*, because they are *moral beings*: the rights of *all* men, grow out of their moral nature; and as all men have the same moral nature, they have essentially the same rights.... Now if rights are founded in the nature of our moral being, then the *mere circumstance of sex* does not give to man higher rights and responsibilities, than to woman.... I recognize no rights but *human* rights—I know nothing of men's rights and women's rights; for in Christ Jesus there is neither male nor female.... Now, I believe it is woman's right to have a voice in all the laws and regulations by which she is to be *governed*, whether in Church or State; and that the present arrangements of society, on these points, are *a violation of human rights, a rank usurpation of power*, a violent seizure and confiscation of what is sacredly and inalienably hers...."

White women abolitionists like Angelina Grimké were accused of being immodest and indelicate because they spoke publicly about the sexual exploitation of enslaved women. The criticisms derived not from the fact of lecturing but because they did it in large public gatherings that included women and men, blacks and whites, and targeted an institution central to the American economic and racial system, slavery. Moreover, they claimed the masculine privilege of using eloquence to persuade audiences of slavery's evils. An 1837 "Pastoral letter" from a group of Congregationalist clergymen in Massachusetts explicitly attacked reformers like the Grimké sisters while praising their counterparts who ran Sunday schools or served as missionaries.

"The appropriate duties and influence of woman are clearly stated in the New Testament. Those duties and that influence are unobtrusive and private, but the sources of mighty power. When the mild, dependent, softening influence of woman upon the sternness of man's opinions is fully exercised, society feels the effects of it in a thousand forms. The power of woman is in her dependence, flowing from the consciousness of that weakness which God has given her for her protection, and which keeps her in those departments of life that form the character of individuals and of the nation....

We appreciate the unostentatious prayers and efforts of woman in advancing the cause of religion at home and abroad; in Sabbath schools; in leading religious inquirers to the pastors for instruction; and in all such associated efforts as becomes the modesty of her sex. . . .

But when she assumes the place and tone of man as a public reformer, our care and protection of her seem unnecessary; we put ourselves in self-defence against her; she yields the power which God has given her for her protection, and her character becomes unnatural. If the vine, whose strength and beauty is to lean upon the trellis work and half conceal its clusters, thinks to assume the independence and the overshading nature of the elm, it will not only cease to bear fruit, but fall in shame and dishonor into the dust. We cannot, therefore, but regret the mistaken conduct of those who encourage females to bear an obtrusive and ostentatious part in measures of reform, and countenance any of that sex who so far forget themselves as to itinerate in the character of public lecturers and teachers.—We especially deplore the intimate acquaintance and promiscuous conversation of females with regard to things which ought not to be named; by which that modesty and delicacy which is the charm of domestic life, and which constitutes the true influence of woman in society is consumed, and the way opened, as we apprehend, for degeneracy and ruin. . . ."

Many women sided with ministers and other critics of abolitionist women's activities. Catharine Beecher articulated a widely held position when she published an essay in 1837 addressed to Angelina Grimké.

"Heaven has appointed to one sex the superior, and to the other the subordinate station, and this without any reference to the character or conduct of either. It is therefore as much for the dignity as it is for the interest of females, in all respects to conform to the duties of this relation. . . . But while woman holds a subordinate relation in society to the other sex, it is not because it was designed that her duties or her influence should be any the less important, or all-pervading. But it was designed that the mode of gaining influence and of exercising power should be altogether different and peculiar. . . .

Woman is to win every thing by peace and love; by making herself so much respected, esteemed and loved, that to yield to her opinions and to gratify her wishes, will be the free-will offering of the heart. . . . [B]ut whatever, in any measure, throws a woman into the attitude of a combatant, either for herself or others—whatever

Catharine Beecher (1800–1878), born into an illustrious family of preachers and writers, became a teacher, school founder, author, advocate for the importance of women's roles as wives and mothers, as well as the necessity of women's higher education, and a major actor in the effort to make teaching a profession for women. Although she never married, Beecher wrote one of the most widely read domestic advice books of the 19th century, *A Treatise on Domestic Economy.* And although she opposed political, and especially partisan, activism by women, Beecher initiated an 1830s petition campaign against Indian removal and in 1854 signed a general petition to Congress opposing the repeal of the Missouri Compromise. Despite these contradictions, Beecher was widely admired for her public work and her writings. Her view that women's self-sacrificing devotion to others was the balm that healed the wounds of industrial society was both influential and long-lived.

finds her in a party conflict—whatever obliges her in any way to exert coercive influences, throws her out of her appropriate sphere...."

In her 1838 book, *Letters on the Equality of the Sexes,* Sarah Grimké rejected the arguments put forth by Catharine Beecher and by the "Pastoral letter" and focused instead on the causes and manifestations of women's *in*equality. She pressed for free women's educational and economic rights, and enslaved women's rights to freedom and protection from sexual abuse, while also making a case for the benefits to men that equality of the sexes would bring.

"During the early part of my life, my lot was cast among the butterflies of the *fashionable* world; and of this class of women, I am constrained to say, both from experience and observation, that their education is miserably deficient; that they are taught to regard marriage as the one thing needful, the only avenue to distinction; hence to attract the notice and win the attentions of men, by their external charms, is the chief business of fashionable girls. They seldom think that men will be allured by intellectual acquirements, because they find, that where any mental superiority exists, a woman is generally shunned and regarded as stepping out of her 'appropriate sphere.'...

[Many girls] are brought up with the dangerous and absurd idea, that *marriage* is a kind of preferment; and that to be able to keep their husband's house, and render his situation comfortable, is the end of her being.... [T]o be married is too often held up to the view of girls as the sine qua non of human happiness and human existence. For this purpose more than for any other, I verily believe the majority of girls are trained. This is demonstrated by the imperfect education which is bestowed upon them, and the little pains taken to cultivate their minds.... In most families, it is considered a matter of far more consequence to call a girl off from making a pie, or a pudding, than to interrupt her whilst engaged in her studies. This mode of training necessarily exalts, in their view, the animal above the intellectual and spiritual nature, and teaches women to regard themselves as a kind of machinery, necessary to keep the domestic engine in order, but of little value as the *intelligent* companions of men....

There is another way in which the general opinion, that women are inferior to men, is manifested, that bears with tremendous effect on the laboring class, and indeed on almost all who are obliged to earn a subsistence, whether it be by mental or physical

"We are thy sisters." This poem by Sarah Forten, an African American friend and co-worker of the Grimké sisters, appeared in the program of the First Anti-Slavery Convention of American Women, held in New York in 1837:

"We are thy sisters. God has truly said,
That of one blood the nation he has made.
O, Christian woman! in a Christian land,
Canst thou unblushing read this great
    command?
Suffer the wrongs which wring our inmost
    heart,
To draw one throb of pity on thy part!
Our skins may differ, but from thee we
    claim
A sister's privilege and a sister's name."

Abolitionists used an image with the caption "Am I Not a Woman and a Sister" to remind viewers of enslaved women's sexual and personal vulnerability and to invoke the ideal of a cross-racial "sisterhood" among antislavery women.

exertion—I allude to the disproportionate value set on the time and labor of men and of women. A man who is engaged in teaching, can always, I believe, command a higher price for tuition than a woman—even when he teaches the same branches, and is not in any respect superior to the woman.... [I]n tailoring, a man has twice, or three times as much for making a waistcoat or pantaloons as a woman, although the work done by each may be equally good. In those employments which are peculiar to women, their time is estimated at only half the value of that of men. A woman who goes out to wash, works as hard in proportion as a wood sawyer, or a coal heaver, but she is not generally able to make more than half as much by a day's work....

There is another class of women in this country, to whom I cannot refer, without feelings of the deepest shame and sorrow. I allude to our female slaves. Our southern cities are whelmed beneath a tide of pollution; the virtue of female slaves is wholly at the mercy of irresponsible tyrants, and women are bought and sold in our slave markets, to gratify the brutal lust of those who bear the name of Christians. In our slave States, if amid all her degradation, and ignorance, a woman desires to preserve her virtue unsullied, she is either bribed or whipped into compliance, or if she dares resist her seducer, her life by the laws of some of the slave States may be, and has actually been sacrificed to the fury of disappointed passion.... But even if any laws existed in the United States ... for the protection of female slaves, they would be null and void, because the evidence of a colored person is not admitted against a white, in any of our Courts of Justice in the slave states.... In Christian America, the slave has no refuge from unbridled cruelty and lust....

[There are] benefits to be derived by men, as well as by women, from the opinions I advocate relative to the equality of the sexes.... Our brethren may reject my doctrine, because it runs counter to some common opinions, and because it wounds their pride; but I believe they would be 'partakers of the benefit' resulting from the Equality of the Sexes, and would find that woman, as their equal, was unspeakably more valuable than woman as their inferior, both as a moral and an intellectual being."

In her 1861 autobiography, Harriet Jacobs, who successfully freed herself from slavery in North Carolina, commented bitterly on enslaved women's sexual vulnerability and lack of the self-ownership and legal protections that free women took for granted.

To the Hon. the Senate and House of Representatives.

The petition of the undersigned Ladies of the County of Erie, (N. Y.) humbly showeth,—That your petitioners feel themselves bound by their duty to their country, to protest against every practical violation of the principles embodied in the memorable Declaration of our Independence, viz. "That all men are created equal, that they are endowed by their Creator with certain inalienable rights, that among these are life, LIBERTY and the pursuit of happiness." Your petitioners, deeply sympathizing with their sisters in bondage, cannot regard themselves as having done their duty to their country—to suffering humanity, and to God, till they have protested against the continuance of Slavery and the Slave Trade in the District of Columbia, and prayed your honorable bodies to exercise your constitutional powers for their immediate abolition.

Remembering that the traffic in human flesh, when practiced upon the ocean, has been solemnly declared piracy by our own, and that it is so considered by almost all christian nations, your petitioners earnestly implore that slavery the necessary cause of that traffic, may no longer be permitted to exist in the capital of this Republic.

NAMES.   NAMES.

To the House of Representatives of the United States of America:

The petition of the undersigned, female citizens of the state of Ohio, respectfully showeth:

That your petitioners would take no measures for the abolition of Slavery which are not reasonable, peaceful, and sanctioned by the Constitution of our country and the dictates of an enlightened humanity. They do not, therefore, ask your honorable body to interfere with those laws which in the several states go to establish and regulate property in human beings. But, as Congress has exclusive power of legislation in and over the District of Columbia, they ask for the exercise of that power totally and immediately to abolish Slavery within said District. They ask it, because Slavery is unjust: Because it violates the rights of both God and man: Because it corrupts public morals: Because it is oppressive to the honest free laborer, and tends to make labor disreputable as well as unprofitable: Because it brands our nation before the world as avaricious, cruel and hypocritical: Because persons have been imprisoned in the District on mere suspicion of their being runaways, and not being proved to be such, have been sold into perpetual slavery for the *payment of their jail fees!* Because, while Slavery continues, there must of necessity be a SLAVE TRADE. Such trade has, by a solemn act of Congress, been declared PIRACY when carried on upon the ocean; your petitioners do not understand why it should be less criminal on land: nor why one man should be licensed to buy and sell the natives of our own country, while another is ignominiously hung for trafficking in the persons of foreigners. Yet, to such a magnitude has this trade grown under the exclusive legislation of Congress, that, if the citizens of the District themselves are to be believed, the capital of our republic is one of the greatest slave marts in the world.

Again, your petitioners ask the immediate abolition of Slavery in the District of Columbia, because they deem it safe and practicable. Safe, because it would make friends of those who now have every reason to be our enemies: Because the government of good laws is always safer than that of arbitrary will: Because every innocent man, in his right senses, is fitter for freedom than for slavery: Because the experiment has been tried elsewhere, and has always been found safe—witness especially the cases of Bermuda and Antigua, where emancipation was immediate and unconditional, and the public peace is now so secure, that the military guards formerly required by slavery, have been entirely dispensed with: And, because the nation has abundant power to enforce order, should there be any disposition to disturb it. Practicable, because it will only exchange an unnatural and forced system of labor for a natural and voluntary one. It will not annihilate the laborers nor their labor, but will merely make it necessary for the employers to pay fair wages.—They ask for them the common protection as well as government of wise and equitable laws.—Finally, your petitioners disclaiming any design of interfering unconstitutionally or unwarrantably with the interests of others; and with the kindest regard for the interests of their southern fellow-citizens, ask for the abolition of slavery in the District of Columbia, because it will furnish a most salutary example to all slave holders throughout the world, teaching them that an immediate abrogation and renunciation of the claim of property in man is safe and profitable, as well as honorable and just. They feel bound as men, as Christians, and as republicans, to urge this subject upon the attention of Congress; and from the exercise of this constitutional right, as well as from the inalienable one of freely expressing their opinions, they can never cease till justice is done.

"O, ye happy women, whose purity has been sheltered from childhood, who have been free to choose the objects of your affections, whose homes are protected by law ... [understand that] if slavery had been abolished, I, also, could have married the man of my choice; I could have had a home shielded by the laws.... Pity me! ... You never knew what it is to be a slave; to be entirely unprotected by law or custom; to have the laws reduce you to the condition of a **chattel [property]**, entirely subject to the will of another.... Still, in looking back, calmly, on the events of my life, I feel that the slave woman ought not to be judged by the same standard as others....

Slavery is terrible for men; but it is far more terrible for women. Superadded to the burden common to all, *they* have wrongs, and sufferings, and mortifications peculiarly their own."

Petition campaigns brought women activists directly into the political arena as they sought to influence state and national legislatures to restrict or abolish slavery. These two examples, pressing Congress to abolish slavery and the slave trade in Washington, D.C., are from Ohio and New York.

Slave women's rights. In 1855, Celia, a nineteen-year-old enslaved woman in Missouri, murdered her owner, Robert Newsom, who had repeatedly raped her. At her trial, Celia's lawyers invoked an 1845 Missouri law making it a crime "to take any woman unlawfully against her will and by force, menace or duress, compel her to be defiled." They argued that "the words 'any woman' . . . [should be interpreted to] embrace slave women, as well as free white women." The judge refused to accept the argument; Celia was convicted and executed.

The Seneca Falls Convention of 1848 in Context

The year 1848 witnessed the first two women's rights conventions in American history: one at Seneca Falls, New York, in July, and a second in Rochester, New York, two weeks later. In 1850, a huge national convention assembled in Worcester, Massachusetts; thereafter, until 1859, conventions were held yearly. A women's rights movement was born.

Most of the three hundred women and men in attendance at the Seneca Falls Convention came from surrounding towns and farms; most were seasoned reformers, used to attending abolitionist and temperance conventions, and skilled in the art of drafting reports and resolutions. Many came in family groups. About a quarter were Quakers, members of the Congregational Friends, a radical group dedicated to what they termed the "co-equality of the sexes" in all areas of life. A few were veterans of a successful and just-completed campaign to get the state legislature in Albany to pass a Married Women's Property Act. Frederick Douglass, who only ten years earlier had been a fugitive from slavery in Maryland, reported approvingly on the proceedings for his newspaper, *The North Star*. The key organizers were Elizabeth Cady Stanton, who was living in Seneca Falls; Lucretia Coffin Mott, who, along with her husband James, was visiting Quaker meetings in upstate New York and staying with Lucretia's sister Martha Coffin Wright in nearby Auburn; Martha Wright; Jane Hunt; and Martha M'Clintock. Together, the five women planned the convention and drafted a document for discussion. That document was the Declaration of Sentiments. Modeled on the Declaration of Independence, it included a preamble; a central section describing the gender hierarchy that created a "tyranny" of "man" over "woman"; and a series of resolutions setting forth the citizenship rights—legal, civil, educational, economic, sexual, and individual—that the signers pledged to pursue.

"When, in the course of human events, it becomes necessary for one portion of the family of man to assume among the people of the earth a position different from that which they have hitherto occupied, but one to which the laws of nature and of nature's God entitle them, a decent respect to the opinions of mankind requires that they should declare the causes that impel them to such a course.

We hold these truths to be self-evident: that all men and women are created equal; that they are endowed by their Creator with certain inalienable rights; that among these are life, liberty, and the pursuit of happiness; that to secure these rights governments are instituted, deriving their just powers from the consent of the governed. Whenever any form of Government becomes destructive of these ends, it is the right of those who suffer from it to refuse allegiance to it, and to insist upon the institution of a new government, laying its foundation on such principles, and organizing its powers in such form as to them shall seem most likely to effect their safety and happiness. Prudence, indeed, will dictate that governments long established should not be changed for light and transient causes; and accordingly, all experience hath shown that mankind are more disposed to suffer, while evils are sufferable, than to right themselves by abolishing the forms to which they are accustomed. But when a long train of abuses and usurpations, pursuing invariably the same object, evinces a design to reduce them under absolute despotism, it is their duty to throw off such government, and to provide new guards for their future security. Such has been the patient sufferance of the women under this government, and such is now the necessity which constrains them to demand the equal station to which they are entitled.

The history of mankind is a history of repeated injuries and usurpations on the part of man toward woman, having in direct object the establishment of an absolute tyranny over her. To prove this, let facts be submitted to a candid world.

He has never permitted her to exercise her inalienable right to the **elective franchise** [**right to vote**].

He has compelled her to submit to laws, in the formation of which she had no voice.

He has withheld from her rights which are given to the most ignorant and degraded men—both natives and foreigners.

Having deprived her of this first right of a citizen, the elective franchise, thereby leaving her without representation in the halls of legislation, he has oppressed her on all sides.

He has made her, if married, in the eye of the law, **civilly dead** [**coverture**].

He has taken from her all right in property, even to the wages she earns.

He has made her, morally, an irresponsible being, as she can commit many crimes **with impunity** [**without punishment**], provided they be done in the presence of her husband. In the covenant of marriage, she is compelled to promise obedience to her husband, he becoming, to all intents and purposes, her master—the law giving him power to deprive her of her liberty, and to administer chastisement.

He has so framed the laws of divorce, as to what shall be the proper causes; and in case of separation, to whom the guardianship of the children shall be given; as to be wholly regardless of the happiness of women—the law, in all cases, going upon a false supposition of the supremacy of man, and giving all power into his hands.

After depriving her of all rights as a married woman, if single and the owner of property, he has taxed her to support a government which recognizes her only when her property can be made profitable to it.

He has monopolized nearly all the profitable employments, and from those she is permitted to follow, she receives but a **scanty remuneration** [**meager wage**].

He closes against her all the avenues to wealth and distinction, which he considers most honorable to himself. As a teacher of theology, medicine, or law, she is not known.

He has denied her the facilities for obtaining a thorough education, all colleges being closed against her.

He allows her in Church, as well as State, but a subordinate position, claiming Apostolic authority for her exclusion from the ministry, and, with some exceptions, from any public participation in the affairs of the Church.

He has created a false public sentiment, by giving to the world a **different code of morals** [**sexual double standard**] for men and women, by which moral delinquencies which exclude women from society, are not only tolerated, but deemed of little account in man.

He has usurped the prerogative of **Jehovah** [**God**] himself, claiming it as his right to assign for her a sphere of action, when that belongs to her conscience and to her God.

He has endeavored, in every way that he could to destroy her confidence in her own powers, to lessen her self-respect, and to make her willing to lead a dependent and abject life.

Now, in view of this entire disfranchisement of one-half the people of this country, their social and religious degradation,—in view of the unjust laws above mentioned, and because women do feel themselves aggrieved, oppressed, and fraudulently deprived of their most sacred rights, we insist that they have immediate admission to all the rights and privileges which belong to them as citizens of the United States.

In entering upon the great work before us, we anticipate no small amount of misconception, misrepresentation, and ridicule; but we shall use every instrumentality within our power to effect our object. We shall employ agents, circulate tracts, petition the State and national Legislatures, and endeavor to enlist the pulpit and the press in our behalf. We hope this Convention will be followed by a series of Conventions, embracing every part of the country.

Firmly relying upon the final triumph of the Right and the True, we do this day affix our signatures to this declaration. . . .

The resolutions . . . were read and taken up separately. Some, from their self-evident truth, elicited but little remark; others, after some criticism, much debate, and some slight alterations, were finally passed by a large majority. . . . :

Whereas, the great precept of nature is conceded to be, 'that man shall pursue his own true and substantial happiness.' Blackstone in his Commentaries remarks, that this law of Nature being coeval with mankind, and dictated by God himself, is of course superior in obligation to any other. It is binding over all the globe, in all countries, and at all times; no human laws are of any validity if contrary to this, and such of them as are valid, derive all their force, and all their validity, and all their authority, mediately and immediately, from this original; therefore;

Resolved, That such laws as conflict, in any way, with the true and substantial happiness of woman, are contrary to the great precept of nature, and of no validity; for this is 'superior in obligation to any other.'

Resolved, That all laws which prevent woman from occupying such a station in society as her conscience shall dictate, or which place her in a position inferior to that of man, are contrary to the great precept of nature, and therefore of no force or authority.

Resolved, That woman is man's equal—was intended to be so by the Creator, and the highest good of the race demands that she should be recognized as such.

Resolved, That the women of this country ought to be enlightened in regard to the laws under which they live, that they may no longer publish their degradation, by declaring themselves satisfied with their present position, nor their ignorance, by asserting that they have all the rights they want.

Resolved, That inasmuch as man, while claiming for himself intellectual superiority, does accord to woman moral superiority, it is pre-eminently his duty to encourage her to speak, and teach, as she has an opportunity, in all religious assemblies.

Resolved, That the same amount of virtue, delicacy, and refinement of behavior, that is required of woman in the social state,

The woman's rights convention met in Seneca Falls because **Elizabeth Cady Stanton** (1815–1902) lived there. After a girlhood in Johnstown, New York, and an education at the Troy Female Seminary, Elizabeth Cady married the abolitionist Henry Stanton in 1840, embarked on a long career in reform activism, and moved with Henry to Seneca Falls in 1847. Her brilliant intellect and powerful analysis of the causes of women's inequality made her a key figure in the developing woman's rights movement, especially after she met Susan B. Anthony in 1851. Often controversial because of her advocacy of equal marriage, "voluntary motherhood," and easy access to divorce, Stanton was an uncompromising radical when it came to women's rights, especially their right to own themselves, or what she termed "self-sovereignty." Over the course of her long life, Stanton bore seven children, argued with colleagues and foes, wrote and delivered scores of speeches, and began the process of compiling the *History of Woman Suffrage*, which eventually ran to six volumes. The *History* preserved her legacy and her version of the major events of the woman's rights movement. Historians today acknowledge its significance but recognize its partial perspective on the events it chronicles, as well as its incomplete—and at times erroneous—version of particular historical episodes.

Frederick Douglass, daguerreotype. Frederick Douglass attended both the Seneca Falls and the Rochester meetings; in reporting on the latter, his newspaper noted: "At a Convention, held in the Unitarian church in the city of Rochester, on the 2nd day of August, 1848, to consider the Rights of Women: politically, socially, religiously, and industriously.... FREDERICK DOUGLASS, remarked, that the only true basis of rights, was the capacity of individuals, and as for himself he dared not claim a right which he would not concede to woman.... He would see her elevated to an equal position with man in every relation of life."

should also be required of man, and the same transgressions should be visited with equal severity on both man and woman.

Resolved, That the objection of indelicacy and impropriety, which is so often brought against woman when she addresses a public audience, comes with a very ill grace from those who encourage, by their attendance, her appearance on the stage, in the concert, or in feats of the circus.

Resolved, That woman has too long rested satisfied in the circumscribed limits which corrupt customs and a perverted application of the Scriptures have marked out for her, and that it is time she should move in the enlarged sphere which her great Creator has assigned her.

Resolved, That it is the duty of the women of this country to secure to themselves their sacred right to the **elective franchise [right to vote]**.

Frederick Douglass

The New York Pictorial Picayune.

WE ARE EQUAL TO MEN, BECAUSE WE ARE THEIR WIVES

WE ARE GREATER THAN MEN, BECAUSE WE ARE THEIR MOTHERS.

FEMALE EMANCIPATION.

OHIO WOMEN'S RIGHTS CONVENTION,
HELD AT AKRON, MAY 28TH AND 29TH, 1851.

A cartoonist lampooned the 1851 Akron Women's Rights Convention with stereotypes of masculine women and feminine men.

Resolved, That the equality of human rights results necessarily from the fact of the identity of the race in capabilities and responsibilities.

Resolved, therefore, That, being invested by the Creator with the same capabilities, and the same consciousness of responsibility for their exercise, it is demonstrably the right and duty of woman, equally with man, to promote every righteous cause, by every righteous means; and especially in regard to the great subjects of morals and religion, it is self-evidently her right to participate with her brother in teaching them, both in private and in public, by writing and by speaking, by any instrumentalities proper to be used, and in any assemblies proper to be held; and this being a self-evident truth, growing out of the divinely implanted principles of human nature, any custom or authority adverse to it, whether modern or wearing the hoary sanction of antiquity, is to be regarded as self-evident falsehood, and at war with the interests of mankind.

[At the last session] Lucretia Mott offered and spoke to the following resolution:

Resolved, That the speedy success of our cause depends upon the zealous and untiring efforts of both men and women, for the overthrow of the monopoly of the pulpit, and for the securing to woman an equal participation with men in the various trades, professions, and commerce."

Early women's rights conventions may have been controversial, but, by 1848, the issue of women's rights had already entered the public consciousness in a variety of ways. In 1846, six women from upstate New York farming families, none of whom is known to have ever attended a women's rights meeting, terming themselves "citizens of the state of New York," sent a plainly worded petition to the men who were meeting in convention to rewrite the state constitution.

"Your Memorialists inhabitants of Jefferson county, believing that civil government has its foundation in the laws of our existence, as moral and social beings, that the specific object and end of civil government is to protect all in the exercise of all their natural rights, by combining the strength of society for the defence of the individual—believing that the province of civil government is not to create new rights, but to declare and enforce those which originally existed. Believing likewise that all governments must derive their just powers from the consent of the governed . . ., therefore respectfully represent: That the present government of this state has widely departed from the true democratic principles upon which all just governments must be based by denying to the female portion of community the right of suffrage and any participation in forming the government and laws under which they live, and to which they are amenable, and by imposing upon them burdens of taxation, both directly and indirectly, without admitting them the right of representation, thereby striking down the only safeguards of their individual and personal liberties. Your Memorialists therefore ask your honorable body, to remove this just cause of complaint, by modifying the present Constitution of this State, so as to extend to women equal, and civil and political rights

"RIGHT IS OF NO SEX—TRUTH IS OF NO COLOR—GOD IS THE FATHER OF US ALL, AND WE ARE BRETHREN"

—Masthead of Frederick Douglass's newspaper, *The North Star*, 1848 with men. In proposing this change, your petitioners ask you to confer upon them no new right but only to declare and enforce those which they originally inherited, but which have ungenerously been withheld from them, rights, which they as citizens of the state of New York may reasonably and rightfully claim. We might adduce arguments both numerous and decisive in support of our position, but believing that a self evident truth is sufficiently plain without argument, and in view of our necessarily limited space, we forbear offering any and respectfully submit it for consideration.

ELEANOR VINCENT,	SUSAN ORMSBY,
LYDIA A. WILLIAMS,	AMY ORMSBY,
LYDIA OSBORN,	ANNA BISHOP.

Aug. 8th, 1846."

In April 1848, three months before the Seneca Falls Convention, the New York State legislature passed a married women's property act.

"The real and personal property of any female [now married and] who may hereafter marry, and which she shall own at the time of marriage, and the rents issues and profits thereof shall not be subject to the disposal of her husband, nor be liable for his debts, and shall continue her sole and separate property, as if she were a single female. . . .

It shall be lawful for any married female to receive, by gift, grant, devise or bequest, from any person other than her husband and hold to her sole and separate use, as if she were a single female, real and personal property, and the rents, issues and profits thereof, and the same shall not be subject to the disposal of her husband, nor be liable for his debts."

New York enacted a revised version in 1860.

"A married woman may bargain, sell, assign, and transfer her separate personal property, and carry on any trade or business, and perform any labor or services on her sole and separate account, and the earnings of any married woman from her trade . . . shall be her sole and separate property, and may be used or invested by her in her own name. . . .

Any married woman may, while married, sue and be sued in all matters having relation to her . . . sole and separate property . . . in the same manner as if she were sole. . . .

"We fully believe in the equality of the sexes, therefore, Resolved, That we hereby invite females hereafter to take part in our deliberations.... Three cheers for woman's rights."

—National Convention of Colored Freemen, Cleveland, September 6, 1849

No bargain or contract made by any married woman, in respect to her sole and separate property ... shall be binding upon her husband, or render him or his property in any way liable therefor.

Every married woman is hereby constituted and declared to be the joint guardian of her children, with her husband, with equal powers, rights, and duties in regard to them, with the husband...."

While traveling in upstate New York in 1848, Lucretia Mott visited a Seneca village, one of the remnants of the once-powerful Iroquois Nation. The group was in the midst of writing a formal constitution that would lead to a loss of older matrons' traditional influence. Under the new constitution, adopted in December, 1848, only men could vote. In a letter to a friend, she relayed her observations.

"The few hundreds left of the Seneca nation at the Cattaraugus reservation, are improving in their mode of living, cultivating their land, and educating their children. They, too, are learning somewhat from the political agitations abroad; and, as man is wont, are imitating the movements of France and all Europe, in seeking larger liberty—more independence.

Their Chieftainship is therefore a subject of discussion in their councils, and important changes are demanded and expected, as to the election of their chiefs, many being prepared for a yearly appointment....

We witnessed their strawberry dance, and ... in observing the profound veneration of the hundreds present, some twenty of whom were performers, and the respectful attention paid to the speeches of their chiefs, women as well as men, it was far from me to say, that our **silent, voiceless worship [Quaker worship services]** was better adapted to their condition....

While in western New York, we attended two Conventions called to consider the relative position of woman in society—one held at Seneca Falls, the other at Rochester....

The attendance and interest manifested, were greatly encouraging; and give hope that this long neglected subject will soon begin to receive the attention that its importance demands.... All these subjects of reform are kindred in their nature; and giving to each its proper consideration, will tend to strengthen and nerve the mind for all."

Mott's reference to "the political agitations abroad" demonstrated American activists' awareness of developments in Europe during the

"Revolutions of 1848" in France and Germany—where radicals sought to overthrow existing monarchies—as well as their familiarity with electoral reform movements in England. That awareness derived from their travels in Europe, the extensive correspondence that many of them carried on with their European counterparts, especially through the international antislavery movement, and the arrival of radical European refugees in the United States in the wake of failed revolutionary efforts. Political discussion crossed back and forth across the Atlantic and along the U.S.-Canada border. An 1851 essay of English feminist Harriet Taylor demonstrated her awareness of developments in the United States.

"Most of our readers will probably learn from these pages for the first time, that there has arisen in the United States,... an organized agitation on a new question.... This question is, the enfranchisement of women; their admission, in law and in fact, to equality in all rights, political, civil, and social, with the male citizens of the community.... It is a political movement, practical in its objects, carried on in a form which denotes an intention to persevere. And it is a movement not merely *for* women, but *by* them.... That women have as good a claim as men have, in point of personal right, to the suffrage, or to a place in the jury-box, it would be difficult for any one to deny. It cannot certainly be denied by the United States of America, as a people or as a community. Their democratic institutions rest avowedly on the inherent right of every one to a voice in the government.... Not only to the democracy of America, the claim of women to civil and political equality makes an irresistible appeal, but also to those Radicals and **Chartists [English advocates of full male suffrage]** in the British islands, and democrats on the continent, who claim what is called universal suffrage as an inherent right, unjustly and oppressively withheld from them.... There are indications that the example of America will be followed on this side of the Atlantic...."

Two French women's rights radicals, Jeanne Deroin and Pauline Roland, imprisoned in Paris for political agitation on behalf of workers, sent this letter to "the Convention of Women in America" in 1851.

"Dear Sisters:

Your courageous declaration of Woman's Rights has resounded even to our prison, and has filled our souls with inexpressible joy.... Sisters of America! your socialist sisters of France are united with you in the vindication of the right of woman to civil and political equality. We have, moreover, the profound conviction that only by the power of association based on solidarity—by the union of the working-classes of both sexes to organize labor—can be acquired, completely and pacifically, the civil and political equality of woman, and the social right for all.

It is in this confidence that from the depths of the jail which still imprisons our bodies without reaching our hearts, we cry to you, Faith, Love, Hope, and send to you our sisterly salutations.

JEANNE DEROIN, PAULINE ROLAND.

PARIS, PRISON OF ST. LA[Z]ARE, *June* 15, 1851."

In 1848, international developments came home to the United States from another direction: through the Treaty of Guadalupe Hidalgo, which ended the highly controversial U.S. war with Mexico and expanded the country's borders to encompass a vast new territory. As with the purchase of Louisiana from France in 1803, the annexation of Mexico's northern lands raised thorny questions about how women who had been governed under a Spanish-derived legal code would fare under American constitutional and civil law. Although gaining access to non-ecclesiastical divorce for the first time, Hispanic married women faced the loss of their accustomed economic and property rights. The discovery of gold in California in 1848 further complicated the picture, bringing thousands of new land-seekers into the territory. María Amparo Ruiz de Burton, one of the wealthy *Californios* (in 1848, residents of modern-day California and Baja California) whose property rights were threatened by U.S. annexation, summarized her view of the treaty in her 1885 novel, *The Squatter and the Don*.

"I think but few Americans know or believe to what extent we have been wronged by Congressional action. And truly, I believe that Congress itself did not anticipate the effect of its laws upon us, and how we would be despoiled, we, the conquered people,' said Don Mariano, sadly.

'It is the duty of law-givers to foresee the effect of the laws they impose upon people,' said Doña Josefa.

'That I don't deny, but I fear that the conquered have always but a weak voice, which nobody hears,' said Don Mariano.

'We have no one to speak for us. By the treaty of Guadalupe Hidalgo the American nation pledged its honor to respect our land titles just the same as Mexico would have done. Unfortunately, however, the discovery of gold brought to California the riff-raff of the world, and with it a horde of land-sharks, all possessing the privilege of voting, and most of them coveting our lands, for which they very quickly began to clamor. . . . They want the land of the Spanish people, because we "have too much," they say. So, to win their votes,

---

"In the said territories, property of every kind, now belonging to Mexicans not established there, shall be inviolably respected. The present owners, the heirs of these, and all Mexicans who may hereafter acquire said property by contract, shall enjoy with respect to it, guaranties equally ample as if the same belonged to citizens of the United States. . . . The Mexicans who, in the territories aforesaid, shall not preserve the character of citizens of the Mexican Republic,. . . shall be incorporated into the Union of the United States and be admitted, at the proper time (to be judged by the Congress of the United States) to the enjoyment of all the rights of citizens of the United States according to the principles of the Constitution; and in the mean time shall be maintained and protected in the free enjoyment of their liberty and property, and secured in the free exercise of their religion without restriction."

—Articles VIII & IX, Treaty of Guadalupe Hidalgo, 1848

"Si me faltasen las fuerzas . . . entonces le suplico de antemano no me juzgue con severidiad. Acuérdese que soy mujer . . . ye mexicana . . . con el alma encerrada en una juala de fierro, pues así nos encierra 'la sociedad' luego que nacemos, como los chinos los pies de sus mujeres."

"If my strength has failed me . . . well, I ask you not to judge me harshly. Remember that I am a woman . . . and a Mexican woman at that . . . and my soul is confined in an iron cage, for that is how 'Society' confines us as soon as we are born, as the Chinese bind the feet of their women."

—María Amparo Ruiz de Burton letter, August 1869

the votes of the squatters, our representatives in Congress helped to pass laws declaring all lands in California open to pre-emption, as in Louisiana, for instance.... While [the] legal proceedings are going on, the squatters locate their claims and raise crops on our lands, which they convert into money to fight our titles.'"

Women's Rights Movements

Women's rights advocates saw the acquisition of Mexico's lands in 1848, following the 1845 annexation of Texas, as opening new areas for the expansion of slavery. Having vigorously opposed the war, they committed themselves to preventing the expansion of slavery into New Mexico, Arizona, California, and the other new territories. At women's rights conventions throughout the 1850s, their work on behalf of both abolitionism and women's rights was evident, as delegates discussed issues ranging from ending slavery, to enhancing the legal rights of married women and working women, to controlling alcohol abuse, and developed lobbying strategies to press state and national legislatures and constitutional conventions for specific legal reforms. The resolutions passed by the 1850 Worcester convention summed up many of the issues.

"*Resolved,* That every human being of full age, and resident for a proper length of time on the soil of the nation, who is required to obey law, is entitled to a voice in its enactments; that every such person, whose property or labor is taxed for the support of government, is entitled to a direct share in such government. Therefore,

Resolved, That women are clearly entitled to the right of suffrage, and to be considered eligible to office;.... Equality before the law, without distinction of sex or color.

Resolved, That political rights acknowledge no sex, and therefore the word 'male' should be stricken from every State Constitution....

Resolved, That as women alone can learn by experience, and prove by works, what is their rightful sphere of duty, we recommend, as *next-steps,* that they should demand and secure—

1. *Education* in primary and high schools, universities, medical, legal, and theological institutions, as comprehensive and exact as their abilities prompt them to seek, and their capabilities fit them to receive;

2. *Partnership* in the labors, gains, risks, and remunerations of productive industry, with such limits only as are assigned by taste, intuitive judgment, or their measure of spiritual and physical vigor, as tested by experiment;

Canada. Women in Lower Canada (modern-day Quebec and Newfoundland) who met the requisite property qualifications had been voting since the 1791 Constitutional Act, which used the term "person" for voters. In 1848, Canada's parliament adopted a law specifying that suffrage was for men only.

"That motley gathering of fanatical mongrels, of old grannies, male and female, of fugitive slaves and fugitive lunatics, called the Woman's Rights Convention, after two day's discussion of the most horrible trash, has put forth its platform and adjourned. The sentiments and doctrines avowed . . . involve all the most monstrous and disgusting principles of socialism, abolition, amalgamation [**marriage across the color line**], and infidelity [**irreligion**]. . . ."

—*New York Herald,* October 28, 1850

"Woman's Right to Labor;"

OR,

LOW WAGES AND HARD WORK:

In Three Lectures,

DELIVERED IN BOSTON, NOVEMBER, 1859.

BY CAROLINE H. DALL.

" Thank God ! a song for the women as well as the men."
CHARLES AUCHESTER.

C. BOSTON:
WALKER, WISE, AND COMPANY,
245, WASHINGTON STREET.
1860.

Caroline Wells Healey Dall, *Woman's Right to Labor: or, Low Wages and Hard Work*; title page.

3. A *co-equal share* in the formation and administration of law, Municipal, State, and National, through legislative assemblies, courts, and executive offices; . . .

Resolved, That a Central Committee be appointed by this Convention, . . . who shall correspond with each other and . . . hold meetings in their respective neighborhoods, gather statistics, facts, and illustrations, raise funds for purposes of publication; and through the press, tracts, books, and the living agent, guide public opinion upward and onward in the grand social reform of establishing woman's co-sovereignty with man. . . .

Resolved, That the cause we are met to advocate,—the claim for woman of all her natural and civil rights,—bids us remember the million and a half of slave women at the South, the most grossly wronged and foully outraged of all women; and in every effort for an improvement in our civilization, we will bear in our heart of hearts the memory of the trampled womanhood of the plantation, and omit no effort to raise it to a share in the rights we claim for ourselves."

The rights of free women workers remained a continuing concern of labor activists and of individuals like Paulina Wright Davis, an abolitionist and women's rights advocate who was the driving force behind the 1850 Worcester convention and a tireless promoter of women's rights conventions throughout the 1850s. As editor of *The Una,* the first newspaper devoted exclusively to the cause of woman's rights, she wrote articles highlighting the economic inequalities that working women faced every day. This one appeared in 1854.

"[T]hat the current rates of remuneration for Woman's Work are entirely, unjustly inadequate, is a proposition which needs only to be considered to insure its hearty acceptance. . . .

Every able bodied Man, inured to Labor, though of the rudest sort, who steps on shore in America from Europe, is worth a dollar per day, and can readily command it. . . .

But the sister of this same faithful worker, equally careful, intelligent, and willing to do anything honest and reputable for a living, finds no such chances proffered *her*. . . . [S]he may think herself fortunate if a week's search opens to her a place where by the devotion of all her waking hours she can earn five to six dollars per month. . . .

Now this disparity between the rewards of Man's and Woman's labor at the base of the social edifice is carried up to its very pinnacle. . . . The mistress who conducts the rural district school in summer, usually receives less than half the monthly stipend that her brother does for teaching that same school in the winter. . . . Between male and female workers in the factories and mills, the same difference is enforced."

Concern about women's economic inequality and their economic dependency within marriage formed a significant part of women's rights advocacy during the 1850s. Campaigns for married women's property and wage laws, along with working women's efforts at collective organization, were ongoing. Strongly supporting the efforts were Elizabeth Cady Stanton and Susan B. Anthony, who met in 1851 and became lifelong co-workers. When they drew connections between women's subordinate role with the family and their secondary citizenship status, and proposed easier divorce as a remedy, they courted controversy. Stanton's 1854 speech to the New York State Legislature directly broached the connections.

"Your laws relating to marriage—founded as they are on the old common law of England, a compound of barbarous usages, but partially modified by progressive civilization—are in open violation of our enlightened ideas of justice, and of the holiest feelings of our nature. . . . The signing of [the marriage] contract is instant civil death to one of the parties. . . . The woman . . . has no civil existence, no social freedom. . . . She can own nothing, sell nothing. She has no right even to the wages she earns; her person, her time, her services are the property of another. . . .

If she have a worthless husband, a confirmed drunkard, a villain, or a vagrant, he has still all the rights of a man, a husband, and a father. Though the whole support of the family be thrown upon the wife, if the wages she earns be paid to her by her employer, the husband can receive them again. . . .

Now, do you candidly think these wives do not wish to control the wages they earn—to own the land they buy—the houses they build? to have at their disposal their own children, without being subject to the constant interference and tyranny of an idle, worthless profligate? Do you suppose that any woman willingly stitches all day for the small sum of fifty cents, that she may enjoy

Dress Reform: "But really, would it not be a curiosity, . . . to see . . . a style of dress for women, comfortable, convenient—in short, one in no wise conflicting with their bodily functions or life's duties? And how much more glorious would it be to see every woman free from *every* fetter that fashion has imposed! Such a day of 'universal emancipation' of the sex would be worthy of a celebration through all coming time."

—"Woman's Dress," by Mrs. R[achel] B[rooks] Gleason, 1851

Gross companionship: A wife's obligation, under coverture, to submit to her husband's sexual demands.

Susan B. Anthony (1820–1906) moved with her family to Rochester, New York, in 1845, where she taught school and immersed herself in reform activism, eventually meeting future co-workers, such as Frederick Douglass. But it was Elizabeth Cady Stanton with whom she forged a lifelong working partnership. Anthony's organizational skills complemented Stanton's skill with the pen; Anthony traveled incessantly in the cause of woman suffrage. In later years, in part because Stanton courted controversy with her views on marriage, divorce, and religion, Anthony came to be venerated as "Aunt Susan" by younger suffragists, who termed the national suffrage amendment "the Susan B. Anthony amendment." After her death, Anthony remained better known and more widely revered than Stanton; only Anthony was chosen to represent the suffrage movement when, in 1979, the U.S. Mint released the Susan B. Anthony dollar.

Susan B. Anthony dollar.

Caroline Cowles Richards at age 18, 1860.

the unspeakable privilege, in obedience to your laws, of paying for her husband's tobacco and rum? Think you the wife of the confirmed, beastly drunkard would consent to share with him her home and bed, if law and public sentiment would release her from such **gross companionship**? Verily, no!"

In 1855, thirteen-year-old schoolgirl Caroline Cowles Richards of Canandaigua, New York, recorded in her diary an encounter with Susan B. Anthony.

"Susan B. Anthony is in town and spoke in Bemis Hall this afternoon. She made a special request that all the seminary girls should come to hear her as well as all the women and girls in town. She had a large audience and she talked very plainly about our rights and how we ought to stand up for them, and said the world would never go right until the women had just as much right to vote and rule as the men. She asked us all to come up and sign our names who would promise to do all in our power to bring about that glad day when equal rights should be the law of the land. A whole lot of us went up and signed the paper. When I told Grandmother about it she said she guessed Susan B. Anthony had forgotten that St. Paul said the women should keep silence. I told her, no, she didn't for she spoke particularly about St. Paul and said if he had lived in these times, instead of 1800 years ago, he would have been as anxious to have the women at the head of government as she was. I could not make Grandmother agree with her at all and she said we might better all of us stayed at home."

Occasionally, a marrying couple publicly rejected the rights that the law conferred upon husbands, making a statement in support of marriage as an equal partnership. One such couple were Lucy Stone and Henry Blackwell, abolitionists who married in 1855. Stone also rejected the custom whereby a wife adopted her husband's name; after marriage, she was "Mrs. Lucy Stone."

"PROTEST.

While acknowledging our mutual affection by publicly assuming the relationship of husband and wife, yet in justice to ourselves and a great principle, we deem it a duty to declare that this act on our part implies no sanction of, nor promise of voluntary obedience to such of the present laws of marriage, as refuse to recognize the wife as an independent, rational being, while they confer upon the husband an injurious and unnatural superiority, investing him with legal powers which no honorable man would exercise, and which no man should possess. We protest especially against the laws which give to the husband:

1. The custody of the wife's person.
2. The exclusive control and guardianship of their children.
3. The sole ownership of her personal, and the use of her real estate, unless previously settled upon her, or placed in the hands of trustees, as in the case of minors, lunatics, and idiots.
4. The absolute right to the product of her industry.
5. Also against laws which give to the widower so much larger and more permanent an interest in the property of his deceased wife, than they give to the widow in that of the deceased husband.
6. Finally, against the whole system by which 'the legal existence of the wife is suspended during marriage,' so that in most States, she neither has a legal part in the choice of her residence, nor can she make a will, nor sue or be sued in her own name, nor inherit property.

We believe that personal independence and equal human rights can never be forfeited, except for crime; that marriage should be an equal and permanent partnership, and so recognized by law; that until it is so recognized, married partners should provide against the radical injustice of present laws, by every means in their power.

We believe that where domestic difficulties arise, no appeal should be made to legal tribunals under existing laws, but that all difficulties should be submitted to the equitable adjustment of arbitrators mutually chosen.

Thus reverencing law, we enter our protest against rules and customs which are unworthy of the name, since they violate justice, the essence of law.

(Signed), HENRY B. BLACKWELL
LUCY STONE."

Gender, Race, and Rights in the Era of Civil War and Reconstruction

The outbreak of Civil War in 1861 led women's rights activists to suspend their conventions and devote themselves to ending slavery and then to guaranteeing full citizenship rights for all Americans. Once Abraham Lincoln issued the Emancipation Proclamation, the Women's Loyal National League became the vehicle for achieving those goals, as reflected in the resolutions passed at the group's first meeting in 1863.

"*Resolved*, 2. That we heartily approve that part of the President's Proclamation which decrees freedom to the slaves of rebel masters, and we earnestly urge him to devise measures for emancipating all slaves throughout the country. . . .

Resolved, 4. That while we welcome to legal freedom the recent slaves, we solemnly remonstrate against all State or National legislation which may exclude them from any locality, or debar them from any rights or privileges as free and equal citizens of a common Republic.

Resolved, 5. There never can be a true peace in this Republic until the civil and political rights of all citizens of African descent and all women are practically established.

Resolved, 7. That . . . we . . . are ready in this war to pledge our time, our means, our talents, and our lives, if need be, to secure the final and complete consecration of America to freedom."

With the Thirteenth Amendment to the Constitution, ratified in 1865, slavery finally came to an end. African American women newly liberated from the bonds of slavery quickly claimed their rights as free people. They particularly cherished the rights prohibited to them as slaves, including the right to marry, earn wages, travel freely, and make choices about the uses of their labor. Taking special joy in motherhood, they fought against any efforts by whites to control their children's lives. Mary Ann Ran's appeal to a white Union Army officer reflected her effort to get her children back from a former owner who had apprenticed them without her consent.

"Baltimore, [Maryland]

Major Gen. Wallace   November 21, 1864

Dear Sir: I, the undersigned your humble servant, beg of you to aid me in the recovery of my two children now in the possession of Thomas R. Brown, my late master. My oldest daughter Susan, about fourteen

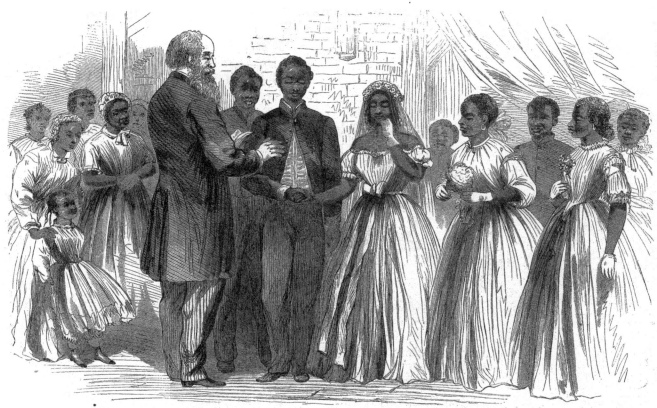

MARRIAGE OF A COLORED SOLDIER AT VICKSBURG BY CHAPLAIN WARREN OF THE FREEDMEN'S BUREAU.

"Marriage of a Colored Soldier at Vicksburg by Chaplain Warren of the Freedmen's Bureau." Freedwomen treasured the right to marry whom they chose and to have their marriages protected by law, two rights that had been denied to them under slavery. An 1866 illustration, drawn for *Harper's Weekly*, reflected the significance that formerly enslaved people gave to marriage, and contrasted with the critiques of unequal marriage being voiced by white women's rights activists.

years of age, he has now on his farm near Chestertown, and the youngest, eight years of age, in service with his family in Baltimore.

He has refused to let me have my children, saying that the courts have bound them to him. May it please your honor that I am able to provide for and with the aid of my husband the father of them to protect them. Hoping that your honor will aid me to recover them,

I am your most ob't servant,

her

Mary Ann   X   Ran

mark"

During the Reconstruction era that followed the Civil War, Congress and the state legislatures confronted the question of what rights former slaves would enjoy. The Fourteenth Amendment, drafted in 1866 and ratified in 1868, settled the issue by defining national citizenship for the first time and extending citizenship rights to "all persons born or naturalized in the United States." Under its terms, all citizens

were guaranteed the same "privileges and immunities" as well as "equal protection of the laws." But was the right to vote a right of citizenship? Through one provision of the Amendment, Congress pressed the former Confederate states to enact *manhood* suffrage laws by cutting seats in the House of Representatives proportionally if state legislatures "denied to any of the male inhabitants of such State" the right to vote. For the first time, the word "male" would be part of the Constitution. As the Amendment wound its way through the ratification process, a new organization, the American Equal Rights Association (AERA), founded in 1866 and uniting abolitionist and women's rights groups, debated whether to endorse it or hold out for universal suffrage without regard to gender. Convinced that suffrage for African American men would be doomed if it were coupled with a demand for woman suffrage, some AERA members supported the Fourteenth Amendment (and then the Fifteenth Amendment). Others, equally convinced that "equal rights" had to include universal adult suffrage, opposed the Amendment. Between 1866 and 1869, members staked out their positions in speeches and in debates at the group's annual meetings. In an 1867 address to the first annual meeting, Sojourner Truth suggested that African American women had the most to lose if only men won voting rights.

"I come from another field—the country of the slave. They have got their liberty—so much good luck to have slavery partly destroyed; not entirely. I want it root and branch destroyed. Then we will all be free indeed. I feel that if I have to answer for the deeds done in my body just as much as a man, I have a right to have just as much as a man. There is a great stir about colored men getting their rights, but not a word about the colored women; and if colored men get their rights, and not colored women theirs, you see the colored men will be masters over the women, and it will be just as bad as it was before. So I am for keeping the thing going while things are stirring; because if we wait till it is still, it will take a great while to get it going again. . . . I want women to have their rights. In the courts women have no right, no voice; nobody speaks for them. I wish woman to have her voice there among the **pettifoggers** [**underhanded lawyers**]. If it is not a fit place for women it is unfit for men to be there. I am above eighty years old; it is about time for me to be going. I have been forty years a slave and forty years free and would be here forty years more to have equal rights for all. I suppose I am kept here because something remains for me to do; I suppose I am yet to help to break the chain. I have done a great deal of work; as much as a man, but did not get so much pay. I used to work in the field... but men doing no more, got twice as much pay.... I suppose I am about the only colored woman that goes about to speak for the rights of the colored women.... Now colored men have the right to vote. There ought to be equal rights now more than ever, since colored people have got their freedom."

With the Fourteenth Amendment ratified, Congress passed and sent to the states the Fifteenth Amendment, which guaranteed citizens' right to vote without regard to "race, color, or previous condition of servitude." Ratified in 1870, the Fifteenth Amendment established suffrage (in principle) as a right of all male citizens. In a speech delivered to the National Woman Suffrage Convention in January, 1869, Elizabeth Cady Stanton proposed a new, Sixteenth Amendment, enfranchising women. The speech reflected her bitter disappointment at the defeat of universal suffrage, as well as her concerns (similar to Truth's) about the persistence of gender hierarchy. But it is especially notable for the racially charged, ethnocentric language in which she expressed her interwoven racial and class assumptions about women and rights.

"Those who represent what is called 'the Woman's Rights Movement,' have argued their right to political equality from every standpoint of justice, religion, and logic, for the last twenty years. They have ... plead the theory of our government; suffrage a natural, inalienable right; shown from the lessons of history, that one class can not legislate for another; that disfranchised classes must ever be neglected and degraded; and that all privileges are but mockery to the citizen, until he has a voice in the making and administering of law....

The Republican party today congratulates itself on having carried the Fifteenth Amendment of the Constitution, thus securing 'manhood suffrage' and establishing an aristocracy of sex on this continent....

This fundamental principle of our government—the equality of all citizens of the republic—should be incorporated in the Federal Constitution, there to remain forever.... Hence, we appeal to the party now in power, everywhere, to end this protracted debate on suffrage, and declare it the inalienable right of every citizen who is amenable to the laws of the land, who pays taxes and the penalty of crime....

I urge a speedy adoption of a Sixteenth Amendment for the following reasons:

A government, based on the principle of caste and class, can not stand. The aristocratic idea, in any form, is opposed to the genius of our free institutions, to our own declaration of rights, and to the civilization of the age.... Of all kinds of aristocracy, that of sex is the most odious and unnatural.... [G]overnment gains no new element of strength in admitting all men to the ballot-box, for we have too much of the man-power there already.... [I]n every department of legislation ... unless some new virtue is infused into our public life the nation is doomed to destruction. Will the foreign element, the dregs of China, Germany, England, Ireland, and Africa supply this needed force, or the nobler types of American womanhood who have taught our presidents, senators, and congressmen the rudiments of all they know? ... Think of Patrick and Sambo and Hans and Yung Tung, who do not know the difference between a monarchy and a republic, who can not read the Declaration of Independence or Webster's spelling book, making laws for Lucretia Mott, Ernestine L. Rose, and Anna E. Dickinson....

Now, when the attention of the whole world is turned to this question of suffrage, and women themselves are throwing off the lethargy of ages,... shall American statesmen, claiming to be liberal, so amend their constitutions as to make their wives and mothers the political inferiors of unlettered and unwashed ditch-diggers, boot-blacks, butchers, and barbers, fresh from the slave plantations of the South, and the effete civilizations of the Old World?... [S]hall the freest Government on the earth be the first to establish an aristocracy based on sex alone? to exalt ignorance above education, vice above virtue, brutality and barbarism above refinement and religion?... Whither is a nation tending when brains count for less than bullion, and clowns make laws for queens?"

The intertwining of assumptions about race, gender, and rights was clearly in evidence at the AERA's annual meeting in May, 1869, where delegates spelled out their positions in impassioned speeches. Frederick Douglass argued that black men's need for voting rights was more urgent than women's. Comments by Susan B. Anthony, Lucy Stone, and Elizabeth Cady Stanton reflected the white members' casual characterization of "the Negro" as male and "woman" as white. In her remarks, Frances Ellen Watkins Harper underlined the extent to which white members ignored the intersecting, and inseparable, concerns of African American women. Ernestine Rose made a ringing argument for universal suffrage.

"[Mr. Douglass:] I must say that I do not see how any one can pretend that there is the same urgency in giving the ballot to woman as to the negro. With us, the matter is a question of life and death, at least, in fifteen states of the Union. When women, because they are women, are hunted down through the cities of New York and New Orleans; when they are dragged from their houses and hung upon lamp-posts; when their children are torn from their arms, and their brains dashed out upon the pavement; when they are in danger of having their homes burnt down over their heads; when their children are not allowed to enter schools; then they will have an urgency to obtain the ballot equal to our own.... Yes, yes, yes; it is true of the black woman, but not because she is a woman, but because she is black.

Miss Anthony: The old anti-slavery school say women must stand back and wait until the negroes shall be recognized. But we say, if you will not give the whole loaf of suffrage to the entire people, give it to the most intelligent first. If intelligence, justice, and morality are to have precedence in the Government, let the question of woman be brought up first and that of the negro last....

Mrs. Lucy Stone: ... Woman has an ocean of wrongs too deep for any plummet, and the negro, too, has an ocean of wrongs that can not be fathomed. There are two great oceans; in one is the black man, and in the other is the woman. But I thank God for that XV. Amendment, and hope that it will be adopted in every State.... But I believe that the safety of the government would be more promoted by the admission of woman as an element of restoration and harmony than the negro....

Mrs. Stanton argued that not another man should be enfranchised until enough women are admitted to the polls to outweigh those already there. She did not believe in allowing ignorant negroes and foreigners to make laws for her to obey.

Mrs. Harper (colored) ... [said that] when it was a question of race, she let the lesser question of sex go. But the white women all go for sex, letting race occupy a minor position.... If the nation could only handle one question, she would not have the black women put a single straw in the way, if only the men of the race could obtain what they wanted.

[Ernestine Rose:] Why is it, my friends, that Congress has enacted laws to give the negro of the South the right to vote? Why do they not at the same time protect the negro woman? If Congress really means to protect the negro race, they should have acknowledged woman just as much as man; not only in the

The American Equal Rights Association fractured in 1869. Two new organizations emerged, both using the term "woman suffrage" instead of "equal rights" in their organizational titles. And so, suffrage, which had been one among many demands of the pre-war women's rights conventions, emerged as the key demand of the post-war organizations. Elizabeth Cady Stanton and Susan B. Anthony joined with others to form the National Woman Suffrage Association (NWSA). Lucy Stone and Henry Blackwell created the competing American Woman Suffrage Association (AWSA). African American supporters of women's full citizenship rights divided their loyalties, with Sojourner Truth becoming a supporter of the NWSA and Frances Harper and Frederick Douglass aligning themselves with the AWSA.

South, but here in the North, the only way to protect her is by the ballot. . . . I ask for the same rights for women that are extended to men—the right to life, liberty, and the pursuit of happiness; and every pursuit in life must be as free and open to me as any man in the land. But they will never be thrown open to me or to any of you, until we have the power of the ballot in our own hands. . . ."

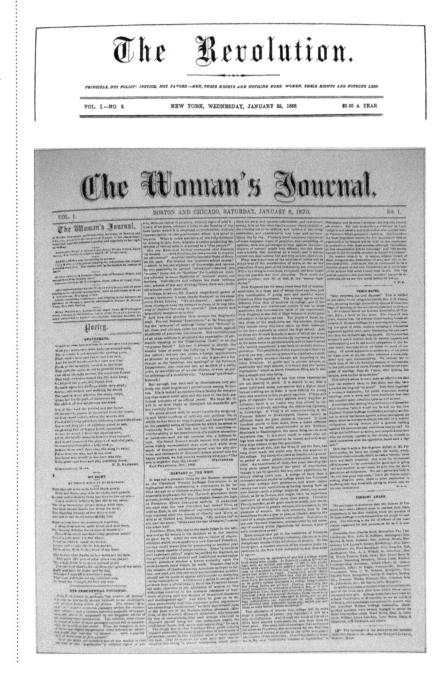

Masthead, *The Revolution*; front page, *Woman's Journal.*

The titles of their competing newspapers, *The Revolution* (1868–1870) and *The Woman's Journal* (1870–1890), along with the contents, reflected the two groups' divergent approaches to women's rights.

"Principle, not Policy; Justice, not Favors—Men, their Rights and Nothing More; Women, their Rights and Nothing Less"—statement of purpose of *The Revolution*, 1868

"Devoted to the interests of woman, to her educational, industrial, legal and political equality, and especially to her right of suffrage"—statement of purpose of *The Woman's Journal*, 1870.

W H Y ?

Why are you paid less than a man?

Why do you wor, in a fire-trap?

Why are your hours so long?

Why are you all strap hangers when you pay or a seat?

Why do you pay the most rent for the worst houses?

Why does the cost of living go up while wages go down?

Why do your children go into factories?

Why do you eat adulterated food?

Why don't you get a square deal in the courts?

Because you are a woman and have no vote.

Votes make the law.

Votes enforce the law.

The law controls conditions.

Women who want better conditions MUST vote.

Join the Wage-Earners' Suffrage League

Meetings the Second and Fourth Mondays of every month, at 8 P. M.

At Headquarters, Room 212 Metropolitan Tower

Fees: Ten Cents a month.

FILL IN THE SLIP BELOW AND COME TO THE NEXT MEETING

I,..

Occupation...

Home Address...... .... Street................. .....City

believing in votes for women, hereby agree to join the Wage-Earners' Suffrage League and work for it.

CHAPTER 4

Suffrage and Women's Rights

Voting moved to the top of advocates' lists of women's rights as a result of the debates over the Fourteenth and Fifteenth Amendments. By 1869, activists had come to see the right to vote as the key to attaining full citizenship. Once all men (in theory at least) could vote, then lack of access to voting became the most visible and obvious way in which women were disadvantaged as citizens. The demand for suffrage thus acquired new importance, and the focus on suffrage acquired new force. As the National Woman Suffrage Association and the American Woman Suffrage Association competed for adherents, while also debating which tactics would be most effective and which other "woman's rights" should have priority, they brought the cause to a broader public.

By the time the two organizations united in 1890 to form the National American Woman Suffrage Association (NAWSA), changes in women's experiences and in state and federal laws had reshaped some terms of the discussion about suffrage and rights. Although only a tiny proportion (3 percent) of college-age Americans attended college in 1890, women made up over one-third of undergraduate students, and more girls than boys were graduating from high school. The creation of national women's clubs and organizations in the 1870s, 1880s, and 1890s was one result of improved educational opportunities. Women were crucial laborers in a changing workforce, too, where farms represented declining opportunity and factories and offices demanded continual new supplies of workers. Their presence in the paid labor force changed both it and them. Yet women's expanded access to educational and economic rights, especially through state property and wage laws, contrasted sharply with contractions in other areas, especially the hostility of courts to workers' efforts to unionize, as well as the growth of censorship laws that imposed a legal silence on public discussions of sexuality, contraception, and human reproduction. New legal limitations fell with special weight onto women and men from racial and ethnic minority groups. By 1890, the states of the former Confederacy had begun systematically to disfranchise African American men and to require legal segregation through "Jim Crow" laws. And immigration restriction was on Congress's agenda, beginning with people of Asian birth, who increasingly were denied the right to enter the United States or, if already in the country, were excluded from becoming naturalized citizens.

Such changes altered the landscape on which a new generation of suffragists planned and executed their campaigns. Creating a broad coalition to press for both state and national woman suffrage laws, they sought allies among individuals and organizations with little else in common except support for suffrage. To be sure, new alliances were significant sources of support, but they also created conflict. Pursuing full suffrage for women at a time when African American men were losing their right to vote, for instance, raised the question of whether the voices of African American suffragists would be drowned out by the demands of Southern white women who supported suffrage but also white supremacy, black disfranchisement, and segregation. Moreover, members of the suffrage coalition who endorsed voting rights for women, but opposed any other expansion of women's citizenship rights, were the polar opposites of those who adopted the new word "feminist" to describe their commitments. Feminism sought the expansive goal of women's "emancipation" from the restrictions of an entrenched gender hierarchy. As the leaders of NAWSA grappled with such issues, the cause assumed a different form from that forged in the Reconstruction era, when suffrage first took center stage in the larger struggle for women's full citizenship rights.

Between 1869 and 1920, suffragists undertook an exhausting number of campaigns (both successful and unsuccessful) on the local, state, and national levels, before they claimed final victory. And claim credit for their victory they could, for they had won the right to suffrage; no one had given it to them.

Seeking Rights: Economic, Educational, Personal

Even as women's rights activists put new emphasis on the right to vote, individuals and groups continued to press for women's freedom to work, seek higher education, travel, and make their own decisions. African American women asserted their economic rights by resisting employers' efforts to reduce them to slave-like conditions, and by taking collective action to improve their wages, as did washerwomen in Jackson, Mississippi (1866); Galveston, Texas (1877); and Atlanta, Georgia (1881). An 1881 strike in Atlanta involved 3,000 washerwomen, who were joined by cooks, nurses, and servants demanding increases in pay. The *Atlanta Constitution* reported on the strike.

"[T]o-day nearly 3,000 negro women are asking their white friends who supported them during the cold, hard winter to pay them a dollar a dozen for washing. Three weeks ago twenty negro women and a few negro men met in Summer Hill Church and discussed the matter. The next night the negro preachers in all the churches announced a mass meeting of the washerwomen. The meeting was a big one and the result was an organization. Officers were elected, committees appointed and time and places for meetings read out. Since then there has been meetings every night or two, and now there is a society or club in every ward in the city.

'What do they do at these meetings?' the reporter asked.

Make speeches and pray. They swear they never will wash another piece for less than one dollar a dozen."

For Native American women, the new federal allotment policy of breaking up reservations, instituted by the Dawes Act in 1887, meant the loss of their traditional rights to the land. In an 1894 petition to the United States Bureau of Indian Affairs, Arizona Hopi women from Moqui village explained their concerns.

"[W]e want to tell you something about this Hopi Land. None of us ever asked that it should be measured into separate lots, and given to individuals for this would cause confusion. The family, the dwelling house and the field are inseparable, because the woman is the heart of these, and they rest with her. Among us the family traces its kin from the mother, hence all its possessions are hers. The man builds the house but the woman is the owner. . . ."

Women of all racial and ethnic backgrounds were increasingly present and visible in the work force during the decades after Reconstruction.

Demand for female workers was especially strong in textile and clothing factories, but women were heavily represented among household servants and laundresses, in growing white-collar occupations such as office work, and in some professional occupations such as teaching. Because poor working conditions, low wages, and limited opportunities were features of most "women's work," working women sought economic justice through individual and collective action. Leonora Barry, an organizer for the Knights of Labor, a national labor union that did not discriminate on the basis of race or sex, described the group's understanding of women's economic rights in an 1888 speech.

"The Knights of Labor were organized openly in 1879.... [T]hey then made known their aims, which were to abolish poverty, to demand that moral and industrial worth and not wealth be made the standard of national and individual greatness. These poor working men ... recognized what your legislators, what your pulpits, what your press have failed to recognize within all the years of your agitation—woman's right to equitable consideration by the side of men in the nation's government. Having recognized this, they inserted in the platform of principles that plank which demands equal pay for equal work; and ere many more years have passed over our heads, there will be another plank inserted not only in the platform of the Knights of Labor, but upon the statute-books of our country, making it a criminal offense for any man to dare employ a woman at less remuneration for labor than will enable her to procure the comforts of life without necessitating **temptation to sin** [**prostitution**]. The Knights of Labor ... are building around our working girls a wall of protection to defend them from the indignities which heretofore they have been subjected to, such as making the **price of their honor** [**sexual harassment**] the possibility of a place to earn their livelihood.

We are trying to teach the outside world that the working woman has feelings, has sensitivities, has her heart's longings and desires for the better things of life, ...

I have, during my connection with the organization, instituted what is known as the Working Women's National Beneficial Fund. This gives to women in sickness not less than $3 nor more than $5 per week, and in case of death not less than $75 nor more than $100. It gives protection to every woman, ... for it is the duty, the aim, and the object of the Knights of Labor to elevate woman, no matter what her nationality, her creed, her color, or her position in life."

In 1876 the Workingmen's Party, a Socialist political party, adopted a statement connecting working women's rights to the rights of working-class people as a whole.

"The emancipation of Labor is a social problem, a problem concerning the whole human race and embracing both sexes. The emancipation of women will be accomplished with the emancipation of *men*, and the so-called woman's rights question will be solved with the labor question. All evils and wrongs of the present society can be abolished only when economical freedom is conquered for men as well as for women.

It is the duty therefore of the wives and daughters of workingmen to organize themselves and take their places within the ranks of struggling labor. To aid and support them in this work is the duty of the *men*. By uniting their efforts they will succeed in breaking the economic fetters and a new and free race of men and women will arise recognizing each other as peers.

We acknowledge the perfect equality of rights of both sexes and in the Workingmen's Party of the United States this equality of rights is a principle and is strictly observed."

Despite being citizens under the Fourteenth Amendment, married women were still subject to the restrictions of coverture. Their right to pursue work or careers separate from their husbands remained in dispute. In the 1873 case of *Bradwell v. Illinois*, the U.S. Supreme Court considered whether Illinois could deny Myra Colby Bradwell, an attorney and editor of *The Chicago Legal News*, the right to practice law. In his brief, Bradwell's lawyer, Matthew Hale Carpenter, made a straightforward case based on Bradwell's citizenship rights. In denying Bradwell's appeal, Justice Joseph Bradley, speaking for the Court, focused almost entirely on her status as a married woman.

"[Mr. Carpenter:] The conclusion is irresistible that the profession of law, like the clerical profession and that of medicine, is an avocation open to every citizen of the United States. And while the legislature may prescribe qualifications for entering upon this pursuit, it cannot, under the guise of fixing qualifications, exclude a class of citizens from admission to the bar. . . .

I maintain the Fourteenth Amendment opens to every citizen of the United States, male or female, black or white, married or single, the honorable professions as well as the servile employments of life; and that no citizen can be excluded from any one of them. . . . [T]he broad shield of the Constitution is over all, and protects each in that measure of success which his or her individual merits may secure."

"We, the undersigned, workingwomen of the city of Boston dependent for our daily bread upon the daily labor of our own hands, humbly make known to your honorable body that we are insufficiently paid for our labor, scantily clothed, poorly fed, and badly lodged."

—Petition of Boston Working Women to the State Legislature, 1869

Cover of *Chicago Legal News.*

"[Justice Bradley:] [T]he civil law, as well as nature itself, has always recognized a wide difference in the respective spheres and destinies of man and woman. Man is, or should be, woman's protector and defender. The natural and proper timidity and delicacy which belongs to the female sex evidently unfits it for many of the occupations of civil life. The harmony ... of interests and views which belong or should belong to the family institution, is repugnant to the idea of a woman adopting a distinct and independent career from that of her husband. So firmly fixed was this sentiment in the founders of the common law that it became a maxim of that system of jurisprudence that a woman had no legal existence separate from her husband . . .; and, not withstanding some recent modifications of this civil status, many of the special rules of law flowing from and dependent upon this cardinal principle still exist in full force in most states. One of these is, that a married woman is incapable, without her husband's consent, of making contracts which shall be binding on her or him. . . .

It is true that many women are unmarried and not affected by any of the duties, complications and incapacities arising out of the married state, but these are exceptions to the general rule. The paramount destiny and mission of woman are to fulfill the noble and benign offices of wife and mother."

Married women like Myra Bradwell had limited citizenship rights. But other women did not have the right to marry partners of their choosing at all. In the South, the establishment of white supremacist governments in the aftermath of Reconstruction, and, in the West, anxieties over Asian immigration led to new "anti-miscegenation" state laws and constitutional provisions prohibiting interracial marriage. By 1900, at least twenty-six states had and enforced such laws. One effect of such laws can be seen in the experience of Ophelia Paquet, a Tillamook Indian, who married Fred Paquet, a white man, in a customary Indian marriage in 1889 and through her labor provided the couple's income and helped buy the land on which they lived. But upon Fred's death, his brother, John, sued to inherit Fred's entire estate, arguing that the marriage was invalid under Oregon's 1866 law. The Oregon Supreme Court agreed and ordered all of Fred's estate transferred to John, "the only relative in the state," even while acknowledging that Ophelia had "lived with [Fred] as a good and faithful wife for more than 30 years."

"[H]ereafter it shall not be lawful within this State [Oregon] for any white person, male or female, to intermarry with any negro, Chinese, or any person having one-fourth or more negro, Chinese, or **Kanaka [Polynesian]** blood, or any person having more than one-half Indian blood; and all such marriages or attempted marriages, shall be absolutely null and void. . . .

If any white person, negro, Chinese, Kanaka, or Indian, within the above forbidden degrees, shall knowingly intermarry or attempt the same by procuring a solemnization of marriage, under any of the forms or circumstances legalized in this State, such person or persons upon conviction thereof, shall be punished by imprisonment in the penitentiary or county jail, not less than three months nor more than one year. . . .

It shall be the duty of the clerks of the several counties in this State, when applied to for a 'license' to marry, to inquire into the facts as to whether either of the parties to such proposed marriage comes within the above forbidden degrees, and for this purpose he may put such applicant on oath, and demand further proof in his discretion. . . ."

Women's right to education came under fire as they took their places in high schools, colleges, and universities in increasing numbers. Were college women damaging their health by sustained study? Harvard Professor Edward H. Clarke thought they were. His 1873 book, *Sex in Education*, provoked a heated debate about the meaning of "equal education" for women and men. Clarke argued that women, because of their "reproductive apparatus," were so physically different from men that they required a separate, different, and less mentally taxing college curriculum than men.

"Neither is there any such thing as inferiority or superiority in this matter. Man is not superior to woman, nor woman to man. The relation of the sexes is one of equality, not of better or worse, or of higher and lower. By this it is not intended to say that the sexes are the same. They are different, widely different from each other, and so different that each can do, in certain directions, what the other cannot; . . . [Yet] many of the efforts for bettering [woman's] education and widening her sphere, seem to ignore any difference of the sexes; seem to treat her as if she were identical with man, and to be trained in precisely the same way; as if her organization, and consequently her function, were masculine, not feminine.

[B]urdening girls . . . with a . . . masculine college regimen . . . is grounded upon the supposition that sustained regularity of action and attendance may as safely be required of a girl as of a boy; that there is no physical necessity for periodically relieving her from walking, standing, reciting, or studying; . . . that she may work her brain over mathematics, botany, chemistry, German, and

"*Miscegenation*" entered the English language in 1863 as a negative term for marriage or sexual relations across the color line.

...not remember the time when I was not sure that studying and going to college were the things above all others which I wished to do. I was always wondering whether it could be really true, as everyone thought, that boys were cleverer than girls. . . . I remember often praying about it, and begging God that if it were true that because I was a girl I could not successfully master Greek and go to college and understand things to kill me at once, as I could not bear to live in such an unjust world."

—M. Carey Thomas, president
of Bryn Mawr College, 1908

the like, with equal and sustained force on every day of the month, and so safely divert blood from the reproductive apparatus to the head; in short, that she, like her brother, develops health and strength, blood and nerve, intellect and life, by a regular, uninterrupted, and sustained course of work. All this is not justified, either by experience or physiology. . . . Girls lose health, strength, blood, and nerve, by a regimen that ignores the **periodical tides [menstrual cycle]** and reproductive apparatus of their organization.

Appropriate education of the two sexes, carried as far as possible, is a consummation most devoutly to be desired; identical education of the two sexes is a crime before God and humanity, that physiology protests against, and that experience weeps over."

Few who responded to Clarke's treatise noted the intertwined racial and class assumptions that he brought to his argument. But in her 1892 book, *A Voice from the South*, Anna Julia Cooper shone a spotlight on the educational restrictions facing African American women because of white women's racial prejudices and black men's gender assumptions.

"Only the BLACK WOMAN can say 'when and where I enter, in the quiet, undisputed dignity of my womanhood, without violence and without suing or special patronage, then and there the whole *Negro race enters with me.*' . . .

[W]ith a view to further enlightenment on the achievements of the century for THE HIGHER EDUCATION OF COLORED WOMEN, I wrote a few days ago to the colleges which admit women and asked how many colored women had completed the B.A. course in each during its entire history. These are the figures returned: Fisk leads the way with twelve; Oberlin next with five; Wilberforce, four; Ann Arbor and Wellesley three each, Livingstone two, Atlanta one, Howard, as yet, none.

I then asked the principal of the Washington High School how many out of a whole number of female graduates from his school had chosen to go forward and take a collegiate course. He replied that but one had ever done so, and she was then in Cornell.

Others ask questions too, sometimes, and I was asked a few years ago by a white friend, 'How is it that the men of your race seem to outstrip the women in mental attainment?' 'Oh,' I said, 'so far as it is true, the men, I suppose, from the life they lead, gain more by contact; and so far as it is only apparent, I think the women are more quiet. They don't feel called to mount a barrel and harangue by the hour every time they imagine they have produced an idea.'

But I am sure there is another reason which I did not at that time see fit to give. The atmosphere, the standards, the requirements of our little world do not afford any stimulus to female development.

It seems hardly a gracious thing to say, but it strikes me as true, that while our men seem thoroughly abreast of the times on almost every other subject, when they strike the woman question they drop back into sixteenth century logic. They leave nothing to be desired generally in regard to gallantry and chivalry, but they actually do not seem sometimes to have outgrown that old contemporary of chivalry—the idea that women may stand on pedestals or live in doll houses, (if they happen to have them) but they must not furrow their brows with thought or attempt to help men tug at the great questions of the world. I fear the majority of colored men do not yet think it worth while that women aspire to higher education. . . ."

As they exercised their citizenship rights, African American women encountered white hostility and racial prejudice, especially on streetcars and railroads, where they were often physically abused or ejected from conveyances on which white women traveled freely. For decades before the Supreme Court decision in the case of *Plessy v. Ferguson* (1896), African American women asserted their right to equal treatment with white women on public transport. Indeed, between 1865 and 1890, women of color were the plaintiffs in over 80 percent of state and federal cases challenging racial segregation on railroads. In her autobiography, Ida B. Wells described her experience when returning to her Memphis school-teaching job in 1884.

"One day while riding back to my school I took a seat in the ladies' coach of the train as usual. There were no jim crow cars then. But ever since the repeal of the Civil Rights Bill by the United States Supreme Court in [1883] there had been efforts all over the South to draw the color line on the railroads.

When the train started and the conductor came along to collect tickets, he took my ticket, then handed it back to me and told me that he couldn't take my ticket there. I thought that if he didn't want the ticket I wouldn't bother about it so went on reading. In a little while . . . he came back and told me I would have to go to in the other car. I refused, saying that the forward car was a smoker, and as I was in the ladies' car I proposed to stay. He tried to drag me out of the seat, but the moment he caught hold of my arm I fastened my teeth in the back of his hand.

Ida B. Wells photograph.

In 1873, the Iowa Supreme Court responded very differently to Emma Coger's suit against the North Western Union Packet Company, employees of which had forcibly removed the African American woman from a steamboat dining room. "Common carriers of passengers . . . have no right . . . to make rules or regulations for their passengers, based upon any distinction as to race or color. A negro woman who purchases a first class dinner ticket on a Mississippi steamboat is entitled to sit at the same table as the other passengers. This is a right secured to her by the laws of the state of Iowa, and the Constitution of the United States."

—*Coger v. N.W. Union Packet Co.*

I had braced my feet against the seat in front and was holding to the back, and as he had already been badly bitten he didn't try it again by himself. He went forward and got the baggage-man and another man to help him and of course they succeeded in dragging me out. They were encouraged to do this by the attitude of the white ladies and gentlemen in the car; some of them even stood on the seats so that they could get a good view and continued applauding the conductor for his brave stand. . . .

I went back to Memphis and engaged a colored lawyer to bring suit against the railroad for me. After months of delay I found he had been bought off by the road, and as he was the only colored lawyer in town I had to get a white one. This man, Judge Greer, kept his pledge with me and the case was finally brought to trial in the circuit court. Judge Pierce, who was an ex-union soldier from Minnesota, awarded me damages of five hundred dollars. . . .

The railroad appealed the case to the state's supreme court, which reversed the findings of the lower court, and I had to pay the costs."

Using the term "voluntary motherhood," advocates of married women's sexual rights argued for the right to choose when and how often to become pregnant. In other words, wives should have the right to say "no" to husbands' sexual demands and to control their own reproduction, though without the use of artificial contraception or abortion to achieve that goal. In an era when the law guaranteed husbands' sexual access to their wives' bodies, and when marital rape was legally unimaginable, claiming the right to voluntary motherhood was radical indeed, so radical that it was mostly associated with freethinkers and advocates of "free love," such as Victoria Woodhull. In an 1874 pamphlet, she set out her views.

"[I]n the new social order of society, . . . there will be no undesired pregnancy; whereas, now, four-fifths of the children who are born are unwelcomed. . . .

All the laws that can be made regarding sex, and be in harmony with the general theory, maintained in everything else, are such as would punish sexual intercourse obtained by force—in other words, rape; and this is the end of the whole question. . . .

[In the current social order], marriage licenses sexuality, while nothing else does; and the horrors that are practiced under this license, are simply demoniacal; almost too horrible to be even thought of without shuddering, how much more so to relate! There is nothing else but marriage that licenses a man to **debauch [rape]**

"GET THEE BEHIND ME, (MRS.) SATAN!"—[SEE PAGE 145.]
WIFE (with heavy burden). "I'D RATHER TRAVEL THE HARDEST PATH OF MATRIMONY THAN FOLLOW YOUR FOOTSTEPS."

A cartoon depicting Victoria Woodhull as "Mrs. Satan" reflected the extreme animosity that her ideas about women's sexual freedom evoked.

Victoria Claflin Woodhull (1838–1927) had several careers behind her by the time she gained public notoriety, but it was her role as the first woman to head a stock brokerage firm—Woodhull, Claflin, and Co.—that gave her the resources and connections to embark on a career in reform and politics. In 1870, she announced her candidacy for the 1872 presidential election and, with her sister Tennie C. (or Tennessee) Claflin, began to publish *Woodhull and Claflin's Weekly*, a reform-oriented newspaper. Her enthusiasm for women's rights and woman suffrage brought her into contact with Elizabeth Cady Stanton and Susan B. Anthony, who were enthralled by her dramatic appearance before a congressional committee in 1871, at which Woodhull staked out her argument that the Fourteenth and Fifteenth Amendments had enfranchised women. Soon, the NWSA adopted Woodhull's constitutional position. After Woodhull's 1872 run for President as the nominee of a new Equal Rights Party, her role in the suffrage movement faded, largely because her private life and her opinions made her seem very scandalous. Not only was she a divorced advocate of "free love," but she exposed charges of adultery against Henry Ward Beecher, then president of the American Woman Suffrage Association, charges that led to counter-charges of "obscenity" against Woodhull. Her later years were spent in England, where she and her sister, along with other family members, moved in 1877.

a woman against her will. There is no sexual license except in marriage. . . .

Perhaps it may be denied that women are slaves, sexually, sold and delivered to man. But I tell you, as a class, that they are, and the conclusion cannot be escaped. Let me convince all doubters of this. Stand before me, all ye married women, and tell me how many of you would remain mistresses of your husbands' homes if you should refuse to cohabit sexually with them? Answer ye this, and

"[There is] a subject which lies deeper down into woman's wrongs than any other. This is the denial of the right to herself. In no historic age of the world ... has the marital union of the sexes been one in which woman has had control over her own body. Enforced motherhood is a crime against the body of the mother and the soul of the child."

—Matilda Joslyn Gage, "Is Woman Her Own?" 1868

then tell me that ye are free, if ye can!... Refuse to yield to the sexual demands of your legal master, and ten to one he will turn you into the street, or in lieu of this, perhaps, give you personal violence, even to compelling you to submit by force...."

Public outrage over any discussion of "free love" and concern about the availability of sexually suggestive materials led Congress to pass the 1873 "Act for the Suppression of Trade in, and Circulation of Obscene Literature and Articles of Immoral Use." Often termed the "Comstock Law," for Anthony Comstock, the New York anti-vice crusader who had lobbied for it, the law covered a broad range of items deemed "obscene," including information on contraception. Enforcement of the law led to arrests for sending such information through the mails.

"Be it enacted ... That whoever, within the District of Columbia or any of the Territories of the United States ... shall sell ... or shall offer to sell, or to lend, or to give away, or in any manner to exhibit, or shall otherwise publish or offer to publish in any manner, or shall have in his possession, for any such purpose or purposes, any obscene book, pamphlet, paper, writing, advertisement, circular, print, picture, drawing or other representation, figure, or image on or of paper or other material, or any cast, instrument, or other article of an immoral nature, or any drug or medicine, or any article whatever, for the prevention of conception, or for causing unlawful abortion, or shall advertize the same for sale, or shall write or print, or cause to be written or printed, any card, circular, book, pamphlet, advertisement, or notice of any kind, stating when, where, how, or of whom, or by what means, any of the articles in this section ... can be purchased or obtained, or shall manufacture, draw, or print, or in any wise make any of such articles, shall be deemed guilty of a misdemeanor, and on conviction thereof in any court of the United States ... he shall be imprisoned at hard labor in the penitentiary for not less than six months nor more than five years for each offense, or fined not less than one hundred dollars nor more than two thousand dollars, with costs of court...."

Women's right to be individuals, to have self-ownership or "self-sovereignty," was a radical proposal in the 19th century. Most women's legal identities were subsumed under coverture, and their personal identities were tied to those of husbands and fathers. Elizabeth Cady Stanton's 1892 lecture "The Solitude of Self" summed up her view of the importance of "self-sovereignty."

"The point I wish plainly to bring before you on this occasion is the individuality of each human soul.... The strongest reason for giving woman all the opportunities for higher education, for the full development of her faculties, her forces of body and mind; for giving her the most enlarged freedom of thought and action; a complete emancipation from all forms of bondage, of custom, dependence, superstition; from all the crippling influences of fear—is the solitude and personal responsibility of her own individual life. The strongest reason why we ask for woman a voice in the government under which she lives; in the religion she is asked to believe; equality in social life, where she is the chief factor; a place in the trades and professions, where she may earn her bread, is because of her birth-right to self-sovereignty; because, as an individual, she must rely on herself."

The Suffrage Effort: New Allies, New Alliances, New Strategies

Although most advocates of women's rights agreed on the centrality of suffrage to their cause, they disagreed about how to win full suffrage and what women would or should do with suffrage once they had won it. Such disagreements formed the core of the division between the National and American Woman Suffrage Associations (NWSA and AWSA). Between 1869 and 1890, the two organizations pursued different goals, used contrasting strategies, sought allies in conventional and unconventional places, and followed different philosophies. The AWSA approached the winning of suffrage at the local and state levels, seeking state constitutional amendments and legislative acts enfranchising women and promoting "school suffrage," whereby women could run for or vote for school board members and state school commissioners. The NWSA, by contrast, pursued a largely national strategy, a "New Departure," encouraging members to go to the polls and vote in order to establish that the Fourteenth Amendment had in fact enfranchised women. Between 1869 and 1872, hundreds of African American and white women voted or attempted to vote. One was Susan B. Anthony, who voted in Rochester, New York, in 1872 and was promptly arrested. In a speech explaining her action, she raised fundamental questions about the nature of women's citizenship.

"Friends and Fellow-Citizens:—I stand before you under indictment for the alleged crime of having voted at the last presidential election, without having the lawful right to vote. It shall be my work this evening to prove to you that in thus doing, I not only committed no crime, but instead simply exercised my citizen's right, guaranteed to me and all United States citizens by the National Constitution beyond the power of any State to deny.

Our democratic-republican government is based on the idea of the natural right of every individual member thereof to a voice and vote in making and executing the laws.... The Declaration of Independence, the United States Constitution, the constitutions of the several States and the organic laws of the Territories, all alike propose to *protect* the people in the exercise of their God-given rights. Not one of them pretends to bestow rights.... [In] the first paragraph of the Declaration, is the assertion of the natural right of all to the ballot; for how can 'the consent of the governed' be given, if the right to vote can be denied? ... The women, dissatisfied as they are with this form of government, that enforces taxation without representation—that compels them to obey laws to which they never have given their consent—that imprisons and hangs them without a trial by a jury of their peers—that robs them in marriage, of the custody of their own persons, wages and children—are this half of the people who are left wholly at the mercy of the other half, in direct violation of the spirit and letter of the declarations of the framers of this government, every one of which was based on the immutable principle of equal rights to all....

It was we, the people, not we, the white male citizens, nor we, the male citizens; but we, the whole people, who formed this Union. We formed it not to give the blessings of liberty but to secure them; not to the half of ourselves and the half of our posterity, but to the whole people—women as well as men. It is a downright mockery to talk to women of their enjoyment of the blessings of liberty while they are denied the only means of securing them provided by this democratic-republican government—the ballot....

[Since] the adoption of the Fourteenth Amendment ... the only question left to be settled now is: Are women persons? ... Being persons, then, women are citizens, and no State has a right to make any new law, or to enforce any old law, which shall abridge their privileges or immunities.... However much the doctors of law may disagree as to whether people and citizens, in the original Constitution, were one and the same, or whether the privileges and immunities in the Fourteenth Amendment include the right of suffrage, the question of the citizen's right to vote is forever settled by the Fifteenth Amendment.... It is upon this just interpretation of the United States Constitution that our National Woman Suffrage Association ... has based all its arguments and action since the passage of these amendments. We no longer petition legislature or

An 1875 cartoon satirized Stanton, Anthony, and the popular suffrage orator Anna Dickinson, depicting them in men's clothing standing before a disapproving female figure labeled "public opinion."

Congress to give us the right to vote, but appeal to women everywhere to exercise their too long neglected 'citizen's right.'"

In 1875, Anthony's argument reached the U.S. Supreme Court when Virginia Minor, founder of the Missouri Woman Suffrage Association, sued a St. Louis registrar for refusing to let her register to vote. Chief Justice Morrison R. Waite delivered the Court's unanimous opinion, rejecting the claim that voting was a right of citizenship, and underscoring that states, not the national government, set the standards for voting.

"The question is presented in this case, whether, since the adoption of the fourteenth amendment, a woman, who is a citizen of the United States and of the State of Missouri, is a voter in that State. . . .

For African American suffragists, the Fourteenth Amendment was critical to securing their inseparable rights as women and as African Americans. A 1908 resolution by the Equal Suffrage League of the National Association of Colored Women illuminated their strategy of pressing Congress and the state legislatures to enforce it and the Fifteenth Amendment: "Resolved: That we, the members of The Equal Suffrage League, representing the National Association of Colored Women through its Suffrage Department, in the interest of Enfranchisement, Taxation with Representation, ask to have enacted such legislation as will enforce the 14th and 15th Amendment[s] of the Constitution of our country, the United States of America, throughout all its sections."

The argument is, that as a woman, born or naturalized in the United States and subject to the jurisdiction thereof, is a citizen of the United States and of the State in which she resides, she has the right of suffrage as one of the privileges and immunities of her citizenship. . . .

There is no doubt that women may be citizens. . . . But, in our opinion it did not need this amendment to give them that position . . . sex has never been made one of the elements of citizenship in the United States. In this respect men have never had an advantage over women. The same laws precisely apply to both. . . .

The direct question is . . . whether all citizens are necessarily voters . . . [and] whether . . . suffrage is necessarily one of [the privileges and immunities of citizens]. It certainly is nowhere made so in express terms. The United States has no voters in the States of its own creation. The elective officers of the United States are all directly elected or indirectly by state voters . . . [and so] it cannot for a moment be doubted that if it had been intended to make all citizens of the United States voters, the framers of the Constitution would not have left it to implication. . . . When the Constitution was adopted . . . all the citizens of the States were not invested with the right of suffrage. In all, save perhaps New Jersey, this right was only bestowed upon men and not upon all of them. . . .

Our province is to decide what the law is, not to declare what it should be. . . . If the law is wrong, it ought to be changed; but the power for that is not with us."

Following the *Minor* decision, the AWSA reaffirmed its state-level and partial-suffrage strategy, as evidenced by the resolutions passed at the group's annual meetings. This resolution is from the tenth convention, 1879.

"*Resolved*, that this Association urges all auxiliary societies to petition their respective Legislatures 1st for the right of women to vote on all school questions, as the public sentiment is now ready to grant this. 2nd, for Presidential and Municipal Suffrage which can be secured by the passage of a law; and 3d for an amendment to the constitution of each State so that women may vote on the same terms as men."

The NWSA's concept of the meaning and uses of suffrage led the group to identify issues and seek alliances in addition to those related specifically to voting. In particular, NWSA leaders Susan B. Anthony and Elizabeth Cady Stanton championed the rights of working women in *The Revolution*, printing articles such as this from 1868.

"The Working Women's Association was organized by Susan B. Anthony, which now numbers over two hundred members. They are to meet once a month to devise ways and means to open to themselves new and more profitable employments, that thus by decreasing the numbers in the few avocations now open to women, they can decrease the supply and raise the wages of those who remain. They propose, also, to demand an increase of wages in all those trades where they now work beside men for half pay. This can only be done by combination, for one person alone demanding higher wages can effect nothing, but 5,000 women in any one employment, striking for higher wages, would speedily bring their employers to terms. Out of the present Association will be formed co-operative unions in every branch of industry, with funds that will enable them to maintain themselves during the period of strike.... As the gods help those who help themselves, we urge on all working women to rouse up from the lethargy of despair and make one combined, determined effort to secure for themselves an equal chance with men in the whole world of work."

The NWSA and AWSA differed sharply on whether to advocate easier access to divorce, at a time when some state legislatures were proposing more restrictive laws. Elizabeth Cady Stanton staked out the NWSA's controversial position in a lecture, first delivered in 1870 and variously titled "Marriage and Divorce" or "Home Life."

"By the laws of several states . . . divorces are granted to day for . . . seventeen reasons. . . . By this kind of legislation . . . we have practically decided two important points: *First*, That marriage is not an indissoluble tie, but may be sundered by a decree of the courts. *Second*, That marriage is not a sacrament of the church, but a civil contract between the parties. . . . It is said that to make divorce respectable by law, gospel and public sentiment, is to break up all family relations. . . . [But] to open the doors of escape to those who dwell in continual antagonism, to the unhappy wives of drunkards, libertines, knaves, lunatics and tyrants, need not necessarily embitter the relations of those who *are* contented and happy, but on the contrary the very fact of freedom strengthens and purifies the bond of union. When husbands and wives do not own each other as property, but are bound together only by affection, marriage will be a life long friendship and not a heavy yoke. . . . The freer the relations are between human beings, the happier."

Lucy Stone (1818–1893) had a long career in reform activism, beginning with her attendance at Oberlin College, where she became the first woman to earn a bachelor's degree in 1847, and continuing through her years as an abolitionist and feminist lecturer. She was an especial advocate of married women's rights, including their rights to their own names. In 1869, along with her husband Henry B. Blackwell, Mary Livermore, and Julia Ward Howe, Stone founded the American Woman Suffrage Association, beginning a long estrangement from her former co-workers, Elizabeth Cady Stanton and Susan B. Anthony. When she edited *The Woman's Journal*, she maintained the organization's focus on state-level suffrage and women's educational and marital rights, while mixing in a range of topics of interest to the middle-class women who were its primary audience. Yet she did not always avoid controversial issues, such as free love and prostitution, and she included essays from members of the NWSA. Convinced by her daughter, Alice Stone Blackwell, that she should endorse a merger between her organization and the NWSA, Stone put aside her animosity toward Stanton and Anthony, and agreed to serve on the executive committee of the new National American Woman Suffrage Association in 1890. She died soon afterward, in 1893.

The NWSA reached out beyond the borders of the United States to connect with activists in other countries. In 1888, on the fortieth anniversary of the Seneca Falls Convention, the group's leaders convened an "International Council of Women" in Washington, D.C.

Leaders of the AWSA, by contrast, refused to endorse easier divorce laws, fearing that support for them made suffragists appear to be hostile to traditional, "til death us do part" marriage and frightened away potential adherents to the cause. Henry Blackwell, who with his wife Lucy Stone had written a "Marriage Protest" in 1855, stated the group's position in an 1870 newspaper notice.

"We observe an increasing disposition upon the part of the newspapers opposed to Woman Suffrage, to charge our movement with hostility to the marriage relation.... So far from Woman Suffrage meaning license, it means exactly the contrary. If Woman Suffrage means anything, it means greater purity and perpetuity in marriage relations.... Freedom of divorce for trifling causes is cruelly unjust to woman. The wife and mother is in no condition to earn her subsistence by labor.... As friends of Woman Suffrage, we protest against being compromised in this matter by the **ultraisms** [**radical positions**] of a few individuals.... We firmly believe the life-long union of one man with one woman to be the law of nature, and the necessity of divorce a rare exception.... Let us confine ourselves to the main question. Let us repudiate side issues. To do this is the aim and intention of the American Woman Suffrage Association."

Other national women's clubs and associations arrived in increasing numbers during the 1870s, 1880s, and 1890s, many of them adding woman suffrage to their groups' other goals. Among the most important were the Woman's Christian Temperance Union (1873) and the National Association of Colored Women (1896). In an 1879 book on "home protection," Frances Willard of the Woman's Christian Temperance Union articulated her concept of the uses to which women suffrage should be put. She believed that "average" women could be drawn to the suffrage issue by an emphasis on protecting children, on women's duties more than women's rights.

"'Home Protection' is the general name given to a movement the object of which is to secure for all women above the age of twenty-one years the ballot as one means for the protection of their homes from the devastation caused by the legalized traffic in strong drink....

During past years the brave women who pioneered the equal suffrage movement, and whose perceptions of justice were keen as a Damascus blade, took for their rallying cry: 'Taxation without representation is tyranny.' But the average woman, who has nothing to be taxed, declines to go forth to battle on that issue. Since the Crusade, plain, practical temperance people have begun appealing to this same average woman, saying 'With your vote we can close the saloons that tempt your boys to ruin'; and behold! they have transfixed with the arrow of conviction that mother's heart, and she is ready for the fray. Not rights, but duties; not her need alone, but that of her children and her country; not the 'woman,' but the 'human' question is stirring women's hearts and breaking down their prejudice today."

Mary Church Terrell, first president of the National Association of Colored Women, saw the relationship between protecting homes and protecting rights in a different light. In an 1898 speech discussing her group's various initiatives, Terrell reminded the white women in the audience that African American women suffered denials of their rights on the basis of *both* race and gender.

"[I rejoice] not only in the prospective enfranchisement of my sex but in the emancipation of my race. . . . By banding themselves together in the interest of education and morality, by adopting the most practical and useful means to this end, colored women have in thirty short years become a great power for good. . . . Believing that it is only through the home that a people can become really good and truly great, the National Association of Colored Women has entered that sacred domain.

Homes, more homes, better homes, purer homes is the text upon which our sermons have been and will be preached. . . . [W]e are working vigorously and conscientiously to establish Mothers' Congresses in every community in which our women may be found. . . . Dotted all over the country are charitable organizations for the aged, orphaned and poor, which have been established by colored women. . . .

Questions affecting our legal status as a race are also constantly agitated by our women. In Louisiana and Tennessee, colored women have several times petitioned the legislatures of their respective States to repeal the obnoxious 'Jim Crow Car' laws, nor will any stone be left unturned until this iniquitous and unjust enactment against respectable American citizens be forever wiped from the statutes of the South. . . .

As an organization of women nothing lies nearer the heart of the National Association than the children, many of whose lives, so sad and dark, we might brighten and bless. It is the kindergarten

Frances Willard (1839–1898), after a childhood in Wisconsin, became a teacher and educator, presiding over the women's college of Northwestern University in Evanston, Illinois, between 1870 and 1873. She found her life's work, however, in the temperance movement, eventually serving as president of the Woman's Christian Temperance Union (WCTU), the largest women's organization in the country, from 1879 until her death in 1898. Under Willard's leadership, the WCTU became a highly organized and effective lobbying group outside of and within the suffrage coalition, promoted the rights of working women, pressed for kindergartens in public schools, and devised a "White Ribbon Campaign" to promote sexual abstinence. Willard's frequent visits to England helped foster an international temperance movement, capped by the founding of the World WCTU in 1883; Willard served as the group's first president. By claiming that women sought the ballot only for "Home Protection," Willard enabled the WCTU to wage political crusades clothed in the language of home and motherhood, and to promote middle-class women's public activism in a variety of social causes.

"LET GO—BUT STAND BY."

At age 53, Willard learned to ride a bicycle, which she named "Gladys." *How I Learned to Ride the Bicycle* promoted bicycle-riding for women's health and independence.

Logo of the National Association of Colored Women.

we need. Free kindergartens in every city and hamlet of this broad land we must have, if the children are to receive from us what it is our duty to give. . . .

And so, lifting as we climb, onward and upward we go, struggling and striving, and hoping that the buds and blossoms of our desires will burst into glorious fruition ere long. With courage, born of success achieved in the past, with a keen sense of the responsibility which we shall continue to assume, we look forward to a future large with promise and hope. Seeking no favors because of our color, nor patronage because of our needs, we knock at the bar of justice, asking an equal chance."

In 1890, the two existing suffrage organizations united, forming the National American Woman Suffrage Association (NAWSA). But suffragists were far from unified in their views about *which women* should have voting rights, and *which rights* (other than suffrage) women should enjoy. That point became clear when Southern white women joined the suffrage coalition in large numbers. They were committed both to woman suffrage and to white supremacy, a position that Mississippian Belle Kearney underscored when she argued, in a speech at the 1903 meeting of NAWSA, for extending voting rights only to educated women, in order to guarantee white supremacy.

"The enfranchisement of women would insure immediate and durable white supremacy, honestly attained, for upon unquestioned authority it is stated that in every Southern State but one, there are more educated women than all the illiterate voters, white and black, native and foreign, combined. As you probably know, of all the women in the South who can read and write, ten out of every eleven are white.... The South is slow to grasp the great fact that the enfranchisement of women would settle the race question in politics.... Some day ... the South [will] be compelled to look to its Anglo-Saxon women as the medium through which to retain the supremacy of the white race over the African."

Could the suffrage umbrella comfortably cover both African American suffragists and white supremacists? In response to the concerns of African American suffragists, the NAWSA leadership made its priorities clear when, at the same 1903 meeting, it responded to a New Orleans newspaper editorial about "the race question." African American women were clearly not included in the letter's definition of "southern women."

"The National American Woman Suffrage Association is seeking to do away with the requirement of a sex qualification for suffrage. What other qualifications shall be asked for it leaves to each State. The southern women most active in it have always in their own State emphasized that granting suffrage to women who can read and write and who pay taxes would insure white supremacy without resorting to any methods of doubtful constitutionality. The Louisiana association asks for the ballot for educated and taxpaying women only and its officers believe that in this lies 'the only permanent and honorable solution of the race question.'"

New Women

At the turn of the 20th century, the term "the New Woman" came into widespread use to represent women who sought to differentiate themselves from an older generation of women's rights advocates. Generally well educated and independent, they endorsed suffrage but demanded more than suffrage as women's due. Calling for women's "emancipation," a word that had been used throughout the 19th century to refer to the freeing of enslaved people from binding shackles, they sought freedoms that transcended political rights. The emancipationist vision encompassed a broad spectrum of issues, ranging from women's economic and sexual freedom to full-blown revolutionary change. Most of its

Mary Church Terrell's life (1863–1954) spanned the years from the Civil War era to the era of the civil rights movement. Born in Memphis, she was educated at Oberlin College in Ohio and then taught school in Washington, D.C., where she met and married Robert H. Terrell. As a founder and first president of the National Association of Colored Women (NACW), Terrell led the organization into a variety of progressive causes, including the improvement of educational, occupational, and social services for African American women and children, antilynching activism, and woman suffrage. She wrote and published widely, traveled often to Europe (she spoke fluent German), and promoted interracial understanding through outreach to white women's groups. When she was in her eighties, Terrell led a successful three-year challenge to restaurant segregation in Washington, D.C., and personally picketed a department store known for its discriminatory practices.

adherents redefined "equality" as a goal, questioning whether securing legal equality alone would work a true transformation in women's subordinate status. In a book published in 1898, the writer and lecturer Charlotte Perkins Gilman tied women's emancipation to both socialist economic principles and an evolutionary specialization of family labor. Her vision of groups of "kitchenless" households served by trained cooks, cleaners, and child-care workers appealed to white professional women and proposed to solve the problem of the "double day"—working wives' need to do home and family care in addition to their paid jobs—through collective means.

"If there should be built and opened in any of our large cities to-day a commodious and well-served apartment house for professional women with families, it would be filled at once. The apartments would be without kitchens; but there would be a kitchen belonging to the house from which meals could be served to the families in their rooms or in a common dining-room, as preferred. It would be a home where the cleaning was done by efficient workers, not hired separately by the families, but engaged by the manager of the establishment; and a roof-garden, day nursery, and kindergarten, under well-trained professional nurses and teachers, would insure proper care of the children. The demand for such provision is increasing daily, and must soon be met, . . . by a permanent provision for the needs of women and children, of family privacy with collective advantage. . . .

In suburban homes this purpose could be accomplished much better by a grouping of adjacent houses, each distinct and having its own yard, but all kitchenless, and connected by covered [walk]ways with the eating-house. . . . Meals could of course be served in the house as long as desired; but, when people become accustomed to pure, clean homes, where no steaming industry is carried on, they will gradually prefer to go to their food instead of having it brought to them."

Thinkers such as Emma Goldman championed the idea of "woman's emancipation" while also challenging women and men to embrace its full possibilities. In a 1906 speech printed in her magazine, *Mother Earth*, Goldman defined emancipation, criticized other advocates' limited understanding of it, and outlined the social restraints that made seeking it so difficult.

"The problem that confronts us today . . . is how to be one's self and yet in oneness with others, to feel deeply with all human beings and still retain one's own characteristic qualities. This seems to me to be the basis upon which the mass and the individual, the true democrat and the true individuality, man and woman, can meet without antagonism and opposition. . . .

Emancipation should make it possible for woman to be human in the truest sense. Everything within her that craves assertion and activity should reach its fullest expression; all artificial barriers should be broken, and the road towards greater freedom cleared of every trace of centuries of submission and slavery.

This was the original aim of the movement for woman's emancipation. But the results so far achieved have isolated woman and have robbed her of the fountain springs of that happiness which is so essential to her. Merely external emancipation has made of the modern woman an artificial being. . . .

What has she achieved through her emancipation? Equal suffrage in a few States. Has that purified our political life, as many well-meaning advocates predicted? Certainly not. . . . There is no hope even that woman, with her right to vote, will ever purify politics.

Emancipation has brought woman economic equality with man; that is, . . . she is often compelled to exhaust all her energy, use up her vitality, and strain every nerve in order to reach the market value. . . . As to the great mass of working girls and women, how much independence is gained if the narrowness and lack of freedom of the home is exchanged for the narrowness and lack of freedom of the factory, sweat-shop, department store, or office? In addition is the burden which is laid on many women of looking after 'home, sweet home'—cold, dreary, disorderly, uninviting—after a day's hard work. Glorious independence! . . .

[Many advanced women] never truly understood the meaning of emancipation. They thought that all that was needed was independence from external tyrannies; the internal tyrants, far more harmful to life and growth—ethical and social conventions—were left to take care of themselves. . . . These internal tyrants, whether they be in form of public opinion or what will mother say, or brother, father, aunt, or relative of any sort; what will **Mrs. Grundy [narrow-minded women]**, Mr. [Anthony] Comstock, the employer, the Board of Education, say? All these busybodies, moral detectives, jailers of the human spirit, what will they say? Until woman has learned to defy them all, to stand firmly on her own ground and to insist upon her own unrestricted freedom, to listen to the voice of her nature. . . . She cannot call herself emancipated."

"The Gibson Girl," named for the illustrator who first sketched her, Charles Dana Gibson, epitomized the "New Woman" of the era. She represented an independent, athletic, and free-spirited creature who threw off the past and strode confidently into the 20th century. Gibson reflected the anxieties that "new women" elicited by depicting a male figure as the object of women's scrutinizing pokes.

In the 1910s, some "new women" and men began to term themselves "feminists," using a French word to signal their interest in combining political activism with personal liberation. Feminists were suffragists, but few believed that the achievement of suffrage was enough to bring about truly fundamental change in women's lives. New York's Greenwich Village feminists formed "Heterodoxy" as a way of opposing "orthodoxy" or conventional ways of thinking. They spelled out their ideas at two 1914 mass meetings.

"Feminists do not think all things will be accomplished through the ballot, but they do see the great value of Woman's Suffrage as the fundamental first step in removing the political discriminations against her. With this removed they feel they will better be able to remove the other discriminations."

—George Middleton, "What Feminism Means to Me," 1914

WHAT IS FEMINISM?
COME AND FIND OUT
FIRST FEMINIST MASS MEETING
at the PEOPLE'S INSTITUTE, Cooper Union
Tuesday Evening, February 17th, 1914, at 8 o'clock, P. M.

Subject: "WHAT FEMINISM MEANS TO ME."
Ten-Minute Speeches by

ROSE YOUNG	GEORGE CREEL
JESSE LYNCH WILLIAMS	MRS. FRANK COTHREN
HENRIETTA RODMAN	FLOYD DELL
GEORGE MIDDLETON	CRYSTAL EASTMAN BENEDICT
FRANCES PERKINS	EDWIN BJORKMAN
WILL IRWIN	MAX EASTMAN

Chairman, MARIE JENNEY HOWE.

SECOND FEMINIST MASS MEETING
at the PEOPLES' INSTITUTE, Cooper Union
Friday, February 20th, 1914, at 8 o'clock, P. M.

Subject: "BREAKING INTO THE HUMAN RACE."

The Right to Work.—
RHETA CHILDE DORR
The Right of the Mother to Her Profession.—
BEATRICE FORBES-ROBERTSON-HALE.
The Right to Her Convictions.—
MARY SHAW.
The Right to Her Name.—
FOLA LA FOLLETTE.
The Right to Organize.—
ROSE SCHNEIDERMAN.
The Right to Ignore Fashion.—
NINA WILCOX PUTNAM.
The Right to Specialize in Home Industries.—
CHARLOTTE PERKINS GILMAN.

Chairman, MARIE JENNEY HOWE.

ADMISSION FREE.   NO COLLECTION.

In the magazine she began editing in 1914, *The Woman Rebel*, Margaret Sanger dismissed Heterodoxy as "a middle-class women's movement" that ignored "the working woman's freedom." Central to the emancipation of all women, but especially of poor women, Sanger believed, was women's right to control their reproductive lives and their right to enjoy sex without worrying about pregnancy. She sought to separate sex from reproduction. To that end, she began to use the newly coined term "birth control," opened a Brooklyn clinic in 1916 to disseminate contraceptive information to immigrants living in the neighborhood (and was promptly arrested under the Comstock laws), and published books and pamphlets setting forth her views. One such work was *Woman and the New Race*, published in 1920.

"To-day, . . . woman is rising in fundamental revolt. Even her efforts at mere reform are . . . steps in that direction. Underneath each of them is the feminine urge to complete freedom. Millions of women are asserting their right to voluntary motherhood. They are determined to decide for themselves whether they shall become mothers, under what conditions and when. This is the fundamental revolt referred to. It is for woman the key to the temple of liberty. . . .

War, famine, poverty and oppression of the workers will continue while woman makes life cheap. They will cease only when she limits her reproductivity and human life is no longer a thing to be wasted.

Two chief obstacles hinder the discharge of this tremendous obligation. The first and the lesser is the legal barrier. Dark-Age laws would still deny to her the knowledge of her reproductive nature. Such knowledge is indispensable to intelligent motherhood and she must achieve it, despite absurd statutes and equally absurd moral canons.

The second and more serious barrier is her own ignorance of the extent and effect of her submission. . . . She [must be] awakened to a knowledge of herself and of the consequences of her ignorance. The first step is birth control. Through birth control she will attain to voluntary motherhood. Having attained this, the basic freedom of the sex, she will cease to enslave herself and the mass of humanity. Then, . . . she will not stop at patching up the world; she will remake it. . . .

The basic freedom of the world is woman's freedom. A free race cannot be born of slave mothers. A woman enchained cannot choose but give a measure of that bondage to her sons and daughters. No woman can call herself free who does not own and control her body. No woman can call herself free until she can choose consciously whether she will or will not be a mother."

Ad for Sanger clinic in three languages, 1916.

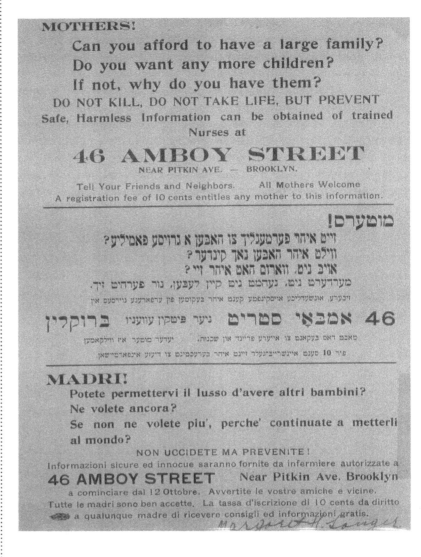

Luisa Capetillo, a feminist political and labor activist and an anarchist, shared some of Sanger's and Emma Goldman's ideas, especially about the need for women to be emancipated from social conventions surrounding sexuality. She stated her views in her 1911 book, *Mi Opinion*.

"The woman who feels wounded in her rights, liberties, and her womanhood, has to recompose and reclaim herself, change her situation, no matter how high the cost. The established morality, or what is called moral, is not what it claims to be; one cannot accept a morality that is against the freedom and rights of each and every human. There is no need to fear a morality that is morality in name only. Let us establish a true morality that does not coerce or is contrary to the rights established by nature. The rest is make-believe, deceitful, and false and we should not continue to permit it. . . .

Woman, ... for the good of future generations place the first stone of the edifice for social equality serenely and resolutely, with all the rights that pertain to you, without bowing your head, since you are no longer the material and intellectual slave you once were....

Oh woman! you will set a great and dignified example by breaking all traditional customs, which are unjust and tyrannical, the symbols of ignorance, in order to establish the realm of Freedom, Equality, and Fraternity, symbols of truth and justice!"

Suffrage-Winning Strategies

In Kansas, where women had voted in school elections since 1867, the legislature approved a suffrage referendum for the 1912 election. Martha Farnsworth, a Sunday school teacher married to postal worker Fred Farnsworth, recorded in her diary the effort that suffragists put forth in 1911 and 1912 to get male voters to approve the referendum, while also casually employing ethnic and racial slurs to refer to some of those voters.

"Tues. 7 [February 1911] O, such a fine day.... [T]his evening Fred and I went to State House to Legislature. House passed Suffrage Amendment.

Wed. 8. An Ideal day and at 9 o'clock, I went to Mrs. Swendson's and she and I walked down to the State House, where we attended the Senate of the Legislature and heard a most tiresome discussion as to whether they should pass the Suffrage Amendment that was passed in the house last night—they succeeded in getting it put off and called for a recess: it's too disgusting.... [T]onight I see by the paper, that the Senate did after all pass the 'Suffrage Amendment' this afternoon....

Thurs 12 [October 1911] Went with Jonesie this afternoon to Good Government Club at Miss Kline's 103 Western Ave. A fine meeting. I was on Program for 'Suffrage Notes': and all said my notes were good.... [J]ust at close of our meeting, Mrs. W. A. Johnston got a Telegram, announcing 'Victory for Women in California.' We all shouted for joy, some hugged and kissed one another, some cried and some jumped 'up and down' for joy and all joined most heartily

Mi Opinion title page.

Between 1890 and 1920, NAWSA pursued a dual strategy for achieving suffrage: campaigns for state-level voting rights and for an amendment to the U.S. Constitution. The success of their local efforts can be seen in a 1908 map produced by the California Equal Suffrage Association showing various types of suffrage that women then exercised. By 1914, women had full suffrage in seven additional states—Washington, California, Oregon, Kansas (Martha Farnsworth's home state), Arizona, Montana, and Nevada—and one territory—Alaska.

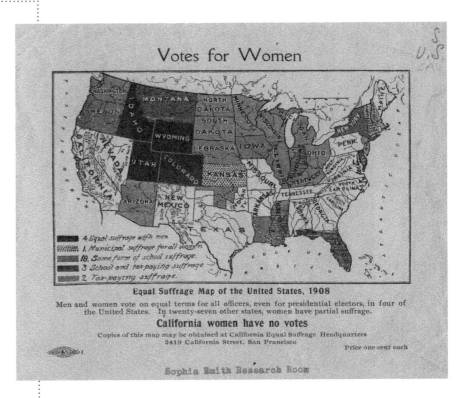

in singing 'Praise God from whom all blessings flow.' O we were a happy lot. . . .

Tues. 8 [October 1912] This afternoon I went to my Bible Class at Y.W.C.A. and at 3:30 to the Auditorium to meet some of Good Gov. Club ladies and distribute our Suffrage Campaign Literature to the crowds of men gathered to see and hear Gov. Woodrow Wilson of New Jersey, the Democratic nominee for President. We found the majority of men for us, and almost every one courteous: occasionally there was a 'smart aleck.' But Wilson's train was delayed and it was almost 6 o'clock when he reached the Auditorium, so I took a look at the man and hiked for home.

Wed. 9 A mighty busy day, but it is nice to be home and busy—no one loves home more than I do, yet we 'Sufferagists' have got to work if we ever get the Ballot. . . .

Thurs. 24 . . . O we 'Sufferagists' are working most strenuously these days—working to the death and praying to win on Nov. 5 at the Ballot Box. . . .

Tues. 5 [November 1912] Up early, got Breakfast, but only took time to eat a wee bite and hurried away to the Polls for it's Election day and we women are to make a last stand for our enfranchisement. I was at the Polling-place (2nd of 6th Ward) before

HOMBRES Y MUJERES

¿Quien Dio Al Hombre El Derecho De Votar Y Cuando?

¶Pueden votar todos los hombres en Los Estados Unidos?

Si, si son mayores de 21 años y son nacidos en el país ó naturalizados. (En algunos Estados deben tambien saber leer).

¶Han pedido todos estos hombres el derecho de votar?

No, Ninguno lo ha pedido. El derecho les ha sido concedido por las leyes del país.

¶Cuando las leyes fueron hechas pidieron todos estos hombres el derecho de votar?

No, los representantes que hicieron las leyes, fueron suficientemente previsores para saber que no podrían formar una república con los pocos ciudadanos, á quienes era permitido votar en los tiempos Coloniales—aquellos hombres que llenaban los requisitos de religion, nacimiento y que tenían propiedades—y en consecuencia todos éstos requisitos fueron suprimidos y á la mayoria de los hombres les fué concedido el derecho de votar.

NOTA, ésto fué hecho por razones políticas y no porque los hombres pidieron el derecho de votar.

LOS DESCENDIENTES de estos hombres han votado desde entonces.

¿Quien Dara a Las Mujeres el Derecho de Votar?

¶Pueden todas las mujeres votar en Los Estados Unidos?

No, solamente aquellas que viven in Los Estados de Colorado, Idaho, Utah, Wyoming y Washington.

¶Han pedido todas las mujeres en Los Estados Unidos el derecho de votar?

No, pero el NUMERO DE MUJERES QUE HAN PEDIDO el derecho de votar es mayor que el NUMERO DE HOMBRES QUE HAN PEDIDO ALGUNA cosa en toda la historia de nuestro país.

Las mujeres son ciudadanas de este país, "aunque sean ó no sean oficialmente reconocidas."

La mujer debe obtener el derecho de votar por las mismas razones politicas por las que el hombre lo ha obtenido y no PORQUE lo pide.

La mujer forma parte del pueblo y nadie se atrevería á negar ésto. Abraham Lincoln definió una república ideal "como un gobierno, formado del pueblo, elegido por el pueblo y para el pueblo," pero el nuestro esta formado del pueblo por la mitad del pueblo.

El país necesita la cooperación de todos sus ciudadanos.

Los hombres y las mujeres necesitan la oportunidad, de trabajar juntos para el mismo fin y en igualdad de condiciones.

Votese por Dar la Mujer de California el Derecho de Votar

EN LA ELECCION DEL 10 DE OCTUBRE, 1911

Political Equality League, Choral Hall, Auditorium Building, Los Angeles, California. Precio, cien por 20 centavos

"Hombres Y Mujeres." California suffragists created Spanish-language leaflets to convince male voters to support the 1911 referendum campaign. The leaflet read, in part: "Men and Women. Who gave men the right to vote, and when? Can all men in the United States vote? Yes, if they are older than 21 years and were born in the country or are naturalized. Did these men petition for the right to vote? No, no one petitioned for it. The right was granted to them by the laws of the country. . . . Women are citizens of this country [and] . . . must get the right to vote for the same political reasons for which men got it. . . . Vote to give the women of California the right to vote in the election of October 11, 1911."

daylight and handing out Cards: no one came to help me for several hours. . . .

Wed. 6 'This is the day after.' And so bright and sunny—a glorious day, and 'there is sunshine in my heart,' for while I went to bed last night a *slave*, I awoke this morning a *free woman*: My vote counts as much as any negro's—as much as any dago's. Oh! it's glorious."

As did Kansas before 1912, a number of states permitted "partial" suffrage whereby women could vote for specific elective offices. In a few instances, such as school board elections, women could run for an office

In 1869, Wyoming had become the first territory to provide full suffrage to women. When Wyoming became a state in 1890, it entered the union with universal suffrage. "Be it enacted by the Council and House of Representatives of the Territory of Wyoming: . . . That every woman of the age of twenty-one years, residing in this Territory, may at every election to be holden under the law thereof, cast her vote. And her rights to the elective franchise and to hold office shall be the same under the election laws of the Territory, as those of electors. . . . Approved December 10, 1869."

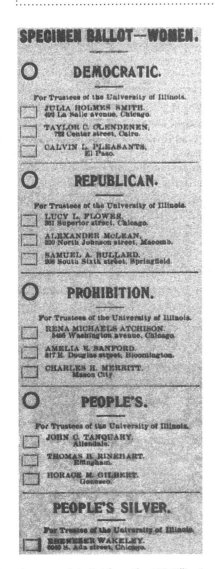

Sample woman's ballot from the 1894 Illinois election for University of Illinois trustees.

Working-class women of all ethnicities entered the suffrage coalition in large numbers during the 1900s and 1910s. As they did, they voiced their ideas about the connections between their rights as workers and their rights as citizens. A 1911 leaflet from the New York Wage Earners' Suffrage League, issued in the aftermath of a devastating fire at the Triangle Shirtwaist Factory, expressed working women's conviction that having the ballot would enable them to pursue their rights to better wages as well as to safer working and living conditions.

but could not vote. Partial suffrage afforded women an entering wedge that enabled them to pry open the suffrage door in increments. In Illinois in 1894, they had their first opportunity to vote for a state-wide office: trustee of the University of Illinois. Ida B. Wells, who already possessed a national reputation as the leader of antilynching activism, recalled in her autobiography how she joined white professionals, social workers, clubwomen, and settlement house workers in organizing to turn out women voters.

"Miss Mary Krout, editor of the women's page of the Chicago *Inter-Ocean*, invited me to be present at a meeting called by the women to organize for the election of a woman to the trustee board of the state university. The women insisted that, as I had been doing public speaking, and they needed public speakers, I should be one of their speaker's bureau. We met ... and organized what was doubtless the first [inclusive] political movement on the part of the

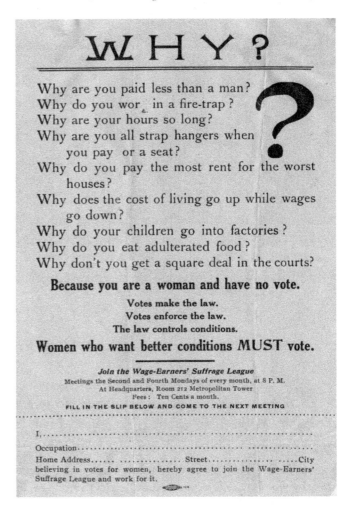

white women of Chicago.... I joined very heartily in the movement, even though the women could only vote for the three trustees elected by the state for the University of Illinois. That took up a great deal of time until the election in November 1894."

Working women who spoke before a 1912 Congressional committee considering a national suffrage amendment used the occasion to explain how their life experiences prompted them to support the suffrage cause. Caroline Lowe of Kansas City, Missouri, and Leonora O'Reilly, a labor organizer, voiced their passionate commitment to suffrage.

"Miss Caroline A. Lowe, of Kansas City, Mo.... Gentlemen of the committee, it is as a wage earner and on behalf of 7,000,000 wage-earning women in the United States that I wish to speak.

I entered the ranks of the wage earners when 18 years of age. Since then I have earned every cent of the cost of my own maintenance, and for several years was a potent factor in the support of my widowed mother.... The need of the ballot for the wage-earning women is a vital one. No plea can be made that we have the protection of the home or are represented by our fathers or brothers. We need the ballot that we may broaden our horizon and assume our share in the solution of the problems that seriously affect our daily lives.... Does the young woman [worker]... need any voice in making the law that sets the hours of labor that shall constitute a day's work?... Receiving a wage of $4.50 a week, has [a working] girl any need of a voice in demanding a minimum-wage law? Has the young woman whose scalp was torn from her head at the Lawrence mill any need of a law demanding that safety appliances be placed upon all dangerous machinery? And what of the working girls who, through unemployment, are denied the opportunity to sell the labor of their hands and are driven to the **sale of their virtue [prostitution]**?

Miss Leonora O'Reilly, of New York City:... We working women need the ballot for self-protection; that is all there is to it. We have got to have it.

We work long, long hours and we do not get half enough to live on. We have got to keep decent, and if we go 'the easy way' you men make the laws that will let you go free and send us into the gutter.... Government, as a whole, rests on industry. You men say to us: 'Go back to the home. Your place is in the home,' yet as children we must come out of the home at 11, at 13, and at 15 years of age to earn a living; we have got to make good or starve...."

We working women want the ballot, not as a privilege, but as a right. You say you have only given the ballot as an expediency; you have never given it as a right; then we demand it as an expediency for the 8,000,000 working women. All other women ought to have it, but we working women must have it."

After 1910, buoyed by an infusion of energy from working women and feminists, NAWSA put increased emphasis on securing an amendment to the U.S. Constitution. Their tactics, drawn from state suffrage campaigns and working women's activism, European examples, and trans-Pacific inspirations (New Zealand had enfranchised women in 1893), encompassed everything from circulating short lists of persuasive arguments to petitioning, to street demonstrations and civil disobedience. Lobbying members of Congress to secure votes for a national suffrage amendment was time-consuming work that required a great deal of preparation and patience. NAWSA prepared detailed instructions for suffrage lobbyists in the 1910s.

"I. PREPARATION:
   1. Read our records of each member before calling on him. Also read biographical sketch in Congressional Directory....

II. INTERVIEWING:
   1. If the member appears busy ask whether he would prefer to see you at some other time.
   2. Be courteous no matter what provocation you may seem to have to be otherwise.
   3. If possible learn the secretary's name and have a little talk with him or her....
   4. If the member is known to be in favor show that you realize that fact and ask him for advice and help with the rest of the delegation. This point is *very important*....
   6. Be a good listener. Don't interrupt.
   7. Try to avoid prolonged or controversial argument. It is likely to confirm men in their own opinion....
   9. Take every possible means to prevent a member from *committing* himself definitely *against* the Federal Amendment. This is *most important*....
   12. Remember to hold each interview confidential....

III. REPORTS:
   1. Do not make notes in offices or halls.

Ad for suffrage film *What 80 Million Women Want*. In 1913, Emmeline Pankhurst, the British suffrage leader, appeared in a dramatic film promoting woman suffrage.

2. Do find opportunity to make notes on one interview before starting another. If necessary step into the 'ladies' dressing room to do this.
3. Write a full report of your interview on the same day, . . ."

Alice Paul and Lucy Burns became the best known American suffragists to use some of the tactics of the British suffragette movement, including civil disobedience. In 1913, they headed up NAWSA's Congressional Committee to push for a national amendment. In 1917, they split from NAWSA, forming the National Woman's Party (NWP), which became famous for its militant tactics. Then, despite NAWSA's agreement to

Working-class women with experience in union organizing and educated women with experience in British suffrage campaigns brought street parades and marches into the suffrage movement. Rose Schneiderman and Harriot Stanton Blatch (daughter of Elizabeth Cady Stanton) were two such veteran organizers. A photo of them together illustrates their use of "street meetings" to mobilize supporters.

suspend its suffrage labors because the United States had entered the First World War, they began picketing the White House and the Capitol, directly challenging President Woodrow Wilson and his party in states where women were already voting, and going on hunger strikes when arrested for obstructing traffic (because crowds had gathered to see the picketing). Using Wilson's wartime rhetoric, they challenged him for his lack of support for democracy at home. In a 1919 magazine article, Doris Stevens described the rationale for the National Woman's Party's tactics.

"[During] the long, forty-year fight . . . woman's suffrage by national action made scant progress. Suffragists had exhausted every form of approach known to human imaginations, such as processions, deputations, resolutions, interviews, mass meetings, open air meetings, drawing room meetings, pamphlets, legislative hearings before congressional committees, bazaars, and the thousand usual forms of campaign.

Smiles, sweet words, promises, weak planks in party platforms, empty eloquence at banquets . . . had been their main reward. . . . [The National Woman's Party said:] 'We must make woman suffrage an immediate issue; we must create a political situation so acute that politicians will have to settle it. National legislators must face suffrage as a question on which they will rise or fall. . . .'

The military strategy of the campaign was based upon the military doctrine of concentrating all one's forces on the enemy's weakest point. The weakest point in our country's political lines, especially during the war, was our boasted crusade for world democracy, with the glaring inconsistency of the denial of democracy at home. . . . Our political strategy consisted of opposing the party in power at elections, which had failed to use its power to free women. . . .

Our simple, peaceful, almost quaint device was a BANNER! A banner on which were inscribed pertinent truths and burning questions, fiery challenges and sedate quotations. . . ."

National Woman's Party leader Alice Paul became a particularly visible symbol of the party's militant tactics when, after her arrest and sentencing in 1917, she went on a hunger strike, was forcibly fed, and was then sent to the prison's psychiatric ward. By smuggling out a note, which the *New York Times* published, dramatically describing her situation, she stirred outrage at the treatment of jailed suffragists and gained public sympathy for the cause.

"We have . . . been deprived of everything else that was included in our demand—letters, books, visitors, decent food, except as they force it upon us through tubes. Two weeks ago they did give us letters like this one, on the back of which I am writing. I was in the psychopathic ward just a week, . . . It was apparently an attempt at intimidation. Dr. Gannon said that if I persisted in hunger-striking he would 'write a prescription' to have me taken to the psychopathic ward and fed forcibly. I was thereupon placed upon a stretcher and taken there [where] Dr. Gannon, another doctor and several nurses then proceeded to feed me forcibly."

Like suffragists, antisuffragists used their citizenship rights to organize, lobby, and agitate for their goal. They emphasized several arguments: that voting was a right properly exercised only by citizens who could physically defend the nation (men); that women did not want to vote; that voting was a failure in states that had suffrage; that woman suffrage was an entering wedge for socialism; and that women voters became pawns of corrupt politicians, thereby losing their ability to be above the political fray. In a 1908 pamphlet entitled "The Anti-Suffrage Movement," Chicagoan Caroline Fairfield Corbin, president of the Illinois Association Opposed to the Extension of Suffrage to Women, gave her group credit for halting the expansion of suffrage, while also outlining antisuffragists' views, particularly their belief that "influential and educated" women were better, non-partisan, citizens precisely because they could not vote.

"The movement of American women in opposition to woman suffrage . . . originated almost simultaneously in the east and the west. . . . About twelve years ago the three associations of Massachusetts, New York and Illinois were formed and since that time there has not

*S*uffragist. Although one group of activists named themselves the "American Suffragettes," the term "suffragette" was generally seen as derogatory in the U.S. context. "Suffragist" was the preferred term.

"*W*ith the four other women who were sentenced with me I was fed food filled with worms and vile with saltpeter; food consisting of cast-off and rotting tomatoes, rotten horse meat and insect-ridden starches."

—Ada Davenport Kendall describing jail conditions for NWP pickets, 1917

Antisuffragists collected petitions and organized to lobby Congress and state legislatures: "Petition from the Women Voters Anti-Suffrage Party of New York," 1917.

been a notable victory for suffrage in the United States, while in almost every state in the north and west, in spite of the boasted organization, large membership and liberal supply of funds of the suffrage associations and their widely advertised activity, their defeats have been almost innumerable. . . .

As in Massachusetts, many leading workers in charity and philanthropy make a special plea for immunity from political responsibilities, on the ground that at present women form a sort of third estate and can carry their claims for legal help to both political parties and be sure of a respectful hearing, while if they were voters they would by their votes be allied with one or the other party and their requests would be subject to party action and the rise and fall of party fortunes. Experience has taught them to prefer

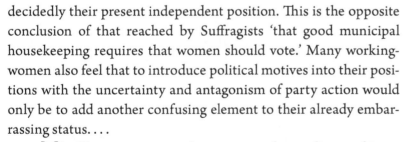

As its members were picketing the White House in 1917, the National Woman's Party reprinted an editorial cartoon drawn by John M. Baer of North Dakota, a member of the U.S. House of Representatives. The cartoon sought to provoke readers' outrage at the pickets' arrest and incarceration in the Occoquan (Virginia) Workhouse by invoking their combined class and race privilege.

decidedly their present independent position. This is the opposite conclusion of that reached by Suffragists 'that good municipal housekeeping requires that women should vote.' Many working-women also feel that to introduce political motives into their positions with the uncertainty and antagonism of party action would only be to add another confusing element to their already embarrassing status. . . .

[T]he Illinois association has . . . secured an audience of interested friends all over the country, which they value more than a large local membership. In 1902 when Socialism was at its height in Germany, they had two of their pamphlets, the Woman Movement in America and The Position of Woman in the Socialistic Utopia, translated into German and sent them . . . to each individual member of the German Reichstag. . . .

In 1919, the Nineteenth Amendment passed both houses of Congress with the necessary two-thirds vote; on August 26, 1920 (later dubbed "Women's Equality Day"), the Secretary of State certified that Tennessee's ratification on August 19 had completed the process; the necessary three-fourths of the states had ratified.

"The right of citizens of the United States to vote shall not be denied or abridged by the United States or by any State on account of sex."

—text of the Nineteenth Amendment

In the [Oregon] campaign the Association Opposed distributed over 1,000,000 pieces of literature and to its energetic efforts the overwhelming victory must be ascribed.... The cause is gaining adherents every day, not only among the influential and educated classes but among practical students of sociology and working men and women."

In June 1920, as the suffrage amendment was moving through the ratification process, Carrie Chapman Catt, president of NAWSA, attended the eighth Congress of the International Woman Suffrage Alliance in Geneva, Switzerland. The group's report summarized the achievements of woman suffrage groups and set out its ongoing objectives and goals.

I. "WOMAN SUFFRAGE...
    [T]his Eighth Congress... desires to place on record its profound gratification that since it last met in 1913 women in twenty-one countries of the world have been enfranchised....

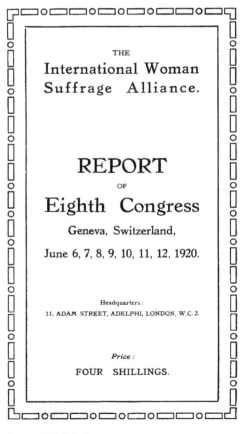

THE
International Woman
Suffrage Alliance.

REPORT
OF
Eighth Congress

Geneva, Switzerland,

June 6, 7, 8, 9, 10, 11, 12, 1920.

Headquarters :
11, ADAM STREET, ADELPHI, LONDON, W.C. 2.

Price :
FOUR SHILLINGS.

Cover of Eighth Congress report.

COUNTRIES IN WHICH WOMEN VOTE

Azerbaijain (Moslem) Republic	1919	Iceland	1919
Australia	1902	Ireland	1918
Austria	1918	Isle of Man	1881
[1]Belgium	1919	Luxembourg	1919
British East Africa	1919	[3]Mexico	1917
Canada	1918	New Zealand	1893
Czecho Slovakia	1918	Norway	1907
Denmark	1915	Poland	1918
[2]England	1918	Rhodesia	1919
Finland	1906	Russia	1917
Germany	1918	Scotland	1918
Holland	1919	[4]Sweden	1919
Hungary	1918	United States	1920
		Wales	1918

[1] *Electoral Reform Bill as passed granted suffrage to widows who have not remarried and mothers of soldiers killed in battle or civilians shot by Germans.*

[2] *Women over age of 30—Bill to reduce age to 21 has passed its second reading.*

[3] *No sex qualification for voting in constitution. Women have so far not availed themselves of their right to vote, but are expected to do so in the coming elections.*

[4] *To be confirmed in 1920.*

List of countries where women were voting by 1920.

II. OBJECT OF THE ALLIANCE...

The object of this Alliance shall be to secure the enfranchisement of the women of all nations by the promotion of Woman Suffrage, and such other reforms as are necessary to establish a real equality of liberties, status, and opportunities between men and women.

III. PROGRAMME OF WOMAN'S RIGHTS

Political Rights.

1. That the suffrage be granted to women, and their equal status with men upon legislative and administrative bodies, both national and international, be recognised.

Personal Rights.

2. That women, equally with men, should have the protection of the law against slavery such as still exists in some parts of Eastern Europe, Asia, and Africa.

3. That a married woman should have the same right to retain or change her nationality as a man.

Domestic Rights.

4. That on marriage a woman should have full personal and civil rights, including the right to the use and disposal of her own earnings and property, . . .

5. That the married mother should have the same rights over her children as the father. . . .

Educational and Economic Rights.

8. That all opportunities of education, general, professional, and technical, should be open to both sexes. . . .

10. That women should receive the same pay as men for the same work.

11. That the right to work of both married and unmarried women be recognised. . . .

Moral Rights.

12. That a higher moral standard, equal for men and women, should be recognised; that the **traffic in women** [**prostitution**] should be suppressed. . . ."

CHAPTER 5

Cartooning for and against Suffrage

Suffragists and antisuffragists debated each other in print, in song, in rhyme, on the lecture platform, and in dramatic works staged for popular audiences. Political cartoons setting forth each side's arguments or lampooning each other's positions were another method of spreading a message. As the movement for women's suffrage gained momentum, both suffragists and their opponents employed cartoons to present their positions in an easy-to-read style. Changes in printing technology facilitated the spread of cartooning; by 1910, not only had the number of weekly magazines increased substantially, but both magazines and newspapers were printing a wide variety of visual materials.

The cartoon form required the artist to boil complicated ideas down to their essences. For that reason, cartoonists employed shorthand devices and recognizable stereotypes to get their points across. Allegorical female figures such as Liberty, Justice, Columbia, and the occasional Mrs. Uncle Sam, for instance, embodied abstract concepts. In both suffrage and antisuffrage cartoons, depictions of actual women often included domestic imagery, such as brooms, babies, aprons, fireplaces, and stoves, representing women's traditional roles as housewives and mothers. Antisuffragist cartoonists employed predictable stereotypes for suffragists: they were ugly and unattractive, mannish and overbearing, or if reasonably pretty, they were simpleminded. Pro-suffrage artists sketched their subjects as modern, attractive, and purposeful individuals, or else they represented "woman" as suffering under the yoke of disfranchisement. Chains and shackles symbolized "woman's" plight. Despite these simplifications, cartoons conveyed ideas quickly to broad audiences. In the battle to shape public opinion, suffragists and antisuffragists alike sought to enlist the power of visual imagery.

Throughout the 19th century, cartoonists generally made sport of women's rights activists, caricaturing them as mannish, dominating ("brassy") crones, and dismissing their claims as preposterous. Drawing on viewers' assumptions about proper gender roles for men and women, they suggested that voting was a masculine undertaking; if women voted, they would break down the supposedly natural distinctions between the sexes, and turn conventional gender roles upside down. The result would be a topsy-turvy world of cigar-smoking female office-holders and emasculated, hen-pecked male baby-minders. Two widely circulated 1869 Currier and Ives lithographs, "The Age of Iron" and "The Age of Brass," summed up the common themes.

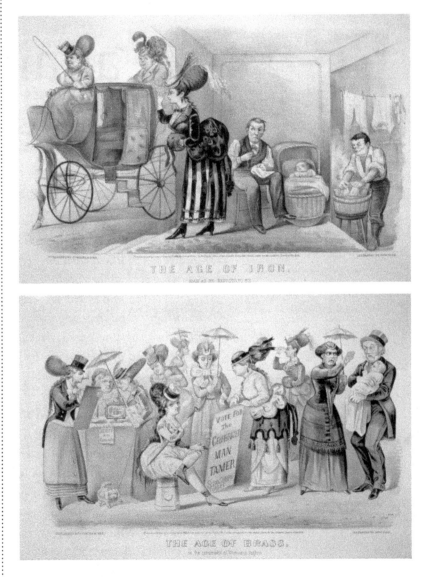

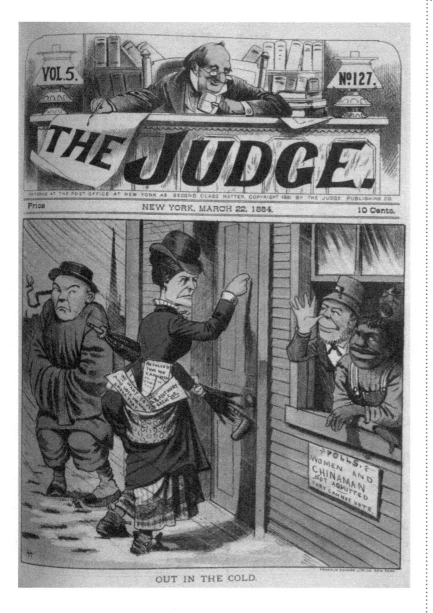

OUT IN THE COLD.

An 1884 *Judge* magazine cartoon employed critical stereotypes of both voters and non-voters to ridicule women's demand for suffrage. A masculine-looking, umbrella-wielding Susan B. Anthony knocks on the door of a cabin marked "Polls," but she is "Out in the Cold" with a "Chinaman" who is barred from voting because he is not permitted to become a citizen. From inside the polling place, under a sign that reads "Women and Chinaman not Admitted. They cannot vote," caricatures of an Irish-American and an African American man taunt the non-voters. Looking down from his desk is "the Judge" of the magazine's title.

Fostering revulsion at potential gender role reversals was a consistent theme of antisuffrage arguments; a 1909 cartoon was typical, depicting a hapless husband left to mind kitchen and babies while his masculine-looking wife goes off to vote on "Election Day."

"Are Not the Women Half the Nation?" asked Mary Taylor's 1915 drawing. Throughout the decades, suffragists consistently argued that suffrage was a natural right of citizens; simple justice demanded that women, as part of "the people" should have the right to vote.

In the late 19th century, some suffragists added another argument to the "natural rights" argument. They claimed that women had special qualities that would improve politics and government, eliminating such horrors as bribery and "white slavery" or "the social evil" (prostitution). Shovels, brooms, and other domestic symbols evoked women's traditional housekeeping responsibilities, suggesting that if women could vote, they would "clean up" political corruption and social problems. "The Dirty Pool of Politics" circulated during the 1911 California referendum.

A corollary argument stressed women's own need, as mothers, for the ballot. Rose O'Neill's cartoon, "Give Mother the Vote," appearing on the cover of the Women's Trade Union League monthly magazine, *Life and Labor*, in 1915, connected voting rights to proper mothering, for how could one be a good mother if she was unable to have a say in her children's health and schooling?

TO THE WOMAN IN THE HOME

How can a mother rest content with this—   When such conditions exist as this?

There are thousands of children working in sweat-shops like the one in the picture. There are
thousands of children working in mines and mills and factories. Thousands more
are being wronged and cheated by Society in countless ways.

IS NOT THIS **YOUR** BUSINESS?

Intelligent citizens WHO CARED could change all this—providing always, of course, that they had
the power of the ballot.

DO **YOU** CARE?

Mothers are responsible for the welfare of children—
all children. Do your duty as a mother and demand

VOTES FOR WOMEN!

NATIONAL AMERICAN WOMAN SUFFRAGE ASSOCIATION
505 FIFTH AVENUE   NEW YORK CITY

In 1912, the National American Woman Suffrage Association addressed a drawing "To the Woman in the Home," arguing that it was the privileged woman's "duty as a mother" to demand the right to vote in order to rescue the children of less-privileged families from the rigors of child labor. The cartoonist made the case that middle-class (white) mothers should extend their maternal concerns into the political arena in order to improve the lives of all children, not merely their own.

In "Woman to the Rescue!" published in 1916 in *The Crisis*, the journal of the National Association for the Advancement of Colored People (NAACP), cartoonist John Henry Adams summarized and endorsed the understanding that for African American suffragists, the Constitution was their primary weapon against restrictions on their rights as citizens. At a time when southern state legislatures were systematically disfranchising African American men and the National American Woman Suffrage Association (NAWSA) was making room in its ranks for white supremacists, African American suffragists stressed the intertwined nature of their racial and gender identities. They defended black men's right to vote while also laboring for the extension of voting rights to all women. Adams's cartoon depicted the strategies African American suffragists employed: a woman uses the Constitution to defend her children against the vultures of segregation, Jim Crow laws, the grandfather clause, mob action (a reference to lynching), and "seduction" (a reference to the rape of African American women). In the background, a man runs away, preferring to "stay in my place" rather than pursue "Citizenship Rights."

Antisuffragists sought to portray suffragists as rejecting women's supposedly "natural" desire for home and children. Cartoonist Laura E. Foster developed those themes in a 1912 cartoon showing an unhappy woman leaving behind flower-strewn steps labeled "home" and "children" to climb the increasingly cracked and unstable stairs leading to "suffrage," "loneliness," and "fame." Foster later changed her mind and began producing a series of pro-suffrage cartoons in 1917.

"Hugging a Delusion" appeared in a 1916 issue of the antisuffrage magazine *Woman's Protest*. The cartoonist sought to suggest that short-haired, mannish "new women" were deluding themselves by cradling "the Ballot" instead of a baby.

Antisuffragists' portrayal of suffragists as unwomanly or mannish easily shaded into homophobic representations of them as a lesbian "third sex." A cartoon entitled "The Three Sexes" by W. Bowles won first prize at a 1911 contest sponsored by the antisuffrage "National League for the Civic Education of Women" and was published in the *New York Times*. (The League's president, Louise Caldwell Jones [Mrs. Gilbert E. Jones] was a daughter-in-law of one of the newspaper's two founders.) Bowles employed imagery that viewers would have recognized: short hair, tailored clothing, and brazen looks for suffragists; demure but sexually revealing attire for their opposites. The man choosing between the two women clearly does not find the suffragist attractive.

The Three Sexes

Suffragists countered antisuffrage imagery with depictions of feminine, maternal figures easily juggling both politics and babies. The Gibson-Girl-like central figure holds a ballot box in her right hand and a cradle in her left. Behind each hand is an oval depicting women as both political activists and mothers. "'I Can Handle Both' says the Lady" appeared in a California newspaper in 1909.

In Southern states, where African American men were disfranchised, antisuffragists had few qualms about using racist imagery to associate woman suffrage with a feared expansion of black voting rights. When pro-suffrage Alabama representative Richmond P. Hobson sought re-election to the House of Representatives in 1916, his support of woman suffrage led his opponents to circulate a cartoon linking black and female suffrage. In the cartoon, Hobson, a hero of the Spanish American War, wears women's shoes and an ill-fitting uniform with an empty scabbard, insinuating that his support for suffrage makes him unmanly. Behind him, white supporters of woman suffrage are either henpecked men or mannish women, while the crude racist drawing of African American suffragists envisions them as ignorant and unthinking. Defeated in the primary election, Hobson lost his bid to rejoin the House.

The Kind of Men Women Will Choose When They Win a Vote

Cartoonist Rueben L. ("Rube") Goldberg repeated a contention at least as old as the 1774 "Edenton Ladies" cartoon: that women voters would choose candidates for frivolous reasons. In his 1912 drawing "The Kind of Men Women Will Choose When They Win a Vote," Goldberg ignored the substantial number of women who were already voting, preferring to imply that suffrage could still be defeated. "The women's vote," in his rendering, was a unified bloc, one that chose male candidates for the shape of their cars or their abilities on the dance floor.

Cartoonist Edwina Dumm's 1917 "Fashion Hints from Darkest Russia" placed the U.S. suffragists' struggle for voting rights within an international context. "Mrs. Russia" enjoys equal suffrage (represented by a feather on her new hat) while "Mrs. Uncle Sam" has to be content with her old plain and plumeless headgear.

FASHION HINTS FROM DARKEST RUSSIA

After the Nineteenth Amendment became part of the Constitution in 1920, fancy hats continued to be useful emblems for cartoonists. In his 1924 drawing, "A Thing of Beauty Should Be a Joy Forever," Dorman H. Smith presented women voters as neither particularly serious nor committed citizens. "The Vote," which the woman in the cartoon receives from a male figure, is beautiful when she doesn't have it, but a "nuisance" when she does. In a way that was not true for men, women voters bore the burden of being model citizens if they wanted to avoid the accusation that they were "civic slackers" because they did not use their hard-won votes.

CHAPTER 6

Women's Citizenship in the Post-Suffrage Era

Once they had secured the Nineteenth Amendment in 1920, suffragists could hardly rest on their laurels. In an era when all adult citizens, in theory, had the right to vote, defining women's citizenship remained a challenging task. There remained significant questions about the effects of coverture on married women's citizenship, for instance, as well as the impact of exclusionary laws and practices based on race, ethnicity, immigrant status, and social class on the citizenship of African American, Asian American, Latina, and poor white women. Moreover, it was not obvious how women would use their votes, to what extent the political parties would welcome their participation, and whether the possession of voting rights would lead to an expansion of women's rights in other arenas, such as economic opportunities and personal freedoms.

The National Woman's Party (NWP), emerging from the suffrage victory as a small, dedicated group of well-educated white feminists, sought to energize former suffragists and female voters by campaigning for an Equal Rights Amendment (ERA) to the Constitution. In their view, an ERA was a logical follow-up to the suffrage amendment, necessary to guarantee that women and men have equal legal and civic status. What "equality" might mean in practice, however, was highly contested, particularly in the economic realm, where most women workers sought opportunity in a job market that was strictly segmented by sex and race and that limited their opportunities to poorly paid jobs labeled "female." For women who did compete with men for jobs, "equality" generally meant attempting to enter male-dominated professions (such as law and medicine) on men's terms. The question remained: Could women and men be both equal to each other and different from each other? The equality debates of the 1920s and 1930s raised more questions than they answered, and succeeded only in dividing former suffrage allies from one another.

The NWP's 1920s version of an ERA-focused feminism was distinctly narrower than the broad vision of women's emancipation that other feminists continued to espouse. Seeking to work a true transformation in women's subordinate status, those individuals combined political activism with a quest for personal freedoms for all women. They demanded economic justice and birth control, promoted peace and international cooperation, rejected unequal marriage arrangements, challenged antiobscenity laws, and called attention to the intersecting oppressions of sex and race that women of color continually confronted. At the same time, many shortened their hair and their skirts, wore makeup in the daytime and smoked cigarettes in public, pursued athletic sports, drove fast cars, and experimented with heterosexual pleasures. A few transformed the 19th-century romantic female friendship into the modern same-sex partnership.

In magazines and movies, however, the "new women" of the 1920s were not feminists, but "flappers." Seeking personal liberation, they nevertheless scorned any broader identification with the emancipation of women as a group. The flapper's rejection of collective political action became part of the 1920s and 1930s debates over the nature of women's citizenship, and how to define and gain equality. Still, the most serious challenge to women's rights activists came less from young women who dismissed them as "old-fashioned" than from antifeminists who tarred their effort as socialist, subversive, and un-American.

The economic crisis of the 1930s cast a clear light on the continuing inequalities facing women, especially married women and working women who were poor, black, or Latina. The new women of that decade pressed for economic as well as political and legal rights. Their ranks included working women and union organizers, a feminist First Lady, the first woman cabinet member, a pioneer aviator, and a comic book heroine.

The Meanings of Citizenship

Despite the Nineteenth Amendment's guarantee that women could not be denied the right to vote "on account of sex," many questions about women's citizenship rights remained. Coverture continued to limit married women's rights in ways large and small, as California-born Ethel Mackenzie learned when she sought to vote. A suffragist active in her state's successful referendum of 1911, Mackenzie had lost her citizenship when she married Gordon Mackenzie, a British subject. Challenging a 1907 federal law providing that "any American woman who marries a foreigner shall take the nationality of her husband," Mackenzie took her case all the way to the Supreme Court. In words that echoed the 1805 case of *Martin v. Massachusetts*, Justice Joseph McKenna delivered the court's decision in 1915.

"[Ethel Mackenzie argues that] under the Constitution and laws of the United States, [citizenship] became a right, privilege and immunity which could not be taken away from her except as a punishment for crime or by her voluntary expatriation. . . .

[But] the identity of husband and wife is an ancient principle of our jurisprudence. It was neither accidental nor arbitrary and worked in many instances for her protection. There has been, it is true, much relaxation of it but in its retention as in its origin it is determined by their intimate relation and unity of interests, and this relation and unity may make it of public concern in many instances to merge their identities, and give dominance to the husband. . . . [Marriage to a foreign man] is as voluntary and distinctive as **expatriation [leaving one's native country permanently]** and its consequences must be considered as **elected [chosen]**."

Also remaining unsettled despite the passage of the Nineteenth Amendment were the rights of women excluded from voting due to race, ethnicity, national origin, or class status. In the southern states, African American women were disfranchised by the same laws and practices that affected men of their race. In a 1920 article in the liberal weekly, *The Nation*, the African American writer and NAACP organizer William Pickens outlined the interconnected obstacles facing southern black women voters.

"The Nineteenth Amendment has become the law of the land and it is constitutionally possible for twenty-five million women to vote. How many of these will actually vote? Three million are colored, and more than three-fourths of them live below Mason and Dixon's line. There the colored man has been cheated out of nine-tenths of his votes. . . . Will the colored women of the south be similarly shut out? . . . [I]n South Carolina, . . . colored women outnumber

After intense lobbying by women's rights groups, led by the National Woman's Party, Congress overturned the *Mackenzie* decision in the 1922 Cable Act, though American-born women who married men ineligible for citizenship (such as men born in China or Japan) continued to lose their citizenship until 1934, when Congress amended the Cable Act.

colored men, . . . and [their] right to vote gives a new concern to the maintainers of 'white supremacy.' . . .

[I]n the city of Columbia, . . . the registrars are white men, sometimes but half-educated. . . . On the first day of the registration in September the colored women who presented themselves evidently took the registrars by surprise, as the latter seemed to have no concerted plan for dealing with colored women except to register them like the white women; . . . While there was apparently no preconcerted plan not to register them, one ready-made discrimination of the South was freely used, that of 'white people first.' The registrars would keep numbers of colored women standing for hours while they registered every white person in sight, man or woman, even the late-comers. . . . Yet many of these colored women bravely stayed and patiently stood from 11:30 in the morning till 8:00 at night in order to register to vote! . . .

On the second day the registrars were assisted by a lawyer, apparently for the special business of quizzing, cross-questioning and harassing the colored women. . . . Well educated colored women were denied the right to register. . . . If a colored woman mispronounced a word in the *opinion* of the half-educated registrar, she was disqualified. . . . Some of the colored teachers of Columbia, licensed by the State to teach colored children, were denied the right to register, as being insufficiently educated to read a ballot! . . .

There was not only insult but threatened and actual violence. . . .—And still the colored people came. The women especially defied all opposition. . . . [S]ome colored women were even stimulated to go and assert their right to register because they heard that others of their race had been unjustly turned away. . . . Will the women of the United States who know something at least of disfranchisement tolerate such methods to prevent intelligent colored women from voting?"

Some women could not vote because they did not have the right to become U.S. citizens. Native American women and men living on reservations did not become U.S. citizens until 1924 (but their counterparts whose reservations had been broken up into allotments under the 1887 Dawes Act had become citizens in the process). Non-Filipino Asian women and men were prohibited by exclusionary laws from becoming naturalized citizens, a restriction that was not lifted until 1943 for Chinese-born Americans, 1952 for Japanese-born Americans. In a 1930 article on "The Legal Status of Chinese Women in China and in Hawaii," University of Hawaii mathematics professor Ruth L. T. Yap

spelled out the ways in which exclusionary laws affected native-born as opposed to foreign-born Asian women. (In 1930, Hawaii was a territory, not a state.)

"The Chinese women born in Hawaii and the United States are American citizens, and as such they have all the rights of the American woman. They have the right to vote; they have equal opportunities in education, business, and other fields. They have the right to own property, to inherit property, and are at liberty to marry anyone they choose. In the case of marrying an American citizen, she does not lose her citizenship, and can travel freely from country to country. Whereas, should she marry an **alien** [**foreign-born man**], she loses her citizenship and she endures hardship while traveling in American territory, for she would be treated as an alien.

By the Immigration Act of 1924, wives of American citizens ineligible to citizenship are excluded from the United States.... The Supreme Court held that the law was constitutional and that the only remedy lies with Congress. Since then the Chinese-American citizens' organizations here and in San Francisco have tried to secure an amendment to the law.... By treaty provision the Chinese merchant, even though he be an alien, can bring into the United States his wife and minor children and make his residence here as long as he maintains the status of merchant. Yet a Chinese who is a citizen is deprived of that right. It is so unjust!"

After 1920, many Native American women continued to struggle to retain traditional voting rights within their villages and tribes. In her 1921 petition to the governor of Maine, a Penobscot woman leader requested a ruling on whether full suffrage for all women meant that Penobscot women could vote on tribal matters.

"Dear Sir:

Now that the women of Maine have full suffrage, we, the wards of the State of Maine, members of the Penobscot tribe, believe that we should have the right to vote in all tribal meetings. We are informed that the present agent of our tribe submitted the question of whether Indian women had such right to the last State administration but that Secretary Ball gave no definitive answer. Local attorney advises that we always had the right to vote and that the agent cannot refuse to accept our votes at election time and sort and count the same, as provided by the statute.

Women who attempted to register to vote in Puerto Rico were refused on the grounds that although they were U.S. citizens, the Nineteenth Amendment did not apply to Puerto Rico. It took until 1929 and a concerted lobbying effort by groups such as the middle-class La Liga Social Sufragista Asociación de Puerto Rico [Puerto Rican Suffrage League] and the working-class Asociación Feminista Popular de Mujeres Obreras Puertoriqueñas [Feminist Association of Puerto Rican Working Women] before Puerto Rican women were enfranchised. Even then, suffrage was restricted to literate women.

Despite a favorable ruling from Maine's attorney general on the matter, and despite both the Nineteenth Amendment and the 1924 Indian Citizenship Act, Penobscot women living on reservations continued to be denied the right to register to vote. As "wards of the state," an ambiguous status indeed, they (and Indian men) could not vote in state and federal elections until 1953 when, as a result of lobbying by Native women, seventy-two year-old Lucy Nicolar, who had become famous as "Princess Watawaso," a lecturer and performer, became the first Penobscot Indian reservation resident to be able to vote.

After 1920, the number of women running for and winning elective office rose. Political parties competed for women's votes and placed women voters on national party committees. Still, as Anne Martin of Nevada, a long-time suffragist, member of the National Woman's Party, and independent candidate for a U.S. Senate seat, argued, while women could vote, they were still held back from full citizenship. An illustration accompanying her 1922 article in *Sunset Magazine* summed up her view.

In 1917, suffragist and peace activist **Jeannette Rankin** (1880–1973) of Montana became the first woman to serve in Congress. Defeated for re-election, largely because of her vote against U.S. entry into the First World War, she devoted two decades to working for peace and for the cause of infant and maternal health. In 1939, she was re-elected; upon her return to Congress, she cast the only vote in the House against U.S. entry into the Second World War. Although she retired in 1943, Rankin returned to public activism in 1968, leading the Jeannette Rankin brigade in a protest against U.S. involvement in Vietnam. She died in 1973, shortly before her ninety-third birthday.

Will you not kindly refer this matter to the attorney general's office that our agent may be fully informed in the premises.

Very truly yours,

(Signed) Mrs. Peter Nicolar"

Poor white southern women were often unable to use their voting rights because their families could not afford to pay the required poll tax, which was cumulative, as sociologist Minnie Steckel pointed out in a 1937 essay on "The Alabama Business Woman as Citizen."

"A consideration of how [poll tax] laws affect women indicates that in many circumstances they do result in limiting women, more than men, in meeting voting qualifications. . . . In many homes, especially during the depression, $1.50 poll tax paid for the husband to vote and also for the wife often meant just that much less food and clothing for the family. If such a family is mindful of the need for voting, in most cases the poll tax will be paid for the man, but not for the woman. . . . According to law, they cannot vote until they have paid all back poll tax; and thus, they are still unable to vote because they are unable to meet the payments."

In a 1928 article, "Women Must Learn to Play the Game as Men Do," Democratic Party activist Eleanor Roosevelt, whose husband was running for Governor of New York, identified key obstacles to women's involvement in political parties.

"[New York] women have been voting for ten years. . . . [But] in those circles which decide the affairs of national politics, women have no voice or power whatever. On the national committee of each party there is a woman representative from every State, and a woman appears as vice-chairman. Before national elections they will be told to organize the women throughout the United States, and asked to help in minor ways raising funds. But when it comes to those grave councils at which possible candidates are discussed, as well as party policies, they are rarely invited in. . . .; [they] are generally 'frozen out' from any intrinsic share of influence in their parties."

At the 1934 "Century of Progress" in Chicago, Florence Bayard Hilles of the National Woman's Party (NWP) gave a speech highlighting the numerous remaining restrictions on women's, especially married women's, full citizenship. Speeches such as Hilles', along with pamphlets setting

out each state's legal discriminatory practices, were central elements in the NWP's effort to focus attention on continuing areas of inequality after 1920.

"Mrs. Hilles astonished her hearers with a recital of some of the existing laws which operate against women. She said that in some States the father may will away the child from the mother; the father is the sole guardian of the child; the child's earnings and services belong to the father alone and if a child is injured in an accident, the father alone may sue and collect damages; a father is sole heir of a child who dies without a will or descendants; the wife's earnings belong to the husband; the wife's personal possessions, jewelry, and clothing belong to her husband; a married woman, even though living apart from her husband, may not sign a contract, as for instance, to go into business without his consent; damages for injury to a married woman belong solely to her husband; divorce laws are much more difficult for the wife than for the husband; inheritance laws discriminate against women; women have not the right to serve on juries; women teachers in public schools have not the same pay for equal work as men; and women are prohibited from working at certain occupations, such as taxi-driver, mining engineer, etc.

Mrs. Hilles said that, as a basis for removing all discriminations against women, the National Woman's Party has for the past several years been making a study of every law, State and national, with every court decision, bearing upon the position of women.

This investigation . . . is for the first time giving to women that knowledge of their legal rights and disabilities which is necessary for a campaign to remove these disabilities."

Women's exclusion from jury service was a particularly visible example of their unequal citizenship. In many states, women were simply barred from serving; in some, women had the right to serve, but unlike men were required to apply for inclusion on lists of potential jurors, or were permitted automatic exemptions. In a 1924 pamphlet, Massachusetts attorney Jennie Loitman Barron, chair of the League of Women Voters' Committee on the Status of Women, outlined the reasons why jury service, as a symbol of equal citizenship, should be required for women as well as men. Defendants' rights required women's inclusion on jury lists, she contended, and she refuted some of the most prevalent arguments against women jurors. Barron later served as the first woman judge on the Massachusetts Superior Court.

"Justice to women, and even to the community, demands that women should be eligible to sit as jurors, for if women are like men,

A historical marker honors Pennsylvania Democrat **Crystal Bird Fauset** (1893–1965), who in 1938 became the first African American woman elected to a state legislature. Long active in interracial causes, in later years Fauset devoted her time to global concerns, becoming a founder of the United Nations Council of Philadelphia in 1945 and in 1950 traveling to India to attend the new nation's independence ceremonies.

"Born in suffrage equal to a man
But on the spiritual plane, much higher,
In moral purity she forms her name
And the Earth goes on in its daily course.
This development, so meritorious . . .
Will cover New Mexico with glory
By sending a woman to Congress: . . .
Behold her here, proclaimed by the people,
The type of the woman, Adelina Otero!
Noble descendant of a Spanish line
And more than that, purely American."
　　　　　—Poem by Felipe Chacón
　　　　　"To Mrs. Adelina Otero-Warren,
　　　　　Republican Candidate for Congress, 1922"

they surely should serve; and if women are unlike men, then their point of view, different from that of men, should be represented on juries. Jury service, whether a privilege or a duty, is an incident of citizenship. Women certainly do not want to be denied it if a privilege, nor evade it if a duty. Every advance in civilization means responsibility as well as privilege. Citizenship implies responsibility. Women are ready to assume the burdens as well as the benefits of citizenship. . . .

The right of trial by jury was intended to give every citizen a trial by an impartial jury and judgment by one's peers. Can we say that a woman or girl on trial is receiving a trial by an impartial jury, when women are not eligible as jurors?

It is contended by some that women do not want to serve as jurors. Since serving on a jury is a civic duty, one should not question whether women want to serve. . . . 'But,' say others, 'women have no time to serve on juries.' How much time does it take? There are different rules in each of the states, but generally one cannot be drafted for jury service more than once in two or three years. . . .

The most common objection to women jurors is that they will be subjected to pass on cases of a disagreeable nature. . . . The opportunity for women to read unsavory stories in **yellow journals [tabloid newspapers]** is greater in one day than jury service would afford them in a lifetime. . . . We have women litigants, women court stenographers, women witnesses, and in some states, even women judges, and these have not suffered from contact with the court room. . . .

The fundamental question is . . . whether it preserves our system of justice. . . . The reasons why women should serve on juries are the same as the reasons why men should serve on juries. All one needs in a jury is sense enough and conscience enough to render honest and intelligent verdicts."

Ordinary women's understanding of their citizenship rights can be glimpsed through the letters that they wrote to the United States Children's Bureau, an agency established in 1912 to promote children's health and welfare. In 1916, "Mrs. H. B." wrote from Illinois to describe her struggles and wonder why bearing children was not seen as a service to the nation.

"God help the poor mothers of today. The cry is Save the babies, but what about the mothers who produce these babies? . . . [W]ould it not be better to enact a law that, when a man marries a woman and she bears his children for him, that he be compelled to provide for the babies he caused to be brought into the world, and permit mothers to properly care for their babies, and give [a man] a life sentence for bringing home disease and inflicting his wife with it. And if possible start an association to protect mothers who are to give birth and after that help them to help themselves, and enable them to do for their babies. The Soldier receive his pension, What do mothers receive? Abuse, torture, slurs, that is the best they receive. Men in long service receive their pension. Mothers deserving receiv[e] nothing."

The Equality Debates

In the post-1920 quest for full citizenship rights, women's rights advocates pursued several strategies. One strategy focused on seeking legal removal of discriminatory practices, using the "equal protection" and "due process" clauses of the Fourteenth Amendment. The other, especially favored by the National Woman's Party (NWP), was to campaign for state and national "equal rights" laws and amendments. In 1921, as the result of a vigorous campaign led by the state's NWP branch, the Wisconsin state legislature passed a "Woman's Rights bill." The bill's text appeared in a 1924 book by Mabel Raef, chair of the NWP's Wisconsin branch.

"Women shall have the same rights and privileges under the law as men in the exercise of suffrage, freedom of contract, choice of residence for voting purposes, jury service, holding office, holding and conveying property, care and custody of children and in all other respects. The various courts, executive and administrative officers shall construe the statutes where the masculine gender is used to include the feminine gender unless such construction will deny to females the special protection and privileges which they now enjoy for the general welfare.... Any woman drawn to serve as a juror upon her request to the presiding judge or magistrate, before the commencement of the trial or hearing, shall be excused from the panel or venire."

In 1923, NWP leader Alice Paul secured introduction into Congress of a proposed new Amendment to the U.S. Constitution, an Equal Rights Amendment (ERA). It immediately provoked a vigorous debate that divided former suffragists into pro-ERA and anti-ERA camps. The debate centered especially on the question of whether achieving equality between men and women was as simple as having "the same rights and privileges" or whether women still needed "special protection and privileges," such as protective labor legislation. Did equality, in the words of

NWP member Florence Kelley, a longtime advocate of working women's rights who left the Party over the issue, require that American women give up "the right to differ," that is, to be different from men? Testimony at a U.S. Senate Committee hearing in 1931 made clear the deep divisions among former suffrage allies over what "equality" meant and how it might be achieved. Speaking in favor of an ERA, lawyer Burnita Shelton Matthews and NWP Vice Chairman Anita Pollitzer emphasized continuing legal restrictions on women's economic opportunities and access to full citizenship rights. Speaking in opposition, labor leaders Rose Schneiderman and Frieda Miller explained why working-class women and women unionists opposed an ERA.

In a 1923 cover of its magazine *Equal Rights,* the NWP provided the text of the proposed ERA, and depicted itself as leading the cause of "equal rights" in general.

VOL. I, No. 28.
FIVE CENTS

OFFICIAL WEEKLY OF
THE NATIONAL WOMAN'S PARTY

SATURDAY, AUGUST 25, 1923

LUCRETIA MOTT
AMENDMENT

MEN AND WOMEN
SHALL HAVE
EQUAL RIGHTS
THROUGHOUT THE
UNITED STATES
AND EVERY PLACE
SUBJECT TO ITS
JURISDICTION.

Drawn by Nina E. Allender

THE MARCH OF THE STATES TOWARD EQUAL RIGHTS

"[Burnita Shelton Matthews]: There are many discriminations in the laws against women. The discriminations show the need for the proposed equal rights amendment. . . . Despite the adoption of the woman suffrage amendment to the National Constitution, the political rights of women are not equal to those of men. . . .

Night work is open to men but closed to women in certain employments in 16 States. . . . Women workers are displaced by men as a result of minimum wage laws setting a standard below which their wages may not fall, but not regulating men's wages. . . .

Another method by which the industrial opportunities of women have been restricted is the limiting of the occupation[s] which women may enter. For instance, a law passed in Ohio in 1919 and still in force bars women from sixteen or more occupations.

The Woman's Party believes that labor legislation should be based on occupation, not the sex of the worker. In that way women will not be placed at a disadvantage in competing with men for employment. . . .

[I]t is not the effort of the Woman's Party at all to wipe out protective legislation but to try to see that the legislation is extended to both and that no handicap is placed on women. . . I don't see why we should be so extremely afraid of the word 'equality.' We have it in a great many State constitutions. Moreover, we have 'equal' protection guaranteed in the fourteenth amendment to the Federal Constitution."

"[Rose Schneiderman]: We are not against equality when we say we oppose the amendment, because most of the 12 organizations [that I represent] are working very diligently to bring about equality among men and women, the widest kind of equality, but we are opposed to this measure because we feel that it is an unwise measure, and that it would cause a great deal of trouble everywhere; we would have a great deal of litigation as to what was equality in particular instances and so on, and we feel that equality can better be brought about by removing specific restrictions through specific laws. . . . We say that protective labor laws go toward that step of bringing the woman's standard up a little toward the standards of men."

"[Frieda Miller]: [M]any of the great basic standards of industry . . . apply equally to both [women and men]; that is, standards of fire protection, standards of lighting and cleanliness, and guarding of machinery which are set for everybody to whom they apply. No one questions those general standards, and we believe that the special standards for women are usually aimed toward bringing up the conditions of women to those already enjoyed by men in industry."

"[Anita Pollitzer]: [I]n no respect should the rights of women be left to the whims of individuals, legislatures or organizations, but, just as men are citizens of this land, knowing that all their rights, privileges, and duties are guaranteed to them by law, so we feel that they should be established for women. . . . [E]qual rights seems a very logical sequence to the suffrage amendment. It seems so right that we really resent having to come to ask for our rights. We are not asking for any special rights. We are not asking for anything but the same opportunity to be human beings in this land of ours."

The issues that American women debated echoed in international settings, as the new League of Nations (which the United States did not join) undertook its work. Reporting from the 1923 Congress of the International Federation of Working Women in Vienna, Austria, for the *International Woman Suffrage News*, the group's secretary, Edith McDonald, pointed to discussions of how to achieve rights for working women: through legislation or through unionization, or both.

"The most important work before the Congress was that dealing with the future development of the Federation and with an agreed policy among working women on such matters as trade union organization, home work, and the low wages paid for it; the system of

"[T]he terms 'rights' and 'equal rights' are subject to diverse constructions. . . . [L]egal rights and other rights are not by any means identical. Legal equality is not necessarily the same as economic equality. It may actually defeat economic equality."

—Elisabeth Christman, national secretary of the National Women's Trade Union League, "What Do Working Women Say?" (c. 1912)

Mississippi-born **Burnita Shelton Matthews** (1894–1988) overcame her father's objections, graduated from law school, and when the local bar association refused to permit her to join, opened her own law office in Washington, D.C. As a member of the National Woman's Party, Matthews picketed the White House in 1919 and then became the NWP's lawyer, devoting much of her time to working on women's legal rights and on the ERA campaign. In 1949, Matthews became the first woman appointed to serve as a federal district judge. When the Senate was considering her nomination, a district court judge and future colleague remarked that while "Mrs. Matthews would be a good judge," there was "just one thing wrong: she's a woman."

family allowances in addition to wages; international labour legislation as it affects women, and the questions of disarmament and world peace. Definite plans were made for trade union work among women. . . .

Factory inspection is down on the agenda for the October meeting of the International Labour Office, and Congress dealt with the matter fully. A resolution adopted declared that nationally and internationally there should be minimum standards of work, such as the eight-hour day. The methods by which such standards are to be obtained, whether by trade union agreement or by law, or by both means, should be determined by the organized workers in all countries according to the conditions prevailing in each. The Congress declared in favour of labour legislation for women where the organized working women wish to work for improvement of industrial conditions along this line. . . .

We were encouraged by the fact that in most countries people are becoming alive to the rights and needs of women workers; we women have grown up as trade unionists. There are nearly three million women trade unionists in Germany, and nearly one million in England. . . . Our aim is to link up with working women in all countries, and this can best be done within a joint international."

Throughout the 1920s and 1930s, advocates on both sides continued to debate the merits of an equal rights amendment and its potential effects on working women. In 1937, the magazine *National Business Woman* provided space to Jane Norman Smith of the NWP and Dorothy Kenyon of the League of Women Voters to state their opposing sides. Jane Norman Smith made the case for "A Blanket Amendment" while Dorothy Kenyon argued instead for "Specific Bills" and encouraged professional women to see the issue from the standpoint of working-class women laboring in factories.

"[Jane Norman Smith]: [T]here are more than one thousand laws which discriminate against women. They exist in every state and touch in every sphere of her life and activities. . . . [T]he surest, quickest and most effective method of removing these discriminations and thus securing equality before the law is by an amendment to the federal Constitution. . . . It would take generations of priceless energy and effort to remove discriminations one by one. . . . Moreover, state legislation is insecure, in that laws passed by one legislature may be modified or repealed by the next.

In many states laws are already in operation on the basis of equality. These apply to support of each other by husband and wife, support of children, alimony, dower, age of consent, . . . eight-hour day in certain occupations in over thirty states, etc. No confusion has resulted and judges have found no difficulty in 'defining equality.'

The amendment is a mandate to the states to equalize their laws. Under it, men and women would have equal rights in any given state but not the same rights in all states. For example, when suffrage was won, California equalized its law by abolishing a poll tax for men, while Mississippi extended its poll tax to women. . . .

We believe that women's opportunities are greatest when they have a fair field in the business and industrial world, unhampered by restrictive legislation *applying to them alone*; that legislation, if necessary, should be based on the nature of the work and not on the sex of the worker."

"[Dorothy Kenyon]: The need today is for . . . some small measure of security and with equal opportunities for all, regardless of race, creed or sex. That is the goal. How to achieve it is one of the most complex questions that a modern democracy can face. Let us not fool ourselves that a magic formula . . . stuck into our Constitution is all we need. . . .

Discriminations against women take all sorts of forms. No one formula, certainly not a mathematical formula like 'equality,' will suffice to cover them all. . . . [I]n the economic field, take the eight hour day and minimum wage laws for women. Men, let us assume, are well unionized in the territory in question and the eight-hour day for them is an accomplished fact. Women are not so unionized and until the hours and wages laws went into effect most of them worked for long hours at pitifully low wages. What is 'equality' in this case? Was it equality *before* the passage of the hours and wages laws when women because of their lack of organizing bargaining power worked only in the **sweated trades [sweatshops]**? Or was it equality *after* the passage of the hours and wages laws, when, the law compensating for their lack of bargaining power, women were pulled out of the slough and their wages and hours more nearly equalized with those of men? . . .

Specific bills for specific ills, that is the answer. Thus and thus only will we gain our common end, the achievement of a fuller life and of equal opportunities for all."

The ERA did not make it to the floor of the U.S. Congress for consideration and debate until 1945. Even then, the first vote by the full Senate, in 1946, fell short of the requisite two-thirds majority. By necessity, the

Throughout the decades after suffrage, **Alice Paul** (1885–1977) continued to advocate for an ERA within the United States and equal rights internationally. She carried that interest to Geneva, Switzerland, in the 1930s, where she worked with women leaders in other nations to promote an equal rights treaty for the League of Nations. These transnational efforts paid off when, after World War II, the United Nations included a statement about equal rights in its founding declaration.

Fourteenth Amendment served as the primary legal mechanism through which women's rights activists worked toward the goal of "equal rights." Yet the Supreme Court sent contradictory messages on the question of what equal rights meant under the Fourteenth Amendment. Two cases involving working women's rights reflected those contradictions. In the 1908 case of *Muller v. Oregon*, the court upheld a state maximum hour law for women workers on the grounds that women alone needed protection.

"That woman's physical structure and the performance of her maternal functions place her at a disadvantage in the struggle for subsistence is obvious. This is especially true when the burdens of motherhood are upon her.... [B]y abundant testimony of the medical fraternity continuance for a long time on her feet at work, repeating this from day to day, tends to injurious effects upon the body, and, as healthy mothers are essential to vigorous offspring, the physical well-being of woman becomes an object of public interest and care in order to preserve the strength and vigor of the race....

Differentiated by these matters from the other sex, she is properly placed in a class by herself, and legislation designed for her protection may be sustained, even when like legislation is not necessary for men, and could not be sustained.... The two sexes differ in structure of body, in the functions to be performed by each, in the amount of physical strength, in the capacity for long continued labor.... This difference justifies a difference in legislation, and upholds that which is designed to compensate for some of the burdens which rest upon her."

A 1923 cartoon by Rollin Kirby for the *New York World* echoed Florence Kelley's words: "As a result of the *Adkins* decision, wages of the most ill-paid women in the District of Columbia have been cut.... It establishes in the practical experience of ... women wage-earners, the constitutional right to starve."

This decision affirms your constitutional right to starve

In 1923, however, in the case of *Adkins v. Children's Hospital*, the Court, now with a different composition, overturned Washington, D.C.'s minimum wage law on the grounds that the Nineteenth Amendment and other legal changes had fundamentally altered women's "contractual, political and civil status." Supporters of the Equal Rights Amendment would have endorsed the Court's argument that working women should exercise their "liberty of contract" rather than seek "special protection."

"[T]he ancient inequality of the sexes, otherwise than physical, as suggested in the Muller Case has continued 'with diminishing intensity.' In view of the great—not to say revolutionary—changes which have taken place since that utterance, in the contractual, political and civil status of women, culminating in the Nineteenth Amendment, it is not unreasonable to say that these differences have now come almost, if not quite, to the vanishing point. . . . [W]e cannot accept the doctrine that women of mature age, . . . require or may be subjected to restrictions upon their liberty of contract which could not lawfully be imposed in the case of men under similar circumstances. . . . [We reject] the old doctrine that [woman] must be given special protection or be subjected to special restraint in her contractual and civil relationships."

The New Deal's 1938 Fair Labor Standards Act, drafted by Secretary of Labor **Frances Perkins** (1880–1965), established the first national minimum wage and maximum hour standards for both women and men workers. It also abolished many forms of child labor.

Feminists, Flappers, and Their Foes

Despite divisions over an ERA, many feminists sustained their emancipationist vision beyond 1920. One who did was Crystal Eastman, a socialist, peace activist, lawyer, and founder of the National Woman's Party whose published essays posited an expansive definition of feminism and women's citizenship. In a 1920 essay entitled "Now We Can Begin," she engaged with Emma Goldman's and Charlotte Perkins Gilman's ideas, looked beyond the recent suffrage victory, and envisioned a feminist future.

"What is the problem of women's freedom? It seems to me to be this: how to arrange the world so that women can be human beings, with a chance to exercise their infinitely varied gifts in infinitely varied ways, instead of being destined by the accident of their sex to one field of activity—housework and child-raising. And second, if and when they choose housework and child-raising, to have that occupation recognized by the world as work, requiring a definite economic reward and not merely entitling the performer to be dependent on some man.

This is not the whole of feminism, of course, but it is enough to begin with. 'Oh, don't begin with economic,' my friends often protest, 'Woman does not live by bread alone. What she needs first of all is a free soul.' And I can agree that women will never be great until they achieve a certain emotional freedom, a strong healthy egotism, and some un-personal sources of joy—that in this inner sense we cannot make woman free by changing her economic status. What we can do, however, is to create conditions of outward freedom in which a free woman's soul can be born and grow. It is these outward conditions with which an organized feminist movement must concern itself.

Freedom of choice in occupation and individual economic independence for women: How shall we approach this next feminist objective? First, by breaking down all remaining barriers, actual as well as legal, which make it difficult for women to enter or succeed in the various professions, to go into and get on in business, to learn trades and practice them, to join trades unions. Chief among these remaining barriers is inequality in pay. . . .

Second, we must institute a revolution in the early training and education of both boys and girls. It must be womanly as well as manly to earn your own living, to stand on your own feet. And it must be manly as well as womanly to know how to cook and sew and clean and take care of yourself in the ordinary exigencies of life. I need not add that the second part of this revolution will be more passionately resisted than the first. Men will not give up their privilege of helplessness without a struggle. The average man has a carefully cultivated ignorance about household matters. . . .

Cooperative schemes and electrical devices will simplify the business of home-making, but they will not get rid of it entirely. As far as we can see ahead people will always want homes, and a happy home cannot be had without a certain amount of rather monotonous work and responsibility. How can we change the nature of man so that he will honorably share that work and responsibility and thus make the home-making enterprise a song instead of a burden? Most assuredly not by laws or revolutionary decrees. Perhaps we must cultivate or simulate a little of that highly prized helplessness ourselves. But fundamentally it is a problem of education, of early training—we must bring up feminist sons.

Sons? Daughters? They are born of women—how can women be free to choose their occupations, at all times cherishing their economic independence, unless they stop having children? This is a further question for feminism. If the feminist program goes to pieces on the arrival of the first baby, it is false and useless. For ninety-nine out of every hundred women want children, and seventy-five out of every hundred women want to take care of their own children. . . .

The immediate feminist program must include voluntary motherhood. Freedom of any kind for women is hardly worth considering unless it is assumed that they will know how to control the size of their families. 'Birth control' is just as elementary and essential in our propaganda as 'equal pay.' Women are to have children when they want them, that's the first thing. That ensures some freedom of occupational choice. . . .

But is there any way of insuring a woman's economic independence while child-raising is her chosen occupation? Or must she sink into that dependent state from which, as we all know, it is so hard to rise again? That brings us to the fourth feature of our program—motherhood endowment. It seems that the only way we can keep mothers free, at least in a capitalist society, is by the establishment of a principle that the occupation of raising children is peculiarly and directly a service to society, and that the mother upon whom the necessity and privilege of performing this service naturally falls is entitled to an adequate economic reward from the political government. . . . [W]ith a generous endowment of motherhood provided by legislation, with all laws against voluntary motherhood and education in its methods repealed, with the feminist ideal of education accepted in home and school, and with all special barriers removed in every field of human activity, there is no reason why woman should not become almost a human thing."

For African American feminists, the term "emancipation" continued to have deeper, more complex, and multi-dimensional meanings than it did for white feminists. In a 1925 magazine essay on "The Double Task: The Struggle of Negro Women for Sex and Race Emancipation," the journalist and teacher Elise Johnson McDougald drew a sketch of the intersecting forms of oppression and daily indignities that faced black women.

"Negro women are of a race which is free neither economically, socially, nor spiritually. Like women in general, but more particularly like those of other oppressed minorities, the Negro woman has been forced to submit to over-powering conditions. Pressure has been exerted upon her, both from without and within her group. . . . The Negro woman does not maintain any moral standard which may be assigned chiefly to qualities of race, any more than a white woman does. Yet she has been singled out as having lower sex standards. . . . This I deny. This is the sort of criticism which predicates of one race, to its detriment, that which is common to all races. Sex irregularities are not a matter of race, but of socio-economic conditions. . . .

With all these forces at work, true sex equality has not been approximated. The ratio of opportunity in the sex, social, economic, and political spheres is about that which exists between white men and women. . . . In this matter of sex equality, Negro women have contributed few outstanding militants, a notable instance being the historic Sojourner Truth.... Their feminist efforts are directed chiefly toward the realization of the equality of the races, the sex struggle assuming a subordinate place....

We find the Negro woman, figuratively, struck in the face daily by contempt from the world about her. Within her soul, she knows little of peace and happiness. Through it all, she is courageously standing erect, developing within herself the moral strength to rise above and conquer false attitudes. She is maintaining her natural beauty and charm and improving her mind and opportunity. She is measuring up to the needs and demands of her family, community, and race, and radiating...a hope that is cherished by her sisters in less propitious circumstances throughout the land. The wind of the race's destiny stirs more briskly because of her striving."

The cause of women's emancipation reverberated internationally through groups such as the Women's International League for Peace and Freedom, founded in 1919, and headed up by Jane Addams. At its 1924 meeting in Washington, D.C., the group combined feminist and pacifist principles in its statement of aims.

"A rewording of its aims was adopted by the League, as follows:

1. Complete and universal disarmament on land, on sea and in the air, abolition of the hunger blockade and of the prostitution of science for destructive purposes.
2. World organization for social, political and economic cooperation.
3. Social, political and economic equality for all, without distinction of sex, race, class or creed.
4. Moral disarmament through education in the spirit of human unity, and through the establishment of social justice."

Many young women in the 1920s and 1930s rejected the feminist vision, taking the position that the Nineteenth Amendment had ushered in a new age, one in which women's political activism was no longer necessary. Although embracing the social and sexual freedoms sought by emancipationist thinkers, they dismissed the activist politics and gender consciousness that was central to feminism. A 1920 film entitled *The Flapper* gave them a label for themselves. In a 1927 essay for *Harper's* magazine, journalist Dorothy Dunbar Bromley summed up the individualistic "modern young woman's" negative view of feminism but dubbed her: "Feminist—New Style."

"The Queen is dead. Long live the Queen! Is it not high time that we laid the ghost of the so-called feminist?

'Feminism' has become a term of opprobrium to the modern young woman. For the word suggests either the old school of fighting feminists who wore flat heels and had very little feminine charm, or the current species who antagonize men with their constant clamor about maiden names, equal rights, woman's place in the world, and many another cause. . . . Indeed, if a blundering male assumes that a young woman is a feminist simply because she happens to have a job or a profession of her own, she will be highly—and quite justifiably insulted: for the word evokes the antithesis of what she flatters herself to be. Yet she and her kind can hardly be dubbed 'old-fashioned' women. What are they, then?

The pioneer feminists were hard-hitting individuals, and the modern young woman admires them for their courage—even while she judges them for their zealotry and inartistic methods. Furthermore, she pays all honor to them, for they fought her battle. But *she* does not want to wear their mantle (indeed, she thinks they should have been buried in it), and she has to smile at those women who wear it today—with the battle cry still on their lips. The worst of the fight is over, yet this second generation of feminists are still throwing hand grenades. They bear a grudge against men, either secretly or openly; they make an issue of little things as well as big; they exploit their sex for the sake of publicity; they rant about equality when they might better prove their ability. Yet it is these women—the ones who do more talking than acting—on whom the average man focuses his microscope when he sits down to dissect the 'new woman.' For like his less educated brethren, he labors under the delusion that there are only two types of women, the creature of instinct who is content to be a 'home-maker' and the 'sterile intellectual' who cares solely about 'expressing herself'—home and children be damned.

But what of the constantly increasing group of young women in their twenties and thirties who are the truly modern ones, those who admit that a full life calls for marriage and children as well as career? . . . [I]n this era of simplified housekeeping they see their opportunity, for it is obvious that a woman who plans intelligently can salvage time for her own pursuits. Furthermore, they are convinced that they will be better wives and mothers for the breadth they gain from functioning outside the home. In short, they are

Married women's names. Bromley considered it "inane" for feminists to challenge the custom whereby brides took their husbands' names upon marriage. Her target was the Lucy Stone League, named in honor of the 19th-century abolitionist and suffragist who had kept her own name throughout her long marriage to Henry Blackwell. During the 1910s and 1920s, the League defended "Lucy Stoners" who sought the right to secure passports, open checking accounts, work for the federal government, claim copyrights, plead legal cases, register at hotels, or purchase property under their own names.

For many young African American women, popular performers such as singer and actress Ethel Waters expressed the feminism of the "New Negro Woman" through earthy songs such as "Shake That Thing" and "No Man's Mamma." They challenged demeaning stereotypes about black female sexuality while also enjoying some of the era's freedoms. Yet, as Elise Johnson McDougald noted in "The Double Task," black women faced much more limited economic opportunities and much greater sexual dangers than white "flappers." Waters herself was conceived from her mother's rape and grew up in dire poverty.

highly conscious creatures who feel obliged to plumb their own resources to the very depths, despite the fact that they are under no delusions as to the present inferior status of their sex in most fields of endeavor.

Numbers of these honest, spirited young women have made themselves heard in article and story. But since men must have things pointed out to them in black and white we beg leave to enunciate the tenets of the modern woman's credo. Let us call her 'Feminist—New Style.' . . .

In brief, Feminist—New Style reasons that if she is economically independent, and if she has, to boot, a vital interest in some work of her own she will have given as few hostages to Fate as it is humanly possible to give. Love may die, and children may grow up, but one's work goes on forever.

She will not, however, live for her job alone, for she considers that a woman who talks and thinks only shop has just as narrow a horizon as the housewife who talks and thinks only husband and children. . . .

Nor has she become hostile to the other sex in the course of her struggle to orient herself. On the contrary, she frankly likes men and is grateful to more than a few for the encouragement and help they have given her. . . .

By the same corollary Feminist—New Style professes no loyalty to women *en masse*, although she staunchly believes in individual women. Surveying her sex as a whole, she finds their actions petty, their range of interests narrow, their talk trivial and repetitious. As for those who set themselves up as leaders of the sex, they are either strident creatures of so little ability and balance that they have won no chance to 'express themselves' (to use their own hackneyed phrase) in a man-made world; or they are brilliant, restless individuals who too often battle for women's rights for the sake of personal glory.

But when a woman in the professions or in public life proves herself really capable, Feminist—New Style will be the first to cheer, and to help her along still farther, by proffering her own support and co-operation. . . .

Finally, Feminist—New Style proclaims that men and children shall no longer circumscribe her world, although they may constitute a large part of it. She is intensely self-conscious whereas the feminists were intensely sex-conscious. . . . She knows that it is her American, her twentieth-century birthright to emerge from a creature of instinct into a full-fledged individual who is capable of molding her own life. And in this respect she holds that she is becoming man's equal."

Psychologists became popular advice-givers in the 1920s, as Freudian ideas percolated into mass media. In his 1927 essay "The Weakness of Women," the influential psychologist John Broadus Watson offered his opinion that women who advocated for women's rights needed psychological help or sexual "adjustment."

"When a woman is a militant suffragist the chances are, shall we say, a hundred to one that her sex life is not well adjusted? Marriage as such brings adjustment in only approximately 20 per cent of all cases, ... [and] among the 20 per cent who find adjustment, I find no militant women, I find no women shouting about their rights to some fanciful career that men—the brutes—have robbed them of.... Most of the terrible women one must meet, women with the blatant views and voices, women who have to be noticed, who shoulder one about, who can't take life quietly, belong to this large percentage of women who have never made a sex adjustment...."

The flapper's apparent sexual freedom belied the continuing power of Comstock and other censorship laws, as well as the difficulty most women had in gaining access to contraceptive information. In 1927, the editors of _Birth Control Review_ took the National Woman's Party to task for neglecting reproductive rights in their definition of "equal rights."

"Until birth control is discussed and until discussion passes into inclusion in its program of women's rights the National Woman's Party will not be in a real sense a Feminist party. For there is one respect in which the average woman of the wage-earning and farming classes—to which belong the great majority of women in the United States—is handicapped by comparison with the average man. Unlimited fatherhood withdraws men in no way from the general life and public activities of humanity. But unlimited motherhood does exactly that for women.... If they aim ... to represent Equal Rights for women of all classes, they must make birth control a foundation demand. Unless they do, the National Woman's Party will represent merely the interests of a favored group, a group who have, all of them who desire it, already gained access to contraceptive information."

Life

Thirty Years of "Progress"!

1896   1926

In drawings for _LIFE_ and other magazines, illustrator John Held, Jr. captured the flapper image with renderings of lean young white women with short hair, short skirts, rolled stockings, and, often, cigarettes and liquor flasks. His 1926 sketch contrasting the free-spirited young woman of his era with her Gibson Girl predecessor revealed certain nostalgia for an idealized Victorian womanhood.

Movies in the 1920s and 1930s provided various interpretations of the possibility of women's freedom. In the hugely popular 1921 film *The Sheik*, based on Edith Hull's romance novel, the heroine, Diana Mayo, seeking her independence, brashly rejects a marriage proposal and her brother's warnings and heads off for a solo adventure in the North African desert, announcing, "I will *never* obey any will but my own." After being abducted and raped by a local sheik, she sees the error of her ways, falls in love with the sheik, and declares to him, "I never lived until you taught me what life was."

Ann Vickers, a popular 1933 film based on the novel by Sinclair Lewis, offers a portrait of an independent woman who enjoys both romance and a fulfilling professional life. Although the film (by screenwriter Jane Murfin) excises the novel's references to Ann's abortion, it does depict two out-of-wedlock pregnancies and an affair with a married man. In focusing on Ann Vickers's admirable career in social work and prison reform, the film refuses to make the main character suffer for her independence and ambition.

By the mid-1930s, Margaret Sanger had backed away from seeing revolutionary feminist potential for women's reproductive freedom in birth control. Her organization, the American Birth Control League, concentrated on founding clinics for married women and seeking to dismantle the Comstock Laws. By 1936, they had won two major Supreme Court cases reinterpreting those laws; by 1938, there were 374 physician-staffed birth control clinics in the United States. In an essay for the liberal weekly, *The New Republic,* Sanger summed up "The Status of Birth Control: 1938."

"At last birth control is legal in the United States. The right to provide contraceptive information and service under medical direction is finally recognized under federal law as now interpreted, and it also is legal under state laws in all but two states, Mississippi and Massachusetts....

It is one of the anomalies of modern civilization that the forces of bigotry, reaction and legalism could so long have kept on the federal statute books a law that classed contraceptive information with obscenity.... It required two-thirds of a century to remove the federal fetters placed upon birth control by Anthony Comstock and a 'reform' group which induced a timid and overawed Congress to pass the overreaching law. That famous, or rather infamous law ... and supplementary laws, prevented the dissemination of birth-control information even by a physician, and barred anything pertaining to the subject from the mails or common carriers. Other sections were even more rigid, forbidding the possession of any article for preventing conception—*and there were no exceptions....* The laws made no distinction between contraception and abortion, though they are as far apart as the poles....

The National Committee on Federal Legislation for Birth Control, Inc., had proceeded along both legislative and legal lines of battle.... [A] particularly strong test case was instituted by the Committee on behalf or Dr. Hannah M. Stone, medical director of the Birth Control Clinical Research Bureau in New York. The government, through the Bureau of Customs, had seized a package containing 120 **pessaries [diaphragms]** to prevent conception,... pessaries [that] had been sent to Dr. Stone by a physician in Japan for trial in her practice....

It was in this case [*U.S. v. One Package of Japanese Pessaries*], on November 20, 1936, that birth control under medical direction was finally recognized as legal. The United States Circuit Court of Appeals for the Second Circuit rendered a decision that the federal obscenity laws do not apply to the legitimate activities of physicians, and that they may prescribe contraceptives in the interests of the health and general well-being of their patients. That enlightened decision brought birth control to the goal it had long sought through legislation and was an emancipation proclamation to the motherhood of America. . . .

However, there is need for clarification of state statutes. . . In Massachusetts the state laws . . . make no exception of any kind. . . . In the summer of 1937 three Massachusetts birth-control clinics were raided. Doctors, nurses, social workers and officials were arrested, convicted, and fined. . . . This reactionary step is a warning that while prohibitory laws of this type remain on the statute books, they constitute a continuing threat to the freedom of the medical profession and the welfare of mothers."

When sociologist Margaret Jarman Hagood interviewed poor Southern white tenant farm women during the 1930s, she found that, despite a desire to limit their childbearing, only a small number had access to physicians or used contraceptive methods. The interviews were complicated by the women's reticence when it came to talking about intimate matters.

"[Mothers express] pride in having borne the number [of children] they have, yet almost never is there expressed a desire for more. The most common example of the first is the ever present suggestion of self-esteem in both words and intonation of answers to the question of how many children the mother of a large family has—'Eleven. I done my share, didn't I'? or 'Ten and all al-living.' . . .

On the other hand, every one of the mothers with babies of two or under, explicitly or by inference, expressed the attitude, 'I hope this is the last one.' So many of them used these identical words. . . .

Certain difficulties inhered in the securing of information on contraceptive practices. In the first place lack of privacy in the interviews prevented discussion of such matters with some mothers. Then, the impossibility of using technical terms because of the mothers' ignorance, or of using 'vulgar, menfolks' words' for fear of offending them made for a lack of concreteness and specificity when contraception or sexual relations were discussed. . . . [Yet] there was almost always a willingness

In 1942, Sanger's organization dropped the term "birth control" and changed its name to the Planned Parenthood Federation of America.

to talk about such matters even though circumlocution made the process of conveying information cumbersome. Of the sixty-nine mothers questioned as to the use of contraceptives, only eight replied in the affirmative. Three use condoms, two douches, one diaphragm and jelly [spermicide], and two practice withdrawal.... [O]ne mother tried to explain that [withdrawal] was the method she and her husband used. Her answer was metaphorical: 'Well, I always say that when you chew tobacco, it don't make so much mess if you spit it out the window.' Another described the same method ...: 'If you don't want butter, pull the dasher out in time!'"

Former antisuffragists, both as individuals and as members of an organized opposition, actively disparaged feminists and flappers alike. Mary Wilson Thompson, who had led the successful effort to prevent Delaware from ratifying the Nineteenth Amendment in 1919, stated her position in a 1937 memoir that revealed her blinkered, class-specific definition of "women."

"I have always opposed votes for women.... It is not that I feel women cannot vote or are not the mental equal of our men folks, but I feel that is duplicating our work. It is putting an extra burden on the women and it has weakened materially our power with the legislatures.

As long as the women of the state came to the legislators of the state to ask for a reform in the laws or an improvement in conditions, our legislators knew we had no ulterior motive and also knew that they could act with a clear conscience, as there was no return vote by which they might benefit. The first question now that arises in their minds is, will she vote for me or will she not? After more than fifteen years of a tryout, what has been accomplished? The cheapening of womanhood, giving her a sort of independence by which she makes it a favor to her husband to attend to the housekeeping and attend to the children....

I say to the women in this country that their first duty is to keep up their man power.... With women all taking up jobs and receiving independent salaries for them, naturally they feel equal if not superior to their husbands. The young woman you see around in public is personally unattractive; she talks too loud and makes herself conspicuous; she is immodest on the beach and in the ballroom; and with her continual loud talking and constant smoking has lost much of her feminine charm. . . . The country has certainly not benefited by the women's vote."

Using their citizenship rights, many former antisuffragists organized to promote a politically conservative, activist agenda, sounding the alarm over what they considered to be the dangers of woman suffrage, feminism, and internationalism. In a 1921 open letter to supporters of *The Woman Patriot*, Katharine T. Balch outlined the concerns that drove antisuffragists to continue their work after 1920.

"We need your help in the fight against Socialism and Feminism, . . .

We are actively working against many radical so-called 'welfare' bills—all of them paternalistic, which, if enacted, would undermine the sturdy self-reliance of our people. Especially we have organized opposition to the **Sheppard-Towner Bill**. We thoroughly believe that the interlocking radical groups in this country are concentrating politically on this bill as the spearhead of their revolutionary thrust.

We are contesting the validity of the 19th Amendment (Federal suffrage), hoping through victory to restore rule by the people. . . .

Our National Association President, Miss [Mary G.] Kilbreth, has lately written one of our members:

'Remember we have with us as allies the Constitution, all the institutions on which . . . Western civilization is based, and all the heritage of beliefs paid for with blood, and wrought out by Anglo-Saxon jurisprudence since the days of the Magna Charta. Our feeble efforts no more measure the strength of our fight than the power of the feminist assault is due to the little band of women radicals. Communism is back of them—they are its tools.'"

The 1921 **Sheppard-Towner Act** provided federal funds to states for programs to improve maternal and infant health care. Under heavy pressure from the American Medical Association and conservative activists, Congress ended funding for it in 1929.

The masthead of *The Woman Patriot* made clear the positions it promoted.

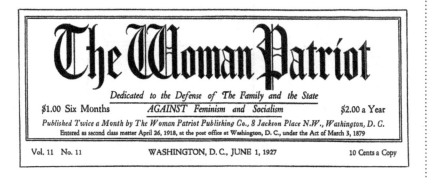

The Woman Patriot

Dedicated to the Defense of The Family and the State

$1.00 Six Months   *AGAINST Feminism and Socialism* $2.00 a Year

Published Twice a Month by The Woman Patriot Publishing Co., 8 Jackson Place N.W., Washington, D. C.
Entered as second class matter April 26, 1918, at the post office at Washington, D. C., under the Act of March 3, 1879

Vol. 11 No. 11   WASHINGTON, D. C., JUNE 1, 1927   10 Cents a Copy

The antifeminist attempt to tar women's rights and feminism with the brush of radicalism proved successful. One of the most effective tactics was the publication of a "Spider-Web" Chart in 1924, claiming that women's organizations represented an insidious, interlocking network of influence with ties to socialist and communist doctrines. The chart was part of a larger "Red Scare" conducted by the U.S. War Department that included post-war deportations of suspected radicals (such as Emma Goldman) and extended into the 1920s.

Women's Rights in an Era of Economic Depression

Economic crises generally push women's rights concerns to the sidelines of politics, and often lead to the eroding of rights already attained. The Great Depression of the 1930s was one such crisis. Although New Deal programs provided some opportunities to women and girls, most beneficiaries were men. Moreover, during the economic crisis, public opinion turned sharply against working women and their economic rights. In a 1940 pamphlet, Ruth Shallcross summarized the results of a survey she conducted for the National Federation of Business and Professional Women's Clubs.

"The Gallup poll found, in 1936, that 82 percent of the people were opposed to married women's working. In 1939, Gallup found that 78 percent were opposed.... In 1936, Fortune made a survey of public opinion and found that 85 percent of the men and 79 percent of the women interviewed thought married women should not work outside the home....

Within the last few years, bills have been introduced in the legislatures of twenty-six states against married women workers. Only one of these passed. This was in Louisiana, and it was later repealed. Six other states have either joint resolutions or governors' orders restricting married women's right to work. Three other states have made a general practice of prohibiting married women from working in public employment....

The bars against married women are of different kinds—all of which exist for some school teachers. They may take the form of refusal to hire married women (the most frequent), or dismissal upon marriage, delay in granting promotion, or actual demotion, and either permanent or temporary dismissal when pregnant....

The National Education Association ... survey, made in 1931, revealed that 77 percent of the cities reporting made a practice of not employing married women as new teachers and 63 percent dismissed women teachers upon marriage....

Few of the people who oppose married women's employment seem to realize that a coal miner or steel worker cannot very well fill the jobs of nursemaids, cleaning women, or the factory and clerical occupations now filled by women...."

The loss of economic rights was particularly devastating for poor and minority women workers, who often lost whatever small gains they had made during prosperous times. Writer and civil rights activist Ella Baker

chronicled for the magazine *The Crisis* the "slave markets" for domestic and child-care workers that she and co-author Marvel Cooke observed in New York City in 1935.

"[T]he Simpson avenue block exudes the stench of the slave market at its worst. Not only is human labor bartered and sold for slave wage, but human love is also a marketable commodity. But whether it is labor or love that is sold, economic necessity compels the sale. . . .

Who are these women? . . . In the boom days before the onslaught of the depression in 1929, many of these women who are now forced to bargain for day's work on street corners, were employed in grand homes in the rich Eighties, or in wealthier homes in Long Island and Westchester, at more than adequate wages. Some are former marginal industrial workers, forced by the slack in industry to seek other means of sustenance. In many instances there had been no necessity for work at all. But whatever their standing prior to the depression, none sought employment where they now seek it. . . . Where once color was the 'gilt edged' security for obtaining domestic and personal service jobs, here, even, Negro women found themselves being displaced by whites. . . ."

Despite the presence of women's rights advocates in Franklin D. Roosevelt's cabinet and administration, New Deal programs often discriminated against women or excluded them from eligibility. When women were included, often white women were the sole or primary beneficiaries. In a 1937 letter to the head of the Works Progress Administration (WPA), Mrs. Mary O'Kelly Albright, writing on behalf of the Workers Council of Colored People in Raleigh, North Carolina, spelled out the issues.

"We . . . wish to state some facts to you about how the colored women, (mostly heads of the families) have been treated by W.P.A. heads here. Also wish you to make investigation about it at once for its pure injustice to us, the way it has been done. . . .

Mr. Hopkins colored women have been turned out of different jobs projects to make us take other jobs we mentioned and white women were hired & sent for & given places that colored women was made to leave or quit.

Let us say that if we cannot work on W.P.A. Projects & be compel to take these poor paying jobs; that food, clothes & rent money be provided for us at once because we are suffering. We the Workers Council understood that no colored women cannot be hired this winter on any of the W.P.A. projects. We wish you to tell us why."

Some women workers benefited from the Roosevelt administration's support for workers' right to unionize, established in law through the National Labor Relations Act (Wagner Act) of 1935. Although unionization of women workers lagged considerably behind that of men, and that of African American women behind that of white women, by 1941, when union official Sabina Martinez wrote an article, "Negro Women in Organization," for *The Aframerican*, she was able to point to some successes.

"Organized labor has rescued the Negro woman from her obscure position in basic industry, where she once toiled and labored from ten to twelve hours a day under most inhuman conditions and at starvation wages. Some women have come timidly, others very sure of their convictions, and some with mental reservations. But all have secured better wages, in many cases as much as 60 per cent increase. All their hours have been reduced to eight hours a day, and all their positions have been rendered more secure. The bosses, who formerly subjected them to their whims and fancies, through their participation in unions, have learned to respect them.

In bringing this about organized labor found it no easy task; not because women did not appreciate unions, but because of the false anti-union propaganda that had been handed out to our women by the bosses ... and because of the definitely Jim-Crow policy of the high executives of the A.F. of L. [American Federation of Labor], which ignored Negro people....

Negro women workers welcomed the birth of the C.I.O. [Congress of Industrial Organizations] and the partially open door of the A.F. of L. and are now a part of such unions as: Laundry, Cleaners, and Dyers, Textiles, Teachers, Domestic and others. Negro women helped to lay the basis for these unions and in many instances were on the first committees that helped to formulate the policies of these unions....

The Laundry workers were unorganized for thirty years in the city of New York. In six months the C.I.O. has organized this industry into a compact body of some 27,000 Laundry workers, the great majority of whom are Negro women. Negro women helped lay the foundation, formulate the policies and now hold executive offices in this union, which is an affiliate of the Amalgamated Clothing Workers of America....

The Cleaners and Dyers Union which is only four years old was given its first impetus toward C.I.O. by Ida J. Dudley, a Negro woman.... The Textile and Domestic workers, who are only

The Social Security Act of 1935 included provisions for old-age pensions, unemployment compensation, disability assistance, and Aid to Dependent Children (ADC) through grants to state social welfare bureaus. Women's rights to claim benefits under the act were restricted in two ways: (1) Many occupations in which women predominated, such as domestic service, were not included. (2) Because benefits were allotted to economic providers (or breadwinners), most women were expected to receive benefits as men's dependents, not as independent citizens. Single (that is, never-married) mothers, for instance, were not entitled to ADC.

partially organized, have brought into the ranks of organized labor hoards of miserable, exploited workers who are denied protection under Social Security or State Labor Laws.... In 1930, 3 out of every 5 Negro women employed were in the field of domestic or personal service....

The Sharecroppers Union, the Tenant League, and many of the new organized unions owe their existence to the unselfish contributions of Negro women.... Organized labor ... must rid itself of the old idea that women must be subordinate to men, or that women do not provide as good leadership as men. Organized labor must make a sincere effort to increase the women personnel of its membership."

Despite the economic crisis, writers, thinkers, and women's organizations sought to keep alive the feminist vision of women's emancipation. Perhaps the most intriguing expression of that vision was the comic-book heroine, Wonder Woman, first introduced in a 1941 issue of *All-Star Comics*. She was the brainchild of a Harvard University–educated psychologist, William Moulton Marston. Soon, a separate *Wonder Woman* comic appeared and the popular character became part of American folklore. In a 1943 article in the journal *American Scholar*, Marston explained the principles that underlay his creation of the character.

Sketched by newspaper artist Harry G. Peter, an illustration of Wonder Woman breaking her chains accompanied Marston's essay.

All-Star Comics promoted Wonder Woman as a role model for girls by means of a popular comic-book feature, "Wonder Women of History." Amelia Earhart was one of those profiled. As a pioneering aviator, Earhart seemed to be a symbol of female emancipation. Her transport pilot's license, issued in 1930 and renewed each year thereafter, reflected her adventurous spirit. While attempting a round-the-world flight in 1937, Earhart was lost at sea.

"It seemed to me, from a psychological angle, that the [existing] comics' worst offense was their blood-curdling masculinity. A male hero, at best, lacks the qualities of maternal love and tenderness which are as essential to a normal child as the breath of life. . . . The obvious remedy is to create a feminine character with all the strength of a Superman plus all the allure of a good and beautiful woman. . . . I wrote Wonder Woman. I found an artist . . . and . . . we created the first successful woman character in comics magazines. After five months the publishers ran a popularity contest between Wonder Woman and seven rival men heroes. . . . The kids who rated Wonder Woman tops in an otherwise masculine galaxy of picture story stars weren't voting for a clever script writer. . . . They were saying by their votes, 'We *love* a girl who is stronger than men, who uses her strength to help others and who allures us with the love appeal of a true woman!'"

The Ladder

OCTOBER, 1957

CHAPTER 7

The Personal
Is Political

The Second World War marked a major change in the understanding that many women had of their citizenship and especially their economic rights. In response to patriotic appeals, some six million women, three-fourths of them married, entered the paid labor force, joining those who had been there throughout the difficult Depression decade. Wartime exigencies made practices differentiating between married and single women in job assignments appear inefficient or retrograde. Because the emerging civil rights movement lobbied for and won new non-discrimination rules in hiring and pay, African American women and Latinas found new economic opportunities. For the first time, women wore the uniforms of the (racially segregated) armed forces and served under military discipline. Chinese-born women benefited from Congress's 1943 ending of exclusion laws, designed to reward China for its wartime alliance with the United States. Along with Chinese-born men, they could now become citizens. Japanese American women and men living on the West Coast, on the other hand, even if they were American citizens, suffered forcible removal from their homes and internment in remote, hastily built camps. As in earlier times, the war and its aftermath brought new pressures for equal rights and prompted fresh ideas about what those who sacrificed for the common good had earned. But, as with earlier wars, the question remained whether women's patriotic service would spark changes that were permanent or temporary.

For many women, wartime gains provided a yardstick against which they measured the post-war world, and they found it wanting. With the return of veterans to civilian life, three-fourths of women workers planned to remain in the labor force but faced policies that relegated them anew to low-paying "women's" jobs with few opportunities for advancement. The contrast between wartime opportunity and post-war discrimination sharpened their awareness of women's rights issues. During the 1950s, however, overt discussion of women's rights remained muted, in part because a Cold War–inspired anticommunist Red Scare targeted progressive causes and people, in part because popular culture tied women and femininity closely to domestic roles. What Betty Friedan termed a "feminine mystique" created a surface appearance of feminine conformity and quiescence. But beneath that surface, a great deal was changing. Activist women whose commitments included labor union membership, civil rights advocacy, grassroots political and community organizing, critiques of conventional heterosexuality, antinuclear agitation, and peace protests formed key constituencies for a women's rights feminism that coalesced during the early 1960s around questions of women's legal "status" and economic and educational opportunities. Younger women, many of them deeply engaged in the civil rights, student protest, and antiwar movements, came together in the late 1960s under the banner of "women's liberation." Women's rights and women's liberation groups often disagreed, especially over how to define and achieve the elusive goal of "equality," and indeed whether equality should be their central goal at all. But together, they created new feminisms that challenged existing legal, social, cultural, and economic institutions and exerted a transformative influence on American life.

Women's Rights in the Eras of Wartime and the "Feminine Mystique"

The U.S. entry into the Second World War opened new opportunities for women workers. Even before the War Labor Board in September 1942 issued an opinion providing that women doing "men's jobs" would get "men's pay," women workers pressed for equitable compensation and won. An article from the Federated Press bureau in May of that year summarized the results of one such case.

"Back wages totaling $55,690 were awarded . . . under the Michigan law requiring equal pay for equal work without discrimination 'on the basis of sex only.' The ruling was made on May 28, 1942.

   This is the first court action carried through to a verdict under the law which had been previously been upheld by the state supreme court. Many settlements out of court had been made in such cases however.

The back pay is shared by 29 women employes [sic] of Olds Motor Works, a General Motors plant in Lansing. They had done men's work in the paint shop, small-press work and on inspection for six years. . . .

Attorney Jack Tucker, . . . general counsel of the UAW-CIO, said in December that the decision would stimulate unions to press for equal rates for women members in revising their contracts."

Wartime contingencies also led women to challenge long-standing practices differentiating between married and single women in employment. The *Boston Herald*, February 18, 1944, covered a school board meeting at which a married Boston teacher sought to overturn a policy requiring women to resign upon marriage.

"Appeals for recognition of merit, rather than marital status, as the basis for retention of teachers and pleas for maintenance of a sixty-year-old ban on married women teachers, based on the charge that 'working wives are a menace to public health, morals and general welfare,' were heard last night by the Boston School Committee.

The occasion was a noisy, frequently heckled public hearing granted [to] the Boston Citizens' Committee for Teachers' Rights, formed recently following the automatic resignation of Grace Lonergan Lorch, a teacher in the second grade, because of her marriage to Pvt. Lee Lorch of the Army Air Forces.

Three [male] members of the committee . . . announced themselves in favor of the retention of the ban. . . .

Pleading her own case as president of the Boston Teachers' Union, . . . Mrs. Lorch was booed when she cautioned several hundred women jammed into the hearing room that the City Council was on record as intending to 'fire every married woman from every city job when the war is over.'

'That means,' she added, 'they intend to rule out marriage, they intend to make marriage a class privilege for the upper classes. They may get away with it for teachers, but not for other women.'

Representative Florence E. Cook, as chairman of the Citizens' Committee, presented representatives of labor, religious, civic and women's organizations [who] supported the appeal for discontinuance of the ban. Most labor leaders asked for suspension of the ban for the duration of the war. . . .

Thomas H. Mahoney, legal adviser for the Citizens' Committee . . . cited the Lorch case. As Grace Lonergan, he said, she had

After the war, **Grace Lonergan Lorch** (1904–1974) and her husband, Lee, moved to New York City, where they became active in the effort to desegregate the city's public housing. When Lee Lorch lost his position teaching math as a result of the controversy surrounding their civil rights advocacy, the couple and their daughter moved (eventually) to Little Rock, Arkansas, where Lee taught math at the historically black Philander Smith College and Grace worked with the local NAACP to help integrate Little Rock High School in 1957. In Massachusetts, the legislature ended the ban on married women teachers in 1953. A historical marker at the Charles Taylor School in Dorchester, Massachusetts, honors Grace Lorch's memory.

In 1940, the Republican Party became the first major party to endorse an ERA in its party platform. The Democratic Party followed suit in 1944. The 1980 Republican platform withdrew the endorsement.

been earning $2,300 a year, was enjoying tenure and pension privileges, then because she married she was automatically retired from the school system, yet permitted to do the same classroom work on a temporary basis at the rate of $5.00 for every working day."

During the war, the National Woman's Party (NWP) continued to focus on the goal of securing an Equal Rights Amendment to the Constitution. Writing in the organization's periodical, *Equal Rights,* in 1944, Alice Paul invoked the wartime context to make the case for an ERA.

"At this moment when the United States is engaged in a war with the avowed purpose of establishing freedom and equality for the whole world, the United States should hasten to set its own house in order by granting freedom and equality to its own women. For the sake of a new and better world, as well as justice to women themselves, [we] ask for the immediate adoption of the Equal Rights Amendment."

In her breezy 1943 book on women and war work, *Why Women Cry, or Wenches with Wrenches*, the clothing designer and fashion critic Elizabeth Hawes summed up the common contemporary view of feminists belonging to the National Woman's Party. She was not alone in depicting them as "Equal-Righters" with little concern for working women.

"A couple of generations or more ago, there was a fanatical group of females known as Feminists. Due to their well-organized and tireless efforts, or at least partially so, we women of the USA have the right to vote.

Once I met six Feminists and it was only then, at the age of 26, that I heard there was a fight between men and women. Later I discovered the Feminists, in their headlong rush for feminine equality, had denied there was any difference between the male and the female. And I mean any difference at all.

They carried this idea to extreme lengths. . . . Today the little group of earnest thinkers who most closely follow the Feminists are now all-out for making women equal with men, not by denying there is a basic difference, but by having the Constitution changed to *say* women are equal with men. . . .

Instead of helping the Nation concentrate on getting equality and better working conditions for everyone, male and female, the Equal-Righters make a loud noise about removing special privileges for women. This is a sure-fire method of losing some of women's present better working conditions and making it harder to get them back for both sexes.

Equality is equality regardless of sex, color, nationality, or religion."

In 1943, at a *New York Times* symposium on "The World after the War," Dorothy Kenyon took an expansive view in answer to the question "What Kind of World Do We Want?"

"[I hope for] the freedom for women, or for anybody, to decide for themselves what they shall do in the world, to exercise freedom of choice in the disposition of their lives, to enjoy the same kind and degree of opportunity to exercise their diverse talents, whether in rocking the cradle or ruling the world, that every other human being has.

A world which freely utilizes the brains and capacities of its women is a complete and rounded world in the sense that a world which keeps its women in **purdah** [**seclusion**] and swathed in veils up to the eyes can never be.

All this seems fairly clear to us, I think, and in our complacent way we American women think we have it. . . . But . . . freedom for ourselves is not enough. We know now that the basic freedoms must be worldwide."

Once the war ended, the contrast between women's wartime experiences and the post-war work world seemed striking indeed. In 1946, the Congress of American Women drew attention to those contrasts. The group, which grew out of an international gathering of some eight hundred women leaders from forty-one countries, brought together a coalition of women's organizations, to develop a women's rights agenda. Its manifesto, "The Position of the American Woman Today," set out the group's view of where post-war women stood in terms of economic, political, social, and individual rights, and envisioned a future of equal citizenship for women regardless of race, class, or marital status.

"The American woman entered World War II hardened and tempered by her experiences during the Great Depression. . . . The terrible manpower needs of the Second World War . . . opened the doors of basic industry . . . wide to women for the first time. . . . Yet it is significant that none of the 'Fair Employment Practices' legislation which came into being during the war included discrimination because of sex. . . .

[I]n the immediate cut-back of war production following V-J day women workers suffered lay-offs more serious than that of any other groups. . . . Of all women the American Negro women have been hit hardest. Job opportunities opened to women during the war were not available to them, except in the dirtiest and

By the time she participated in the symposium, **Dorothy Kenyon** (1888–1972) was widely known for her skills as a lawyer and judge and for her women's rights activism. A consistent opponent of employment discrimination on the basis of sex and race, she advocated for the rights of married women workers and for military commissions for female physicians during World War II. Despite having opposed an ERA in the 1930s because of its potentially destructive effects on working-class women, by 1970 she had come to agree that it was necessary to end legal sex discrimination. In her later career, she was a global advocate for women's rights, serving as a delegate to the United Nations Commission on the Status of Women and actively opposing the U.S. war in Vietnam.

lowest-paying groups. Now many of these Negro women have been forced back into domestic service. . . .

The problem of the working woman . . . does not end with equal pay, equal upgrading or the end of discrimination in employment. Freedom to work means freedom to do two full-time jobs[,] . . . a full shift in industry or office and . . . then . . . another full day's work, cooking, cleaning, washing, mending. . . . [T]he American woman has been found capable of doing most jobs as well as men, but her difficulties arise when she tries to do two jobs as well as the man does only one.

Politically, . . . twenty-six years after the American woman secured the right to vote, with a numerical voting superiority, . . . only seven women are in the House of Representatives and four in the Senate. . . . Women are now becoming aware of the necessity of united political action, and for the election of more women to office. The Congress of American Women plans to fight for '48 Women in Congress in '48.'

Legally, too, the American woman is only 'half free.' . . . For example, in . . . 15 states a woman can become the natural guardian of her child only if it is born out of wedlock, but in three of those states she can go to jail if she does not reveal the name of the father. . . . In six states she is not entitled to her wages—they belong to her husband as part of the marriage property. In three states a married woman's will is automatically revoked by her marriage. . . .

Until the day when the American woman is free to develop her mind and abilities to their fullest extent, without discrimination because of her sex, is free to work without neglecting her children, to live with her husband on an equal level, with adequate provision made for the care [of] that home without injury to her health; until she takes her full responsibilities as citizen and individual, supporting herself if necessary and her family where she has a family, at a decent wage, paid equally with men for the work she does; until she is freed from the terror of war, and lives in a world of peaceful friendship between nations, in a society without prejudice against Negro, Jew, national groups or women—her long struggle for emancipation must continue."

Calling attention to the specific challenges facing African American women, as the Congress of American Women did, was unusual in postwar America. Even more unusual was the approach taken by writer and activist Claudia Jones, who singled out for comment the multiple,

overlapping forms of discrimination they faced. Her essay, published in the Communist Party journal *Political Affairs* in 1949, was entitled "An End to the Neglect of the Problems of the Negro Woman!"

"Negro women—as workers, as Negroes, and as women—are the most oppressed stratum of the whole population.

In 1940, two out of every five Negro women, in contrast to two out of every eight white women, worked for a living. By virtue of their majority status among the Negro people, Negro women not only constitute the largest percentage of women heads of families, but are the main breadwinners of the Negro family. The large proportion of Negro women in the labor market is primarily a result of the low-scale earnings of Negro Men. This disproportion also has roots in the treatment and position of Negro women over the centuries.

Following emancipation, and persisting to the present day, a large percentage of Negro women—married as well as single— were forced to work for a living. But despite the shift in employment of Negro women from rural to urban areas, Negro women are still generally confined to the lowest-paying jobs. . . . [W]hite women workers [have] median earnings more than twice as high as those of non-white women, and non-white women workers (mainly Negro women) [earn] less than $500 a year! In the rural South, the earnings of women are even less. . . . The super-exploitation of the Negro woman worker is thus revealed not only in that she receives, as woman, less than equal pay for equal work with men, but in that the majority of Negro women get less than half the pay of white women. Little wonder, then, that in Negro communities the conditions of ghetto-living—low salaries, high rents, high prices, etc.— virtually become an iron curtain hemming in the lives of Negro children and undermining their health and spirit! Little wonder that the maternity death rate for Negro women is triple that of white women! Little wonder that one out of every ten Negro children born in the United States does not grow to manhood or womanhood! . . .

During the anti-Axis war, Negro women for the first time in history had an opportunity to utilize their skills and talents in occupations other than domestic and personal service. They became trail blazers in many fields. Since the end of the war, however, this has given way to growing unemployment, to the wholesale firing of Negro women, particularly in basic industry. . . .

The anticommunist Red Scare of the post-war years silenced the voices of women like Claudia Jones and decimated the ranks of progressive groups like the Congress of American Women. When the House Un-American Activities Committee (HUAC) claimed that the Congress's purpose was "not to deal primarily with women's problems . . . but rather to serve as a specialized arm of Soviet political warfare in the current 'peace' campaign to disarm and demobilize the United States," the Department of Justice demanded that the group register as "foreign agents." Rather than fight a lengthy legal battle, the group disbanded in 1950.

Inherently connected with the question of job opportunities where the Negro woman is concerned, is the special oppression she faces as Negro, as woman, and as worker. . . .

A developing consciousness on the woman question today, therefore, must not fail to recognize that the Negro question in the United States is *prior* to, and not equal to, the woman question; that only to the extent that we fight all chauvinist expressions and actions as regards the Negro people, and fight for the full equality of Negro people, can women as a whole advance their struggle for equal rights. For the progressive women's movement, the Negro woman, who combines in her status the worker, the Negro, and the woman, is the vital link to this heightened political consciousness."

Despite the repressive political climate of the late 1940s and 1950s, labor activists and working-class women in progressive unions were strong advocates for women's rights. In 1952, the United Electrical, Radio, and Machine Workers of America issued a pamphlet entitled "UE Fights for Women Workers," written by Betty Goldstein, who later gained fame under her married name, Betty Friedan.

"In advertisements across the land, industry glorifies the American woman—in her gleaming GE kitchen, at her Westinghouse Laundromat, before her Sylvania television set. Nothing is too good for her—unless she works for GE, or Westinghouse, or Sylvania or thousands of other corporations throughout the U.S.A.

As an employee, regardless of her skill she is rated lower common labor (male). She is assigned to jobs which, according to government studies, involve greater physical strain and skill than many jobs done by men—*but she is paid less than the underpaid sweeper, the least skilled men in the plant.* She is speeded up until she may faint at her machine, to barely earn her daily bread.

Wage discrimination against women workers exists in every industry where women are employed. . . . It is no accident that big business all over the world fought the movement for votes and equal rights for women. For in their factories, the public acceptance of women's equality would mean the loss of a huge source of labor they could segregate and exploit for extra profits, and as a means to hold down the wages of all workers. . . .

The situation of Negro women workers today is even more shocking. Even more than white women, Negro women have to work to live. For the discrimination that keeps Negro men at the bottom of the pay scale forces their wives to work to supplement the pitifully inadequate income of the family.

But Negro women are barred from almost all jobs except low-paying domestic service in private homes, or menial outside jobs as janitresses and scrubwomen. . . .

UE's fair practices committees in many local unions have been fighting the discrimination against hiring the Negro women in the electrical and machine industry, and the discriminatory practices that restrict Negro women to the most menial, lowest-paid jobs. . . . Negro women workers have a real stake in the UE's fight to end rate exploitation of women in industry, but their problems also require a special fight to lift the double bars against hiring of Negro women."

Recalling her work with women farmworkers, organizer Jessie Lopez de la Cruz told an interviewer in the late 1970s.

"When I became involved in the [farmworkers'] union, I felt I had to get other women involved. Women have been behind men all the time, always. . . . Then some women I spoke to started attending the union meetings, and later they were out on the picket lines. . . . I told them about how we . . . had no benefits, no minimum wage, nothing out in the fields—no restrooms, nothing. . . . I said, 'Well! Do you think we should be putting up with this in this modern age?'"

Speaking to an interviewer in 1986, Packinghouse Workers Union official Addie Wyatt recalled how her union's cross-race and cross-gender alliances facilitated activism for women's economic rights.

"[I]n 1953, I think it was, I went to . . . an anti-discrimination and women's conference held by our union, the United Packinghouse Workers. At that conference I saw women and men, black, white, and brown, take a leadership role. I also heard appeals to other blacks, Hispanics, and women like myself to run for positions in our local unions. . . . The union embraced the practice and the policies of equal pay for equal work. . . . The union really did an effective job of helping workers to understand that 'an injury to one is an injury to all.' The Packinghouse Workers Union was the strongest force and the strongest voice for minorities and for women and for wage earners. . . . We were pioneers in the equal rights movement. We were winning equal rights for women before the movement of the '60s and '70s really took off."

Women's rights advocates participated in the formation of the new United Nations in 1945 and served actively to shape its agenda. One result was the 1948 Universal Declaration of Human Rights; its provisions reflected the inclusion of women's rights as human rights, as well as the optimism for a better future that the UN's creation sparked.

The 1954 film *Salt of the Earth*, based on a successful strike at a zinc mine in New Mexico, dramatized women's rights in labor struggles. In the film, when the men are enjoined by a judge from picketing, the women take their places while the men assume their wives' family labor, trying to cook and care for children without indoor plumbing or hot water. As a result, the strike settlement includes both higher wages and improved sanitation and utility services in company-owned housing. Few Americans saw the film in the 1950s, however. Because of anticommunist hysteria, it was banned from distribution, many of the participants were blacklisted, and the female lead, Rosaura Revueltas, was deported to her native Mexico.

"Whereas recognition of the inherent dignity and of the equal and inalienable rights of all members of the human family is the foundation of freedom, justice and peace in the world . . .

Whereas, the peoples of the United Nations have in the Charter reaffirmed their faith in fundamental human rights, in the dignity and worth of the human person and in the equal rights of men and women . . .

Now, Therefore, THE GENERAL ASSEMBLY proclaims THIS UNIVERSAL DECLARATION OF HUMAN RIGHTS as a common standard of achievement for all peoples and all nations. . . .

Article 2. Everyone is entitled to all the rights and freedoms set forth in this Declaration, without distinction of any kind, such as race, colour, sex, language, religion, political or other opinion, national or social origin, property, birth or other status. . . .

Article 16. Men and women of full age, without any limitation due to race, nationality or religion, have the right to marry and to found a family. They are entitled to equal rights as to marriage, during marriage and its dissolution."

Eleanor Roosevelt devoted much of the last two decades of her life to service as an American delegate to the United Nations. In that capacity, she helped draft the Universal Declaration of Human Rights. In a 1951 statement on a subsequent "Convention on the Political Rights of Women," she stressed the need to move beyond suffrage to full inclusion of women in countries' policy-making bodies.

"As most of you know, the subject of this convention—equal suffrage for women—is very close to my heart. I believe in active citizenship, for men and women equally, as a simple matter of right and justice. I believe we will have better government in all of our countries when men and women discuss public issues together and make their decisions on the basis of their differing areas of experience and their common concern for the welfare of their families and the world.

In the United States, and in most countries today, women have equal suffrage. Some may feel for that reason this convention is of little importance to them. I do not agree with this view. It is true, of course, that the first objective of this convention is to encourage equal political rights for women in all countries. But its significance reaches far deeper into the real issue of whether in fact women are recognized fully in setting the policies of our governments.

While it is true that women in 45 of our 50 member nations vote on the same terms as men, and in 7 [additional member nations women] have partial voting rights, too often the great decisions are originated and given form in bodies made up wholly of men, or so completely dominated by them that whatever of special value women have to offer is shunted aside without expression. Even in countries where for many years women have voted and been eligible for public office, there are still too few women serving in positions of real leadership. I am not talking now in terms of paper parliaments and honorary appointments. . . . What I am talking about is whether women are sharing in the direction of the policy making in their countries; whether they have opportunities to serve as chairmen of important committees and as cabinet ministers and delegates to the United Nations."

During the post-war era, women and girls received a variety of mixed messages about womanhood, women's rights, and those who advocated for change. In their best-selling 1947 book, *Modern Woman: The Lost Sex*, the journalist Ferdinand Lundberg and the psychiatrist Marynia Farnham employed a crude version of Freudian theory to represent feminists as neurotic, needy, and unfulfilled, and to suggest that agitation for rights was unnecessary.

Sculptor Penelope Jencks's statue of Eleanor Roosevelt, dedicated in 1996, stands in Riverside Park, New York City.

"[I]t is our view, based on historic utterances of feminists, contemporary clinical data relating to women and psychiatric insight, that the entire feminist campaign was fundamentally about something quite other than it appeared to be about on the surface: woman's suffrage, woman's property laws and woman's education. . . .

It was fundamentally about something much deeper, of greater social and psychological consequence. . . . Unconsciously, the feminists were more interested in what we term the 'feminist ideology' than in the program of women's rights and privileges. And although the rights have since been won, the ideology lingers on and is frequently encountered today in the psychoanalysis of women. It is an intellectual construction growing out of deep emotional maladjustment and bewilderment.

This ideology . . . bespoke fierce hatred of the male. . . . The feminists, in brief, were out to get rid of their femaleness and to limit male privileges. It was their femaleness, they concluded, that was at the root of their many tribulations—political, economic, social and sexual. . . . Most of the social and political program of feminism . . . was an ego-prop, sought by the most articulate and

Wedding rings: "There was a time when it was considered odd in the U.S. for males to wear wedding rings. But those who indulge in the practice can now be assured of being perfectly acceptable. Since 1939, the percentage of double-ring—as against single-ring—marriages has increased from 15 to at least 80 per cent."—"Ring Twice," *Fortune Magazine*, November, 1947. Historically, only women wore wedding rings. The symbolism was profound: the wife's encirclement in the bonds of matrimony signaled to other men that she was "taken"—not sexually available. The post-war change to double-ring weddings represented new gender ideals by which men as well as women were to commit themselves to marriage and family life.

1950s Working Mothers: Popular images of "typical" 1950s women as housewives conflicted with a striking increase in the workforce presence of wives and mothers during the decade. The contradiction between image and reality was evident in the lives of working mothers such as Barbara Billingsley (June Cleaver on "Leave It to Beaver") and Lucille Ball ("I Love Lucy") who played stay-at-home mothers on TV. Ball not only starred as Lucy Ricardo, she was also the show's co-producer and co-owner of Desilu Studios. In the 1950s, Phyllis Schlafly raised six children, ran for Congress, published several books, served in state and national offices with the Daughters of the American Revolution, and was president of the Illinois Federation of Republican Women. In 1978, she completed her law degree. Working mother Betty Friedan had an active career as a journalist for labor and popular magazines during the 1950s.

A 1957 cover of *The Ladder* encouraged lesbians to "take off the mask" and be themselves.

emotionally deprived women as a way of restoring their self-esteem and self-confidence.... In the woman of feminist orientation (masculinity complex), the penis-envy defect has succeeded...in showing itself more or less clearly. Such a woman lives out her neurosis, expresses it for all to see by celebrating whatever is peculiarly male and deprecating whatever is peculiarly female....She is almost certain to have 'man trouble' of one kind or another."

Table 7.1 The Female Labor Force, 1940–1956

In the midst of mixed messages about women's roles, in 1957, the National Manpower Council published a report, *Womanpower,* that called attention to "a revolution in women's employment." A particularly striking table demonstrated clearly that in the post-war era, the proportion of women in the paid labor force had risen consistently.

Year	Thousands	Percent of Women Aged 14 and Over	Percent of All Workers
1940	13,840	27.6	25.4
1941	13,930	27.4	25.3
1942	15,460	30.1	27.7
1943	18,100	34.9	33.0
1944	18,450	35.2	34.0
1945	19,570	37.0	36.1
1946	16,590	30.9	29.4
1947	16,320	30.0	27.6
1948	17,155	31.2	28.3
1949	17,167	30.9	28.2
1950	18,063	32.1	29.0
1951	16,607	32.7	30.1
1952	18,798	32.7	30.4
1953	19,296	33.1	30.6
1954	19,726	33.4	30.8
1955	20,154	33.8	31.2
1956	21,194	35.1	31.8

Despite the repressive political climate of the 1950s, when homosexuality was routinely described as an illness, in 1955 four San Francisco lesbian couples founded a lesbian civil rights organization, the Daughters of Bilitis. The group listed its goals in a 1957 issue of its publication, *The Ladder*.

"A Women's Organization for the Purpose of Promoting the Integration of the Homosexual into Society by:

1. Education of the variant, with particular emphasis on the psychological, physiological and sociological aspects, to

enable her to understand herself and make her adjustment to society in all its social, civic and economic implications. . . .

2. Education of the public at large through acceptance first of the individual, leading to an eventual breakdown of erroneous conceptions, taboos and prejudices; through public discussion meetings aforementioned; through dissemination of educational literature on the homosexual theme.

3. Participation in research projects by duly authorized and responsible psychology, sociology and other such experts directed toward further knowledge of the homosexual.

4. Investigation of the penal code as it pertains to the homosexual, proposal of changes to provide an equitable handling of cases involving this minority group, and promotion of these changes through due process of law in the state legislatures."

SCIENCE

THE VICE PRESIDENT
WASHINGTON
March 15, 1962

Dear Jim:

I have conferred with Mrs. Philip Hart and Miss Jerrie Cobb concerning their effort to get women utilized as astronauts. I'm sure you agree that sex should not be a reason for disqualifying a candidate for orbital flight.

Could you advise me whether NASA has disqualified anyone because of being a woman?

As I understand it, two principal requirements for orbital flight at this stage are: 1) that the individual be experienced at high speed military test flying; and 2) that the individual have an engineering background enabling him to take over controls in the event it became necessary.

Would you advise me whether there are any women who meet these qualifications?

If not, could you estimate for me the time when orbital flight will have become sufficiently safe that these two requirements are no longer necessary and a larger number of individuals may qualify?

I know we both are grateful for the desire to serve on the part of these women, and look forward to the time when they can.

Sincerely,

Lets stop this now!

Lyndon B. Johnson

File

Mr. James E. Webb
Administrator
National Aeronautics and Space Administration
Washington, D. C.

COPY LBJ LIBRARY

Vice-President Lyndon Johnson refused to sign a 1962 letter drafted by his assistant, Liz Carpenter, approving the training of women astronauts. His peremptory order, "Let's stop this now!" dashed the hopes of the thirteen women pilots who had expected to pioneer in space. Not until 1983 did astrophysicist Sally Ride become the first American woman in space.

Feminism: Women's Rights

Post-war women's rights activists achieved an important victory when in 1961, as a result of the pressure they brought to bear upon him, President John F. Kennedy created the President's Commission on the Status of Women (PCSW), led by longtime labor feminist Esther Peterson and chaired by Eleanor Roosevelt. The commission's twenty-six core members, many of them with lengthy histories in grassroots women's organizations, issued a landmark report in 1963. In it, the commissioners mentioned the considerations that shaped their approach. The commission's three-hundred-page report, plus additional supporting volumes, replete with charts, tables, and statistics detailing widespread sex and race discrimination, laid out in detail a variety of areas in which women's

legal and civil status was unequal to that of men, giving particular attention to the disabilities married women still faced under coverture.

"Throughout its deliberations, the Commission has kept in mind certain women who have special disadvantages. Among heads of families in the United States, 1 in 10 is a woman. At least half of them are carrying responsibility for both earning the family's living and making the family's home. . . .

Seven million nonwhite women and girls belong to minority racial groups. Discrimination based on color is morally wrong and a source of national weakness. Such discrimination currently places an oppressive dual burden on millions of Negro women. . . .

Hundreds of thousands of other women face somewhat similar situations: American Indians, for instance; and Spanish-Americans, many of whom live in urban centers but are new to urban life and burdened with language problems. . . .

The Commission strongly urges that in the carrying out of its recommendations, special attention be given to difficulties that are wholly or largely the products of this kind of discrimination. [Recommendations:]

PERSONAL AND PROPERTY RIGHTS. . . . In the [42] separate property states [that follow English common law practices], a wife has no legal rights to any part of her husband's earnings or property during the existence of the marriage, aside from the right to be properly supported. Hence, if she does not have earnings or property of her own, she is completely dependent upon his largesse for anything above and beyond the money she needs for support. On the other hand, under [the 8 state] community-property systems, a wife has an interest in the commonly owned property, but a husband generally has exclusive authority to manage and control that property. . . . A number of states limit [a married woman's] right to sue or be sued in her own name . . . . A few states still restrict the right of a wife to engage in a separate business. . . .

DOMICILE. A person's domicile or legal residence is important because it may determine many personal rights and obligations, . . . [such as where] the right to vote may be exercised, where an individual may run for public office, . . . where a divorce may be filed, . . . where one may receive welfare benefits, and where one may be eligible for admission to . . . state institutions [such as universities]. A person's domicile generally is the place which he intends to be his permanent home. However, this rule does not normally apply to married women . . . [because] her domicile . . . is her husband's, without regard to her intent or actual residence.

GUARDIANSHIP OF CHILDREN. . . . 6 states . . . still provide by statute that the father is the preferred natural guardian of a minor child.

[An invitation to action:]

HOME AND COMMUNITY: For the benefit of children, mothers, and society, child-care services should be available for children of families at all economic levels. . . .

WOMEN IN EMPLOYMENT: Equal opportunity for women in hiring, training, and promotion should be the governing principle in private employment. . . .

LABOR STANDARDS: . . . State laws should establish the principle of equal pay for comparable work. State laws should protect the rights of workers to join unions of their own choosing and to bargain collectively.

SECURITY OF BASIC INCOME: A widow's benefit under the federal old-age insurance system [Social Security] should be equal to the amount that her husband would have received at the same age had he lived. . . . Paid maternity leave or comparable insurance benefits should be provided for women workers. . . .

WOMEN UNDER THE LAW: Early and definitive court pronouncement, particularly by the United States Supreme Court, is urgently needed with regard to the validity under the Fifth and Fourteenth Amendments of laws and official practices discriminating against women, to the end that the principle of equality become firmly established in constitutional doctrine. . . . State legislatures . . . concerned with the improvement of state statutes affecting family law and personal and property rights of married women, . . . should move to eliminate laws which impose legal disabilities on women.

WOMEN AS CITIZENS: Women should be encouraged to seek elective and appointive posts at local, state, and national levels. . . ."

The year 1963 also marked the publication of *The Feminine Mystique*, Betty Friedan's best-selling book detailing the discontents of educated middle-class suburban women. Despite her own background as a labor journalist and advocate for working women's economic rights, Friedan focused the book on the concerns of women coping with what she termed "the problem that has no name" and issued a call to action.

"On the ERA question, we ultimately settled on a carefully worded compromise. . . . The report stated first that equal rights for all persons is basic to democracy and must be reflected in the law of the land. But we argued that the principle of equality was embodied in the Fifth and 14th Amendments to the Constitution and that a separate Equal Rights Amendment was not necessary. . . . I strongly believed that specific legislation targeting specific problems—specific bills for specific ills—was a far more effective way of getting focused results and reforms than a one-sentence addition to the Constitution."

—Esther Peterson on why the Commission report refused to endorse an ERA

"Gradually, without seeing it clearly for quite a while, I came to realize that something is very wrong with the way American women are trying to live their lives today. I sensed it first as a question mark in my own life, as a wife and mother of three small children, half-guiltily, and therefore half-heartedly, almost in spite of myself, using my abilities and education in work that took me away from home. . . . The problems and satisfactions of [my Smith College classmates'] lives, and mine, and the way our education had contributed to them, simply did not fit the image of the modern American woman as she was written about in women's magazines, studied and analyzed in classrooms and clinics, praised and damned in a ceaseless barrage of words ever since the end of World War II. There was a strange discrepancy between the reality of our lives as women and the image to which we were trying to conform, the image that I came to call the feminine mystique. . . .

The problem lay buried, unspoken, for many years in the minds of American women. It was a strange stirring, a sense of dissatisfaction, a yearning that women suffered in the middle of the twentieth century in the United States. Each suburban wife struggled with it alone. As she made the beds, shopped for groceries, matched slipcover material, ate peanut butter sandwiches with her children, chauffeured Cub Scouts and Brownies, lay beside her husband at night—she was afraid to ask even of herself the silent question—'Is this all?' . . .

[T]here was no word of this yearning in the millions of words written about women, for women, . . . telling women that their role was to seek fulfillment as wives and mothers. Over and over women heard in voices of tradition and of Freudian sophistication that they could desire no greater destiny than to glory in their own femininity. . . . They were taught to pity the neurotic, unfeminine, unhappy women who wanted to be poets or physicists or presidents. They learned that truly feminine women do not want careers, higher education, political rights—the independence and the opportunities that the old-fashioned feminists fought for. . . . [They learned that] all they had to do was devote their lives from earliest girlhood to finding a husband and bearing children. . . . Nobody argued whether women were inferior or superior to men; they were simply different. Words like 'emancipation' and 'career' sounded strange and embarrassing; no one had used them for years. . . . The 'woman problem' in America no longer existed.

If a woman had a problem in the 1950s and 1960s she knew that something must be wrong with her marriage, or with herself. Other women were satisfied with their lives, she thought. What kind of a woman was she if she did not feel this mysterious fulfillment waxing the kitchen floor? She was so ashamed to admit her dissatisfaction that she never knew how many other women shared it. . . . But . . . suddenly they realized they all shared the same problem, the problem that has no name. They began, hesitantly, to talk about it. . . .

[E]very woman . . . must create, out of her own needs and abilities, a new life plan, . . . Not until a great many women move out of the fringes into the mainstream will society itself provide the arrangements for their new life plan. But every girl who manages to stick it out through law school or medical school, who finishes her M.A. or Ph.D. and goes on to use it, helps others to move on. Every woman who fights the remaining barriers to full equality which are masked by the feminine mystique makes it easier for the next woman. The very existence of the President's Commission on the Status of Women, under Eleanor Roosevelt's leadership, creates a climate where it is possible to recognize and do something about discrimination against women, in terms not only of pay but of the subtle barriers to opportunity. Even in politics, women must make their contribution not as 'housewives' but as citizens."

Between 1963 and 1965, Congress passed three laws with significant consequences for women's rights.

1963 Equal Pay Act: "No employer having employees subject to any provisions of this section shall discriminate, within any establishment in which such employees are employed, between employees on the basis of sex by paying wages to employees in such establishment at a rate less than the rate at which he pays wages to employees of the opposite sex in such establishment for equal work on jobs the performance of which requires equal skill, effort, and responsibility, and which are performed under similar working conditions, . . . "

1964 Civil Rights Act: [Title VII] "It shall be unlawful employment practice for any employer—

1. to fail or refuse to hire or to discharge any individual or otherwise to discriminate against any individual with respect to his compensation, terms, conditions, or privileges

Long before Title VII became part of the 1964 Civil Rights Act, lawyer and human rights activist **Pauli Murray** (1910–1985) had coined the term "Jane Crow," to refer to discriminatory practices based on race and sex. By pressing for an interpretation of civil rights laws that linked the two intersecting forms of exclusion, she suggested a new legal strategy to bring together two movements—civil rights and women's rights—that had largely operated separately since the early 20th century. Murray spent her adult life challenging restrictive policies based on race and gender. Turned down for admittance to the University of North Carolina Law School because of her race, she attended Howard University, and upon graduation was refused admittance to Harvard University Law School's graduate program because of her sex. She went to the University of California, writing her 1945 graduate thesis on "The Right to Equal Opportunity in Employment." As a practicing lawyer, she made important contributions to constitutional legal theory on race and sex discrimination, serving on the President's Commission on the Status of Women and helping to found the National Organization for Women in 1966. Responding to a deeply spiritual sense of calling, she shifted careers in the 1970s, attending divinity school and pressing the Episcopal Church to change its policy on the ordination of women. In 1977, she became one of the first women to be ordained by the church, and its first African American female priest. Until her final illness, Rev. Murray served churches in Washington, D.C., and Baltimore, Maryland.

of employment, because of such individual's race, color, religion, sex, or national origin; or,

2. to limit, segregate, or classify his employees in any way which would deprive or tend to deprive any individual of employment opportunities or otherwise adversely affect his status as an employee, because of such individual's race, color, religion, sex, or national origin."

1965 Voting Rights Act: "No voting qualification or prerequisite to voting, or standard, practice, or procedure shall be imposed or applied by any State or political subdivision to deny or abridge the right of any citizen of the United States to vote on account of race or color."

Dissatisfaction with the slow pace at which the President's Commission's recommendations were being implemented boiled over at a 1966 meeting of state Commissions on the Status of Women. Twenty-eight attendees became the founding group for a new National Organization for Women (NOW). The group set out its goals in a 1968 "Bill of Rights for 1969."

"We demand:

I. That the United States Congress immediately pass the Equal Rights Amendment to the Constitution . . . and that such then be immediately ratified by the several states.

II. That equal employment opportunity be guaranteed to all women, as well as men, by insisting that the Equal Employment Opportunity Commission enforces the prohibitions against sex discrimination in employment under Title VII of the Civil Rights Act of 1964 with the same vigor as it enforces the prohibitions against racial discrimination.

III. That women be protected by law to ensure their rights to return to their jobs within a reasonable time after childbirth without loss of seniority or other accrued benefits, and be paid maternity leave as a form of social security and/or employee benefits.

IV. Immediate revision of tax laws to permit the deduction of home and child care expenses for working parents.

V. That child care facilities be established by law on the same basis as parks, libraries, and public schools, adequate to the needs of children from the preschool years through adolescence, as a community resource to be used by all citizens from all income levels.

VI. That the right of women to be educated to their full potential equally with men be secured by Federal and State legislation, eliminating all discrimination and segregation by sex, written and unwritten, at all levels of education. . . .

VII. That the right of women in poverty to secure job training, housing, and family allowances on equal terms with men, but without prejudice to a parent's right to remain at home to care for his or her children; revision of welfare legislation and poverty programs which deny women dignity, privacy and self-respect.

VIII. The right of women to control their own reproductive lives by removing from penal codes laws limiting access to contraceptive information and devices and laws governing abortion."

Like the founders of NOW, those who created the National Welfare Rights Organization (NWRO) defined welfare as a women's rights issue. In a 1972 article, the group's chairperson, Johnnie Tillmon, explained the connection.

"Welfare's like a traffic accident. It can happen to anybody, but especially it happens to women. And that is why welfare is a women's issue. . . .

Forty-four per cent of all poor families are headed by women. . . . [But] 99 per cent of [families on welfare] are headed by women. That means there is no man around. In half the states there really can't be men around because A.F.D.C. [Aid to Families with Dependent Children] says if there is an 'able-bodied' man around, then you can't be on welfare. If the kids are going to eat, and the man can't get a job, then he's got to go . . . So his kids can eat. . . .

On A.F.D.C., . . . you give up control of your own body. It's a condition of aid. You may even have to agree to get your tubes tied so you can never have more children just to avoid being cut off welfare. . . .

The truth is a job doesn't necessarily mean an adequate income. A woman with three kids— not twelve kids, mind you, just three kids—that woman earning the full Federal minimum wage of $1.60 an hour, is still stuck in poverty. She is below the Government's own official poverty

"We, men and women who hereby constitute ourselves as the National Organization for Women, believe that the time has come for a new movement toward true equality for all women in America, and toward a fully equal partnership of the sexes, as part of the world-wide revolution of human rights now taking place within and beyond our national borders. The purpose of NOW is to take action to bring women into full participation in the mainstream of American society now. . . . "
—NOW Statement of Purpose, 1966

Some founders of NOW. They are, from left, Michigan's Dorothy Haener of the United Auto Workers; Sister Mary Joel Read, a member of the School Sisters of St. Francis and later president of Alverno College in Wisconsin; Anna Arnold Hedgeman, an African American civil rights activist and Methodist churchwoman; Betty Friedan; Brooklyn-born Inez Casiano, who worked for the Puerto Rican Community Development Project and later was an advisor to the U.S. Secretary of Labor; Richard Graham, an EEOC commissioner and later president of Goddard College; and Inka O'Hanrahan of the California Commission on the Status of Women. Absent from the photograph was Pauli Murray, who stepped out of camera range in order to push Anna Hedgeman forward.

line. There are some ten million jobs that now pay less than the minimum wage, and if you're a woman, you've got the best chance of getting one. . . .

Maybe it is we poor welfare women who will really liberate women in this country. We've already started on our own welfare plan.

Along with other welfare recipients, we have organized together so we can have some voice. Our group is called the National Welfare Rights Organization (N.W.R.O.). We put together our own welfare plan, called Guaranteed Adequate Income (G.A.I.) which would eliminate sexism from welfare. . . .

If I were president, I would solve this so-called welfare crisis in a minute and go a long way toward liberating every woman. I'd just issue a proclamation that 'women's' work is real work.

In other words, I'd start paying women a living wage for doing the work we are already doing—childraising and housekeeping. And the welfare crisis would be over, just like that. Housewives would be getting wages, too—a legally determined percentage of their husband's salary—instead of having to ask for and account for money they've already earned. . . .

No woman in this country can feel dignified, no woman can be liberated, until all women get off their knees. That's what N.W.R.O. is all about—women standing together, on their feet."

With the support of organizations such as NOW, women's rights activists challenged women's unequal legal, political, economic, and personal status in both legislative halls and courts. In the arena of reproductive rights, they sought an end to the practice of involuntarily sterilizing poor women, and championed repeal of laws restricting women's right to acquire contraceptives and to seek abortions. In the 1965 case of *Griswold v. Connecticut*, the Supreme Court overturned one of the last vestiges of the old Comstock laws, a Connecticut statute dating to 1879 making it illegal for married couples to use contraceptives.

"[Mr. Justice Douglas]: The present case, then, concerns a relationship lying within the zone of privacy created by several fundamental constitutional guarantees. And it concerns a law which, in forbidding the use of contraceptives, rather than regulating their manufacture or sale, seeks to achieve its goals by means having a maximum destructive impact upon that relationship. Such a law cannot stand in light of the familiar principle, so often applied by this Court, that a 'governmental purpose to control or prevent activities constitutionally subject to state regulation may not be achieved by means which sweep unnecessarily broadly and thereby invade the area of protected freedoms.' . . . Would we allow the police to search the sacred precincts of marital bedrooms for telltale signs of the use of contraceptives? The very idea is repulsive to the notions of privacy surrounding the marriage relationship. We deal with a right of privacy older than the Bill of Rights—older than our political parties, older than our school system. . . . "

Women's obligations as citizens remained different from men's in the area of jury service, where a few states still systematically exempted them from jury duty. A 1961 Supreme Court decision had permitted the practice on the grounds that, whereas for male citizens, jury service was a duty, for female citizens, it was a privilege because "woman is still regarded as the center of home and family life." Arguing that equal legal status included equal obligations, lawyers working with the Women's Rights Law Project of the American Civil Liberties Union, founded by Ruth Bader Ginsburg in 1972, won a reversal of that decision in the 1975 case of *Taylor v. Louisiana*.

"[Mr. Justice Byron White]: [When this case was tried], . . . the Louisiana Code of Criminal Procedure provided that a woman should not be selected for jury service unless she had previously filed a written declaration of her desire to be subject to jury service. The constitutionality of these provisions is the issue in this case. . . . The Louisiana jury selection system does not disqualify women from jury service, but in operation its conceded systematic impact is that only a very few women . . . are called for jury service. . . . The issue we have, therefore, is whether a jury selection system

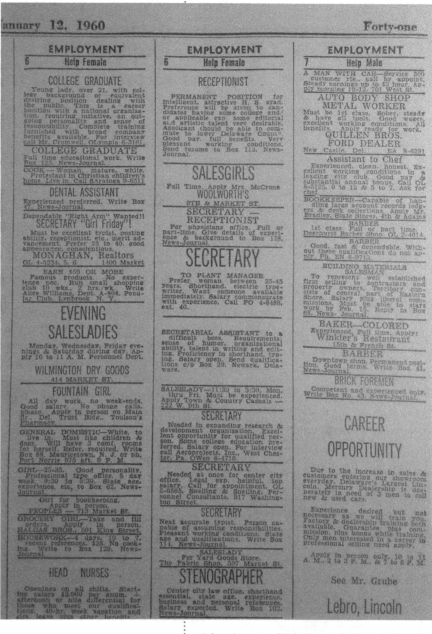

Advertisement: "Help Wanted—Female." Until women's rights activists won a ruling from the Equal Employment Opportunity Commission in 1969, women's economic opportunities were restricted by race- and sex-specific advertising, such as this 1960 employment ad from the *Wilmington (Delaware) Every Evening*. In 1960, it was legal to advertise jobs restricted to "women" or "white" women.

which operates to exclude from jury service an identifiable class of citizens constituting 53% of eligible jurors in the community comports with the Sixth and Fourteenth Amendments. . . . [As the Court held in *Ballard v. United States*], 'if the shoe were on the other foot, who would claim that a jury was truly representative of the community if all men were intentionally and systematically excluded from the panel? The truth is that the two sexes are not fungible; a community made up exclusively of one is different from a community composed of both' . . . . If the fair cross-section rule is to govern the selection of juries . . . women cannot be systematically excluded from jury panels. . . ."

Feminism: Women's Liberation

Believing that the fundamental causes of women's inequality lay deeper than law and public policy could reach, younger women began to talk about "women's liberation." Rejecting what they saw as the gradualist approach of women's rights feminists and organizations like NOW, they traced their new-found feminism to their personal experiences in the civil rights and New Left student protest groups ("the Movement"), and connected their struggle to liberation movements around the world. A 1967 "Statement of Principles" created by a group of Chicago women summing up some of their views echoed earlier calls for women's "emancipation."

M*ale chauvinism*: The term referred to male assumptions of the superiority of their sex, and the continuing power of gender hierarchy in American society. Its use by women's liberation feminists reflected their familiarity with the terms and concepts used earlier in the century by members of left-wing political groups.

"Our political awareness of our oppression has developed . . . as we sought to apply the principles of justice, equality, mutual respect and dignity which we learned from the Movement . . . only to come up against the solid wall of **male chauvinism**. Realizing that this is a social problem of national significance not at all confined to our struggle for personal liberation, within the Movement we must approach it in a political manner. Therefore it is incumbent on us, as women, to organize a movement for woman's liberation. . . . The liberation of women cannot be divorced from the larger revolutionary struggle. . . . [W]e identify with those groups now in revolutionary struggle within our country and abroad. Until the movement recognizes the necessity that women be free and women recognize the necessity for all struggles of liberation, there can be no revolution."

Women's Liberation feminists burst into public awareness when New York Radical Women mounted a protest against the Miss America Pageant in Atlantic City, New Jersey, in 1968. One of the organizers, journalist Carol Hanisch, explained the rationale for the protest in a document entitled "A Critique of the Miss America Protest."

"The protest of the Miss America Pageant in Atlantic City in September told the nation that a new feminist movement is afoot in the land. Due to the tremendous coverage in the mass media, millions of Americans now know there is a Women's Liberation Movement. The action brought many new members into our group and many requests from women outside the city for literature and information. A recurrent theme was, 'I've been waiting so long for something like this.' . . . The idea for the protest came out of the method used first in New York Radical Women of analyzing women's oppression by analyzing our own experiences, called consciousness-raising. . . . We decided to go around the room with each woman telling how she felt about the pageant. We discovered that many of us who had always put down the contest still watched it. Others had consciously identified with it. . . .

[We] agreed that the main point in the demonstration would be that all women are hurt by beauty competition—Miss America as well as ourselves. . . . We tried to carry the democratic means we used in planning the action into the actual doing of it. We didn't want leaders or spokesmen. It makes the movement not only *seem* stronger and larger if everyone is a leader, but it actually *is* stronger if not dependent on a few. And of course, many voices are more powerful than one."

The slogan "the personal is political" became a shorthand way to say that changing power relationships in both women's personal lives and within social institutions was the key to women's liberation. The technique of "consciousness raising" was widely used by women's liberation feminist groups to make the slogan an actuality. In a 1970 pamphlet entitled "What We Do at Meetings," the members of the Gainesville, Florida, Women's Liberation group explained the technique.

"[Our meetings center] around a question that each woman can answer by giving her own experiences. Sometimes we decide on a question that has been used successfully in other groups, but most often we think up our own . . ., ask[ing] how we feel about something, not just what happened. . . . In answering the question we sit in a circle (of sorts) and go around the room. Each woman answers the question from her personal experiences, instead of what she read in a book somewhere, or what she heard somebody else say about it. . . . We need to change what causes our problems, not just adjust to those bad conditions. One of the first things we discovered in the [consciousness-raising] group is that personal problems are really political problems. That is, there is no way out by ourselves.

Although protesters simply threw various "instruments of torture," such as hair curlers, false eyelashes, girdles, and bras into a "Freedom Trash Can," the media epithet that they were "bra-burners" stuck.

We need collective action for a collective solution. This is not to deny that these sessions make us feel better about ourselves. When we hear other women have the same problems we say, 'Wow! It's not my fault. There's nothing wrong with ME.'"

In her 1970 essay on "The Politics of Housework," Pat Mainardi echoed themes first articulated by early 20th-century feminists and provided a concrete example of how personal experience with something as ordinary as housework could reveal broader societal ideas about women's work and men's work. Using humor and wit, she dissected the assumptions underlying the allocation of tasks at home, assumptions that permitted men to enjoy leisure time while women performed unpaid labor.

"Liberated women—very different from women's liberation! The first signals all kinds of goodies, to warm the hearts (not to mention other parts) of the most radical men. The other signals—*housework*. The first brings sex without marriage, sex before marriage, cozy housekeeping arrangements... and the self-content of knowing that you're not the kind of man who wants a doormat instead of a woman....

On the other hand is women's liberation—and housework. What? You say this is all trivial. Wonderful! That's what I thought. It seemed perfectly reasonable. We both had careers, ... so why shouldn't we share the housework? So I suggested it to my mate and he agreed—most men are too hip to turn you down flat. 'You're right,' he said. 'It's only fair.'

Then an interesting thing happened. I can only explain it by stating that we women have been brainwashed more than even we can imagine. Probably too many years of seeing television women in ecstasy over their shiny waxed floors or breaking down over their dirty shirt collars. Men have no such conditioning.... All of us have to do [dirty chores], or get someone else to do them for us. The longer my husband contemplated these chores the more repulsed he became, and so proceeded the change from the normally sweet considerate Dr. Jekyll into the crafty Mr. Hyde, who would stop at nothing to avoid the horrors of—*housework*.... Housework trivial? Not on your life! Just try to share the burden.

So ensued a dialogue that's been going on for several years. Here are some of the high points:

'I don't mind sharing the housework, but I don't do it very well. We should each do the things we're best at.'

Meaning: Unfortunately I'm no good at things like washing dishes or cooking. What I do best is a little light carpentry, changing light bulbs, moving furniture (*how often do you move furniture?*) . . .

'I *hate* it more than you. You don't mind it so much.'

Meaning: Housework is . . . the worst crap I've ever done. It's degrading and humiliating for someone of *my* intelligence to do it. But for someone of *your* intelligence. . . .

'Housework is too trivial to even talk about.'

Meaning: It's even more trivial to do. Housework is beneath my status. My purpose in life is to deal with matters of significance. . . . You should do the housework. . . .

'Man's accomplishments have always depended on getting help from other people, mostly women. What great man would have accomplished what he did if he had to do his own housework?'

Meaning: Oppression is built into the System and I as the white American male receive the benefits of this system. I don't want to give them up. . . .

I was just finishing this when my husband came in and asked what I was doing. Writing a paper on housework. *Housework?* Oh my god how trivial can you get. A paper on housework."

The group Redstockings staked out a radical feminist position on male-female relations in its 1969 "Manifesto" identifying "male supremacy" (or gender hierarchy) as the root cause of women's historical and contemporary condition.

"I. After centuries of individual and preliminary political struggle, women are uniting to achieve their final liberation from male supremacy. Redstockings is dedicated to building this unity and winning our freedom.

II. Women are an oppressed class. Our oppression is total, affecting every facet of our lives. We are exploited as sex objects, breeders, domestic servants, and cheap labor. We are considered inferior beings, whose only purpose is to enhance men's lives. Our humanity is denied. Our prescribed behavior is enforced by the threat of physical violence.

Because we have lived so intimately with our oppressors, in isolation from each other, we have been kept from seeing our personal suffering as a political condition. This creates the illusion that a woman's relationship with her man is a matter of interplay between two unique personalities, and can be worked out. In reality, every such relationship is a *class* relationship, and the conflicts between individual women and men are *political* conflicts that can only be solved collectively.

III. We identify the agents of our oppression as men. Male supremacy is the oldest, most basic form of domination. All other forms of exploitation and oppression (racism, capitalism, imperialism, etc.) are extensions of male supremacy; men dominate women, a few men dominate the rest. All power structures throughout history have been male-dominated and male-oriented. Men have controlled all political, economic and cultural institutions and back up this control with physical force. They have used their power to keep women in an inferior position. *All men* receive economic, sexual, and psychological benefits from male supremacy. *All men* have oppressed women.

IV. Attempts have been made to shift the burden of responsibility from men to institutions or to women themselves. We condemn these arguments as evasions. Institutions alone do not oppress; they are merely tools of the oppressor. To blame institutions implies that men and women are equally victimized, obscures the fact that men benefit from the subordination of women, and gives men the excuse that they are forced to be oppressors. On the contrary, any man is free to renounce his superior position, provided that he is willing to be treated like a woman by other men.

We also reject the idea that women consent to or are to blame for their own oppression. Women's submission is not the result of brain-washing, stupidity or mental illness but of continual, daily pressure from men. We do not need to change ourselves, but to change men.

The most slanderous evasion of all is that women can oppress men. The basis for this illusion is the isolation of individual relationships from their political context and the tendency of men to see any legitimate challenge to their privileges as persecution.

V. We regard our personal experience, and our feelings about that experience, as the basis for an analysis of our common situation. We cannot rely on existing ideologies as they are all products of male supremacist culture. We question every generalization and accept none that are not confirmed by our experience.

Our chief task at present is to develop female class consciousness through sharing experience and publicly exposing the sexist foundation of all our institutions. Consciousness-raising is not 'therapy,' which implies the existence of individual solutions and falsely assumes that the male-female relationship is purely personal, but the only method by which we can ensure that our program for liberation is based on the concrete realities of our lives.

The first requirement for raising class consciousness is honesty, in private and in public, with ourselves and other women.

VI. We identify with all women. We define our best interest as that of the poorest, most brutally exploited women.

We repudiate all economic, racial, educational or status privileges that divide us from other women. We are determined to recognize and eliminate any prejudices we may hold against other women.

We are committed to achieving internal democracy. We will do whatever is necessary to ensure that every woman in our movement has an equal chance to participate, assume responsibility, and develop her political potential.

VII. We call on all our sisters to unite with us in struggle.

We call on all men to give up their male privilege and support women's liberation in the interest of our humanity and their own.

In fighting for our liberation we will always take the side of women against their oppressors. We will not ask what is 'revolutionary' or 'reformist,' only what is good for women.

The time for individual skirmishes has passed. This time we are going all the way."

Members of the group Radicalesbians, in their 1970 manifesto, embraced the term "lesbian," challenged readers to do the same, and claimed the radical feminist mantle for themselves.

"What is a lesbian? A lesbian is the rage of all women condensed to the point of explosion. She is the woman who . . . acts in accordance with her inner compulsion to be a more complete and freer human being than her society . . . cares to allow her. . . . But lesbianism is also different from male homosexuality, and serves a different function in the society. . . . Lesbian is the word, the label, the

"Redstockings" chose a name that rejected the old slur that intellectual women were unfeminine "blue-stockings"; the "red" in the group's name signaled their self-identification as Marxist feminists.

"It's hard to convey to people who didn't go through that experience how radical, how unpopular and difficult and scary it was just to get up and say, 'Men oppress women. Men have oppressed me. . . .' We were laughed at, patronized, called frigid, emotionally disturbed man-haters."

—Ellen Willis, a founder of Redstockings, 1992

In 1973, responding to challenges from lesbian and gay rights groups, and acknowledging the lack of any evidence for its categorization as a "mental disorder," the American Psychiatric Association removed homosexuality from the *Diagnostic and Statistical Manual of Mental Disorders*.

condition that holds women in line. When a woman hears this word tossed her way, she knows she is stepping out of line. She knows that she has crossed the terrible boundary of her sex role. She recoils, she protests, she reshapes her actions to gain approval. Lesbian is a label invented by the man to throw at any woman who dares to be his equal, who dares to challenge his prerogatives, . . . who dares to assert the primacy of her own needs. . . . For in this sexist society, for a woman to be independent means she *can't* be a *woman*—she must be a *dyke*."

In a 1969 essay, black feminist Frances Beal, whose personal experience had been shaped by her activism within the Student Non-Violent Coordinating Committee (SNCC) and the black power movement, analyzed the "double jeopardy" or intersecting oppressions that African American women faced and the pressure they felt to defer to male leadership.

"[I]t is idle dreaming to think of black women simply caring for their homes and children like the middle class white model. Most black women have to work to help house, feed, and clothe their families. Black women make up a substantial percentage of the black working force and this is true for the poorest black family as well as the so-called 'middle-class' family. . . . [B]lack women are not resentful of the rise to power of black men. We welcome it. We see in it the eventual liberation of all black people from this oppressive System of capitalism. Nevertheless, this does not mean that you have to negate one for the other. This kind of thinking is a product of miseducation; that it's either X or it's Y. It is fallacious reasoning that in order for the black man to be strong, the black woman has to be weak. . . . [W]e must begin talking about the elimination of all kinds of oppression. . . . We need our whole army out there dealing with the enemy and not half an army. . . . It becomes essential . . . to realize that the exploitation of black people and women works to everyone's disadvantage and that the liberation of these two groups is a stepping stone to the liberation of all oppressed people in this country and around the world."

Emphasizing women's personal freedom, women's liberation feminists created alternative, woman-oriented institutions that emphasized self-help. The Boston Women's Health Book Collective, deeply critical of how the existing health care system treated women, produced a major work in 1970 entitled *Our Bodies, Ourselves*. Its explicit discussion of issues ranging from abortion to lesbian sex was both shocking and empowering. The group explained its approach in the work's first edition.

"A year ago, a group of us . . . got together to work on a laywoman's course on health, women and our bodies. . . . [S]everal of us developed a questionnaire about women's feelings about their bodies and their relationship to doctors. We discovered there were no 'good' doctors and we had to learn for ourselves. We talked about our own experiences and we shared our own knowledge. We went to books and to medically trained people for more information. We decided on the topics collectively. (Originally, they included: Patient as Victim; Sexuality; Anatomy; Birth Control; Abortion; Pregnancy; Prepared Childbirth; Postpartum and Childcare; Medical Institutions; Medical Laws; and Organizing for Change.) . . .

It was exciting to learn new facts about our bodies, but it was even more exciting to talk about how we felt about our bodies, how we felt about ourselves, how we could become more autonomous human beings, how we could act together on our collective knowledge to change the health care system for women and for all people."

As women's rights feminists worked through the courts and legal system to legalize abortion, women's liberation feminists in Chicago created a women's healthcare center and established a network to assist women seeking safe (illegal) abortions. They called their service "Jane." Laura Kaplan, a founding member of Jane, recalled its work and foundational principles in her 1995 book *The Story of Jane*.

"Jane was the contact name for a group in Chicago officially known as The Abortion Counseling Service of Women's Liberation. Every week desperate women of every class, race and ethnicity telephoned Jane. . . .

As members of the women's liberation movement, the women in Jane viewed reproductive control as fundamental to women's freedom. The power to act had to be in the hands of each woman. Her decision about an abortion needed to be underscored as an active choice about her life. . . .

When a woman came to Jane for an abortion, the experience she had was markedly different from what she encountered in standard medical settings. She was included. She was in control. Rather than being a passive recipient, a patient, she was expected to participate. . . . By letting each woman know beforehand what to expect during the abortion and the recovery stage, and then talking with her step by step through the abortion itself, group members attempted to give each woman a sense of her own personal power in a situation in which most women felt powerless. Jane tried to create an environment in which women could take back their bodies, and by doing so, take back their lives. . . .

Jane developed at a time when blind obedience to medical authority was the rule. There were no patient advocates or hospital ombudsmen, no such person as a health consumer. Few women understood their reproductive physiology or had any idea where to get the information they needed. The special knowledge doctors had was deliberately made inaccessible, couched in language incomprehensible to the lay person. We did not have a right to it. . . .

Now many of us know that we can get the medical information we need in a library or bookstore, but this was unheard of twenty-five years ago. . . .

Women's liberation groups organized speak-outs at which women testified to their own illegal abortions. They marched and demonstrated and disrupted legislative hearings on abortion that excluded women. They demanded that women, the true experts on abortion, be heard and recognized. They brought abortion out of the closet, where it had been shrouded in secrecy and shame. . . . [They] framed the issue, not in terms of privacy in sexual relations, and not in the neutral language of choice, but in terms of a woman's freedom to determine her own destiny as she defined it, not as others defined it. Abortion was a touchstone. If she did not have the right to control her own body, which included freedom from forced sterilizations and unnecessary hysterectomies, gains in other areas were meaningless. . . .

While the public struggle was underway, every day women who tried to find abortions put their lives at risk. Their suffering could not be ignored. Women's groups and networks of the clergy organized to meet these women's immediate needs. Based on a moral imperative, Howard Moody, a Baptist minister, founded the first clergy group, the New York Clergy Consultation Service on Abortion [in 1967]. He encouraged clergymen throughout the country to set up similar networks to help women get safe abortions. . . .

Both the clergy and women's liberation groups sought out competent abortionists, negotiated the price, raised money to pay for abortions and counseled thousands of distraught women. Not only did they help women but, by breaking the law, they also undermined it. They followed the tradition of the Underground Railroad which defied another immoral law, the Fugitive Slave Act, and helped to undermine the institution of chattel slavery. Like the scores of people who were part of the Underground Railroad, the stories of those who participated in these referral services are part of our hidden history."

On the fiftieth anniversary of the Nineteenth Amendment, August 26, 1970, the National Organization for Women sponsored Women's Strike for Equality. In her draft message calling on women to participate, Betty Friedan made clear her view that women had not yet achieved full citizenship.

"Our movement toward true equality for all women in America in fully equal partnership with men has reached this year a point of critical mass. The chain reaction of events and breakthroughs against sex discrimination and the denigration of women as we begin this new decade is unmistakable evidence that the unfinished revolution of women towards full human freedom, dignity, self determination and full participation in the mainstream of society has exploded into the consciousness, into the actions of millions of women across the lines of generation, across the lines of nation, of color, of man-made politics.

It is only three years since employers and even government commissioners empowered to enforce the civil rights act's ban on sex discrimination in employment were treating it as a slightly dirty joke.... It is only two years ago that we dared to say that the right of a woman to control her own body's reproductive process should be an inalienable human right for the time—women's voice was heard on the question of abortion, up until then, completely decided by men. I still remember the courage it took for us to dare to confront this question in terms of the basic principle involved and how even the abortion reformers laughed when we changed the terms of the debate from reform to repeal....

All of us this past year have learned in our gut that sisterhood is powerful. The awesome power of women united, the awesome political power of 53% of the population, is visible now and is being taken seriously, as all of us who define ourselves as people now take the actions that need to be taken in every city and state, and together make our voices heard....

And so we face now the awesome responsibility of this beautiful miracle of our own power as women to change society, to change the conditions that oppress us in government, industry, the professions, the churches, the political parties, the unions, in education, in medicine and in our own homes, in the very images that confine us. I think it is urgent that we confront in all seriousness the power we have to make this revolution happen now, not in some abstract future, . . . but in our own lives, in the mainstream of our own society. We have the power to restructure the institutions and conditions that oppress all women now, and it is our responsibility to history, to ourselves, to all who will come after us, to use this power NOW. . . .

We must use our power to end the war between the sexes by confronting politically the conditions, the institutions that keep women in this impotent state. If we confront the real conditions that oppress men now as well as women and translate our rage into action, then and only then will sex really be liberated to be an active joy and a receiving joy for women and for men, when we are both really free to be all we can be. This is not a war to be fought in the bedroom, but in the city, in the political arena. . . .

I propose that on Wednesday, August 26, we call a 24-hour general strike, a resistance both passive and active, of all women in America against the concrete conditions of their oppression. On that day, 50 years after the amendment that gave women the vote became part of the Constitution, I propose we use our power to declare an ultimatum on all who would keep us from using our rights as Americans. I propose that the women who are doing menial chores in the offices cover their typewriters and close their notebooks and the telephone operators unplug their switchboards, the waitresses stop waiting, cleaning women stop cleaning, and everyone who is doing a job for which a man would be paid more—stop; every woman pegged forever as "assistant-to," doing jobs for which men get the credit, stop. In every office, every laboratory, every school, all the women to whom we get word will spend the day discussing, analyzing the conditions which keep us from being all we might be. And if the condition that keeps us down is the lack of a child care center, we will bring our babies to the office that day and sit them on our bosses' laps. We do not know how many will join our day of abstention from so-called women's work, but I expect it will be millions. We will then present concrete demands to those who so far have made all the decisions.

And when it begins to get dark, instead of cooking dinner or making love, we will assemble, and we will carry candles symbolic of that flame of the passionate journey down through history—relit anew in every city—to converge the visible power of women at city hall—at the political arena where the larger options of our life are decided. If men want to join us, fine. If politicians, if political bosses, if mayors and governors wish to discuss our demands, fine, but we will define the terms of the dialogue. And we will send our most skillful scouts to track down senators one by one, until we have his commitment to the equal rights of women. And by the time these 24 hours are ended, our revolution will be a fact."

Native Women's Reproductive Rights Agenda

"Empowerment Through Dialogue", a historical three-day meeting was held in Pierre, South Dakota, on May 16, 17, and 18, 1990. More than 30 Native Women, representing over eleven (11) Nations from the Northern Plains came together in a collective decision making process to form a Reproductive Rights Coalition. Their efforts resulted in an Agenda for Native Women's Reproductive Rights.

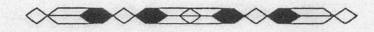

CHAPTER 8

Women's Rights after 1970

The August 26, 1970, Women's Strike for Equality signaled the arrival of a full-fledged "women's movement." Despite differences among activists over goals, strategies, and philosophies, the term became shorthand used by journalists and others seeking to encapsulate the myriad events and groups working for women's rights and equal citizenship. Like all umbrella terms, "the women's movement" collected under one rubric a wide variety of disparate groups, organizations, and individuals, with both conflicting and overlapping interests and goals. For a time during the 1970s, it appeared that members of the "movement" shared one goal, securing an Equal Rights Amendment (ERA) to the Constitution. But just as the terms "woman movement" and "suffrage movement" had concealed some fundamental disagreements among women's rights activists earlier in the century, especially over how to define and achieve the elusive goal of "equality," the shorthand use of "women's movement" or, more disparagingly, "women's lib" conferred a false unity upon advocates of gender equity.

To an extent, some feminists contributed to the blurring of differences by claiming a universal "sisterhood" among like-minded activists. In the heady early days of the women's liberation movement in particular, invocations of women's common experiences as women overshadowed the reality that differences in the social experiences of race, class, ethnicity, and sexuality separated women as often as the mere fact of shared womanhood united them. Within both women's rights and women's liberation groups, feminists of color, along with white working-class and lesbian feminists, bore the burden of challenging easy assumptions about sisterhood and pressing for feminisms that confronted differences among women while also dismantling the intersecting racial, class, and sexual privileges that gave some women more rights than other women.

The struggle for an ERA brought those internal divisions to the surface; it also revived well-organized antifeminist efforts and sparked a significant backlash against gains in women's rights. When Congress passed and sent the ERA to the states for ratification in 1972, a nine-year effort to gain approval ensued but ultimately failed; the amendment fell three states short of the three-quarters needed to ratify. Nevertheless, during those years, advocates for women's full citizenship won a number of victories in the areas of educational, economic, reproductive, and personal liberties. When some twenty thousand delegates to a Congressionally funded National Women's Conference came together in Houston in 1977, the platform they built and voted upon reflected the successes that advocates had won, the topics on which they agreed, and the divisions that remained. Neither successes nor divisions disappeared once the delegates went home, but a continuing backlash during the 1980s meant that women's rights advocates had to expend time and energy merely to maintain gains that had been won during the heady early days of the women's movement. When members of a younger generation—the first generation to reap the benefit of those gains—came of age in the 1980s and 1990s, they brought new perspectives, ideas, and priorities to their advocacy of women's rights.

In recent decades, as American feminists participated in international Women's Conferences sponsored by the United Nations, they encountered women around the world making equal rights demands based on their own experiences, cultures, and political positions. The establishment of global connections among women's rights advocates carried echoes of earlier international meetings. In the context of the 21st century, however, global ties carried both the promise of common undertakings and the peril of miscommunication and misunderstanding. As women's rights advocates sought common ground with colleagues from around the world, it remained to be seen whether and how they would learn from the past.

"Sisterhood" and Its Challengers

In 1970, writer and radical feminist Robin Morgan published an influential collection entitled *Sisterhood Is Powerful: An Anthology of Writings from the Women's Liberation Movement*. Its title seemed to say it all: that

when women spoke from personal experience, then united and worked together to seek social change, they had great power. It also captured an ideal that captivated many activists at the time: that women could form a "sisterhood" across racial, class, and sexual lines, one that would transform social, economic, and political institutions. In the book's introduction, Morgan situated herself politically, differentiated the women's liberation approach to women's rights from that of the National Organization for Women, and summarized the rapid pace of change occurring even as she wrote.

"[W]hen I first began work on this book, . . . I was a so-called 'politico,' who shied away from admitting (on any but a superficial level) that *I* was oppressed, and who put all other causes above and ahead of my own. . . . [But] it isn't until you begin to fight in your own cause that you (a) become really committed to winning, and (b) become a genuine ally of other people struggling for their freedom. I also nurtured a secret contempt for other women who weren't as strong, free, and respected (by men) as I thought I was (that's called 'identifying yourself with the oppressor' . . .). Especially threatening were the women who admitted that they were simply unable to cope with the miserable situation we were all in, and needed each other and a whole movement to change that.

Well, somewhere during that year, I became such a woman—and it's been a radicalizing experience. . . . It makes you very sensitive—raw, even—this consciousness. . . . You begin to see how all-pervasive a thing is sexism—the definition of and discrimination against half the human species by the other half. Once started, the realization is impossible to stop, and it packs a daily wallop. . . . (The monies from the book's sales, by the way, will go to the women's movement, for day-care and abortion projects, bail and defense funds, etc.). . . .

The women's movement is a non-hierarchical one. It does things collectively and experimentally. It is also the first movement that has the potential of cutting across all class, race, age, economic, and geographical barriers—since women in every group must play essentially the same role. . . .

[The National Organization for Women] fights *within* the System, lobbying legislators, concentrating on job discrimination, etc. NOW helped win the airline stewardesses' fight against mandatory retirement when a woman married or reached the age of thirty-five; the group was almost solely responsible for the Equal Employment Opportunities Commission ruling that segregated male-female help-wanted ads in newspapers were discriminatory and illegal. They have worked hard to change abortion laws and to call attention to educational discrimination against women.

NOW is essentially an organization that wants reforms about the second-class citizenship of women—and this is where it differs drastically from the rest of the Women's Liberation Movement. Its composite membership [which includes men] ... determines, of course, its politics, which are not radical. . . . The only hope of a new feminist movement is some kind of only now barely emerging politics of *revolutionary feminism*, . . .

Alternative institutions are springing up: women's liberation child-care centers and cooperative nurseries; all-women's communes; halfway houses for women separating, divorcing, or recently widowed; abortion counseling and referral services; women's liberation books, magazines, newspapers and theater groups that can create our own new media, and bail funds to free our political prisoners—among them, prostitutes. . . . [T]he general consciousness about the oppression of women is spreading through all groups and classes, . . . partly because the women's movement has set itself the task of analyzing divisions (race, class, age, hetero- and homosexuality) that keep us apart from each other, and is working very concretely to break down those divisions. . . .

It is now the spring of 1970. During the past few months, wildcat strikes by women workers at General Electric, Bendix, and the New York Bell Telephone Company surprised both management and labor; . . . The first serious woman jockey was pelted by rocks before a major race. Housewives in Stockton, California, went on strike for wages and for a clear definition of their 'job'—in writing. Women's caucuses have been formed or are forming in . . . established professional gatherings. Welfare mothers have been disrupting welfare centers all over the country to protest the bureaucracy that robs them of human dignity. Roman Catholic women are in revolt over the Pill, and Catholic nuns demand greater autonomy from the male clerical hierarchy. . . . Women are marching, picketing, and mounting a variety of actions against abortion laws in every state. Boycotts have been started against billionaire corporations like Procter & Gamble or Lever Brothers, which manipulate women as consumers but are blatantly discriminatory in their own hiring and salary practices. . . . Women's Liberation Centers are being set up by local groups all around the country, to try to deal with the women who are pouring into the movement every day. Nurses are organizing. Women in the Armed Forces are organizing. Women have attacked, disrupted, seized, or completely taken over certain media institutions.... *Newsweek* women employees brought suit against the magazine for discrimination in salaries, promotions, and assignments....

We know that it is not enough to look around in awe at the rising tide of anger over the lack of 'women's rights.' We know that we want something more, much more, than the same gray, meaningless, alienating jobs that men are forced to sacrifice their lives to.... We know that the vote proved useless for our needs (perhaps those of men, too). We know that the so-called sexual revolution was only another form of oppression for women.... We know that 'hip culture' and 'radical life style'—whatever those mean—have been hip and radical for the men, but filled with the same old chores, harassment, and bottling-up of inner rage for the women, as usual....

More and more, I begin to think of a worldwide Women's Revolution as the only hope for life on the planet. It follows, then, that where women's liberation is, *there* is, for me, the genuine radical movement.... The Women's Liberation Movement exists ... in your mind, and in the political and personal insights that you can contribute to change and shape and help its growth. It is frightening. It is very exhilarating. It is creating history, or rather, *herstory.*"

Not everyone agreed that sisterhood was possible. In a 1977 statement, a group of African American lesbian feminists terming themselves the Combahee River Collective (after an 1863 action that Harriet Tubman undertook to free slaves) underlined their commitment to the struggle for racial equality (hence their rejection of feminist separatism) and reminded white feminists about the blinders they too often wore about their own racial privilege.

"We are a collective of black feminists who have been meeting together since 1974.... [W]e are actively committed to struggling against racial, sexual, heterosexual, and class oppression and see as our particular task the development of integrated analysis and practice based upon the fact that the major systems of oppression are interlocking. The synthesis of these oppressions creates the conditions of our lives. As black women we see black feminism as the logical political movement to combat the manifold and simultaneous oppressions that all women of color face....

Although we are feminists and lesbians, we feel solidarity with progressive black men and do not advocate the fractionalization that white women who are separatists demand. Our situation as black people necessitates that we have solidarity around the fact of race. . . . We struggle together with black men against racism, while we also struggle with black men about sexism. . . . [W]e are not just trying to fight oppression on one front or even two, but instead to address a whole range of oppressions. We do not have racial, sexual, heterosexual, or class privilege to rely upon, nor do we have even the minimal access to resources and power that groups who possess any one of these types of privilege have. . . .

One issue that is of major concern to us and that we have begun to publicly address is racism in the white women's movement. As black feminists we are made constantly and painfully aware of how little effort white women have made to understand and combat their racism, which requires among other things that they have a more than superficial comprehension of race, color, and black history and culture. Eliminating racism in the white women's movement is by definition work for white women to do, but we will continue to speak to and demand accountability on this issue."

Margaret Sloan, a founder of the National Black Feminist Organization in 1973, described the ways in which African American feminists conceptualized their work, emphasizing the "duality" (or intersectionality) of their experiences.

"Black women comprise over half of the black population in this country. We see ourselves as strengthening the black community by calling upon all the talents of an entire people to combat racism. We feel that there can't be liberation for less than half a race. We want *all* black people in this country to be free, and by organizing around our needs as black women, we are making sure that we won't be left out. . . . Many of us come out of the Women's Movement, and are still active in a variety of its organizations, but we felt that the duality of being black and female made us want to organize around those things which affect us most."

In an essay published in 1971, a group of California Asian American feminists identified themselves as "Third World" women and described how they experienced gender, racial, and class status; oppressions overlapped, making their layers inseparable.

"American society is broken up into different levels based on economic income, education, politics, color, and sex. . . . At the bottom of these varying gradations are women of color. Third World women face domination by both racism and sexism (discrimination based

Intersectionality: Coined by the legal theorist Kimberlé Crenshaw in 1989, the term "intersectionality" became widely used to refer to the "multidimensional" aspects of women's experiences as members of racial, sexual, class, and ethnic groups. Although Crenshaw's original formulation sought to "demarginalize" the "intersection of race and sex" for black women, scholars have found her work extraordinarily fruitful as a way to describe how women can experience either oppression and marginalization or privilege and power in their relationships with other women—and with men.

on sex). Both racism and sexism are means by which American society controls and oppresses everyone. Everyone is forced to conform to the values and roles established by the dominant group in order to 'succeed.' For the Asian movement to progress, it must have a clear understanding of sexism, racism, and imperialism; and deal with them simultaneously."

At the same time that they contended with myopia within feminism, feminists active in ethnic and racial liberation movements continued to struggle with the assumption of masculine superiority within those movements. The comments of Jennie V. Chavez in a 1972 essay reflected those frustrations.

"It has taken what I consider a long time for [Chicanas] to realize and to speak out about the double oppression of the Mexican-American woman. . . . As the social revolution for all people's freedoms has progressed, so Chicanas have caught the essence of freedom in the air. The change has occurred slowly. Mexican-American women have been reluctant to speak up, afraid that they might show up the men in front of the white man—afraid that they may think our men not men. Now, however, the Chicana is becoming as well educated and as aware of oppression, if not more so, as the Mexican-American male. . . . As the new breed of Mexican-American women, we have been, and probably will continue to be, ridiculed by our men for attempting the acrobatics of equality. . . . [B]ut I believe that this new breed of bronze womanhood, as all women today, will be a vanguard for world change."

Naming Wrongs, Seeking Rights

As they sought to define women's rights, feminists identified and named women's wrongs. A group calling themselves simply "The Feminists" made the inequities of marriage and the persistence of coverture their target when they handed out an in-your-face leaflet at the New York marriage license bureau in 1969.

"Women: Do You Know the Facts about Marriage?
DO YOU KNOW THAT RAPE IS LEGAL IN MARRIAGE?
According to law, *sex* is the purpose of marriage. You have to have sexual intercourse in order to have a valid marriage.
DO YOU KNOW THAT LOVE AND AFFECTION ARE NOT REQUIRED IN MARRIAGE?
If you can't have sex with your husband, he can get a divorce or annulment. If he doesn't love you, that's *not* grounds for divorce.

"[A] pervasive feeling of mistrust toward the women in the movement is fairly representative of a large group of women who live in the psychological place we now call Asian Pacific America. A movement that fights sexism in the social structure must deal with racism, and we had hoped the leaders in the women's movement would be able to see the parallels in the lives of the women of color and themselves, and would 'join' *us* in our struggle and give *us* 'input.'"
—writer Mitsuye Yamada, 1979

Mitsuye Yasutake Yamada (1923–) is a poet, women's rights activist, and feminist whose work reflects her experiences being interned with her Japanese American family at the Minidoka Camp during World War II and her belief that Asian American women in the United States experience double invisibility as Asians and as women. Her essays and poems have appeared in a number of venues, including the anthology *This Bridge Called My Back: Radical Writings from Women of Color* (1981), and along with the poet Nellie Wong, she has been the subject of a documentary film, *Mitsuye and Nellie: Asian American Poets.*

No-fault divorce: In 1969, California became the first state to reject the centuries-old notion that one party must be "at fault" when individuals sought to dissolve a marriage. By 1977, nine states had "no-fault" divorce statutes.

DO YOU KNOW THAT YOU ARE YOUR HUSBAND'S PRISONER?

You have to live with him wherever *he* pleases. If he decides to move someplace else, either you go with him or he can charge you with desertion, get a divorce and, according to law, you deserve nothing because *you're the guilty party.*

DID YOU KNOW THAT, ACCORDING TO THE UNITED NATIONS, MARRIAGE IS A 'SLAVERY-LIKE PRACTICE'?

According to the marriage contract, your husband is entitled to more household services from you than he would be from a live-in maid. So, why aren't you getting paid? Under law, you're entitled only to 'bed and board.'"

Feminist activism in legislatures and courthouses opened the floodgates to women's grievances. Soon, ordinary women and men began to name the wrongs they had experienced and claim their rights. Sharron Frontiero was an Air Force officer who challenged inequitable rules on dependents' benefits whereby men but not women could automatically claim their spouses as dependents. In its 1973 decision in the case of *Frontiero v. Richardson*, the Supreme Court agreed with Frontiero's lawyer, Ruth Bader Ginsburg, that distinctions based on sex, like those based on race, were legally "suspect."

"The question before us concerns the right of a female member of the uniformed services to claim her spouse as a 'dependent.' . . . [A]ppellants contend that classifications based upon sex, like classifications based upon race, alienage, and national origin, are inherently suspect and must therefore be subjected to close judicial scrutiny . . . We agree. There can be no doubt that our Nation has had a long and unfortunate history of sex discrimination. Traditionally, such discrimination was rationalized by an attitude of 'romantic paternalism' which, in practical effect, put women, not on a pedestal, but in a cage. . . . [T]he position of women in America has improved markedly in recent decades. Nevertheless, . . . women still face pervasive, although at times more subtle, discrimination in our educational institutions, in the job market, and perhaps most conspicuously, in the political arena. . . ."

Girls' and women's unequal access to education and training was a key target of women's rights agitation. Title IX of the 1972 Education Amendments Act was a major victory for equal rights and became a powerful tool for addressing widespread discrimination in educational institutions, including everything from quotas on women's admission to elite law and medical schools (usually 5 percent), to unequal pay for female

college professors, to girls' almost non-existent opportunities for athletic competition. In 1975 Congressional testimony opposing an effort to exempt "revenue-producing" sports (such as football) from Title IX coverage, Senator Birch Bayh of Indiana, who had sponsored Title IX in the Senate, took the opportunity to note the many still-existing disparities between women's and men's opportunities in college sports. In the process, he identified arguments made by those who sought to limit Title IX's coverage.

"[I take] the opportunity to testify here today on legislation which seeks to fundamentally alter the original goals of Title IX, goals which included equal opportunity for women in athletics and physical education. . . . Congress's decision to uphold the coverage of athletics by Title IX has been buttressed by a number of court decisions which mandated equal opportunity for women in high school and college athletics based upon the due process guarantees of the Fourteenth Amendment. . . .

The question . . . is whether the Congress should retreat from the full commitment it has given to provide equal opportunity for women in athletics by exempting revenue-producing sports from Title IX. . . . [I]t is interesting to me that . . . no one is making the argument that there is not discrimination against women. No football coach or athletic director is denying that this is something fundamentally wrong with a college or university that relegates its female athletes to second-rate facilities, second-rate equipment, or second-rate schedules, solely because they are women. No one seriously disputes the fact that athletic budgets for women are a fraction of those provided for the men. Instead, the argument has focused on the ability of certain intercollegiate sports to withstand the financial burdens imposed by the equal-opportunity requirements of Title IX. . . .

What does Title IX require of colleges and universities in order to meet their equal opportunity guidelines in intercollegiate athletics? . . .

[O]ne example of how Title IX would change things is that . . . if the men are trying out for the [basketball] team, and the university feels that buying the shorts and the shirts and the attendant equipment is a university expense, but the women, to try out for the women's team, must bear the expense themselves. . . .

[F]rom the college coed to the ten-year-old longing to play Little League baseball, American women have been consistently denied adequate athletic opportunities. Funding, coaching, scheduling,

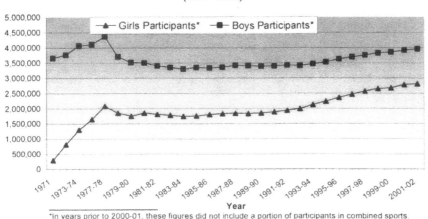

Athletics Participation Totals - All Sports
(1971 - 2002)

*In years prior to 2000-01, these figures did not include a portion of participants in combined sports.
Source: National Federation of State High School Associations 2002 Participation Survey

A chart demonstrates Title IX's impact on women's athletics.

"No person in the United States shall, on the basis of sex, be excluded from participation in, be denied the benefits of, or be subjected to discrimination under any education program or activity receiving federal financial assistance."

—Title IX

In 1973, the National Organization for Women created a Rape Task Force to develop statutes revising existing state laws. The task force challenged laws requiring rape victims to prove that they had been "chaste" before the rape and had resisted the rape with "utmost force." Susan Brownmiller's 1975 book, *Against Our Will*, exposed the ways in which rape had historically been used to subjugate women, including the use of mass rape as a weapon in wartime. By 1978, feminists were holding "Take Back the Night" marches to claim women's right to freedom of access and safety on public streets.

scholarships, and access to facilities are only a few of the areas where inequities are glaring.

Title IX attempts to address these inequities, not through rigid requirements of equal expenditures for males and females, but through an assessment of a variety of factors including student interest and participation, past history of athletic opportunities for members of both sexes, and current fiscal constraints that will vary from institution to institution. . . .

It is unbelievable to me that sports programs so steeped in tradition as [are] most of our big-ten schools[,] are suddenly going to disintegrate or even be seriously damaged or even slightly damaged by permitting women to attend these same fine institutions and have an equal opportunity to participate in athletic programs and programs of physical education."

Feminists highlighted women's vulnerability to sexual assault and shone a spotlight on the often dismissive treatment of rape victims by the police and courts. Writer Susan Griffin contributed an important conceptual analysis of rape in a 1971 essay by identifying it as a signal example of the pervasiveness of violence against women, and a mechanism whereby men control women and maintain gender hierarchy.

"Rape is an act of aggression in which the victim is denied her self-determination. It is an act of violence which, if not actually followed by beatings or murder, nevertheless always carries with it the threat of death. And finally, rape is a form of mass terrorism, for the victims of rape are chosen indiscriminately, but the propagandists for male supremacy broadcast that it is women who cause rape by being unchaste or in the wrong place at the wrong time—in essence, by behaving as though they were free.

The threat of rape is used to deny women employment. (In California, the Berkeley Public Library . . . refused to hire female shelvers because of perverted men in the stacks.) The fear of rape keeps women off the streets at night. Keeps women at home.

Keeps women passive and modest for fear that they be thought provocative."

Calling attention to the plight of women victimized by spousal abuse, feminists gave domestic violence a name—"battering." They analyzed it both as evidence of the inequities of coverture in marriage and as a mechanism for maintaining male supremacy. In her 1979 book, *The Battered Woman*, Lenore E. Walker provided a succinct introduction to the issue, offering women's stories to help personalize the issue.

"Denise: After we got married, every little thing would set him right off. It seemed he needed extra special loving at all times, and I kept throwing hurdles because I wasn't doing that. Evidently, that was causing him to be very upset. I always got the impression that I wasn't loving enough, giving enough, that there was something defective in my character as far as giving love. That's basically the message he gave to me.

There was physical abuse right away. He would slap me a lot, and I would fight back. Sometimes I didn't, because I thought if I didn't, it might cure him.... In the beginning, I couldn't tell anyone what was happening; yet it was terrorizing me. I had one girl friend I told about it, and it turned out she was being slapped, too. She could sympathize with me, but it was something that I couldn't and wouldn't talk to anyone else about. Every time I went to my parents, I wouldn't tell them. My brothers and sisters . . . I wouldn't tell anyone. It was very, very embarrassing to me. To them, he was still this gentle, kind, charming man."

Working women's experiences of sexual teasing, propositions, jokes, and forced intimacies from male supervisors and employers had long been dismissed as one of the hazards of the workplace. In May 1975, while working at Cornell University, feminist activist Lin Farley and several colleagues held the first "speak out" to discuss those experiences. A new term—sexual harassment—enabled participants to describe what they had endured. After *New York Times* reporter Enid Nemy used the term in an August article, it gained wide currency.

"For years, many women accepted it as a job hazard. Now, with raised consciousness and increased self-assurance, they are speaking out against the indignities of work-related sexual advances and intimidation, both verbal and physical.

'Sexual harassment of women in their place of employment is extremely widespread. It is literally epidemic,' said Lin Farley,

In 1994, the Violence Against Women Act became law. A landmark provision stated: "All persons within the United States shall have the right to be free from crimes of violence motivated by gender." In 2000, 2005, and again in 2013, Congress reauthorized the law. The 2013 reauthorization explicitly included gay, bisexual, and transgender women in its provisions.

First performed in 1996, *The Vagina Monologues*, a play by Eve Ensler, became a significant mechanism for calling attention to the issue of violence against women. It led to the designation of February 14 (St. Valentine's Day) as "V-Day," when college students and activists around the world stage productions of the play.

After enduring continual sexual harassment from her supervisor, a vice-president of Meritor Savings Bank who eventually raped her, Mechelle Vinson took her case to the Equal Employment Opportunity Commission (EEOC) and, with the legal backing of women's rights advocates, to the courts. The result was a redefinition of harassment as a form of sex discrimination, prohibited under the 1964 Civil Rights Act. In the 1986 case of *Meritor Savings Bank v. Vinson*, the Supreme Court unanimously agreed that "unwelcome sexual advances that create an offensive or hostile working environment violate Title VII [of the 1964 Civil Rights Act].... [A] claim of 'hostile environment' sex discrimination is actionable under Title VII."

In 1991, sexual harassment became a topic of widespread public discussion when President George H. W. Bush nominated a former head of the Equal Employment Opportunity Commission, Clarence Thomas, to a seat on the Supreme Court. One of Thomas's former employees, law professor Anita Hill, testified at the Senate confirmation hearings that years earlier Thomas had sexually harassed her. Because she had never formally complained about Thomas's behavior, Hill found her credibility attacked, with Democratic Senator Howell Heflin of Alabama questioning whether she was a "scorned woman" who possessed "a martyr complex." The Senate confirmed Thomas's nomination.

director of the women's section of the Human Affairs Program at Cornell University.

She listed the forms such harassment could take:

- Constant leering and ogling of a woman's body.
- Continually brushing against a woman's body.
- Forcing a woman to submit to squeezing or pinching.
- Catching a woman alone for forced sexual intimacies.
- Outright sexual propositions, backed by threat of losing a job.
- Forced sexual relations.

Miss Farley, in testimony given before the Commission on Human Rights of New York City, noted that, in the past, women ... were ... humiliated or intimidated, and had watched 'the ridicule and condescension' heaped upon women who did complain. ...

The women of Tompkins County, N.Y., who have banded together to form Working Women United, agree that sexual harassment is humiliating. They do not believe it is trivial. They have now launched a campaign to expose the problems of sexual exploitation of women on the job.

'[M]en think ... they have a right to touch me, or proposition me because I'm a waitress,' said Janet Oestreich, ... 'Why do women have to put up with this sort of thing anyway? You aren't in any position to say "get your crummy hands off me" because you need the tips, that's what a waitress job is all about. Women are the ones who are punished. They have to leave a job because of a man's behavior and the man is left there, sitting pretty.'"

Women's rights to autonomy and self-ownership at work and in personal relationships extended to reproductive decisions as well. Building upon the *Griswold v. Connecticut* case (1965), women's rights lawyers won the *Roe v. Wade* case in 1973. The Supreme Court, invoking the constitutional right to privacy, found blanket restrictions on abortion unconstitutional.

"The Constitution does not explicitly mention any right of privacy. In a line of decisions, however ... the Court has recognized that a right of personal privacy, or a guarantee of certain areas or zones of privacy, does exist under the Constitution. This right ... is broad enough to encompass a woman's decision whether or not to terminate her pregnancy. ... We ... conclude that the right of personal privacy includes the abortion decision, but that this right is not unqualified and must be considered against important state interests in regulation."

Speaking at a Black Women's Community Development Foundation Conference in Washington, D.C., in 1974, Naomi Gray of Black Women Organized for Action offered specific examples of the denial to black women of reproductive autonomy.

"Over the years I have come in contact with a substantial number of women who have been sterilized, either by tubal ligation or hysterectomy. Many, at the time, were unaware that this had occurred, because they never consented to have the operation performed. For instance, the majority of these women signed a medical consent form, not to be sterilized but rather placing their faith in the doctor to discover and rectify the so-called trouble. This is not informed consent; instead these women have been sterilized through means of deceit and trickery. Many of us were aware through the black grapevine that black women had been forced to undergo involuntary sterilizations in the South and elsewhere. However, it was not until recently that it was possible to document the extent to which black women have suffered involuntary sterilization. . . . As is always the case with such laws, it is the poor and more often the black female, including minors, who are victimized."

With her 1978 poster, artist Rachael Romero highlighted the denial of reproductive rights to poor and minority women by pointing to laws permitting women to be sterilized without their consent.

Critics of the *Roe v. Wade* decision worked to undermine its impact by seeking state and national legislation restricting women's access to abortion. Through the Hyde Amendment (1977), Congress eliminated all federal funding for abortions. When the Pennsylvania legislature passed a series of new restrictions on that state's abortion rights statute, lawyers defending women's reproductive rights challenged the legislation. The end result was a 1992 Supreme Court case, *Planned Parenthood of Southeastern Pennsylvania v. Casey*. In rendering its 5–4 decision, the court permitted many of the restrictive provisions to stand, but reaffirmed the *Roe v. Wade* decision and overturned one of the last vestiges of coverture, a requirement in the law that wives, but not single women, notify their sexual partners before having an abortion.

"Liberty finds no refuge in a jurisprudence of doubt. Yet 19 years after our holding that the Constitution protects a woman's right to terminate her pregnancy in its early states . . . that definition of liberty is still questioned. . . . After considering the fundamental constitutional questions resolved by *Roe*, . . . we are led to conclude this: the essential holding of *Roe v. Wade* should be retained and

Native Women's Reproductive Rights Agenda

"Empowerment Through Dialogue", a historical three-day meeting was held in Pierre, South Dakota, on May 16, 17, and 18, 1990. More than 30 Native Women, representing over eleven (11) Nations from the Northern Plains came together in a collective decision making process to form a Reproductive Rights Coalition. Their efforts resulted in an Agenda for Native Women's Reproductive Rights.

In 1990, Native American women from the Northern Plains held a three-day meeting in South Dakota that resulted in the formation of an Agenda for Native American Women's Reproductive Rights.

In the 2000 case of *Stenberg v. Carhart*, the Supreme Court upheld Congress's restriction on a particular abortion method, "intact dilation and extraction," termed "partial birth" abortion by opponents.

once again reaffirmed.... Constitutional protection of the woman's decision to terminate her pregnancy derives from the Due Process Clause of the Fourteenth Amendment.... It is a premise of the Constitution that there is a realm of personal liberty which the government may not enter....

Men and women of good conscience can disagree, and we suppose some always shall disagree, about the profound moral and spiritual implications of terminating a pregnancy, even in its earliest stage. Some of us as individuals find abortion offensive to our most basic principles of morality, but that cannot control our decision. Our obligation is to define the liberty of all, not to mandate our own moral code....

Our law affords constitutional protection to personal decisions relating to marriage, procreation, contraception, family relationships, child rearing, and education.... These matters ... are central to the liberty protected by the Fourteenth Amendment. At the heart of liberty is the right to define one's own concept of existence, or meaning, or the universe, and of the mystery of human life. Beliefs about these matters could not define the attributes of personhood were they formed under compulsion of the State. The woman's right to terminate her pregnancy before viability is the most central principle of *Roe v. Wade*. It is a rule of law and a component of liberty we cannot renounce."

Religious feminists challenged women's exclusion from spiritual leadership in their denominations. At a 1975 meeting of about 1,200 Catholics held in Detroit to discuss women's ordination, Margaret Farley, RSM, a member of the Sisters of Mercy, articulated her views on the topic.

"I ... wish to argue that the question of the ordination of women to the priesthood must indeed be central to any considerations of roles for women in the Church, and that the many moral imperatives which confront the Church regarding women and ministry unavoidably converge in the imperative to ordain women to the priesthood. The office of priesthood, in fact, offers a particularly potent focus for addressing directly the sources of sexism in Christian thought. Reasons and attitudes which have kept women from the office of priesthood are remarkably similar to reasons and attitudes which continue to keep them from full participation in the general priesthood of the faithful.... [T]he Church ought to open its ordained sacramental ministry to women. It ought to do so because not to do so is to affirm a policy, a system, a structure, whose presuppositions are false (for the nonordination of women is premised on the denial in women of a capacity for leadership, a call to represent God in the community and the community to God, and a worthiness to approach the sacred in the fullness of their womanhood)."

Working women's advocacy groups, especially "9 to 5," founded in 1973, and the Coalition of Labor Union Women (CLUW), founded in 1974, advocated for women workers, homemakers, and women who faced job discrimination. At a 1980 Labor Day rally in Washington, D.C., they put forward a fifteen-point "Working Women's Platform," later reported by writer Lorraine Sorrel in the feminist journal *Off Our Backs*.

"Because the concerns of working women are still not addressed by the major political parties in their 1980 platforms, four national women's labor organizations proclaimed the Working Women's Platform [today.] ... The working women's organizations sent copies of the platform to their local groups and national women's organizations. They want these issues raised to public debate, and each candidate for public office to state where they stand on the specific issues....

1. RECOGNITION. Recognize, understand and value the strong tradition and increasing importance of women as workers in all aspects of social, political and economic life in America....
2. MINORITY WOMEN. Recog[n]ize the special needs, concerns and problems of minority women workers who face both sexism and racism....
3. JOB OPTIONS. Eliminate job segregation by sex [which] is a major factor in the overall low status of women in the work force....
4. WAGES. Eliminate wage discrimination by sex....
5. EDUCATION AND TRAINING. Eliminate sex-stereotyping and other barriers to equity in all publicly funded educational, employment and training programs, and promote equal access to these programs....
6. EMPLOYMENT PROGRAMS. Expand and create special programs to improve employment opportunities

Although women are barred from being ordained in the Catholic Church, local parishes opened the door for girls to be altar servers in the 1980s; in 1994 the Vatican signaled its consent, subject to the approval of the local diocesan bishop.

Women's rights concerns made their way into popular media. In the 1980 comedy *Nine to Five*, three women stuck in low-paying jobs outwit their sexist boss and introduce numerous changes into the office, including a merit-based promotional system for female employees and an on-site day care center. The 1982 comedy *Tootsie* puts a man in women's clothing at a job; through it he discovers the kinds of sexist put-downs and stereotyping that women deal with daily. The 1984 film *The Burning Bed* exposed the phenomenon of wife battering, and the 1988 drama *The Accused* dramatized the way the legal system dealt with rape. In the television series *Remington Steele*, which aired from 1982 until 1987, a smart and feisty female private investigator has little luck getting clients until she invents a male figurehead, whom she names "Remington Steele." Audience members empathized with her as clients insist on dealing only with her "boss" and with her effort to maintain the fiction that he, and not she, has solved complicated crimes.

Unlike women in most western European countries, American women did not have the right to maternity leave (let alone paid leave); syndicated cartoonist Cathy Guisewite used humor in a 1986 comic strip to make that point.

Passed by Congress but vetoed by President George H. W. Bush in 1991, the Family and Medical Leave Act was re-passed in 1993 and signed by President Bill Clinton. It protects qualified employees' jobs for up to twelve weeks of unpaid family leave. As of 2014, the United States remained the only industrialized country without provisions for paid parental leave for the birth or adoption of a child.

for all women (including young women, women on welfare, ex-offenders, displaced homemakers, handicapped, older and minority women), providing them with career development, skills training (including nontraditional work), supportive services, and access to upwardly mobile jobs. . . .

7. ENFORCEMENT. Enforce laws and regulations mandating equal employment opportunities for women. . . .

8. HEALTH AND SAFETY. Promote healthy and safe working conditions. . . .

9. SEXUAL HARASSMENT. Maintain work environments free of sexual harassment and intimidation. According to several recent surveys, approximately 60–75% of the women questioned experienced sexual harassment on the job. Economic dependency and the fear of losing jobs or promotions make women particularly vulnerable to sexual harassment.

10. DEPENDENT CARE. Provide accessible, quality care for children and other dependents. . . .

11. ORGANIZING. Support the organization of the millions of unorganized women workers, and strengthen the role and participation of women in labor unions. . . .

12. HOMEMAKING. Recognize homemakers as an important segment of the country's labor force and recognize unpaid labor in the home as a significant contribution to the national economy. . . .

13. BENEFITS. Promote equitable benefits for women, including pensions, social security, paid maternity leave, health care and health insurance. . . .

14. WORK SCHEDULES. Promote alternative work schedules (including flex-time, part-time, compressed work week, and job sharing) with appropriate benefits. . . .

15. PUBLIC POLICY. Promote the participation of women in the formulation and evaluation of public policy affecting employment. . . ."

"Equality of Rights under the Law": The ERA Revived

The National Organization for Women (NOW) endorsed a new Equal Rights Amendment (ERA) to the Constitution in 1967. In 1969, Representative Shirley Chisholm of New York, the first African American woman to serve in Congress, introduced the ERA into the House with a speech entitled "Equal Rights for Women."

"As a black person, I am no stranger to race prejudice. But the truth is that in the political world I have been far oftener discriminated against because I am a woman than because I am black.

Prejudice against blacks is becoming unacceptable although it will take years to eliminate it. But it is doomed because, slowly, white America is beginning to admit that it exists. Prejudice against

All the Women Are White, All the Blacks Are Men, But Some of Us Are Brave

Black Women's Studies

Edited by Gloria T. Hull, Patricia Bell Scott, and Barbara Smith

Girls' and women's right to know their own history and to make women the subject of academic study led to the creation of courses in Women's History and Women's Studies during the 1970s. These, in turn, created a demand for works by and about women. The anthology, *All the Women Are White, All the Blacks Are Men, But Some of Us Are Brave* (1982), was a landmark book in Black Women's Studies published by The Feminist Press, which had been founded in 1970.

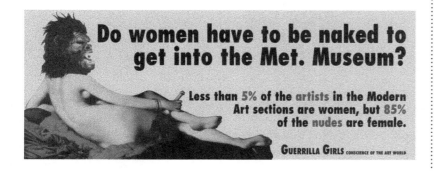

A group of feminist artists calling themselves Guerrilla Girls called attention to the vastly unequal opportunities afforded women within the art world with posters such as this one from 1989. In it, they reproduced a painting by Ingres but added the group's trademark signature: a gorilla mask and some telling statistics.

Born in Brooklyn in 1924, **Shirley Anita St. Hill Chisholm** (1924–2005) was the daughter of a factory worker and a seamstress. After spending part of her childhood during the Depression with her maternal grandparents in Barbados, she completed her education at Brooklyn College, where she excelled as a debater, and then earned a master's degree in elementary education at Columbia University. She first won political office on the state level, serving in the New York State Legislature, and in 1968 was elected to the U.S. House from her Brooklyn district, defeating a well-known civil rights leader who referred to her as "a little schoolteacher" and argued that the district needed "a man's voice in Washington." Focusing on issues such as women's rights, early childhood education, educational funding, and the concerns of poor people, she served until 1983 and was a founding member of the Congressional Black Caucus (1971) and the Congressional Women's Caucus (1977). In 1972, Shirley Chisholm became the first woman to seek a major party's nomination for the presidency, running in Democratic Party primaries against better known and better funded candidates. Although she won no primaries, she garnered 152 delegate votes, about 10 percent of the total. Her slogan, "unbought and unbossed," reflected both her personal feistiness and a lifetime of political independence.

women is still acceptable. There is very little understanding yet of the immorality involved in double pay scales and the classification of most of the better jobs as 'for men only.'

More than half of the population of the United States is female. But women occupy only 2 percent of the managerial positions. They have not even reached the level of tokenism yet. No women sit on the AFL-CIO council or Supreme Court. There have been only two women who have held Cabinet rank, and at present there are none. Only two women now hold ambassadorial rank in the diplomatic corps. In Congress, we are down to one Senator and 10 Representatives. . . .

As in the field of equal rights for blacks, Spanish-Americans, the Indians, and other groups, laws will not change such deep-seated problems overnight. But they can be used to provide protection for those who are most abused, and to begin the process of evolutionary change by compelling the insensitive majority to re-examine its unconscious attitudes.

It is for this reason that I wish to introduce today a proposal that has been before every Congress for the last 40 years and that sooner or later must become part of the basic law of the land—the equal rights amendment."

Once the ERA had been introduced, NOW devoted substantial resources to getting Congress to pass it and send it to the states for ratification, which it did in 1972, establishing a seven- and then nine-year limit on the ratification process. Within NOW, however, not everyone agreed on how to define and achieve "equality." At its 1970 annual meeting, as Karla Jay recalled in her autobiography, the issue of whether equal rights should include lesbian rights proved contentious.

"Conservative elements of the women's movement were openly hostile to lesbians. For instance, Betty Friedan had branded us a 'lavender menace.' Lesbians, she believed, would blight the reputation of the National Organization for Women if its members were labeled 'man-haters' and 'a bunch of dykes.' The very threat of such appellations led NOW to deny the number of lesbians in its ranks. . . . Calls for attention to lesbian issues were attacked as divisive. . . . By the spring of 1970 many lesbian/feminists were frustrated at feeling ignored by both the women's and gay [liberation] movements. . . . A large group of us began to meet regularly . . . and . . . set about crafting the now-famous manifesto called 'The Woman-Identified Woman.' . . . It has become an oft-reprinted classic because it summed up so much of what we as radical lesbians thought about ourselves. . . . We . . . called ourselves 'woman-identified women'—that is, those

EQUALITY OF RIGHTS UNDER THE LAW SHALL NOT BE DENIED OR ABRIDGED BY THE UNITED STATES OR BY ANY STATE ON ACCOUNT OF SEX

At a 1978 "March for Equality" in Washington, D.C., participants carried a banner with the twenty-four-word text of the ERA.

who chose to work with and for others of our gender. It was a term even heterosexuals could feel comfortable claiming. . . . We knew we could no longer accept second-class status in the women's movement or the gay movement. We would be equal partners, or we would leave the straight women and gay men behind."

By 1977, when twenty thousand women, men, and children of all racial, ethnic, religious, political, sexual, and class identities gathered in Houston for a three-day National Women's Conference sponsored and financed by Congress, resolutions endorsing both an ERA and lesbian rights were on the agenda. Both passed. But, as a summary of the "National Plan of Action" included in the official report suggests, there were intense discussions and heated exchanges among the two thousand delegates over those and other controversial questions.

"The main work of the delegates was to vote on a proposed National Plan of Action, a 26-plank program that was itself the product of a lengthy democratic process that had taken almost a year. . . .

In 1971 NOW adopted a resolution acknowledging that lesbian rights are "a legitimate concern of feminism"; in 1984, it held a Lesbian Rights Conference.

Delegates to the Houston Convention wore buttons connecting their 1977 conference with the 1848 Seneca Falls Conference and identifying their state affiliations. The letters IWY referred to the United Nations International Women's Year, celebrated two years earlier.

Only one of the 26 planks was unchanged [from the year-long discussions]. Approved by 41 State meetings, it stated simply: 'The Equal Rights Amendment should be ratified.'

All 26 planks in the National Plan of Action were open to debate on the floor at the Houston meeting. . . .

With only 20 percent of the delegates opposing some or most of the planks, there emerged from Houston a consensus on what American women need and want to achieve equal rights, equal status, and equal responsibilities with men.

At the heart of the consensus was the belief that final ratification of the Equal Rights Amendment is needed, as one speaker said, 'to put women in the Constitution' and to establish a framework of justice for their efforts to remove remaining barriers to equality.

Their other demands . . . ran the gamut of issues that touch women's lives: equal opportunities for women in the arts and humanities, in the media, in elective and appointive office, in credit and insurance, in business and education, in formulating foreign policy; extension of social security benefits to homemakers and programs to provide counseling and other services for displaced homemakers; assistance to battered women, disabled women, minority women, older women, rural women, and women in prison; concern for women's health needs and the right to choose abortion, with Federal and State Medicaid benefits for those who cannot afford it; pregnancy disability benefits for employed women; civil rights for lesbians; protection against rape and child abuse; comprehensive child care facilities; welfare reform, educational and job programs for poor women; an end to all discrimination in employment and an opening up of new job opportunities for women."

Ann Follis, president of the Homemakers' Equal Rights Association, commented in 1977 on the Amendment's importance to the women in her organization.

"When I began to work for ERA, I was appalled at the laws regarding the married woman. The law essentially regards the married woman as the property of her husband. Well, ERA is not going to send policemen into everybody's house to make sure that everything is being done equally. It is just a legal situation that will recognize that the wife, under law, will be a partner in the family enterprise."

Disagreements among the delegates to the Houston Conference were not confined to disputes among supporters of women's rights. Some

delegates opposed all of the main resolutions, especially those support- ing an ERA, abortion rights, and lesbian rights. They circulated a "Call to Action" but did not formally submit it to the Conference Resolutions Committee.

"We are unalterably opposed to any extension of the ratification period for ERA. If the amendment cannot be ratified within seven years, it obviously has no significant or worthwhile merit.

While we wholeheartedly favor equal pay, equal educational opportunities, and job opportunities for women, we cannot sup- port this dangerous amendment.

It will do nothing to solve any of woman's real problems. . . . Instead, constitutional scholars and attorneys have warned us re- peatedly that ERA can:

Remove the legal requirement that husbands support wives . . .;

Require the legalization of homosexual marriages and allow these couples to adopt children . . .;

Constitutionally mandate the 'right' to kill unborn babies . . .;

Subject women to compulsory military service and combat duty on a par with men . . .;

Forbid any religious body which has a tax-exempt status from refusing certain roles within their body to women or homosexuals. . . ."

Chief among the opponents of the Houston Conference "Plan of Action" and especially the ERA was Phyllis Schlafly, founder of STOP-ERA and leader of a political organization entitled Eagle Forum. In a 1976 inter- view with the Washington (D.C.) *Star*, she explained her views.

"[T]he voters recognized ERA as a fraud, and they're against it. They recognize it as a takeaway of women's rights; they recognize it won't do anything good for women, and so they're against it. . . . ERA will take away the right of the wife to be supported and to have her minor children supported. Obviously, this is an attack on the rights of the wife and on the family. The principal thing that ERA does is to take away the right of the wife in an ongoing mar- riage, the wife in the home. . . . I think our laws are entitled to re- flect the natural differences and the role assigned by God, in that women have babies and men don't have babies.

Therefore, the wife has the right to support, and the husband has the duty to pay for the groceries on the table. Anything that ERA does to that is a takeaway of what she has now. It's a reduction in those rights. . . .

ERA Ratification 1972-1982

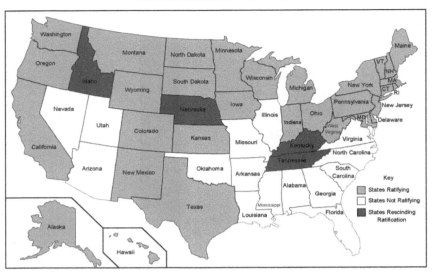

Key
- States Ratifying
- States Not Ratifying
- States Rescinding Ratification

Thirty-eight states were needed to ratify the ERA. In 1977, Indiana became the thirty-fifth state to ratify, but no other states did so before the 1982 deadline. The amendment failed.

[T]he women's movement . . . is destructive and antifamily. I think their goals can be summed up as, first, for ERA, which is a takeaway of the legal rights that wives now have. Second, it is pro-abortion on demand and government-financed abortion and abortion in government hospitals or any hospitals. Third, it's for state nurseries, to get the children in the nurseries and off the backs of the mothers.

Fourth, it is for prolesbian legislation, which is certainly an antimarriage movement. And fifth, it is for changing the school textbooks in order to eliminate what they call the stereotype of woman in the home as wife and mother. So I consider that all five of their princip[al] objectives are antifamily."

The ERA campaign had brought women's rights issues, including the question of what equal rights might mean, into regular public discussions and provoked a serious backlash. In the early 1980s, Gloria Steinem, editor of *Ms.* magazine, took stock of what had—and had not—occurred in the 1970s as a result of feminist activism, and outlined ideas about next steps.

"[W]e might see the seventies as a time of massive consciousness-raising: of breaking the conspiracy of silence on the depth of sex-based inequities, both nationally and internationally, and of achieving token victories that raised women's hopes. Having forged a majority change in consciousness, we are now ready for more institutional, systematic change in the eighties. A redistribution of power in families, a revolution in the way children are raised and by whom, flexible work schedules outside the home, a lessening of the violence that is rooted in the cult of masculinity, the redistribution of wealth that would begin if we actually got comparable pay: all these structural changes are possible because hopes were raised in the seventies.

If, on the other hand, we are simply among the millions of women struggling to survive the double burden of working outside the home, yet carrying the major responsibility for homemaking and raising children, we might describe the seventies as the decade in which we advanced *half* the battle. We've learned that women can and should do 'men's jobs,' for instance, and we've won the principle (if not the fact) of getting equal pay. But we haven't yet established the principle (much less the fact) that men can and should do 'women's jobs': that homemaking and child-rearing are as much a man's responsibility, too, and that those jobs in which women are concentrated outside the home would probably be better paid if more men became secretaries, file clerks, and nurses, too.... If men become flight attendants but women don't become pilots and airline executives, ... women will still be on the losing end.

Politicians and organizers would surely measure the success of the seventies ... by the force of the right-wing backlash against all of these majority changes in hopes and values. Representatives of a social order that depends mostly on sex, race, and class privilege for its power, and is often justified by the mythic economic force of patriarchal religions, are feeling endangered. They have paid this feminism the honor of opposing it very seriously indeed...."

Susan Faludi's 1991 book, *Backlash: The Undeclared War Against American Women*, offered a stinging critique of how various media portrayed the gains women had made in seeking equal rights, and dissected claims that equality between the sexes had been fully realized.

"Just when women's quest for equal rights seemed closest to achieving its objectives, the backlash struck it down. Just when a 'gender gap' at the voting booth surfaced in 1980, and women in politics began to talk of capitalizing on it, the Republican party elected Ronald Reagan and both political parties began to shunt women's rights off their platforms. Just when support for feminism and the Equal Rights Amendment reached a record high in 1981, the amendment was defeated the following year. Just when women were starting to mobilize against battering and sexual assaults, the federal government stalled funding for battered-women's programs, defeated bills to fund shelters, and shut down its Office of Domestic Violence—only two years after opening it in 1979. Just when record numbers of younger women were supporting feminist goals in the mid-'80s (more of them, in fact, than older women) and a majority of all women were calling themselves feminists, the media declared the advent of a younger 'post-feminist'

Gender Gap: Introduced into the language during the 1970s, when electoral polling data first showed that women's voting patterns diverged significantly from men's, the term came into wide use to describe persistent differences between women and men in areas such as job opportunities and pay equity. The National Committee on Pay Equity (http://www.pay-equity.org/info-time.html) found that in 2013, full-time, year-round women workers earned, on average, about 78% of what men earned. For African American women, the figure was 68%, for Latinas 60%, and for Asian American women, it was 85% of all men's earnings.

generation that supposedly reviled the women's movement. Just when women racked up their largest percentage ever supporting the right to abortion, the U.S. Supreme Court moved toward reconsidering it.

In other words, the antifeminist backlash has been set off not by women's achievement of full equality but by the increased possibility that they might win it. . . .

Although the backlash is not an organized movement, that doesn't make it any less destructive. In fact, the lack of orchestration, the absence of a single string-puller, only makes it harder to see—and perhaps more effective. A backlash against women's rights succeeds to the degree that it appears *not* to be political, that it appears not to be a struggle at all. It is most powerful when it goes private, when it lodges inside a woman's mind and turns her vision inward, until she imagines the pressure is all in her head, until she begins to enforce the backlash, too—on herself."

Journalist Barbara Ehrenreich reflected on what "equality" meant, and should mean, in a 1993 magazine article covering "women's progress in the last couple of decades."

"How far did we get and is there anything left over for anybody else to do? When we assess this progress, we have to remember that there were always at least two goals for the women's movement. The first goal is equality, which is a simple, though not necessarily easy, goal. It means simply that women's life chances must not be diminished by male supremacist beliefs and practices.

The second goal, which often gets lost or forgotten, involves challenging oppression based on race and class and all the other dimensions of potential inequality and injustice. . . .

We want equality, but we also want a world worth being equal in—a world in which repression and rigid forms of hierarchy would be seen as ugly relics. It's pointless even to imagine what equality for women would mean or could mean in the context of racial and class inequalities for both women and men. We reject . . . the idea of equality for women as a category, so long as there is inequality along these other lines, on the lines of color, ethnicity, and class."

Young women, referring to themselves as a "Third Wave" of feminism and often proudly calling themselves "girls," wondered how much had

really changed as they experienced the backlash against feminist gains, especially in popular culture. In a 1998 article, fifteen-year-old Jessica Rosenberg explained the philosophy of Riot Grrrls, a "loosely connected group of punk feminists who publish zines and play in bands " such as *Bikini Kill.*

"Riot Grrrl is much angrier than was the second wave of feminism of the 1970s. Riot Grrrls are loud and, through zines, music, and spoken word, express themselves honestly and straightforwardly. Riot Grrrl does not shy away from difficult issues and often addresses painful topics such as rape and abuse. Riot Grrrl is a call to action, to 'Revolution Girl-Style now.' At a time in their lives when girls are taught to be silent, Riot Grrrl demands that they scream.... Riot Grrrl, although remaining staunchly political, also pays attention to the personal and the everyday. It focuses more on the individual and the emotional than on marches, legislation, and public policy....

Across the country and even internationally, girls produce countless zines. Riot Grrrl sees zine writing and publishing as a basic method of empowerment; zine production is self-motivated, political activism that a girl can do entirely independently. Zines subvert standard patriarchal mainstream media by critiquing society and the media without being censored....

More recently, Riot Grrrl has formed a community on the Internet.... Because the feminism of Riot Grrrl is self-determined and grassroots, its greatest power is that it gives girls room to decide for themselves who they are. It provides a viable alternative to the skinny white girls in *Seventeen* and *YM* (*Young and Modern*) magazines."

A 1992 report from the American Association of University Women (AAUW) documented *How Schools Shortchange Girls* **and challenged "the common assumption that girls and boys are treated equally in our public schools."**

"Girls and boys enter school roughly equal in measured ability. Twelve years later girls have fallen behind their male classmates in key areas such as higher-level mathematics and measures of self-esteem. Yet gender equity is still not a part of the national debate on educational reform....

What Happens in the Classroom?
- Girls receive significantly less attention from classroom teachers than boys.

After the turn of the century, Internet-based social networks, blogs, Twitter, and other social media sites became increasingly important as forums for feminist debates, as well as means for organizing and mobilizing around women's rights issues.

- African American girls have fewer interactions with teachers than do white girls, despite evidence that they attempt to initiate interactions more frequently. . . .

A large body of research indicates that teachers give more classroom attention and more esteem-building encouragement to boys. . . . In a study . . . boys in elementary and middle school called out answers eight times more often than girls. When boys called out, teachers listened. But when girls called out, they were told to 'raise your hand if you want to speak.' Even when boys do not volunteer, teachers are more likely to encourage them to give an answer or an opinion than they are to encourage girls. . . .

What Do We Teach Our Students?
- The contributions and experiences of girls and women are still marginalized or ignored in many of the textbooks used in our nation's schools. . . .

Perhaps the most evaded issue of all topics in schools is the issue of gender and power. As girls mature they confront a culture that both idealizes and exploits the sexuality of young women while assigning them roles that are clearly less valued than male roles. If we do not begin to discuss more openly the ways in which ascribed power—whether on the basis of race, sex, class, sexual orientation, or religion—affects individual lives, we cannot truly prepare our students for responsible citizenship. . . .

The formal school curriculum must include the experiences of women and men from all walks of life. Girls and boys must see women and girls reflected and valued in the materials they study."

Cartoonist Gary Trudeau illustrated the findings of the AAUW report in his comic strip "Doonesbury."

In an anthology published in 1995, writer JeeYeun Lee contributed her thoughts on how the feminism of young "women of color" like herself differed from that of their predecessors.

"I want to emphasize that the feminism that I and other young women come to today is one that is at least sensitive to issues of exclusion. If perhaps twenty years ago charges of racism, classism and homophobia were not taken seriously, today they are the cause of extreme anguish and soul-searching. I am profoundly grateful to older feminists of color and their white allies who struggled to bring U.S. feminist movements to this point. . . . Women of color do not struggle in feminist movements simply to add cultural diversity, to add the viewpoints of different kinds of women. Women of color feminist theories challenge the fundamental premises of feminism, such as the very definition of 'women,' and call for recognition of the constructed racial nature of all experiences of gender. . . . Sisterhood may be global, but who is in that sisterhood? None of us can afford to assume anything about anybody else. This thing called 'feminism' takes a great deal of hard work, and I think this is one of the primary hallmarks of young feminists' activism today: We realize that coming together and working together are by no means natural or easy."

Perhaps the best-known work by younger feminists who identified themselves as members of a "Third Wave" was the 2000 book *Manifesta* (with a new edition in 2010) by the journalists Jennifer Baumgardner and Amy Richards. They conceived their "Third Wave MANIFESTA: A Thirteen-Point Agenda" as a modern-day "declaration of sentiments," comparable to that first issued at Seneca Falls in 1848.

"1. To out unacknowledged feminists, specifically those who are younger, so that **Generation X [a popular term for Americans born in the 1980s and 1990s]** can become a visible movement, and, further, a voting block of eighteen- to forty-year-olds.

2. To safeguard a woman's right to bear or not to bear a child, regardless of circumstances, including women who are younger than eighteen or impoverished. To preserve this right throughout her life and support the choice to be childless.

3. To make explicit that the fight for reproductive rights must include birth control; the right for poor women and lesbians to have children; partner adoption for gay couples; subsidized fertility treatments for all women who choose them; and freedom from sterilization abuse. . . .

4. To bring down the double standard in sex and sexual health, and foster male responsibility and assertiveness in the following areas: achieving freedom from STDs; more fairly dividing the burden of family planning as well as responsibilities such as child care; and eliminating violence against women.

5. To tap into and raise awareness of our revolutionary history, and to the fact that almost all movements began as youth movements. To have access to our intellectual feminist legacy and women's history; . . .

6. To support and increase the visibility and power of lesbians and bisexual women and trans people in the feminist movement, in high schools, colleges, and the workplace. To recognize that queer women have always been at the forefront of the feminist movement, and that there is nothing to be gained—and much to be lost—by downplaying their history, whether inadvertently or actively.

7. To . . . see activism not as a choice between self and community but as a link between them that creates balance.

8. To have equal access to health care, regardless of income, which includes coverage equivalent to men's. . . .

9. For women who so desire to participate in all reaches of the military, including combat, and to enjoy all the benefits (loans, health care, pensions) offered to its members for as long as we continue to have an active military. . . .

10. To liberate adolescents from slut-bashing, listless educators, sexual harassment, and bullying at school, as well as violence in all walks of life, . . .

11. To make the workplace responsive to an individual's wants, needs, and talents. This includes valuing (monetarily) stay-at-home parents, aiding employees who want to spend more time with family and continue to work, equalizing pay for jobs of comparable worth, enacting a minimum wage that would bring a full-time worker with two children over the poverty line, and providing employee benefits for freelance and part-time workers.

12. To acknowledge that, although feminists may have disparate values, we share the same goal of equality, and of supporting one another in our efforts to gain the power to make our own choices.

13. To pass the Equal Rights Amendment so that we can have a constitutional foundation of righteousness and

equality upon which future women's rights conventions will stand."

On August 26, 2008, Women's Equality Day (marking the date in 1920 when the Nineteenth Amendment was ratified), retired factory supervisor Lilly Ledbetter gave a speech to the Democratic National Convention explaining how, despite the provisions of the 1964 Civil Rights Act, she was systematically, and legally, underpaid for nineteen years. The inequities she described were rectified for future workers by the 2009 Lilly Ledbetter Fair Pay Act.

"I'm here to talk about America's commitment to fairness and equality, and how people like me—and like you—suffer when that commitment is betrayed.

How fitting that I speak to you on Women's Equality Day, when we celebrate ratification of the amendment that gave women the right to vote. Even as we celebrate, let's also remind ourselves: The fight for equality is not over. I know that from personal experience. I was a trailblazer when I went to work as a female supervisor at a Goodyear tire plant in Gadsden, Alabama.

My job demanded a lot, and I gave it 100 percent. I kept up with every one of my male co-workers. But toward the end of my nineteen years at Goodyear, I began to suspect that I wasn't getting paid as much as men doing the same job. An anonymous note in my mailbox confirmed that I was right. Despite praising me for my work, Goodyear gave me smaller raises than my male co-managers, over and over.

Those differences affected my family's quality of life then, and they affect my retirement [income] now. When I discovered the injustice, I thought about moving on. But in the end, I couldn't ignore the discrimination. So I went to court. A jury agreed with me. They found that my employer had violated the law and awarded me what I was owed.

I hoped the verdict would make my company feel the sting, learn a lesson and never again treat women unfairly. But they appealed, all the way to the Supreme Court, and in a 5-to-4 decision our highest court sided with big business. They said I should have filed my complaint within six months of Goodyear's first decision to pay me less, even though I didn't know that's what they were doing. . . .

My case is over. I will never receive the pay I deserve. But there will be a far richer reward if we secure fair pay. For our children and grandchildren so that no one will ever again experience the discrimination that I did. Equal pay for equal work is a fundamental American principle."

In 2013, the Secretary of Defense lifted barriers to women in the military serving in combat.

Global Connections

American women's rights advocates established connections with their counterparts around the globe at United Nations conferences where women's rights were on the agenda. Among the most important were the International Women's Year Conference in Mexico City, Mexico, in 1975, the UN World Women's Conference in Copenhagen, Denmark, in 1980, the Third World Women's Conference in Nairobi, Kenya, in 1985, and the 1995 UN World Conference on Women in Beijing, China. As a result of these meetings, and building on its 1948 Universal Declaration of Human Rights, in 1979, the UN General Assembly adopted the Convention on the Elimination of all forms of Discrimination Against Women (CEDAW) and established a committee to study the Convention's implementation. The United States' UN representative signed CEDAW, but because the Senate did not ratify it, it has no force in the United States.

"[T]he Charter of the United Nations reaffirms faith in fundamental human rights, in the dignity and worth of the human person and in the equal rights of men and women, . . . [yet] extensive discrimination against women continues to exist . . . . [Such discrimination] violates the principles of equality of rights and respect for human dignity, is an obstacle to the participation of women, on equal terms with men, in the political, social, economic and cultural life of their countries. . . .

[T]he eradication of apartheid, all forms of racism, racial discrimination, colonialism, neo-colonialism, aggression, foreign occupation and domination and interference in the internal affairs of States is essential to the full enjoyment of the rights of men and women. . . .

Article 1. For the purposes of the present Convention, the term 'discrimination against women' shall mean any distinction, exclusion or restriction made on the basis of sex which has the effect or purpose of impairing or nullifying the recognition, enjoyment or exercise by women, irrespective of their marital status, on a basis of equality of men and women, of human rights and fundamental freedoms in the political, economic, social, cultural, civil or any other field.

Article 2. State Parties condemn discrimination against women in all its forms, agree to pursue by all appropriate means and without delay a policy of eliminating discrimination against women. . . .

Article 3. State parties shall take in all fields, in particular in the political, social, economic and cultural fields, all appropriate measures, including legislation, to ensure the full development and advancement of women, for the purpose of guaranteeing them the exercise and enjoyment of human rights and fundamental freedoms on a basis of equality with men."

Implementing the lofty goals of the CEDAW treaty required U.S. feminists to learn how to work with feminists from around the globe, who held diverse perspectives on women's rights. In a talk delivered at the 2011 Berkshire Conference on Women's History, American feminist Charlotte Bunch reflected upon her activist history, her education in working on global women's issues, and the role of the UN in shaping "transnational feminist activism."

"The four UN World Conferences on Women—Mexico City 1975, Copenhagen 1980, Nairobi 1985, and Beijing 1995—became avenues and opportunities for many feminists to discover each other and to learn and struggle together as we engaged in what has come to be called transnational feminist activism. . . . The United Nations certainly did not create feminism, and its conferences, women's units, declarations, or other activities are not substitutes for women's movements nor should they be expected to be so. However, the UN has provided an invaluable international focus on women's lives and rights, thus expanding the public space in which feminists could work. Women developed international contacts and political savvy, exchanged strategies, and engaged with governments; all of these activities strengthened the impact of their work on the ground.

These events profoundly affected my life and work as a feminist as they did many of my generation, both in the U.S. and elsewhere. I entered UN-sponsored women's space in 1975 as an anti-imperialist U.S. feminist from the women's liberation strand of the women's movement, with its roots in the 1960s U.S. civil rights and anti-war movements. . . . As a member of the women's caucus of the Board of the National Gay (and Lesbian) Task Force, I helped organize 'lesbian visibility' activities around the World Conference in Mexico City, but I did not attend the conference mostly because I thought too many 'gringas' crossing the border would dominate the event, . . . but wished I had gone and vowed never to miss another of these conferences. . . .

[The Mexico City Conference] was a massive global consciousness-raising moment, even if a painful one, as women learned how women's issues were seen in other countries. . . . [It] introduced activists to the potential of pursuing their interests through the UN, at a time when there were few international venues for women's rights, . . . [and led to] the International Tribunal on

Crimes Against Women ... [and] several parallel tribunals.... [Women's testimonies] forecasted many women's rights concerns that have made their way onto the UN agenda over the past three decades, from forced motherhood to economic crimes to femicide and violence against women in many forms....

The ... Conference on Women in Copenhagen in 1980 was overwhelmed by ... debate over which factors—sexism, racism, or the economy—were more important to women's subordination.... Of particular importance to me was the debate over 'what is a women's issue,' which initially was polarized between a predominantly 'western' tendency to separate out a limited specific gendered list of women's issues and a more 'southern' approach that saw all issues as women's issues, but often left women open to manipulation by governments or political parties.... I observed that in sessions on violence against women we were most able to talk across various lines of division, ... Women mobilizing against gendered violence could work concretely from a feminist political perspective that acknowledged the many differences among us, while affirming commonality in our struggles....

In the preparations for the Copenhagen conference, I met Roxanna Carrillo from Peru, the woman who would later become my life partner and my closest colleague in the work we began together on global feminism and human rights.... Through my time with her in Latin America, I developed [my understanding] that the ideas we call 'feminism' have many historical roots in every part of the world and that global feminist transnational work must be grounded in, and learn from, the particularities of each locale....

The Nairobi World Conference was particularly important for global feminism as it was the place where it became clear that the movement indeed was global.... Women's diversity was embraced as strength even when diversity produced conflict. A growing consensus was that all issues were indeed women's issues and needed a gendered or feminist lens applied to them....

The Fourth World Conference on Women in Beijing was a highlight for the global women's movement and consolidated its gains on the UN agenda.... The Beijing Platform for Action took up the new framework of women's rights as human rights ... and included 'the girl child'—a topic African women added to the agenda....

Women's transnational feminist activism has continued since Beijing both at the UN and in other arenas.... But many challenges continue to face feminist transnational activism as backlash and anti-feminist forces have gained ground in a number of countries and often at the UN as well. The polarizations of the world post-9/11 have made women's alliances across cultural lines more difficult.... In the globalized world of today, transnational feminist activism is not only a choice but a necessity for women's rights as local and global actions are so interconnected."

At the Fourth World Conference on Women, held in Beijing in 1995, First Lady Hillary Rodham Clinton led the United States delegation. Her speech on that occasion included a ringing declaration that "women's rights are human rights."

"By gathering in Beijing, we are focusing world attention on issues that matter most in our lives—the lives of women and their families: access to education, health care, jobs and credit, the chance to enjoy basic legal and human rights and to participate fully in the political life of our countries....

The great challenge of this conference is to give voice to women everywhere whose experiences go unnoticed, whose words go unheard. Women comprise more than half the world's population, 70% of the world's poor, and two-thirds of those who are not taught to read and write. We are the primary caretakers for most of the world's children and elderly. Yet much of the work we do is not valued—not by economists, not by historians, not by popular culture, not by government leaders....

Our goals for this conference, to strengthen families and societies by empowering women to take greater control over their own destinies, cannot be fully achieved unless all governments—here and around the world—accept their responsibility to protect and promote internationally recognized human rights.... Tragically, women are most often the ones whose human rights are violated. Even now, in the late 20th century, the rape of women continues to be used as an instrument of armed conflict. Women and children make up a large majority of the world's refugees. And when women are excluded from the political process, they become even more vulnerable to abuse. I believe that now, on the eve of a new millennium, it is time to break the silence. It is time for us to say here in Beijing, and for the world to hear, that it is no longer acceptable to discuss women's rights as separate from human rights....

If there is one message that echoes forth from this conference, let it be that human rights are women's rights and women's rights are human rights once and for all."

Established in 1976, UNIFEM was a United Nations agency working to promote women's rights around the world. In 2011, it was merged into UN Women.

Further Reading

General Works

Baumgartner, Jennifer, and Amy Richards. *Manifesta: Young Women, Feminism, and the Future.* 2nd ed. New York: Farrar, Straus, and Giroux, 2010.

Cobble, Dorothy Sue, Linda Gordon, and Astrid Henry. *Feminism Unfinished: A Short, Surprising History of American Women's Movements.* New York: Liveright, 2014.

Collins, Gail. *When Everything Changed: The Amazing Journey of American Women from 1960 to the Present.* New York: Little, Brown, 2009.

Cushman, Clare, *Supreme Court Decisions and Women's Rights.* Washington, D.C: Congressional Quarterly Press, 2001.

DeLuzio, Crista, ed. *Women's Rights: People and Perspectives.* Santa Barbara, CA: ABC-CLIO Press, 2010.

Echols, Alice. *Daring to Be Bad: Radical Feminism in America, 1965–1975.* Minneapolis: University of Minnesota Press, 1989.

Evans, Sara. *Personal Politics: The Roots of Women's Liberation in the Civil Rights Movement and the New Left.* New York: Knopf, 1979.

Faulkner, Carol, and Alison M. Parker, *Interconnections: Gender and Race in American History.* Rochester: University of Rochester Press, 2012.

Flexner, Eleanor, and Ellen Fitzpatrick. *Century of Struggle: The Woman's Rights Movement in the United States.* Cambridge, MA: Harvard University Press, 1996.

Freedman, Estelle. *No Turning Back: The History of Feminism and the Future of Women.* New York: Ballantine Books, 2002.

———. *Redefining Rape: Sexual Violence in the Era of Suffrage and Segregation.*
Cambridge, MA: Harvard University Press, 2013.

Freeman, Jo. *We Will Be Heard: Women's Struggles for Political Power in the United States.* Lanham, MD: Rowman and Littlefield, 2008.

Giddings, Paula. *When and Where I Enter: The Impact of Black Women on Race and Sex in America.* New York: Morrow, 1984.

Gilmore, Stephanie, ed. *Feminist Coalitions: Historical Perspectives on Second-Wave Feminism in the United States.* Urbana: University of Illinois Press, 2008.

Harrison, Cynthia. *On Account of Sex: The Politics of Women's Issues, 1945–1968.* Berkeley: University of California Press, 1988.

Hewitt, Nancy, ed. *No Permanent Waves: Recasting Histories of U.S. Feminism.* New Brunswick, NJ: Rutgers University Press, 2010.

Kerber, Linda K. *No Constitutional Right to be Ladies: Women and the Obligations of Citizenship.* New York: Hill & Wang, 1998.

Kessler-Harris, Alice. *In Pursuit of Equity: Women, Men and the Quest for Economic Citizenship in 20th-Century America.* New York: Oxford University Press, 2001.

Mayeri, Serena. *Reasoning from Race: Feminism, Law, and the Civil Rights Revolution.* Cambridge, MA: Harvard University Press, 2011.

Perdue, Theda, ed. *Sifters: Native American Women's Lives.* New York: Oxford University Press, 2001.

Rosen, Ruth. *The World Split Open: How the Women's Movement Changed America.* New York: Penguin Books, 2000.

Springer, Kimberly, *Living for the Revolution: Black Feminist Organizations, 1968–1980.* Durham, NC: Duke University Press, 2005.

Stansell, Christine. *The Feminist Promise: 1792 to the Present.* New York: Modern Library, 2010.

Van Burkleo, Sandra F. *"Belonging to the World": Women's Rights and American Constitutional Culture.* New York: Oxford University Press, 2001.

Wayne, Tiffany K. *Women's Rights in the United States: A Comprehensive Encyclopedia of Issues, Events, and People.* 4 vols. Santa Barbara, CA: ABC-CLIO Press, 2014.

Zaeske, Susan. *Signatures of Citizenship: Petitioning, Antislavery, & Women's Political Identity.* Chapel Hill: University of North Carolina Press, 2003.

Suffrage and Equal Rights

Baker, Jean, ed. *Votes for Women: The Struggle for Suffrage Revisited.* New York: Oxford University Press, 2002.

Bausum, Ann. *With Courage and Cloth: Winning the Fight for a Woman's Right to Vote.* Washington, DC: National Geographic Society, 2004.

Berry, Mary Frances. *Why the ERA Failed: Women's Rights and the Amending Process of the Constitution.* Bloomington: Indiana University Press, 1988.

Bredbenner, Candice Lewis. *A Nationality of Her Own: Women, Marriage, and the Law of Citizenship.* Berkeley: University of California Press, 1998.

Cole, Johnnetta Betsch, and Beverly Guy-Sheftall. *Gender Talk: The Struggle for Women's Equality in African American Communities.* New York: Ballantine Books, 2003.

Collins, Patricia Hill. *Black Feminist Thought: Knowledge, Consciousness, and the Politics of Empowerment.* New York: Routledge, 1990.

Cott, Nancy. *The Grounding of Modern Feminism*. New Haven: Yale University Press, 1987.

DuBois, Ellen. *Feminism and Suffrage: The Emergence of an Independent Women's Movement in America, 1848–1869*. Ithaca, NY: Cornell University Press, 1978.

Dudden, Faye. *Fighting Chance: The Struggle over Woman Suffrage and Black Suffrage in Reconstruction America*. New York: Oxford University Press, 2011.

Ginzberg, Lori D. *Untidy Origins: A Story of Woman's Rights in Antebellum New York*. Chapel Hill: University of North Carolina Press, 2005.

Gordon, Ann, and Bettye Collier-Thomas, eds. *African American Women and the Vote, 1837–1965*. Amherst: University of Massachusetts Press, 1997.

Hoffert, Sylvia. *When Hens Crow: The Women's Rights Movement in Antebellum America*. Bloomington: Indiana University Press, 1995.

Isenberg, Nancy. *Sex and Citizenship in Antebellum America*. Chapel Hill: University of North Carolina Press, 1998.

Jones, Martha. *All Bound Up Together: The Woman Question in African American Public Culture, 1830–1900*. Chapel Hill: University of North Carolina Press, 2007.

Kraditor, Aileen. *The Ideas of the Woman Suffrage Movement: 1890–1920*. Chicago: Quadrangle Books, 1968.

Lunardini, Christine. *From Equal Suffrage to Equal Rights: Alice Paul and the National Woman's Party, 1910–1928*. New York: New York University Press, 1986.

Mansbridge, Jane, *Why We Lost the ERA*. Chicago: University of Chicago Press, 1986.

Marshall, Susan. *Splintered Sisterhood: Gender and Class in the Campaign against Suffrage*. Madison: University of Wisconsin Press, 1997.

Mathews, Donald, and Jane Sherron DeHart. *Sex, Gender, and the Politics of ERA: A State and the Nation*. New York: Oxford University Press, 1990.

Mead, Rebecca. *How the Vote Was Won: Woman Suffrage in the Western United States, 1868–1914*. New York: New York University Press, 2004.

Rupp, Leila, and Verta Taylor, *Survival in the Doldrums: The American Women's Rights Movement, 1945 to the 1960s*. New York: Oxford University Press, 1987.

Schwarz, Judith. *The Radical Feminists of Heterodoxy: Greenwich Village, 1912–1940*. Lebanon, NH: New Victoria Publishers, 1982.

Scott, Anne Firor, ed. *One Half the People: The Fight for Woman Suffrage*. Urbana: University of Illinois Press, 1982.

Terborg-Penn, Rosalyn. *African American Women in the Struggle for the Vote, 1850–1920*. Bloomington: Indiana University Press, 1998.

Tetrault, Lisa. *The Myth of Seneca Falls: Memory and the Women's Suffrage Movement, 1848–1898*. Chapel Hill: University of North Carolina Press, 2014.

Wheeler, Marjorie Spruill. *New Women of the New South: The Leaders of the Woman Suffrage Movement in the Southern States*. New York: Oxford University Press, 1993.

———. *One Woman, One Vote: Rediscovering the Woman Suffrage Movement*. Troutdale, OR: New Sage Press, 1996.

White, Deborah Gray. *Too Heavy a Load: Black Women in Defense of Themselves, 1894–1994*. New York: W.W. Norton, 1999.

Useful Texts and Documentary Collections

Alexander, M. Jacqui, ed. *Third Wave: Feminist Perspectives on Racism*. Brooklyn, NY: Kitchen Table Press, 1994.

Anzaldúa, Gloria. *Making Face, Making Soul/Haciendo Caras: Creative and Critical Perspectives by Feminists of Color*. San Francisco: Aunt Lute Books, 1990.

Baer, Judith A., and Leslie Friedman Goldstein, eds. *The Constitutional and Legal Rights of Women*. 3rd ed. Los Angeles: Roxbury, 2006.

Blumenthal, Karen. *Let Me Play: The Story of Title IX, the Law That Changed the Future of Girls in America*. New York: Atheneum, 2005.

Buhle, Mari Jo, and Paul Buhle, eds. *The Concise History of Woman Suffrage*. Urbana: University of Illinois Press, 1978.

DuBois, Ellen Carol, ed. *Elizabeth Cady Stanton, Susan B. Anthony: Correspondence, Writings, Speeches*. Boston: Northeastern University Press, 1991.

DuPlessis, Rachel Blau, and Ann Snitow. *The Feminist Memoir Project: Voices from Women's Liberation*. New York: Three Rivers Press, 1998.

Foner, Philip S., ed. *Frederick Douglass on Women's Rights*. Westport, CT: Greenwood Press, 1976.

Foster, Frances Smith, ed. *A Brighter Coming Day: A Frances Ellen Watkins Harper Reader*. New York: Feminist Press, 1990.

García, Alma M, ed. *Chicana Feminist Thought: The Basic Historical Writings*. New York: Routledge, 2007.

Gordon, Ann, ed. *The Selected Papers of Elizabeth Cady Stanton and Susan B. Anthony.* 5 vols. New Brunswick, NJ: Rutgers University Press, 1997–.

Gordon, Linda, and Rosalyn Baxandall, eds. *America's Working Women: A Documentary History, 1600–Present.* New York: W. W. Norton, 1995.

———. *Dear Sisters: Dispatches from the Women's Liberation Movement.* New York: Basic Books, 2000.

Guy-Sheftall, Beverly, ed. *Words of Fire: An Anthology of African-American Feminist Thought.* New York: New Press, 1995.

Hole, Judith, and Ellen Levine, eds. *The Rebirth of Feminism.* New York: Quadrangle Books, 1971.

hooks, bell. *Feminist Theory from Margin to Center.* Cambridge, MA: South End, 1984.

Hine, Darlene Clark, ed. *Black Women in America: An Historical Encyclopedia.* Brooklyn, NY: Carlson, 1993.

Jones, Beverly Washington. *Quest for Equality: The Life and Writings of Mary Eliza Church Terrell, 1863–1954.* Brooklyn, NY: Carlson, 1990.

Keetley, Dawn, and John Pettegrew, eds. *Public Women, Public Words: A Documentary History of American Feminism.* 3 vols. Madison, WI: Madison House, 1997, and Lanham, MD: Rowman and Littlefield, 2002.

Kimmel, Michael S., and Thomas E. Mosmiller, eds. *Against the Tide: Pro-Feminist Men in the United States, 1776–1990: A Documentary History.* Boston: Beacon Press, 1992.

Kraditor, Aileen, ed. *Up from the Pedestal: Selected Writings in the History of American Feminism.* Chicago: Quadrangle Books, 1968.

Maclean, Nancy, ed., *The American Women's Movement, 1945–2000.* New York: Bedford Books, 2009.

Mathews, Donald, and Jane Sherron DeHart. *Sex, Gender, and the Politics of the ERA: A State and a Nation.* New York: Oxford University Press, 1990.

McClymer, John F., ed. *This High and Holy Moment: The First National Woman's Rights Convention, Worcester, 1850.* Orlando, FL: Harcourt Brace, 1999

Moraga, Cherríe, and Gloria Anzaldúa, eds. *This Bridge Called My Back: Writings by Radical Women of Color.* New York: Kitchen Table, 1983.

Richardson, Marilyn, ed. *Maria W. Stewart, America's First Black Woman Political Writer: Essays and Speeches.* Bloomington: Indiana University Press, 1987.

Rossi, Alice, ed. *The Feminist Papers: From Adams to de Beauvoir.* New York: Columbia University Press, 1973.

Roth, Benita. *Separate Roads to Feminism: Black, Chicana, and White Feminist Movements in America's Second Wave.* New York: Cambridge University Press, 2004.

Ruiz, Vicki L., and Virginia Sánchez Korrol, eds. *Latinas in the United States: A Historical Encyclopedia.* Bloomington: Indiana University Press, 2006.

Rupp, Leila J., and Verta Taylor, *Survival in the Doldrums: The American Women's Rights Movement, 1945 to the 1960s.* New York: Oxford University Press, 1987.

Schneir, Miriam, ed. *Feminism: The Essential Historical Writings.* New York: Vintage Books, 1994.

———. *Feminism in Our Time: The Essential Writings, World War II to the Present.* New York: Vintage, 1994.

Sheppard, Alice. *Cartooning for Suffrage.* Albuquerque: University of New Mexico Press, 1994.

Sklar, Kathryn Kish, ed. *Women's Rights Emerges within the Antislavery Movement.* Boston: Bedford/ St. Martin's, 2000.

Smith, Barbara, ed. *Homegirls: A Black Feminist Anthology.* New Brunswick, NJ: Rutgers University Press, 2000.

Stanton, Elizabeth Cady, et al., eds. *The History of Woman Suffrage,* 6 vols. New York: Fowler & Wells, 1881–1922.

Strom, Sharon Hartman, ed. *Women's Rights.* Westport, CT: Greenwood Press, 2003.

Biographies of Key Figures

Baker, Jean. *Margaret Sanger: A Life of Passion.* New York: Hill & Wang, 2011.

Barry, Kathleen. *Susan B. Anthony: A Biography of a Singular Feminist.* New York: New York University Press, 1995.

Bataille, Gretchen and Laurie Lisa. *Native American Women: A Biographical Dictionary.* New York: Garland, 1993.

Bay, Mia. *To Tell the Truth Freely: The Life of Ida B. Wells.* New York: Hill & Wang, 2009.

Bordin, Ruth. *Frances Willard: A Biography.* Chapel Hill: University of North Carolina Press, 1986.

Critchlow, Donald. *Phyllis Schlafly and Grassroots Conservatism: A Woman's Crusade.* Princeton, NJ: Princeton University Press, 2005.

Falk, Candace. *Love, Anarchy, and Emma Goldman.* New Brunswick, NJ: Rutgers University Press, 1984.

Gallman, J. Matthew. *America's Joan of Arc: The Life of Anna Elizabeth Dickinson.* New York: Oxford University Press, 2006.

Ginzberg, Lori D. *Elizabeth Cady Stanton: An American Life.* New York: Hill & Wang, 2009.

Hoffert, Sylvia. *Alva Vanderbilt Belmont: Unlikely Champion of Women's Rights.* Bloomington: Indiana University Press, 2012.

Horowitz, Daniel. *Betty Friedan and the Making of the Feminine Mystique.*

Amherst: University of Massachusetts Press, 1998.

Hine, Darlene Clark, ed. *Black Women in America: An Historical Encyclopedia*. Brooklyn, NY: Carlson, 1993.

Hoffert, Sylvia D. *Jane Grey Swisshelm: An Unconventional Life, 1815–1884*. Chapel Hill: University of North Carolina Press, 2004.

James, Edward T., et al., eds, *Notable American Women: A Biographical Dictionary*. 5 vols. Cambridge, MA: Harvard University Press, 1971–2004.

Lepore, Jill. *The Secret History of Wonder Woman*. New York: Random House, 2014.

Lerner, Gerda. *The Grimké Sisters from South Carolina: Pioneers for Women's Rights and Abolition*. New York: Houghton Mifflin, 1967.

Lunardini, Christine. *Alice Paul: Equality for Women*. Boulder, CO: Westview Press, 2013.

May, Vivian M., *Anna Julia Cooper, Visionary Black Feminist: A Critical Introduction*. New York: Routledge, 2007.

McDuffie, Erik S. *Sojourning for Freedom: Black Women, American Communism, and the Making of Black Left Feminism*. Durham: Duke University Press, 2011.

McMillen, Sally. *Lucy Stone: An Unapologetic Life*. New York: Oxford University Press, 2015.

Moynihan, Ruth Barnes. *Rebel for Rights, Abigail Scott Duniway*. New Haven, CT: Yale University Press, 1983.

Painter, Nell Irvin. *Sojourner Truth: A Life, a Symbol*. New York: W. W. Norton, 1996.

Ransby, Barbara. *Ella Baker and the Black Freedom Movement: A Radical Democratic Vision*. Chapel Hill: University of North Carolina Press, 2003.

Ruiz, Vicki L., and Virginia Sánchez Korrol, eds., *Latina Legacies: Identity, Biography, and Community*. New York: Oxford University Press, 2005.

Sklar, Kathryn Kish. *Florence Kelley and the Nation's Work: The Rise of Women's Political Culture, 1830–1900*. New Haven, CT: Yale University Press, 1995.

Venet, Wendy Hamand. *A Strong-Minded Woman: The Life of Mary Livermore*. Amherst: University of Massachusetts Press, 2005.

Washington, Margaret. *Sojourner Truth's America*. Urbana: University of Illinois Press, 2009.

Winslow, Barbara. *Shirley Chisholm: Catalyst for Change*. Boulder, CO: Westview Press, 2013.

Global Connections

Anderson, Bonnie. *Joyous Greetings: The First International Women's Movement, 1830–1860*. New York: Oxford University Press, 2000.

Berkovitch, Nitza. *From Motherhood to Citizenship: Women's Rights and International Organizations*. Baltimore: Johns Hopkins University Press, 1999.

D'Itri, Patricia Ward. *Cross Currents in the International Women's Movement, 1848–1948*. Bowling Green, OH: Bowling Green State Press, 1999.

Jain, Devaki. *Women, Development, and the UN: A Sixty-Year Quest for Equality and Justice*. Bloomington: Indiana University Press, 2005.

McFadden, Margaret. *Golden Cables of Sympathy: The Transatlantic Sources of Nineteenth-Century Feminism*. Lexington: University of Kentucky Press, 1999.

Moynagh, Maureen, with Nancy Forestall, eds. *Documenting First Wave Feminisms. Vol. 1, Transnational Collaborations and Crosscurrents*. Toronto: University of Toronto Press, 2012.

Offen, Karen. *Globalizing Feminisms, 1789–1945*. New York: Routledge, 2010.

Paisley, Fiona. *Glamour in the Pacific: Cultural Internationalism and Race Politics in the Women's Pan-Pacific*. Honolulu: University of Hawaii Press, 2009.

Rupp, Leila J. *Worlds of Women: The Making of an International Women's Movement*. Princeton, NJ: Princeton University Press, 1997.

"UN Activist Forum." *Journal of Women's History*, 24 (Winter 2012): 175–221.

Wu, Judy Tzu-Chun. *Radicals on the Road: Internationalism, Orientalism, and Feminism during the Vietnam Era*. Ithaca, NY: Cornell University Press, 2013.

Web Sites

National Women's History Project
http://www.nwhp.org/

An excellent starting point for resources, collectibles, and teaching materials on women's history in general.

Women and Social Movements in the United States, 1600–2000
http://womhist.alexanderstreet.com/

A vast archive of projects and documents relating to the history of women's activism in social movements, ranging from temperance to transnational feminist organizing. Of particular note are the recent additions of materials from the 1960s Commissions on the Status of Women, the 1977 Houston Conference, and the ongoing Black Women Suffragists project.

Women Working, 1800–1930
http://ocp.hul.harvard.edu/ww/

Digitized primary sources from the vast collections of Harvard University's Libraries. Includes a selection of anti-suffragist writings.

Schomburg Library of African American Women Writers
http://digital.nypl.org/schomburg/writers_aa19/toc.html

Digitized primary sources from a number of women writers whose documents are included here.

Library of Congress "Votes for Women"
http://memory.loc.gov/ammem/naw/nawshome.html

Part of the Library of Congress's "American Memory" project, the site includes a huge collection of materials on the suffrage crusade from the records of the National American Woman Suffrage Association.

Library of Congress "Photographs from the Records of the National Woman's Party"
http://memory.loc.gov/ammem/collections/suffrage/nwp/

This section of the "American Memory" project offers striking photographs.

National Archives "Teaching with Documents: Woman Suffrage and the 19th Amendment"
http://archives.gov/education/lessons/woman-suffrage/

Documents and lesson plans from the National Archives' collection on suffrage.

Suffragists Oral History
http://bancroft.berkeley.edu/ROHO/projects/suffragist/

Transcribed versions of a rare set of 1970s interviews with seven women suffrage leaders, including Alice Paul, along with four rank-and-file suffragists.

"Remember the Ladies!" Women Struggle for an Equal Voice
http://www.tennessee.gov/tsla/exhibits/suffrage/struggle.htm

Maintained by the Tennessee State Library and Archives, this site includes some excellent visuals on the suffrage struggle.

Women of the West Museum
http://theautry.org/research/women-of-the-west

Maintained by the Autry Center in Los Angeles, California, this site is dedicated to the history of women of all cultures in the American West.

No Turning Back: The History of Feminism and the Future of Women
http://noturningback.stanford.edu/

Stanford historian Estelle Freedman created this site in conjunction with her book, *No Turning Back*. It includes a great deal of material on the history of feminism worldwide.

Elizabeth Cady Stanton and Susan B. Anthony Papers
http://ecssba.rutgers.edu/

Rutgers University's project is publishing the papers of the two women. The site includes sample documents and links to many research sources on them.

Emma Goldman Papers
http://ucblibrary3.berkeley.edu/goldman/

The University of California at Berkeley is publishing Emma Goldman's papers. The site includes a great deal of information on Goldman, including sample documents, as well as links to related topics, such as Jewish women's activism for women's rights.

Eleanor Roosevelt Papers
http://www.gwu.edu/~erpapers/

This George Washington University site provides a guide to Eleanor Roosevelt's life, as well as to the project that is publishing her papers. It includes lesson plans and materials focusing on her work for women's rights and human rights.

Margaret Sanger Papers
http://www.nyu.edu/projects/sanger/

New York University sponsors the publication project for Margaret Sanger's papers. The web site provides biographical background on Sanger, documents, and links to research sources.

Anna Julia Cooper Center on Gender, Race, and Politics in the South
http://cooperproject.org/

Named for the 19th-century black feminist, the center provides materials for studying the intersection of gender and race in the history of the U.S. South.

Sewall Belmont House & Museum
http://www.sewallbelmont.org/

The historic home of the National Woman's Party (NWP), the Sewall-Belmont House maintains a web site with extensive resources on the history of the NWP and its founder, Alice Paul.

Chicago Women's Liberation Union History
http://www.cwluherstory.org/

Duke University "Documents from the Women's Liberation Movement"
http://scriptorium.lib.duke.edu/wlm/

Both sites provide numerous documents from the women's liberation branch of 1960s–1970s feminism.

United Nations Women Watch
http://www.un.org/womenwatch/

This United Nations site offers quick access to information on women around the world, as well as UN resources on women's rights.

International Museum of Women
http://www.imow.org/

Part of the Global Fund for Women, the museum maintains lively and interesting digital exhibits on a variety of topics related to global women's issues and provides links to other web sites that address gender equity around the world.

Third Wave Foundation
http://www.thirdwavefoundation.org/

A good starting point for learning about "Third Wave" feminism.

9 to 5 National Association of Working Women
http://9to5.org/

The web site of the advocacy group "9 to 5" provides useful statistics on women in the workforce.

National Committee on Pay Equity
http://www.pay-equity.org/

Founded in 1979, the National Committee on Pay Equity advocates for women's rights in the workforce.

Her Hat Was in the Ring!
http://www.herhatwasinthering.org/web/index.aspx

Dedicated to identifying and profiling women candidates for office, starting with the earliest women elected to school boards in the 1850s.

Center for American Women and Politics
http://www.cawp.rutgers.edu/

The go-to site for detailed information on women's experiences in politics, both historically and today.

Gender Equity in Sports
http://bailiwick.lib.uiowa.edu/ge/

Gender Equality in Athletics and Sports
http://www.feminist.org/sports/titleIXb.asp

Two sites cover the history of Title IX (1972) and advocate for gender equity in sports by providing news, data, and surveys.

National Organization for Women
http://www.now.org/

Independent Women's Forum
http://www.iwf.org/about

Two groups on opposite sides of contemporary feminist issues.

Timeline

1636
Massachusetts tried Anne Hutchinson for heresy.

1648
Margaret Brent requested a vote in the Maryland house.

1662
Virginia law established that slavery will be inherited matrilineally.

1662, 1668
Virginia laws differentiated between white and black women for purposes of taxation.

1667
Connecticut's legislature passed a law permitting divorce.

1691
Virginia's legislature passed a law punishing marriage across the color line.

1718
Pennsylvania's legislature passed a "feme sole trader" law.

1724
French "Code Noir" applied in Louisiana to marriages between whites and blacks.

1765
Blackwell's *Commentaries* summed up English Common law on women's rights.

1773
Phillis Wheatley published *Poems on Various Subjects*.

1774
Fifty-one Edenton Ladies signed a consumer boycott of tea.

1776–1782
Abigail Adams wrote letters to John Adams regarding women's rights.

1776
Free adult property-owning single women permitted to vote in New Jersey.

1780
Esther DeBerdt Reed and the Ladies Association of Philadelphia organized to express their support for the Patriot cause and the Continental Army.

1781
Elizabeth Freeman (Mumbet) sued for her freedom from slavery under the new Massachusetts state constitution.

1785
Pennsylvania's legislature passed a liberalized divorce law.

1790
Judith Sargent Murray published her essay "On the Equality of the Sexes."

1792
A Vindication of the Rights of Woman by Mary Wollstonecraft published in the United States.

1793
Priscilla Mason gave her rights-oriented salutatory oration at the Young LadiesAcademy of Philadelphia.

1798
Charles Brockden Brown discussed women's rights in his novel *Alcuin*.

1804
Thomas Jefferson assured a group of Louisiana nuns that their property rights would be protected despite the change from French to U.S. law.

1805
In *Martin v. Massachusetts*, a state court considered wives' citizenship rights.

1807
New Jersey revoked the voting rights of women.

1816
Tapping Reeve's *Law of Baron and Feme* adapted Blackstone's *Commentaries* for Americans.

1817
Cherokee women penned a petition to the group's all-male leadership regarding their customary property rights.

1818
Hannah Mather Crocker published *Observations on the Real Rights of Women*.

1827
The Constitution of the Cherokee Nation restricted voting to men alone.

1829
Frances Wright delivered her "Course of Popular Lectures" in New York.

1831–1832
Maria W. Stewart delivered lectures in Boston.

1835
Oberlin College admitted students without regard to race or sex.

1836
Sarah Grimké wrote *Letters on the Equality of the Sexes*.

1837
Ernestine Rose and Thomas Herttell circulated petitions advocating a married women's property law for New York.

1837–1839
Three Anti-Slavery Conventions of American Women considered the rights of women—enslaved and free.

1839
Mississippi enacted the first Married Women's Property Act.

1840
World's Anti-Slavery Convention in London refused to seat women delegates.

1846
Six women petitioned the New York State Constitutional convention for women's rights, including voting rights.

1848
New York State legislature passed a Married Women's Property Act.

Women's Rights Conventions held at Seneca Falls and Rochester, New York.

Treaty of Guadalupe Hidalgo raised questions about merging Spanish legal practices with English-derived common law.

Revolutions in Europe brought radical women to the United States as refugees.

Lower Canada adopted a law restricting voting rights to men.

Iroquois Nation Constitution restricted voting rights to men.

1848–1860
A Woman's Rights Convention held almost every year.

States began to criminalize abortion.

1851
Elizabeth Cady Stanton and Susan B. Anthony met.

1855
Lucy Stone and Henry Blackwell issued their marriage "protest."

1863
Women's rights activists formed Women's Loyal National League to work for slavery's end.

1865
Thirteenth Amendment abolished slavery.

1866
American Equal Rights Association founded.

1868
Fourteenth Amendment defined national citizenship but also introduced the word "male" into the Constitution.

1869
National Woman Suffrage Association and American Woman Suffrage Association founded.

Wyoming Territory enfranchised women.

1870
Fifteenth Amendment guaranteed voting rights to all men.

1870–1887
Woman suffrage approved in the territories of Utah, Washington, Montana.

1872
Susan B. Anthony arrested for illegal voting; several hundred other women, including Virginia Minor, attempted to vote.

1873
Congress passed the first Comstock Act.

Woman's Christian Temperance Union founded.

1875
In *Minor v. Happersett* the Supreme Court ruled that the Fourteenth Amendment did not enfranchise women.

1884
Belva Lockwood ran for President on the Equal Rights Party ticket.

1887
The Dawes Severalty Act undercut women's property rights among Native groups whose land was broken up into allotments.

1888
International Council of Women met in Washington, D.C.

1890
National American Woman Suffrage Association formed.

Wyoming entered the Union with full suffrage.

1890–1912
Women enfranchised in the states of Colorado, Utah, Idaho, Washington, California, Arizona, Oregon, and Kansas.

1896
National Association of Colored Women founded.

1906
Emma Goldman published *Mother Earth*.

1908
In *Muller v. Oregon*, the Supreme Court upheld a state maximum hour law for women workers.

1910
First woman suffrage parade held in New York City.

1911
National Association Opposed to Woman Suffrage founded.

The Triangle Factory fire brought attention to working women's rights.

New York Wage Earners League encouraged working women's suffrage.

1912
Heterodoxy founded in New York; members termed themselves "Feminists."

1914
Margaret Sanger began publishing *The Woman Rebel*, including information on birth control.

1915
In *Mackenzie v. Hare*, the Supreme Court held that American-born women who married foreign men lost their citizenship (but men who married foreign women did not).

1916
Jeannette Rankin of Montana became the first woman to serve in the U.S. House of Representatives.

1917
Alice Paul and Lucy Burns formed the National Woman's Party, began picketing the White House; when arrested, NWP members undertook hunger strikes.

1919
Women's International League for Peace and Freedom founded.

1920
Nineteenth Amendment ratified.

1921
The Sheppard–Towner Act provided grants to states to improve maternal and infant health.

1923
The National Woman's Party proposed an Equal Rights Amendment to the Constitution.

In *Adkins v. Children's Hospital*, the Supreme Court ruled unconstitutional a Washington, D.C., law providing minimum wages for women workers.

1929
Puerto Rican territorial legislature enfranchised literate women.

1933
Frances Perkins appointed Secretary of Labor, the first woman to serve in a president's cabinet.

1935
Ella Baker described the "Bronx slave market."

1935
National Council of Negro Women founded.

1936
U.S. v. One Case of Japanese Pessaries court case won approval for the use of pessaries (diaphragms) as birth control.

1938
Crystal Bird Fauset became the first African American woman elected to a state legislature.

The Fair Labor Standards Act established the first national minimum wage and maximum hour laws for women and men.

1941
Wonder Woman figure introduced in *All-Star Comics*.

1944
Grace Lonergan Lorch challenged Massachusetts's prohibition on hiring married women teachers.

1946
The Congress of American Women founded.

1948
U.N. Universal Declaration of Human Rights adopted.

1952
The Second Sex by Simone de Beauvoir published in the United States.

United Electrical Workers union published "U.E. Fights for Women Workers."

1955
Daughters of Bilitis, a lesbian rights organization, founded.

1957
The National Manpower Commission published its study of women in the workforce, *Womanpower*.

1961
President's Commission on the Status of Women (PCSW) established.

(continued)

1963

Equal Pay Act signed into law.

PCSW report, *American Women,* published.

Feminine Mystique published.

1964

Title VII of the 1964 Civil Rights Act outlawed discrimination in employment on the basis of race or sex and set up Equal Employment Opportunity Commission (EEOC).

1965

In *Griswold v. Connecticut,* the Supreme Court established that married couples have a right to privacy in decisions about contraception.

1966

National Organization for Women (NOW) founded.

National Welfare Rights Organization (NWRO) founded.

1967

Loving v. Virginia invalidated the last remaining laws prohibiting marriage across color lines.

1968

First national Women's Liberation conference held in Illinois.

Women's Equality Action League (WEAL) founded.

1969

National Association to Repeal Abortion Laws (NARAL) founded.

Redstockings founded.

In *Weeks v. Southern Bell,* the Supreme Court ruled that the telephone company had illegally discriminated against female employees.

1970

New York, Hawaii, and Alaska liberalized abortion laws.

Women's Strike for Equality held on the fiftieth Anniversary of the Nineteenth Amendment.

1971

First regular college courses on women's history and literature offered.

National Women's Political Caucus (NWPC) founded.

In *Rosenfeld v. Southern Pacific,* a federal appeals court ruled that protective laws for women workers violated Title VII of the 1964 Civil Rights Act.

In *Reed v. Reed,* the Supreme Court invalidated as "arbitrary" state laws preferring men over women as administrators of estates.

1972

ERA passed by Congress and sent to the states for ratification.

Title IX of the Higher Education Amendments passed.

Equal Employment Opportunity Act extended Title VII

protections to public employees.

First rape crisis centers and battered women's shelters established.

Phyllis Schlafly founded STOP-ERA.

Ms. magazine began publication.

Shirley Chisholm ran for the Democratic Party presidential nomination.

In *Eisenstadt v. Baird,* the Supreme Court extended to single people the right to purchase contraceptives.

1973

Roe v. Wade decriminalized abortion.

National Right to Life Committee founded.

National Black Feminist Organization (NBFO) founded.

In the case of *Frontiero v. Richardson,* the Supreme Court ruled that differential dependents' benefits for husbands and wives are unconstitutional.

1974

Coalition of Labor Union Women (CLUW) founded.

Equal Credit Opportunity Act ensured women access to credit cards, bank loans, and mortgages.

Women's Educational Equity Act provided funding for projects to ensure sexual equality in schools and universities.

1975

Taylor v. Louisiana found the exclusion of women from juries unconstitutional.

1976

Nebraska passed the United States's first marital rape law.

1977

Women Against Pornography (WAP) founded.

1978

Pregnancy Discrimination Act signed into law.

First "Take Back the Night" marches held in Boston and Los Angeles.

1979

Women Against Pornography divided anti-porn and "pro-sex" feminists.

First National March for Lesbian and Gay Rights.

UN adopted Convention on the Elimination of All Forms of Discrimination Against Women (CEDAW).

1981

In *Rotsker v. Goldberg,* the Supreme Court ruled that Congress could require the registration of men, but not women, for the military draft.

1982

ERA failed to be ratified.

1985

Guerilla Girls began exposing sexism in the art world.

Wilma Mankiller became first female principal chief of the Cherokee Nation.

1986

In *Meritor Savings Bank v. Mechelle Vinson,* the Supreme Court established that sexual harassment constitutes illegal sex discrimination.

Congress designated March as Women's History Month.

1989

Feminist Futures conference held by and for women in their twenties.

1991

Anita Hill testified at his confirmation hearing that Supreme Court nominee Clarence Thomas had sexually harassed her.

1992

Planned Parenthood v. Casey case decided.

Riot Grrrl convention held in Washington, D.C.

AAUW issued report *How Schools Shortchange Girls.*

1993

Family and Medical Leave Act re-passed by Congress and signed into law.

1994

Violence Against Women Act signed into law.

1995

UN's Fourth World Conference on Women held in Beijing.

1996

Third Wave Foundation created by young feminists.

Eve Ensler created *The Vagina Monologues*.

1997

First Lilith music fair.

2003

In *Lawrence v. Texas*, the Supreme Court held that state laws may not criminalize private sexual intimacy for homosexuals but not heterosexuals.

2007

Nancy Pelosi became the first female Speaker of the U.S. House of Representatives.

Young Feminist Leadership Institute held at national NOW conference.

2008

In the case of *Schroer v. Library of Congress*, a federal district court ruled that discriminating against someone for changing genders constitutes sex discrimination under federal law.

2009

The Lilly Ledbetter Fair Pay Act extended the statute of limitations on challenging pay discrimination under Title VII.

2013

The Secretary of Defense lifted restrictions on combat duty for women in the military.

In the case of *U.S. v. Windsor*, the Supreme Court ruled that the 1996 Defense of Marriage Act, by restricting the rights of married same-sex couples, violated the Constitution's guarantee of "equal protection."

Laverne Cox became the first openly transgender actor to star in a television series ("Orange is the New Black").

2014

As of December, thirty-six states permitted same-sex couples to marry; fourteen states banned same-sex marriage.

Text Credits

12: William Wood, *New England's Prospect* (London: T. Coates, 1634).

14: Pierre de Charlevoix, *Journal of a Voyage to North America* (orig. written, 1721; London: R & J. Dodsley, 1761).

15: Joseph-François Lafitau, *Customs of the American Indians Compared with the Customs of Primitive Times,* ed. and trans. William N. Fenton and Elizabeth L. Moore, 2 vols. (1724; Toronto: The Champlain Society, © 1974, 1977), I: 69–70. Reprinted by permission from University of Toronto Press (www.utpjournals.com).

16: *Archives of Maryland, I: Proceedings and Acts of the General Assembly, January 1637/8–September 1664* (Baltimore: Maryland Historical Society, 1883).

17: William Blackstone, *Commentaries on the Laws of England* (Oxford: Clarendon Press, 1765–1769), I: 430–33; II: 433–35, 498.

18: *Probate Records of Essex County, Massachusetts* (Salem: Essex Institute, 1917), II: 1665–1674.

19: "An Act Concerning Feme-Sole Traders," 1718; *Laws of the Commonwealth of Pennsylvania* (Philadelphia: John Bioren, 1810), I: 99–101.

21: *The Public Records of the Colony of Connecticut* (Hartford: Printed by Case, Lockwood, and Brainerd, 1874).

22: Gustavus Schmidt, *The Civil Law of Spain and Mexico, Arranged on the Principles of the Modern Code* (New Orleans: T. Rea, 1851), 13.

22: *Testimonio de escriptura,* Monclova, Sánchez Navarro Papers, Nettie Lee Benson Latin American Collection, University of Texas at Austin; translation courtesy of Jesus Cruz.

23: Gustavus Schmidt, *The Civil Law of Spain and Mexico, Arranged on the Principles of the Modern Code* (New Orleans: T. Rea, 1851), 11–12.

24: *The Statutes at Large: Being a Collection of All the Laws of Virginia from the First Session of the Legislature in 1619,* ed. William Waller Hening (New York: Printed for the editor, 1819–1823).

25: Louisiana's Code Noir, 1724, reprinted in Louis Sala-Molins, *Le Code noir, ou, Le Calvaries de Canaan* (Paris: Presses Universitaires de France, 1987), article 6:109; translation courtesy of Jennifer Spear.

26: John Lawson, *A New Voyage to Carolina, Containing an Exact Description and Natural History of That Country* (London, 1709).

27: *The Public Records of the Colony of Connecticut* (Hartford: Printed by Case, Lockwood, and Brainerd, 1874).

28: Text of Ruth Crary divorce petition, RG #003, Box 326, State Archives, Connecticut State Library.

28: *Archives of Maryland: Proceedings of the Council of Maryland, 1671–1681,* ed. William Hand Browne (Baltimore: Historical Society, 1896), XV (October 24, 16 78): 206–7.

30: *Pennsylvania Gazette,* June 30, 1768; August 11, 1768; September 29, 1768.

32: *The Statutes at Large: Being a Collection of All the Laws of Virginia from the First Session of the Legislature in 1619,* ed. William Waller Hening (New York: Printed for the editor, 1819–1823).

33: Thomas Hutchinson, *The History of the Colony and Province of Massachusetts-Bay from the First Settlement Thereof in 1628....* (London: Printed for M. Richardson, 1765).

35: [Anne Bradstreet], *The Tenth Muse Lately Sprung Up in America* (London, 1650).

36: Richardson Manuscript, Quaker Collection, Haverford College Library (Haverford, PA).

37 and 38: *Voices from an Early American Convent: Marie Madeleine Hachard and the New Orleans Ursulines, 1727–1760,* ed. Emily Clark (Baton Rouge: Louisiana State University Press, 2007), 70–72, 82–84. Reprinted and edited with permission.

42: Boston *Evening Post,* February 12, 1770.

43: Samuel Ashe, *History of North Carolina* (Greensboro, NC: Van Noppen, 1908–1925), I: 428–29.

43: "The Female Patriots. Addressed to the Daughters of Liberty in America, 1768," *Pennsylvania Chronicle* (December 25, 1769): 392.

45: *Virginia Gazette and Weekly Advertiser,* Richmond, October 26, 1782.

45: *Virginia Gazette and Weekly Advertiser,* Richmond, February 2, 1782.

47: Reprinted by permission of the publisher from *The Adams Papers: Adams Family Correspondence, Volume I: December 1761–May 1776,* ed. L. H. Butterfield (Cambridge, MA: The Belknap Press of Harvard University Press), 369–70, 381–83. Copyright © 1963 by the Massachusetts Historical Society.

49: Susanna Wright, "To Eliza Norris, at Fairhill," *Signs,* 6 (1981): 799–800; University of Chicago Press Journals. Reprinted by permission of the Library Company of Philadelphia.

50: Phillis Wheatley, *Poems on Various Subjects, Religious and Moral* (London: A. Gell, 1773).

51: *Massachusetts Magazine,* March 1790, 132–35; and *The Gleaner: A Miscellaneous Production in Three Volumes* (Boston: I. Thomas and E. T. Andrews, 1798), III: 188–96.

53: *Rise and Progress of the Young-Ladies' Academy of Philadelphia* (Philadelphia: Stewart & Cochran, 1794), 90–95.

55: *Philadelphia General Advertiser,* January 24, 1791. Reprinted in *Salem* [MA] *Gazette,* March 1, 1791.

56: *Martin v. Commonwealth of Massachusetts,* 1 Mass. Reports 348 (1805) .

57: Reprinted from Vol. I, p. 401 of the Grafton County (N.H.) Superior Court Records, at the New Hampshire State Archives, with permission.

59: Tapping Reeve, *Law of Baron and Femme....* (New Haven, CT: Oliver Steele, 1816), 49, 102, 139, 150.

60: Catherine Maria Sedgwick, "Slavery in New England," *Bentley's Miscellany,* 34 (1853): 417–24.

61: *True American,* October 18, 1802.

62: Gaillard Hunt, ed., *The First Forty Years of Washington Society, Portrayed by the Family Letters of Mrs. Samuel Harrison Smith (Margaret Bayard), from the Collection of her Grandson, J. Henley Smith* (New York: Scribner, 1906).

63: Cherokee Women's Petition to the Cherokee Council, May 2, 1817; Library of Congress Presidential Papers in Microfilm, Andrew Jackson, series 1, reel 22. Courtesy of the Library of Congress.

65: Courtesy of the Ursuline Convent Collection, Archives and Museum, New Orleans, Louisiana.

66: Hannah Mather Crocker, *Observations on the Real Rights of Women* (Boston: Printed for the Author, 1818).

70: Frances Wright, *Course of Popular Lectures* (New York: Office of the Free Enquirer, 1829), 41–62.

71: *New York Daily Sentinel,* June 25, 1831.

72: Writings and speeches of Maria W. Stewart, *The Liberator* 1831–1833.

74: Thomas Herttell, *Remarks Comprising in Substance Judge Herttell's argument in the House of Assembly of the State of New York in the Session of 1837 to Restore to Married Women "The Right of Property" as Guaranteed by the Constitution of This State* (New York: H. Durrell 1839).

74: Angelina Grimké, *Letters to Catherine E. Beecher; in reply to An Essay on Slavery and Abolitionism* (Boston: Isaac Knapp, 1836).

75: *New England Spectator,* July 12, 1837.

76: Catharine E. Beecher, *Essay on Slavery and Abolitionism, with Reference to the Duty of American Females* (Philadelphia: H. Perkins, 1837).

77: Sarah E. Grimké, *Letters on the Equality of the Sexes and the Condition of Woman* (Boston: Isaac Knapp, 1838).

78: Harriet E. Jacobs, *Incidents in the Life of a Slave Girl* (Boston: Published for the Author, 1861), chapter x.

80: *History of Woman Suffrage,* ed. Elizabeth Cady Stanton, Susan B. Anthony, and Matilda Joslyn Gage(New York: Fowler & Wells, 1881), I: 70–71.

86: William G. Bishop and William H. Attree, *Report of the Debates and Proceedings of the Convention for the Revision of the Constitution of the State of New York, 1846* (Albany Argus, 1847).

87: *Laws of the State of New-York, Passed at the Seventy-First Session of the Legislature . . .* (Albany: Charles Van Benthuysen, 1848), 307–308.

87: *Laws of the State of New York, Passed at the Eighty-Third Session of the Legislature . . .* (Albany: Printed by E. Croswell, 1860), 157–59.

88: *Selected Letters of Lucretia Coffin Mott,* ed. Beverly Wilson Palmer and Carol Faulkner (Urbana: University of Illinois Press, 2002), 165–67.

89: Harriet Taylor, "Enfranchisement of Women," *Westminster and Foreign Quarterly Review* (July 1851), in *The Complete Works of Harriet Taylor Mill,* ed. Jo Ellen Jacobs (Bloomington: Indiana University Press, 1998), 51–73. Courtesy of Indiana University Press. All rights reserved.

89: *History of Woman Suffrage,* ed. Elizabeth Cady Stanton, Susan B. Anthony, and Matilda Joslyn Gage (New York: Fowler & Wells, 1881), I: 234–37.

90: C. Loyal [pseud.], *The Squatter and the Don* (San Francisco: S. Carson & Co., 1885): 17–18.

91: *Proceedings of the Woman's Convention Held at Worcester, October 23rd and 24th, 1850* (Boston: Prentiss Sawyer, 1851).

92: "Woman and Work," *Una,* 2 (January 1854): 203–4.

93: Elizabeth Cady Stanton, "Address to the Legislature of New York on Women's Rights," February 14, 1854, *History of Woman Suffrage,* ed. Elizabeth Cady Stanton, Susan B. Anthony, and Matilda Joslyn Gage (New York: Fowler & Wells, 1881), I: 595–605.

94: *Village Life in America,* ed. Margaret E. Sangster (New York: H. Holt & Co., 1913), 49–50.

94: "Marriage of Lucy Stone Under Protest," *History of Woman Suffrage,* ed. Elizabeth Cady Stanton, Susan B. Anthony, and Matilda Joslyn Gage (New York: Fowler & Wells, 1881), I: 260–61.

96: "Resolutions," Women's Loyal National League Meeting, New York City, May 14, 1863, *History of Woman Suffrage,* ed. Elizabeth Cady Stanton, Susan B. Anthony, and Matilda Joslyn Gage (Rochester: C. Mann, 1887), II: 57–66.

96: Mary Ann Ran letter, from Lew Wallace, *Communication from Major Gen'l Lew Wallace in Relation to the Freedmen's Bureau to the General Assembly of Maryland* (Annapolis: Richard P. Bayly, 1865).

98: Speech of Sojourner Truth to the American Equal Rights Association, May 10, 1867; *History of Woman Suffrage,* ed. Elizabeth Cady Stanton, Susan B. Anthony, and Matilda Joslyn Gage (Rochester: C. Mann, 1887), II: 381–89.

99: Elizabeth Cady Stanton, "Address to the National Woman Suffrage Convention, Washington, D.C., January 19, 1869," *History of Woman Suffrage,* ed. Elizabeth Cady Stanton, Susan B. Anthony, and Matilda Joslyn Gage (Rochester: C. Mann, 1887), II, 348–55.

100: Frederick Douglass, Susan B Anthony, Lucy Stone, Elizabeth Cady Stanton, and Frances E. W. Harper speeches at the American Equal Rights Association Meeting, May 12–14, 1869, *History of Woman Suffrage,* ed. Elizabeth Cady Stanton, Susan B. Anthony, and Matilda Joslyn Gage (Rochester: C. Mann, 1887), II: 381–89.

103: *The Revolution,* 1868; and *Woman's Journal,* 1870.

107: *Atlanta Constitution,* July 29 and August 3, 1881.

107: Moqui [Hopi] petition; Records of the Bureau of Indian Affairs, RG 75, National Archives.

107: Leonora Barry, "What the Knights of Labor Are Doing for Women," *Report of the International Council of Women, Assembled by the National Woman Suffrage Association* (Washington, DC: R. H. Darby, 1888).

109: From Michael Schaack, *Anarchy and Anarchists: A History of the Red Terror and the Social Revolution in America and Europe* (Chicago: F. J. Schulte, 1889), 56.

109: *Bradwell v. Illinois,* 83, U.S. 130 (1873).

110: *Oregonian,* November 2, 1866; Oregon Historical Society: www.ohs.org

111: Edward T. Clarke, *Sex in Education; or, a Fair Chance for the Girls* (Boston: J. R. Osgood & Co., 1873).

112: Anna Julia Cooper, *A Voice from the South* (Xenia, OH: Aldine, 1892).

113: Excerpts from Alfreda M. Duster, ed., *Crusade for Justice: The Autobiography of Ida B. Wells.* (London: University of Chicago Press, Ltd., © 1970 by The University of Chicago.) All rights reserved. Published 1970.

114: Victoria Woodhull, "The Scare-Crows of Sexual Slavery," an Oration Delivered at Silver Lake, Mass., Camp Meeting, Sunday, August 17, 1873 (New York: Woodhull & Claflin, 1874).

116: *Public Laws of the United States of America, Passed at the Third Session of the Forty-Second Congress* (Boston: Little Brown, 1873), 598.

116: "The Solitude of Self," *The Woman's Column,* January 1892: 2–3.

117: Susan B. Anthony, "Constitutional Argument," in *Life and Work of Susan B. Anthony,* ed. Ida H. Harper (Indianapolis: Bowen Merrill, 1898), II: 977–92.

119: *Minor v. Happersett,* 88 U.S. 162 (1875).

120: "Tenth Annual Meeting of the American Woman Suffrage Association," *The Woman's Journal,* X (November 15, 1879): 365.

120: "The Working Woman's Association," *Revolution,* November 5, 1868: 280.

121: Paulina W. Davis, comp., *A History of the National Woman's Rights Movement, for Twenty Years, with the Proceedings of the Decade Meeting, Held at Apollo Hall, October 20, 1870 . . .* (New York: Journeymen Printers' Cooperative Association, 1871), 66–67, 71.

122: Henry B. Blackwell, "Woman Suffrage and Divorce," *The Woman's Journal,* I (June 4, 1870): 173.

122: Frances E. Willard, *Home Protection Manual: Containing an Argument for the Temperance Ballot for Woman . . .* (New York: The Independent Office, 1879).

123: Mary Church Terrell, *The Progress of Colored Women: An Address Delivered before the National American Woman Suffrage Association . . .* (Washington, DC: Smith Brothers, 1898).

124: Belle Kearney, "The South and Woman Suffrage," *Woman's Journal,* April 4, 1903.

125: Letter to the New Orleans *Times-Democrat,* 1903, *History of Woman Suffrage,* ed. Ida H. Harper (New York: National American Woman Suffrage Association, 1922), V: 59–60.

125: Charlotte Perkins Gilman, *Women and Economics: A Study of the Economic Relation between Men and Women as a Factor in Social Evolution* (Boston: Small, Maynard, & Company, 1898).

126: Emma Goldman, "The Tragedy of Woman's Emancipation," *Mother Earth,* 1 (March 1906): 9–18.

128: "What is Feminism" broadsides, George Middleton Papers, Box 84. Courtesy of the Library of Congress.

129: Margaret Sanger, *Woman and the New Race* (New York: Brentano's, 1920), 5, 7, 25.

130: "Mi Opinion" is reprinted with permission from the publisher of *A Nation of Women* by Luisa Capetillo (© 2004 Arte Público Press–University of Houston).

131: *Plains Woman: The Diary of Martha Farnsworth,* ed. Marlene Springer and Haskell Springer (Bloomington: Indiana University Press), 202–17.

133: Alfreda M. Duster, ed., *Crusade for Justice: The Autobiography of Ida B. Wells* (Chicago: University of Chicago Press, 1970), 234.

135: Joint Committee, 62nd Congress, 2nd session; Senate Document 601: 16–20.

136: *Victory: How Women Won It, A Centennial Symposium, 1840–1940* (New York: H. W. Wilson Co., 1940). Used by permission of EBSCO Information Services, Ipswich, MA.

137: Doris Stevens, "The Militant Campaign," *The Suffragist,* July 19, 1919.

139: *New York Times,* November 19, 1917.

139: Caroline Fairfield Corbin, "The Anti-Suffrage Movement," *Chicago Daily News,* November 24, 1908.

142: International Woman Suffrage Alliance, *Report of Eighth Congress Geneva Switzerland* (London, 1920): 49–50.

161: *Mackenzie v. Hare,* 239 U.S. 299 (1915).

161: William Pickens, "The Woman Voter Hits the Color Line," *The Nation,* October 6, 1920: 372–73.

162: Ruth Yap, "The Legal Status of Chinese Women in China and in Hawaii," *Mid-Pacific Magazine,* 40 (1930).

163: "Indian Woman Desires Right of Suffrage," *Sprague's Journal of Maine History,* vol. 9 (Dover: John Francis Sprague, 1921), 44.

164: Minnie L. Steckel, *The Alabama Business Woman as Citizen," Alabama College Bulletin,* XXX (July, 1937): 24, 29.

164: Eleanor Roosevelt, "Women Must Learn to Play the Game as Men Do," *Red Book,* 50 (April 1928).

164: "Century of Progress Hears Equal Rights Speeches," *Equal Rights,* 20 (July 28, 1934): 203.

165: Jennie Loitman Barron, *Jury Service for Women* (Washington, DC: League of Women Voters, 1924). Reprinted by permission of the League of Women Voters.

166: Children's Bureau records. National Archives, Record Group 102.

167: Mabel Raef Putnam, *The Winning of the First Bill of Rights for American Women* (Milwaukee: Frank Putnam, 1924), 65–66.

167: Senate Committee hearing; 71st Congress, 3rd Session on S.J. Res 52, a Joint Resolution Proposing an Amendment to the Constitution of the United States Relative to Equal Rights for Men and Women, January 6, 1931.

169: Edith McDonald, "International Federation of Working Women, Vienna Congress," *International Woman Suffrage News* (October, 1923): 2.

170: "To End Discriminations against Women," *National Business Woman,* 5 (May 1937): 132, 151, 159. Reprinted by permission of the Business and Professional Women's Foundation.

171: *Muller v. Oregon,* 208 U.S. 412 (1908).

172: *Adkins v. Children's Hospital,* 261 U.S. 525 (1923).

173: Crystal Eastman, "Now We Can Begin," *The Liberator,* 3 (1920): 20-23.

175: Elise Johnson McDougald, "The Double Task: The Struggle of Negro Women for Sex and Race Emancipation," *Survey,* 53 (March 1, 1925): 689–91.

176: Women's International League for Peace and Freedom, statement of purpose, 1924.

176: Dorothy Dunbar Bromley, "Feminist—New Style," *Harper's,* 155 (October 1927). Copyright © 1927 by Harper's Magazine. All rights reserved. Reproduced from the October issue by special permission.

179: John Watson, "The Weakness of Women." Reprinted with permission from the July 6, 1927, issue of *The Nation.* For subscription information call 1-800-333-8536. Portions of each week's *Nation* magazine can be accessed at http://www .thenation.com.

179: Birth Control Review, as quoted in *Equal Rights,* August 20, 1927, 220. Courtesy of the Sewall-Belmont House, Home of the Historic National Woman's Party.

180: Margaret Sanger, "The Status of Birth Control," *New Republic,* 94 (April 20, 1938): 324–26. Copyright © by Alexander Sanger; reprinted by permission.

181: From Margaret Hagood, *Mothers of the South: Portraiture of the White Tenant Farm Woman.* Copyright © 1939 by the University of North Carolina Press, renewed 1967 by Margaret Benaya. www.uncpress.unc.edu.

182: Mary Wilson Thompson Memoir, Delaware Historical Society, Wilmington, Delaware. Courtesy of the Delaware Historical Society. Reprinted by permission.

182: *The Woman Patriot,* 30/5 (1921): 4.

185: Ruth Shallcross, "Shall Married Women Work?" National Federation of Business and Professional Women's Clubs, Public Affairs Pamphlet #40, New York City, 1940. Reprinted by permission of the Business and Professional Women's Foundation.

185: Ella Baker and Marvel Cooke, "The Bronx Slave Market," *The Crisis,* 42 (November 1935). The author wishes to thank the Crisis Publishing Co., Inc., the publisher of the magazine of the National Association for the Advancement of Colored People, for the use of the material first published in the November 1935 issue of *The Crisis.*

186: Mary O'Kelly Albright letter; Works Progress Administration files W89; Box 11; Moorland-Spingarn Research Collection, Howard University.

187: Sabina Martinez, "Negro Women in Organization—Labor," *The Aframerican Woman's Journal,* 2 (1941). Reprinted by permission of Bethune House, Washington, D.C.

188: From *The American Scholar,* 13 (No. 1, Winter 1943–44). Copyright © 1943 by the Phi Beta Kappa Society. Reprinted by permission.

192: "Michigan Court Orders Equal Pay for Women," Federated Press Bureau, May, 1942.

193: "Right to Wed Hotly Debated at Hearing— Teachers Fight Ban," *Boston Herald,* February 18, 1944.

194: Alice Paul, quoted in Cecelia O'Neal, "Equal Rights Is a Basic Principle," *Equal Rights,* 30 (June– July, 1944). Courtesy of the Sewall-Belmont House, Home of the Historic National Woman's Party.

194: Elizabeth Hawes, *Why Women Cry* (New York: Reynal & Hitchcock, 1943), 21–23.

195: Dorothy Kenyon, "What Kind of World Do We Want?" April 9, 1943. Dorothy Kenyon Papers, Sophia Smith Collection, Smith College, Northampton, Mass.

195: Congress of American Women; original in Communism Collection, Box 2, Folder 20a; Sophia Smith Collection, Smith College.

196: Claudia Jones, "An End to the Neglect of the Problems of the Negro Woman," *Political Affairs,* 28 (June 1949). Reprinted by permission of *Political Affairs.*

198: "UE Fights for Women Workers," 1952; IUE Archives, University of Pittsburgh Library.

199: Excerpted from Ellen Cantarow with Susan Gushee O'Malley and Sharon Hartman Strom, *Moving the Mountain: Women Working for Social Change* (© 1980 by the Feminist Press at the City University of New York). Feministpress.org

199: Rick Halpern and Roger Horowitz, "'An Injury to One Is an Injury to All': Addie Wyatt Remembers the Packinghouse Workers' Union," *Labor's Heritage,* 12 (March 2003), 24–33. Published by the George Meany Memorial Archives. Reprinted by permission.

199: United Nations, Universal Declaration of Human Rights: www.un.org.

200: Eleanor Roosevelt, "Convention on the Political Rights of Women," State Department Bulletin, December 31, 1951.

201: Quotes from pp. 168–79 from Ferdinand Lundberg and Marynia F. Farnham, *Modern Woman: The Lost Sex.* © 1947 by Ferdinand Lundberg and Marynia F. Farnham. Copyright renewed © 1974 by Ferdinand Lundberg. Reprinted by permission of HarperCollins Publishers.

202: *The Ladder,* 1 (March 1957), 2.

203: *American Women: Report of the President's Commission on the Status of Women* (Washington DC: U.S. Government Printing Office, 1963).

205: From Betty Friedan, *The Feminine Mystique.* Copyright © 1983, 1974, 1973, 1963 by Betty Friedan. Used by Permission of W. W. Norton & Company, Inc.

207: Texts of Equal Pay Act of 1963, Civil Rights Act of 1964, and Voting Rights Act of 1965.

208: National Organization for Women, "Bill of Rights for 1969," 1968. Reprinted with permission of the National Organization for Women. This is a historical document and may not reflect the current language or priorities of this organization.

209: Johnnie Tillmon, "Welfare Is a Women's Issue," *Liberation News Service,* 415 (Feb. 26, 1972). Courtesy of the LNS News Service, Inc.

210: *Griswold v. Connecticut,* 381 U.S. 479 (1965).

211: *Taylor v. Louisiana,* 419 U.S. 522 (1975).

212: Chicago Women's Liberation, "To the Women of the Left," *New Left Notes* (November 13, 1967).

212: Excerpt from "A Critique of the Miss America Protest." Reprinted by permission of Carol Hanisch. To see a complete version of the document, visit http://carolhanisch.org/CHwritings/ MissACritique.html

213: Excerpted from Gainesville (Florida) Women's Liberation, "What We Do in Meetings," mimeographed pamphlet, 1970. This document and other materials from the 1960s rebirth years of feminism are available from the Redstockings Women's Liberation Archives for Action at www .redstockings.org or P.O. Box 744 Stuyvesant Station, New York, NY, 10009. For more on Gainesville Women's Liberation, now a founding chapter of National Women's Liberation, go to www .womensliberation.org or write to P.O. Box 14017, Gainesville, FL, 32604.

214: Pat Mainardi, "Politics of Housework," in *Sisterhood Is Powerful,* ed. Robin Morgan (New York: Vintage, 1970). Copyright © 1970 Patricia Mainardi. Reprinted by permission.

215: The Redstockings Manifesto was issued in New York City on July 7, 1969. It first appeared as a mimeographed flyer, designed for distribution at women's liberation events. Further information about the Manifesto and other materials from the 1960s rebirth years of feminism is available from the Redstockings Women's Liberation Archives for Action at www.redstockings.org or P.O. Box 744, Stuyvesant Station, New York, NY, 10009.

217: Out of the Closets: Voices of Gay Liberation, ed. Karla Jay and Allen Young (New York: New York University Press, 1992). Reprinted by permission of the editors.

218: Frances Beal, "Women in Black Liberation," in Sisterhood Is Powerful (New York: Vintage, 1970), 342–46. © Robin Morgan. By permission of Edite Kroll Literary Agency Inc.

218: "Our Bodies Ourselves," 1970, from Dear Sisters: Dispatches from the Women's Liberation Movement, ed. Linda Gordon and Rosalyn Baxandall (New York: Basic Books, 2000), 120–21. Reprinted by permission.

219: Excerpt from Laura Kaplan, The Story of Jane: The Legendary Underground Feminist Abortion Service, copyright © 1995 by Laura Kaplan. Used by permission of Pantheon Books, an imprint of the Knopf Doubleday Publishing Group, a division of Random House LLC. All rights reserved.

221: Betty Friedan Papers, Schlesinger Library, Radcliffe Institute, Harvard University. Reprinted by permission of Curtis Brown, Ltd.

226: Robin Morgan, "Introduction," Sisterhood Is Powerful (New York: Vintage, 1970), xiv–xxxvi. © Robin Morgan. Reprinted by permission of Edite Kroll Literary Agency Inc.

229: Combahee River Collective Statement, from Zillah R. Eisenstein, Capitalist Patriarchy and the Case for Socialist Feminism (New York: Monthly Review Press, 1978), 362–72. Reprinted by permission.

230: Margaret Sloan, "Black Feminism: A New Mandate," Ms, May 1974: 99ff. Reprinted by permission of Ms. magazine, © 1974.

230: "Women in the Asian Movement," from Roots: An Asian American Reader, ed. Amy Tachiki (Los Angeles: Continental Graphics,1971). Copyright © 1971 UCLA Asian American Studies Center Press.

231: Alma M. Garcia ed., Chicana Feminist Thought: The Basic Historical Writings (New York: Routledge, 1997). Reprinted by permission.

231: The Feminists, "Do You Know the Facts about Marriage?" (leaflet), in Sisterhood Is Powerful, ed. Robin Morgan (New York: Vintage, 1970), 536–37. © 1970 by Robin Morgan. Used by permission of Edite Kroll Literary Agency Inc.

232: Frontiero v. Richardson, 411 U.S. 677 (1973).

232: "Statement of Senator Birch Bayh," Hearings before the Subcommittee on Education of the Committee on Labor and Public Welfare, Senate, 94th Congress, 1st Session (September 16 and 18, 1975).

234: Susan Griffin, "Rape: The All-American Crime" (essay), Ramparts, 10 (September 1971): 26–35. Reprinted by permission of Susan Griffin.

235: Brief excerpt from Lenore E. Walker, The Battered Woman (New York: HarperCollins, 1979), 84–85. Copyright © 1979 by Lenore E. Walker. Reprinted by permission of HarperCollins Publishers.

235: Enid Nemy, "Women Begin to Speak out Against Sexual Harassment," New York Times, August 19, 1975. Reprinted by permission of PARS International Corp.

236: Roe v. Wade, 410 U.S. 113 (1973).

236: Naomi Gray quoted in "Stresses and Strains on Black Women," Ebony, 29 (June 1974): 36, 38.

237: Planned Parenthood Southeastern Pennsylvania v. Casey, 505 U.S. 833 (1992).

238: Excerpts from Anne Marie Gardiner, S.S.N.D., Women and Catholic Priesthood an Expanded Vision: Proceedings of the Detroit Ordination Conference (New York: Paulist Press, 1976). Copyright © 1976 by the Missionary Society of St. Paul the Apostle in the State of New York. Paulist Press, Inc., New York/Mahwah, NJ. Used with permission of Paulist Press. www.paulistpress.com.

239: "Working Women's Platform," Off Our Backs (October 1980): 19–21.

241: Shirley Chisholm speech; Congressional Record, May 21, 1969 (E4165-6).

242: Karla Jay, Tales of the Lavender Menace: A Memoir of Liberation (New York: Basic Books, 1999), 137–45; Copyright 1999 © by Karla Jay. Reprinted by permission.

243: The Spirit of Houston: The First National Women's Conference (Washington, DC: National Commission on the Observance of International Women's Year, 1978).

244: Ann Follis in Woman Alive! (newsletter), April 1977.

244: "Call to Action," in The Spirit of Houston: The First National Women's Conference (report). (Washington, DC: National Commission on the Observance of International Women's Year, 1978), 265–72.

245: Phyllis Schlafly interview, Washington Star, January 18, 1976.

246: Gloria Steinem, "The Way We Were—And Will Be," Ms., December 1979. Reprinted by permission of East Toledo Press.

247: Susan Faludi, Backlash: The Undeclared War against American Women: (New York: Crown, 1991). Reprinted by permission.

248: Barbara Ehrenreich, "Beyond Gender Equality: Toward the New Feminism," Democratic Left, July/August 1993. Reprinted by permission of International Creative Management, Inc. Copyright © 1993 by Barbara Ehrenreich.

248: Jessica Rosenberg and Gitana Garofalo, "Riot Grrrl: Revolution from Within," Signs, 23:3 (1998): brief excerpt, 810–11. Copyright © 1998 by The University of Chicago. All rights reserved.

249: American Association of University Women, How Schools Shortchange Girls (Washington, D.C.: AAUW Educational Foundation, 1992), Executive Summary, 1–8. Reprinted by permission.

251: JeeYeun Lee, "Beyond Bean Counting," in Listen Up: Voices from the Next Feminist Generation, ed. Barbara Findlen (Seattle, WA: Seal Press, 1995), 67–73. Reprinted by permission.

251: "Third Wave Manifesta: A Thirteen-point Agenda," from "What Is Activism?" in Jennifer Baumgardner and Amy Richards, eds., Manifesta: Young Women, Feminism, and the Future (New York: Farrar, Straus and Giroux, 2010). Copyright © 2000, 2010 by Jennifer Baumgardner and Amy Richards. Reprinted by permission of Farrar, Straus and Giroux, LLC.

253: Lilly Ledbetter, Grace and Grit (New York: Crown Archtype, 2012), 239–40. Reprinted by permission.

254: CEDAW: www.un.org

255: Charlotte Bunch, "Opening Doors for Feminism: UN World Conferences on Women." Journal of Women's History 24:4 (2012): 213–217, 220. Copyright © 2012 Journal of Women's History. Adapted and reprinted with permission of The Johns Hopkins University Press.

257: http://www.americanrhetoric.com/speeches/hillaryclintonbeijingspeech.htm.

Sidebars

14: James E. Seaver, A Narrative of the Life of Mrs. Mary Jemison (Canadaigua, NY: J. D. Bemis & Co., 1824).

16: Oneida leader Good Peter's address to Governor DeWitt Clinton, New York, 1788, from William W. Campbell, The Life and Writings of DeWitt Clinton (New York: Baker and Scribner, 1849), Appendix 3.

16: Lois Green Carr, "Brent, Margaret" in Notable American Women, 1607-1850, ed. Edward T. James, Janet Wilson James, and Paul S. Boyer (Cambridge, MA: Harvard University Press, 1971), I, 237–38.

25: From Ramon Guiterrez, When Jesus Came, The Corn Mothers Went Away: Marriage, Sexuality, and Power in New Mexico, 1500–1846 (Stanford, CA: Stanford University Press, 1991), 334.

27: John Heckewelder, An Account of the History, Manners and Customs of the Indian Nations who Once Inhabited Pennsylvania and the Neighboring States (Philadelphia: A. Small, 1819).

28: Windham Superior Court Records, Connecticut State Library.

33: Sarah Driggers petition, August 14, 1688, Maryland Historical Society.

35: James Kendall Hosmer, ed., Winthrop's Journal, "History of New England," 1630–1649 (New York:Charles Scribner's Sons , 1908), II: 225.

36: Ola Elizabeth Winslow, "Bradstreet, Anne," in Notable American Women, 1607-1950, ed. Edward T. James, Janet Wilson James, and Paul S. Boyer (Cambridge, MA: Harvard University Press, 1971), I, 222–23.

53: Elizabeth Sandwith Drinker diaries [Collection 1760], The Historical Society of Pennsylvania.

54: Manigault Family Papers, South Caroliniana Library, University of South Carolina, Columbia, SC.

54: Janet Wilson James, "Murray, Judith Sargent," in Notable American Women, 1607-1950, ed. Edward T.

James, Janet Wilson James, and Paul S. Boyer (Cambridge: Harvard University Press, 1971), II, 604–06.

57: Mitchill papers, December 8, 1804. Library of Congress.

59: James Kent, *Commentaries on American Law* (New York, 1827), II: 180.

60: Reprinted by permission of the publisher from *The Adams Papers: Adams Family Correspondence, Volume 4: October 1780–September 1782.* ed. L. H. Butterfield (Cambridge, MA: The Belknap Press of Harvard University Press, 1973), 328. Copyright © 1973 by the Massachusetts Historical Society.

65: Ben Harris McClary, "Ward, Nancy," in *Notable American Women, 1607–1950*, ed. Edward T. James, Janet Wilson James, and Paul S. Boyer (Cambridge, MA: Harvard University Press, 1971), III, 541–43,

71: *Free Enquirer,* IV: 141.

71: *Commercial Advertiser,* November 7, 1829.

72: *Salem Gazette,* Friday, February 25, 1831.

73: Margaret Fuller, "The Great Lawsuit," *The Dial,* July 1843.

74: *History of Woman Suffrage,* ed. Elizabeth Cady Stanton, Susan B. Anthony, and Matilda Joslyn Gage (New York: Fowler & Wells, 1881), I: 689–99.

76: Kathryn Kish Sklar, *Catharine Beecher: A Study in American Domesticity* (New Haven, CT: Yale University Press, 1973); Susan Zaeske, *Signatures of Citizenship: Petitioning, Antislavery, & Women's Political Identity* (Chapel Hill: University of North Carolina Press, 2003).

78: *Proceedings of the Anti-Slavery Convention of American Women. . .* (Philadelphia: Printed by Merrihew and Gunn 1838).

80: Melton McLaurin, *Celia, A Slave* (Athens: University of Georgia Press, 1991).

84: Lori D. Ginzberg, *Elizabeth Cady Stanton: An American Life* (New York: Hill & Wang, 2009).

86: *The North Star,* August 11, 1848.

88: *Report of the Proceedings of the Colored National Convention Held at Cleveland, Ohio, on Wednesday, September 6, 1848* (Rochester: printed by John Dick, at the *North Star* Office, 1848).

90: Articles VIII & IX, Treaty of Guadalupe Hidalgo, 1848.

90: Reprinted with permission from the publisher of Rosaura Sánchez and Beatrice Pita Cofer, *Conflicts of Interest: The Letters of María Amparo Ruiz de Burton.* (Copyright © 2001 Arte Público Press—University of Houston). English translation courtesy of John Felix Boylan.

92: *New York Herald,* October 28, 1850.

93: *Water-Cure Journal,* 11 (February 1851): 30–31.

93: Kathleen Barry, *Susan B. Anthony: A Biography of a Singular Feminist* (New York: New York University Press, 1995).

109: *Workingman's Advocate,* 5 (April 24, 1869).

112: M. Carey Thomas, "Women's College and University Education." Address Delivered at the Quarter-Centennial Meeting of the Association of Collegiate Alumnae, Boston, November 6, 1907 (New York: Education Review, 1908).

114: *Coger v. North West Union Packet Co. American Law Register,* 22 (March 1874): 161–62.

115: Geoffrey Blodgett, "Woodhull, Victoria Claflin," in *Notable American Women, 1607-1850,* ed. Edward T. James, Janet Wilson James, and Paul S. Boyer (Cambridge, MA: Harvard University Press, 1971), III, 653–55.

116: Matilda Joslyn Gage, "Is Woman Her Own?" *The Revolution,* April 9, 1868.

120: Mary Church Terrell Papers. Courtesy of the Library of Congress.

121: Sally McMillen, *Lucy Stone: An Unapologetic Life* (New York: Oxford University Press, 2015).

123: Ruth Bordin, *Frances Willard: A Biography* (Chapel Hill: University of North Carolina Press, 1986).

125: Beverly Washington Jones, ed., *Quest for Equality: The Life and Writings of Mary Eliza Church Terrell, 1863–1954* (Brooklyn, NY: Carlson, 1990).

128: George Middleton, speech delivered at the Cooper Union, February 17, 1914. George Middleton Papers. Courtesy of the Library of Congress.

139: Ada Davenport Kendall, quoted in Inez Haynes Irwin, *The Story of the Woman's Party* (New York: Harcourt, Brace, 1921), 288.

161: Nancy F. Cott, "Marriage and Women's Citizenship in the United States, 1830–1934," *American Historical Review,* 103 (December 1998).

163: María de Fátima Barceló-Miller, "Halfhearted Solidarity: Women Workers and the Women's Suffrage Movement in Puerto Rico During the 1920s," in *Puerto Rican Women's History: New Perspectives,* ed. Félix V. Matos Rodríguez and Linda C. Delgado (Armonk, NY: M. E. Sharpe, 1998), pp. 126–42.

163: Bunny McBride, "Lucy Nicolar: The Artful Activism of a Penobscot Performer," in *Sifters: Native American Women's Lives,* ed. Theda Perdue (New York: Oxford University Press, 2001), 141–59.

164: Joan Hoff Wilson, "Rankin, Jeannette Pickering," in *Notable American Women: The Modern Period,* ed. Barbara Sicherman and Carol Hurd Green (Cambridge, MA: Harvard University Press, 1980), 567–69.

165: Felipe Chacón, *Obras de Felipe Maximiliano Chacón, El Cantor Neomexicano: Poesía y prosa*

[The Works of Felipe Maximiliano Chacón, New Mexican Singer: Poetry and Prose] (Albuquerque: n.p., 1924). Translation courtesy of John Felix Boylan.

169: Elisabeth Christman, "What Do Working Women Say?" National Women's Trade Union League Collection, Series III, Tamiment Library & Robert F. Wagner Archives, New York University.

169: Linda Greenhouse, "Burnita Shelton Matthews Dies at 93," *New York Times,* April 28, 1988, D27.

171: Amelia Roberts Fry, "Paul, Alice," in *Notable American Women: Completing the Twentieth Century,* ed. Susan Ware and Stacy Lorraine Braukman (Cambridge, MA: Harvard University Press, 2004).

194: www.dorchesteratheneum.org

195: Susan M. Hartmann, "Kenyon, Dorothy," in *Notable American Women: The Modern Period,* ed. Barbara Sicherman and Carol Hurd Green (Cambridge, MA: Harvard University Press, 1980), 396–97.

201: "Ring Twice," *Fortune* (November 1947): 147–48.

205: Esther Peterson with Winifred Conkling, *Restless: The Memoirs of Labor and Consumer Activist Esther Peterson* (Washington, DC: Caring Publishing, 1995), 112. Reprinted by permission of Winifred Conkling.

208: Patricia Bell-Scott, "Murray, Anna Pauline (Pauli)," in *Notable American Women:Completing the Twentieth Century,* ed. Susan Ware and Stacy Lorraine Braukman (Cambridge, MA: Harvard University Press, 2004).

209: "NOW Statement of Purpose," in Aileen Hernandez, ed. *The First Five Years, 1966–1971* (Chicago: National Organization for Women, 1971), 5. Reprinted with permission of the National Organization for Women. This is a historical document and may not reflect the current language or priorities of this organization.

217: Ellen Willis, *No More Nice Girls: Countercultural Essays* (Hanover, NH: University Press of New England, 1992), 120.

231: Mitsuye Yamada, "Asian Pacific American Women and Feminism," in *This Bridge Called My Back: Writing by Radical Women of Color,* ed. Cherríe Moraga and Gloria Anzaldúa (Watertown, MA: Persephone Press, 1981): 73.

234: Text of Title IX (Public Law No. 92318, 86 Stat. 235, June 23, 1972).

236: *Meritor Savings Bank v. Vinson,* 477 U.S. 57 (1986).

236: *The Complete Transcripts of the Clarence Thomas-Anita Hill Hearings,* ed. Anita Miller (Chicago: Academy Chicago, 1994).

242: Barbara Winslow, *Shirley Chisholm: Catalyst for Change* (Boulder, CO: Westview Press, 2013).

Picture Credits

Cover Reprinted with permission of the DC Public Library, Star Collection, © Washington Post; 14: Thomas Campanius Holm, *Kort Beskrifning om Provincien Nya Swerige utk America...* (Stockholm, 1702); Courtesy the University of Delaware Library Special Collections; 23: Nettie Lee Benson Latin American Collection, University of Texas Libraries, The University of Texas at Austin; 26: Museo de America, Madrid, Spain/Bridgeman Images; 31: *Providence Gazette and Country Journal* [Jonathan Staples Advertisement], Providence, RI. May 19, 1764. Image Ref. No. RHi X17 1719. Courtesy of the Rhode Island Historical Society; 32: *New-York Weekly Journal*, September 23, 1735. Courtesy, American Antiquarian Society; 38: Drawing of Nuestra Señora de Guadalupe on hide, courtesy of Museum of International Folk Art, IFAF Collection, FA. 1966.56.1. Santa Fe, New Mexico; 39: Ataresta Learned 1756 sewing sampler; courtesy of the Governor Stephen Hopkins House, Providence, RI, a member of the National Society of the Colonial Dames of America; 43: Handbill. Courtesy of the Library of Congress; LC-USZ62-43568; 44: Courtesy of the Library of Congress; 45: *Diary of Anna Green Winslow: A Boston School Girl of 1777*, ed. Alice Morse Earle (Boston: Houghton, Mifflin, 1894); 46: "The Sentiments of an American Woman," Call No. AB [1780]-4, Courtesy of the Historical Society of Pennsylvania; 51: Phillis Wheatley, *Poems on Various Subjects*, 1773, frontispiece/Bridgeman Images; 52: Courtesy of the Library Company of Philadelphia; 53: Courtesy, American Antiquarian Society; 55: American; Miniature Panorama: Scenes from a Seminary for Young Ladies (detail, two young women studying a globe), c. 1810–1820; watercolor and ink on silk; 7 1/16 × 96 5/8 in. (17.9 × 245.4 cm); Saint Louis Art Museum, Museum Purchase and funds given by the Decorative Arts Society 89:1973; 58: From Volume I, page 401 of the Grafton County (N.H.) Superior Court Records, at the New Hampshire State Archives, with permission; 59: *Providence Gazette*, October 1, 1803; Courtesy, American Antiquarian Society; 61: Portrait of Elizabeth "Mumbet" Freeman (c. 1742–1829), 1811 (w/c on ivory), Sedgwick, Susan Anne Livingston Ridley (fl.1811) / © Massachusetts Historical Society, Boston, MA, USA / Bridgeman Images; 66: Jefferson's letter. Courtesy of the Ursuline Convent Collection, Archives and Museum, New Orleans, Louisiana; 67: Courtesy, Winterthur Museum, Engraving, *Keep Within Compass*, 1785–1805, England, gift of Henry Francis du Pont, 1954.93.1; 73: Courtesy of the New-York Historical Society; 78: Courtesy of the Friends Historical Library of Swarthmore College; 79: Records of the U.S. House of Representatives, National Archives and Records Administration; 79: Records of the U.S. House of Representatives, National Archives and Records Administration; 84: Frontispiece and title page to "My Bondage and My Freedom," by Frederick Douglass (1818–1895) published 1855 (print), American School (19th century) / American Antiquarian Society, Worcester, Massachusetts, USA / Bridgeman Images. Image cropped with permission; 85: Courtesy of the Library of Congress and Gary L.

Bunker; 92: Courtesy of University of Delaware Library; 94: U.S. Treasury; 94: *Village Life in America*; 97: "Marriage of a Colored Soldier," *Harper's Weekly*, June 30, 1866, Courtesy of HarpWeek LLC; 102: Courtesy of the University of Delaware Library; 110: Courtesy of the Chicago History Museum, ICHi-35122; 114: Photograph of Ida B. Wells, courtesy Special Collections Research Center, University of Chicago; 115: "Get Thee Behind Me (Mrs.) Satan," *Harper's Weekly*, February 1872. Courtesy of the Library of Congress: C-USZ62-1-1-54; 119: Courtesy of the Library of Congress and Gary L. Bunker; 122: Courtesy of the University of Delaware Library Special Collections; 124: Courtesy of the University of Delaware Library; 124: NACW logo; Courtesy of the University of Delaware Library; 128: Courtesy of University of Delaware Library Special Collections; 128: George Middleton Papers, Box 84, Library of Congress. Reprinted by permission; 130: Flyer for 46 Amboy Street clinic in three languages, Brownsville, Brooklyn, NY, circa 1916. From the Margaret Sanger Papers, Sophia Smith Collection, Smith College (Northhampton, MA). Reprinted by permission; 131 Courtesy of the University of Delaware Library; 133: Leaflet: "Hombres y Mujeres," Sophia Smith Collection, Smith College. Translation courtesy of John Felix Boylan; 134: Chicago *Inter-Ocean*, November 2, 1894, 2; 134: Leaflet: Wage Earners' League for Woman Suffrage, March 22, 1911, Leonora O'Reilly Papers, A-39, folder 111, Schlesinger Library, Radcliffe Institute, Harvard University; 137: *Moving Picture World*, November 8, 1913; 138: Courtesy of the Tamiment Library, New York University; 140: Petition from the Women Voters Anti-Suffrage Party of New York, c. 1917, SEN65A-K11 (box 129, folder 2), Senate Judiciary Committee, Records of the U.S. Senate, National Archives; 141: Courtesy of Sewall-Belmont House, Museum Home of the Historic National Woman's Party; 142: Cover of *Report of Eighth Congress Geneva Switzerland* (London, 1920); 142: Doris Stevens, *Jailed for Freedom* (New York: Boni & Liveright, 1920): 350. 146: "Age of Iron," Courtesy of the Library of Congress; 146: "Age of Brass." Courtesy of the Library of Congress; 147: Cartoon from *Judge* magazine, March 22, 1884. Courtesy of the Library of Congress, LC USZC4-4119; 148: "Election Day, 1909." Courtesy of the Library of Congress, LC-USZ62-51821; 149: "Are Not Women Half the Nation?," *Maryland Suffrage News*, August 7, 1915. Courtesy of the University of Delaware Library; 149: "The Dirty Pool of Politics," call number: BANC MSS C-B 773:7. Courtesy of The Bancroft Library, University of California, Berkeley; 150: "Give Mother the Vote," *Life and Labor*, 1915. Courtesy of the University of Delaware Library; 151: "To the Woman in the Home," *Woman's Journal* July 27, 1912. Courtesy of the University of Delaware Library; 152: "Woman to the Rescue!" *The Crisis*, May 1916. Courtesy of the University of Delaware Library; 153: "Looking Back." Courtesy of the Library of Congress; 153: "Hugging a Delusion," *Woman's Protest*, April 1916. Courtesy of the University of Delaware Library; 154: "The Three Sexes," *New York Times*, February 5, 1911; 154: Back cover of *San Francisco Sunday Call*, Magazine section, July 4, 1909, Color illustration, "'I can handle both,' says the lady," Suffrage Collection, Sophia Smith Collection, Smith College (Northampton, MA); 155: Alabama Department of Archives and History, Montgomery, Alabama, Woman Suffrage Files 1915-1920, v8416; 155: Dorman H. Smith, "The Kind of Men Women Will Choose," *Philadelphia Inquirer*, August 12, 1912; 156: Edwina Dumm Collection, The Ohio State University Billy Ireland Cartoon Library & Museum. *Columbus Daily Monitor*, March 30, 1917, Courtesy of the Ohio State University Libraries; 157: Dorman H. Smith, "A Thing of Beauty," *Muncie Evening Press*, September 29, 1924. Courtesy of the *Star Press* of Muncie, Indiana; 164: Anne Martin, "Woman's Vote and Woman's Chains," *Sunset Magazine* (April, 1922), 12; courtesy of the University of Delaware Library; 165: *The historical marker is a registered trademark of the Pennsylvania Historical and Museum Commission, and the marker text is copyright protected. Used with permission; 168: *Equal Rights*, I, August 23, 1923. Courtesy of the Sewall-Belmont House, Museum Home of the Historic National Woman's Party; 172: Courtesy of the Library of Congress, LC-DIG-ppmsca-02945; 178: Courtesy of the Library of Congress, LIC-DIG-ppmsca-08326; 179: LIFE Magazine, October 7, 1926, Courtesy of the University of Delaware Library; 183: *Woman Patriot* masthead. Courtesy of the University of Delaware Library; 188: *The American Scholar*, Vol. 13, No. 1, Winter 1943–44. Copyright © 1943 by The Phi Beta Kappa Society; 188: Courtesy of Purdue University Libraries, Karnes Archives and Special Collections; 201: Eleanor Roosevelt Memorial, Penelope Jencks, sculptor. Photo by Daniel Avila, NYC parks. Courtesy of City Parks Foundation; 202: Image courtesy of the Lesbian Herstory Archives. Cover art by Kay Somers; 203: Courtesy of the Lyndon B. Johnson Presidential Library; 209: Group portrait of some founding members of NOW at NOW's organizing Conference in Washington, D.C., 1966. Photo by Vince Graas. MC 575-7-18. Courtesy of Schlesinger Library, Radcliffe Institute, Harvard University; 211: "Help Wanted" *Every Evening*, Wilmington, Delaware, January 12, 1960. Courtesy of the Delaware Historical Society; 237: Courtesy of Rachael Romero http:// rachaelromero.com; 238: Cover of pamphlet "Native Women's Reproductive Rights Agenda" published by the Native American Women's Health Education Resource Center, ca. 1990. J. R. Rouse, Sophia Smith Collection, Smith College; 240: Cartoons: "Cathy," 1986, Andrews McMeel Publishing. Reprinted by permission; 241: Book Cover: Gloria Hull, et al., eds., *All the Women Are White, All the Blacks Are Men, But Some of Us Are Brave* (© 1980 by The Feminist Press at the City University of New York) www.feministpress.org; 241: Copyright © Guerrilla Girls. www.guerrillagirls.com; 243: Reprinted with permission of the DC Public Library, Star Collection, © Washington Post; 244: Courtesy of Jo Freeman, www.jofreeman.com; 250: Gary Trudeau, "Doonesbury," April 27, 1992. Reprinted by permission of Universal UClick; 257: www.unwomen.org.

Map Credits

132: "Suffrage map published by California Equal Suffrage, 1908." From Suffrage Collection, Sophia Smith Collection, Smith College (Northampton, MA). Reprinted by permission.

246: Adapted by Angela Hoseth, with permission, from Janet K. Boles, *The Politics of the Equal Rights Amendment: Conflict and the Decision Process* (United Kingdom: Longman Group, 1979).

Chart Credits

184: *Woman Patriot,* June 1, 1927. Courtesy of the University of Delaware Library.

234: U.S. Department of Education, Secretary's Commission for Opportunity in Athletics, *Open to All: Title IX at Thirty*, Washington, D.C., 20202, 18.

Table Credits

202: Table on Women's Employment, National Manpower Council, *Womanpower* (Columbia University Press, 1957).

Acknowledgments

For their assistance in conceptualizing and developing this volume, I am especially grateful to the series editors, Carol Karlsen and Sarah Deutsch. Carol read two full versions, offering excellent suggestions and providing much-needed moral support at every juncture. I want her to know how much I appreciated her efforts on my behalf. Nancy Toff first commissioned the book for Oxford; Brian Wheel took over editorial duties when the series moved to the College division, and Karen Omer and Gina Bocchetta shepherded the manuscript through the publication process. Many librarians and archivists responded most helpfully to my requests for document or illustration permissions; I thank them all. My colleague, Jesús Cruz, and my brother, John Felix Boylan, supplied translations of Spanish-language documents; and my colleague, Angela Hoseth of the University of Delaware's History Media Center, gave unstintingly of her photographic expertise. Christine Sears and her University of Alabama–Huntsville student, Whitney Reid, directed me to a key document for Chapter 5, and Micah Pawling of the University of Maine helped me track down an important Native woman's petition for Chapter 6. University of Delaware students Sarah Conroy and Mary Woodruff, along with my sister Bridget Boylan, assisted with research and proofreading. I valued enormously the consistent encouragement offered by my family, friends, and colleagues, and benefited from the helpful feedback provided by my students, and by Susannah Walker of Virginia Wesleyan College and the anonymous readers who vetted the manuscript for the press. Above all, I want to acknowledge the work of feminist historians who, over the past five decades and more, have produced path-breaking scholarship on women's history and women's rights. Without them, I could not have written this book.

Index

About the Author

Anne M. Boylan is Professor of History and Women and Gender Studies at the University of Delaware. She is the author of *The Origins of Women's Activism: New York and Boston, 1797–1840* (University of North Carolina Press, 2002), which was awarded a Certificate of Merit by the American Association for State and Local History, and *Sunday School: The Formation of an American Institution, 1790–1880* (Yale University Press, 1988), as well as articles in *The Journal of American History, Feminist Studies, American Quarterly,* and other scholarly journals.